# The Rise of the English Regions?

Drawing on the rich tradition of regional and economic geography, this book provides a theoretically informed analysis of 'devolution' in general – and the English regions in particular – from the perspective of uneven development and its geographical manifestation. *The Rise of the English Regions?* will be important reading for anyone studying the English regions, or involved in regional studies from academic, policy and practice standpoints.

The regions of England are currently governed from London, the location of national political power and the epicentre of the UK economy. The first part of the book looks at how this apparently colonial relationship has arisen and analyses the contemporary situation from a range of theoretical perspectives. Contributors discuss the nature of regional problems and governance, the institutions involved in regional governance and regional approaches to economic development.

In the second part of the book, one chapter is devoted to each English region, examining a particular region's characteristics, and the opportunities created for it by devolution. This highly detailed approach sheds light on the question of whether the post-1997 regional devolution of governance benefits the regions, or simply rescales governance to introduce another layer of bureaucracy.

**Irene Hardill** is Professor of Economic Geography at the Nottingham Trent University Graduate School, Business, Law and Social Sciences, and is currently Secretary and Vice Chair of the Regional Studies Association. She has a long-standing research interest in the meaning of 'work' (paid and unpaid) in its broadest sense to individuals, households and communities.

**Paul Benneworth** is a Research Councils UK Academic Fellow in Territorial Governance at the Centre for Urban and Regional Development Studies, University of Newcastle upon Tyne, and a Visiting Fellow at the Institute for Governance Studies, University of Twente, the Netherlands.

**Mark Baker** is a Senior Lecturer in Planning Policy & Practice and the current Head of Planning and Landscape within the School of Environment and Development at Manchester University. He is a chartered town planner with previous professional planning experience in UK local and central government. His teaching and research interests focus on the operation of the UK planning system and, especially, regional and strategic planning.

**Leslie Budd** is Reader in Social Enterprise at the Business School at the Open University. He is an economist who has written widely on the relationship between regional economic development and growth and international financial markets. He has worked at a number of universities and research centres in the UK, France and Germany, and is currently Chair of the Regional Studies Association. He was born in London, where he still lives.

## Regions and Cities

*Series editors: Ron Martin, University of Cambridge, UK;*
*Gernot Grabher, University of Bonn, Germany; Maryann Feldman,*
*University of Georgia, USA*

**Regions and Cities** is an international, interdisciplinary series that provides authoritative analyses of the new significance of regions and cities for economic, social and cultural development, and public policy experimentation. The series seeks to combine theoretical and empirical insights with constructive policy debate and critically engages with formative processes and policies in regional and urban studies.

### Geographies of the New Economy
Peter Daniels, Michael Bradshaw, Jon Beaverstock and Andrew Leyshon (eds)

### The Rise of the English Regions?
Irene Hardill, Paul Benneworth, Mark Baker and Leslie Budd (eds)

### Regional Development in the Knowledge Economy
Philip Cooke and Andrea Piccaluga (eds)

### Clusters and Regional Development
*Critical reflections and explorations*
Bjørn Asheim, Philip Cooke and Ron Martin (eds)

### Regions, Spatial Strategies and Sustainable Development
Graham Haughton and David Counsell

### Geographies of Labour Market Inequality
Ron Martin and Philip Morrison (eds)

### Regional Development Agencies in Europe
Henrik Halkier, Charlotte Damborg and Mike Danson (eds)

### Social Exclusion in European Cities
*Processes, experiences and responses*
Ali Madanipour, Goran Cars and Judith Allen (eds)

**Regional Innovation Strategies**
*The challenge for less-favoured regions*
Kevin Morgan and Claire Nauwelaers (eds)

**Foreign Direct Investment and the Global Economy**
Nicholas A. Phelps and Jeremy Alden (eds)

**Restructuring Industry and Territory**
*The experience of Europe's regions*
Anna Giunta, Arnoud Lagendijk and Andy Pike (eds)

**Community Economic Development**
Graham Haughton (ed.)

**Out of the Ashes?**
*The social impact of industrial contraction and regeneration on Britain's mining communities*
David Waddington, Chas Critcher, Bella Dicks and David Parry

*Forthcoming:*
**Devolution, Regionalism and Regional Development**
Jonathan Bradbury and John Mawson (eds)

# The Rise of the English Regions?

Edited by Irene Hardill,
Paul Benneworth, Mark Baker
and Leslie Budd

Routledge
Taylor & Francis Group

LONDON AND NEW YORK

Learning Resources
Centre

# 13046330

First published 2006
by Routledge
2 Park Square, Milton Park, Abingdon, Oxon OX14 4RN

Simultaneously published in the USA and Canada
by Routledge
270 Madison Ave, New York, NY 10016

*Routledge is an imprint of the Taylor & Francis Group, an informa business*

Typeset in Bembo by Keystroke, 28 High Street, Tettenhall, Wolverhampton
Printed and bound in Great Britain by The Cromwell Press, Trowbridge, Wiltshire

*British Library Cataloguing in Publication Data*
A catalogue record for this book is available from the British Library

*Library of Congress Cataloging in Publication Data*
The rise of the English regions? / Irene Hardill . . . [et al.]. – 1st ed.
p. cm. – (Regions and cities)
Includes bibliographical references and index.
ISBN 0–415–33632–5 (hb : alk. paper)
1. Regionalism–England. 2. Decentralization in government–England. 3.
England–Administrative and political divisions. 4. Local government–Great Britain. I. Hardill,
Irene, 1951– II. Title. III. Series.
JN297.R44R57 2006
320.8′30942–dc22
2006004537

ISBN10: 0–415–33632–5 (hbk)
ISBN10: 0–203–42150–7 (ebk)

ISBN13: 978–0–415–33632–1 (hbk)
ISBN13: 978–0–203–42150–5 (ebk)

# Contents

## 7 The North West: cultural coherence and institutional fragmentation 120

CHRISTOPHER WILSON AND MARK BAKER

## 8 Yorkshire and the Humber 137

TONY GORE AND CATHERINE JONES

## 9 The West Midlands: the 'hinge' in the middle 156

ANNE GREEN AND NIGEL BERKELEY

## 10 The East Midlands: the missing middle? 168

IRENE HARDILL, CHRIS BENTLEY AND MIKE CUTHBERT

## 15 Conclusions 267

PAUL BENNEWORTH, IRENE HARDILL, PETER ROBERTS,
MARK BAKER AND LESLIE BUDD

# Illustrations

## Figures

## Tables

## Boxes

# Illustrations

## Figures

## Tables

## Boxes

# Contributors

**Mark Baker** is a Senior Lecturer in Planning Policy & Practice within the School of Environment and Development at Manchester University. He is a chartered town planner with previous professional planning experience in UK local and central government. His teaching and research interests focus on the operation of the UK planning system, especially regional and strategic planning, and he is currently Chair of the Town and Country Planning Association (TCPA)'s Regional Planning Task Team.

**Paul Benneworth** is a Research Councils UK Academic Fellow at the Centre for Urban and Regional Development Studies at the University of Newcastle, and a Visiting Fellow at the University of Twente, the Netherlands. He is a board member of the Regional Studies Association, and edits *Regions*, the newsletter of the RSA. His research concerns knowledge-based regional economic development in old industrial regions, particularly the role of universities in regional economic development and high-technology entrepreneurship in less successful places.

**Chris Bentley** is currently responsible for Regional Planning at the Government Office for the East Midlands. He is a chartered town planner who has previously worked for local authorities in both England and Scotland, and in a parallel existence has also worked in Japan, most recently as an instructor at the Institute for International Mineral Resource Development in Fujinomiya, Shizuoka Prefecture.

**Nigel Berkeley** is Director of the Centre for Local Economic Development, part of the Faculty of Business, Environment and Society at Coventry University. He has extensive experience of managing research projects in the field of local economic development, with a particular focus on issues of urban regeneration and sustainability in the West Midlands Region. His particular research interests concern restructuring and diversification in the region's 'mature' sectors/clusters, notably the regional automotive sector.

**Leslie Budd** is a Reader in Social Enterprise and Convenor of the ESRC Research Seminar Series 'The New Regional Management: A Consequence of Multi-level and Meta-Governance?' His research interests are varied, covering social enterprise, regional economic development in global context, international financial markets, urban economics, public policy and public management. He is currently Chair of the Regional Studies Association, and his recent published works include *eEconomy: Rhetoric or Business Reality?* (with L. Harris (eds)), *Key Concepts in Urban Studies* (with M. Gottdiener) and *Making Policy Happen* (with J. Charlesworth and R. Paton (eds)).

**Dave Byrne** is Professor of Sociology and Social Policy at the University of Durham. He is joint editor of *Sociology*. His research interests are in the transition to post-industrialism and the application of complexity theory to social science. Other relevant publications include *Understanding the Urban* (Palgrave, 2001).

**Allan Cochrane** is Professor of Public Policy at the Open University. He has researched and published on a wide range of topics relating to urban and regional policy and politics. He is particularly interested in the ways in which they connect into wider processes of political and social change. He has recently been undertaking research on the reshaping and re-imagining of Berlin, as well as on the contemporary redefinition of British urban policy and the invention of the South East of England as an object of policy. He was co-author (with John Allen and Doreen Massey) of *Re-Thinking the Region* (Routledge, 1998) and joint editor (with John Clarke and Sharon Gewirtz) of *Comparing Welfare States* (Sage, 2001).

**Mike Cuthbert** is Senior Tutor in Law in the School of Social Sciences at the University of Northampton. He is Treasurer of the East Midlands branch of the Regional Studies Association. His research is mainly in the area of EU law, including the constitutional impact of regionalism.

**Tony Gore** is a Senior Research Fellow at the Centre for Regional Economic and Social Research (CRESR), Sheffield Hallam University. His main research interests are the EU Structural Funds, coalfields regeneration, labour markets, and connections between places of need and areas of growth. His work also emphasises governance and policy-making, particularly inter-institutional relationships both at sub-regional and regional scales and between local, regional, national and supranational levels.

**Mia Gray** is an economic geographer at the Department of Geography, University of Cambridge. Her current work includes a socially oriented analysis of occupational and job segregation; research on skill formation, diffusion of knowledge, and innovation in elite labour markets; and investigation of new types of labour organising in low-paid service sector occupations.

**Anne Green** is a Principal Research Fellow at the Institute for Employment Research, University of Warwick. Her research focuses on the geography of employment and non-employment, local and regional labour market issues, and on spatial dimensions of economic, social and demographic change more broadly. Much of her research is funded by government departments and research councils and foundations.

**Irene Hardill** is Professor of Economic Geography at the Graduate School, College of Business, Law and Social Sciences, Nottingham Trent University. She is Secretary and Vice Chair of the Regional Studies Association, and Chair of the East Midlands branch. Her research concerns the juggling of paid and unpaid work (unpaid caring activity as well as voluntary action) and household decision-making. Recent publications include *Gender, Migration and the Dual Career Household* (Routledge, 2002).

**Dr Amer Hirmis** is currently Director of Research and Consulting at DTZ Bahrain. Previously, he has worked with Skidmore, Owings & Merrill on the master planning for the Kingdom of Bahrain as well as other high-profile assignments in Saudi Arabia. He holds a Ph.D. in economic development from the University of Manchester and was previously Senior Economist at SERPLAN; Chief Economist at the London Chamber of Commerce; Executive Chair of Londonomics; and Chief Economist at the South West Regional Development Agency. His previous publications include *Global Cities Benchmarking* (London Development Partnership), *How London Works: London's Economy and its Labour Markets* (Kogan Page) and *Conceptual Framework for Regional Competitiveness* (Regional Studies). He writes here in a personal capacity.

**Catherine Jones** is a Research Associate at the Centre for Regional Economic and Social Research (CRESR), Sheffield Hallam University. Her main interests are in social and economic regeneration, and she has worked extensively on the National Evaluation of New Deal for Communities for the Neighbourhood Renewal Unit. She will shortly be starting a Ph.D. at the University of Sheffield, which will be exploring socio-economic and geographical employment barriers.

**Ron Martin** is Professor of Economic Geography at the University of Cambridge, UK, and Research Associate of the Centre for Business Studies and a Fellow of the Cambridge–MIT Institute there. His research interests include regional growth and competitiveness; financial markets and regional development; economic theory and economic geography; local labour markets; the geographies of the 'new economy'; and the geographies of public policy. He has published some 25 books and more than 135 papers on these and related topics. He has undertaken research for the European Commission and the UK government on clusters, regional growth and city competitiveness. He is an Academician of the Academy of Social Sciences and a Fellow of the British Academy, and is listed by the American Economic Association as one of the world's most cited economists.

**Nick Phelps** is Reader in Economic Geography at the School of Geography, University of Southampton. His main interests are in the local and regional economic development impacts of multinational companies and the theory of agglomeration and the economic basis of city-regions. Recent work includes *The New Competition for Inward Investment*, co-edited with Phil Raines (Edward Elgar, 2003).

**Mike Raco** is Senior Lecturer in Human Geography in the Department of Geography, King's College London. He is co-editor of the journal *Local Economy* and is a Principal Investigator in the EPSRC's Sustainable Urban Brownfield Regeneration: Integrated Management (SUBR:IM) Research Consortium. His research has examined the theories and practices of urban governance in Western cities; the form and character of devolution in the UK; and the discourses and practices of sustainable community-building in the EU.

**Peter Roberts** OBE is currently Professor in Sustainable Spatial Development in the School of Earth and Environment at the University of Leeds. He holds senior positions with several national organisations and in 2005 was appointed Chair of the UK's Academy for Sustainable Communities with responsibility for overseeing strategy and policy relating to sustainable communities, skills and knowledge. His research interests include European, national and regional strategic spatial planning, regeneration and development, policy formulation and evaluation, economy–environment interaction and local and regional governance.

**Pete Shirlow** is a Senior Lecturer in the School of Environmental Sciences at the University of Ulster. He has published papers on political economy and violence in journals such as *Capital and Class*, *Urban Studies*, *Regional Studies*, *Antipode*, *Environment and Planning A* and *Area*, and is on the international editorial board of *Capital and Class*. He is currently leading the research project 'Forward to the Past? Loyalism and the Future of Loyalist Violence', funded by the ESRC.

**Peter Tyler** is Professor in Urban and Regional Economics at the University of Cambridge, and a Fellow of St Catharine's College. He is an urban and regional economist specialising in urban and regional economic development and the evaluation of policies designed to regenerate declining areas. He is a member of the National Evaluation of Sure Start panel, an Academician of the Learned Society for Social Sciences and an expert adviser to the ODPM National Evaluation of Housing Market Renewal Pathfinders.

**David Valler** is Associate Professor and Associate Chair at the Department of Community and Regional Planning, Iowa State University. He was previously Senior Lecturer in Economic Development at the Department of Town and Regional Planning, University of Sheffield. His research has focused on local and regional economic development, the politics of business representation, and urban governance and policy. Between 2001 and 2003 he led a UK Economic and Social Research Council research project entitled

'Devolution and the Politics of Business Representation' which formed part of the ESRC's £4.7m Devolution and Constitutional Change Programme. He is co-editor (with Dr A. Wood) of *Governing Local and Regional Economies: Institutions, Politics and Economic Development* (Ashgate, 2004).

**Christopher Wilson** is qualified as a town planner and has worked on a short-term basis for several Manchester-based planning consultancy firms on a number of key projects throughout the North West, as well as for several local authorities. In 2003 he completed a one-year Master's in social research and is currently undertaking a Ph.D. on community engagement in the Housing Market Renewal initiative at Manchester University.

**Andrew Wood** is an Associate Professor of Geography at the University of Kentucky. His major research interests are in globalisation, urban politics and governance, and the dynamics of local and regional economic change. He has recently published in *Economic Geography*, *Political Geography* and *Urban Studies* and is co-editor (with Dave Valler) of *Governing Local and Regional Economies: Institutions, Politics and Economic Development* (Ashgate, 2004).

# Preface

It is apposite that the fortieth year of the Regional Studies Association, the learned society that seeks to promote understanding of regional development through policy and research, should be marked by its third book on the English regions. The first was produced in the 1980s, when the Association undertook an *Inquiry into the UK Regional Problem*. The second, *Regional Development in the 1990s*, which appeared in this very series, was produced in the early 1990s, was edited by Ron Martin and Peter Townroe, and was a mix of thematic and regional analysis of key issues facing the UK economy of the day.

This third book is different in that the focus is not the UK but England, and this is deliberate because while much has been written in academic spheres about the institutional and political arrangements for English devolution post-1997, there has been a lacuna in work seeking to understand in an empirically 'deep' manner the interaction between this primarily national-centred regionalisation process and the way it is unfolding in the English regions with their very distinctive economic, political, social and cultural structures. This book has had a long gestation period, and a number of RSA branch events were held in 2002 and 2003 in the North West, East Midlands and North East. More recently, in 2005 we organised a session within the 2005 RGS–IBG conference Flows and Spaces in a Globalised World. In between these events, a number of other regional teams emerged with the enthusiasm to write engaging portraits of their 'home' regions, and to explore how local characteristics have interwoven with the national agenda to produce very place-specific versions of English regionalism.

*Irene Hardill, Nottingham*
*Paul Benneworth, Newcastle*
*Mark Baker, Manchester*
*Les Budd, London*
*September 2005*

# Acknowledgements

We must acknowledge the contribution of a number of people without whose support we would never have produced this finished book. We would like to thank Sally Hardy at the Regional Studies Association for supporting the project, and helping us sustain our momentum. We would like to thank the editor of the book series, Professor Ron Martin, Caroline Mallinder, Georgina Johnson of Routledge, and Professor Peter Roberts, who was rapporteur for a session on the book within the 2005 RGS–IBG conference Flows and Spaces in a Globalised World. A number of people also contributed in a more technical capacity to assembling the book, and we are profoundly grateful for their time and effort: Chris Bentley, Government Office for the East Midlands, for the regional statistics at the opening of Part II; Stephen Hincks, University of Liverpool, for the regional maps; Anthony Plumridge, University of the West of England, Bristol; Eric McVittie and Rachel Fryett, University of Plymouth Business School, who helped in the production of Chapter 12; and Sally Lewis of Nottingham Trent University, for her work in assembling, preparing and formatting the manuscript. We are also indebted to all the authors for their contributions and for participating in the RGS–IBG session. In recognising our debt of gratitude to all these individuals, we of course absolve them for any errors or omissions, which remain the responsibility of the editorial team.

# Abbreviations

| | |
|---|---|
| A1 | Great North Road |
| AC | Autonomous Communities |
| AWM | Advantage West Midlands |
| BBC | British Broadcasting Corporation |
| BCC | British Chambers of Commerce |
| CAN | Campaign for a Northern Assembly |
| CBI | Confederation of British Industry |
| CORDIS | EU research database |
| CRESR | Centre for Regional Economic and Social Research |
| CSWP | Coventry, Solihull and Warwickshire Partnership |
| CURDS | Centre for Urban and Regional Development Studies |
| DEA | Department of Economic Affairs |
| DETR | Department of Environment Transport and Regions |
| DIRFT | Daventry International Rail Freight Terminal |
| DTI | Department of Trade and Industry |
| DTLR | Department of Transport, Local Government and the Regions |
| EC | European Community |
| EEC | European Economic Community |
| EEDA | East of England Development Agency |
| ESDP | European Spatial Development Perspective |
| EU | European Union |
| EUREGIO | evaluation of cross-border regions in the European Union |
| FDI | Foreign Direct Investment |
| FE | Further Education |
| FIRE | Fire, Insurance and Real Estate |
| FSB | Federation of Small Businesses |
| FUR | Functional Urban Region |
| G&M | General and Municipal workers union |
| GCP | Greater Cambridgeshire Partnership |
| GCSE | General Certificate of Secondary Education |
| GDP | Gross Domestic Product |
| GFCF | Gross Fixed Capital Formation |

| | |
|---|---|
| GLA | Greater London Assembly |
| GLA | Greater London Authority |
| GLC | Greater London Council |
| GOL | Government Office for London |
| GONW | Government Office North West |
| GOR | government office region |
| GOSE | Government Office of the South East |
| GOWM | Government Office for the West Midlands |
| GREMI | groupe de recherche européen sur les milieux innovateurs |
| GVA | Gross Value Added |
| HBF | House Builders Federation |
| HMR | Housing Market Renewal |
| ICT | information and communication technologies |
| ILO | International Labour Office |
| INTERREG | Inter-Regional Cooperation Fund of the European Union |
| IoD | Institute of Directors |
| IT | Information Technology |
| LAD | Local Authority District |
| LCC | London County Council |
| LDA | London development agency |
| LDP | London Development Partnership |
| LPAC | London Planning Advisory Council |
| MAFF | Ministry of Agriculture, Food and Fisheries |
| MCR | Mega-City Region |
| MEP | Member of the European Parliament |
| MORI | Market and Opinion Research International |
| MP | Member of Parliament |
| MSP | Member of the Scottish Parliament |
| AM | Assembly Member |
| MUR | Mega/Macro Urban Region |
| NATO | North Atlantic Treaty Organisation |
| NDC | Northern Development Corporation |
| NDPB | Non-Departmental Public Bodies |
| NEA | North East Assembly |
| NEPC | North East Planning Council |
| NUM | National Union of Mineworkers |
| NVQ | National Vocational Qualification |
| NWDA | North West Development Agency |
| NWMA | North West Metropolitan Area |
| NWRA | North West Regional Assembly |
| ODPM | Office of the Deputy Prime Minister |
| OECD | Organisation for Economic Cooperation and Development |
| OLPC | Office of the Lord President of Council |
| ONS | Office of National Statistics |

| | |
|---|---|
| CEO | Chief Executive Officer |
| PAFT | Policy Appraisal and Fair Treatment |
| PPP | Public Private Partnership |
| PSA | Public Service Agreement |
| PUR | Polycentric Urban Regions |
| R&D | Research and Development |
| RAF | Royal Air Force |
| RDA | regional development agency |
| RES | Regional Economic Strategy |
| RPG | Regional Planning Guidance |
| RSCP | Regional Skills and Competitiveness Partnership |
| RSS | Regional Spatial Strategy |
| SCIB | Sustainable Communities and Infrastructure Board |
| SEEDA | South East of England Economic Development Agency |
| SEEDS | South East Economic Development Strategy |
| SEERA | South East of England Regional Assembly |
| SIS | South East Region Social Inclusion Strategy |
| SOA | Super Output Area |
| SWRDA | South West Regional Development Agency |
| TFP | Total Factor Productivity |
| TIM | Territorial Innovation Models |
| UA | Unitary Authority |
| UK | United Kingdom |
| UNISON | The Public Services Trade Union |
| USA | United States of America |
| WMRO | West Midlands Regional Observatory |
| Y&H | Yorkshire and the Humber |
| YHRA | Yorkshire and the Humber Regional Assembly |

# Part I

The English regions are extremely complex entities, and attempting to explain the significance of the changes through which they progress is a complex process. Our argument in this book is that regions are systematically overlooked within England because of a preoccupation with a nationhood which has evolved with a peculiar myopia for its regions. However, both political and academic agendas have turned back towards the region as a unit of economic competitiveness, as a space of social inclusion, and scale for environmental protections. These pressures have manifested themselves in other countries through the increasing importance accorded to regional structures, both formally through devolution processes and through the capture of non-devolved institutions by regional interests. Regional devolution is not the only significant socio-economic change currently under way, and recent moves to regional devolution must be seen in the context of attempts to achieve gender equality, and the greater ease with which newer regional bodies have been able to implement such equality, binding those two issues tightly together. Our aspiration in this book is thus to take a fresh look at the English regions to understand the significance of these changes, in economic, social and political terms, and to try to find commonalities of process in the divergences of experiences across the English regions.

In doing so, Part I of this volume first establishes more clearly several different perspectives on the English regionalisation process. First, a contribution from Peter Roberts and Mark Baker (Chapter 2) begins from an organic, bottom-up conception of regional governance. In this chapter, the details of the English regional mobilisations are explored through a historical perspective of English regional identity. The starting point for this chapter is the concept of the existence of particular 'problems' which articulate at a regional scale, and to which 'regional institutions' emerge as the solution. This produces a very different conception of region, regional autonomy and regional actors to an efficiency (Chapter 3) or democracy (Chapter 4) perspective, and focuses much more on the necessities from which regions have emerged.

In Chapter 3 Paul Benneworth highlights an unresolved tension in the devolution process within England, namely between using regions as a tool to promote economic efficiency and using them as an appropriate political space for the democratic representation and resolution of conflicting interests. The key tension is that there are very different roles for institutions in each of these conceptions. From an economic efficiency perspective, institutions help to promote adaptation and renewal, or inhibit innovation through processes of lock-in. From a political perspective, institutions are much more amorphous and free-flowing entities, which evolve in response to the demands of the various interest groups seeking representation. Whilst much of what has been written to date about the English regions takes the first perspective, the neo-Lamarckian outlook implicit in our approach requires that the second is taken.

In the third theoretical contribution, Andy Wood *et al.* reflect in Chapter 4 on the notion of regional coherence. It is too easy to take regional institutions for granted, and to assume that particular sectional interests will engage with regional institutions if they wish to achieve regional ends. They observe that in the UK, business representation has been extremely slow – and indeed reluctant – to develop any kind of meaningful regional capacity, and has instead engaged collectively with the 'regional agenda'. Peak interest organisations have therefore chosen to shape the business environment primarily through engagement with ministers rather than through the new regional arrangements. This is a consequence of the centralisation of Britain, and has been finessed to some extent by not requiring regional institutions to engage with regional business representatives.

One of the issues to emerge in the course of the other chapters in this volume is that the interplay of gender tensions has an important – if unappreciated – shaping effect on the form that particular places take. This is explored further by Hardill, Gray and Benneworth in Chapter 5.

These more conceptual contributions are intended to set the scene for Part II of the book, which, through a series of regional essays, subsequently develops a number of themes relating to the increasing significance of regions within England.

# 1 The rise of the English regions

## An introduction

*Paul Benneworth, Irene Hardill, Mark Baker and Leslie Budd*

## Setting the scene

To be a student of English regions is to live on something of an intellectual rollercoaster. Despite, or perhaps because of, the pre-eminence of London in the political, economic and cultural life of the United Kingdom, the status of regional studies has never really progressed past a precarious and transitory existence. The creation of the Ministry of Economic Affairs in the 1960s and Regional Economic Planning Councils in the 1970s, and the post-1997 moves towards regional forms of governance, might suggest that the English regions are a fashion that rise and fall like hem lines. But the Ministry and the Planning Councils were never successful under their promoting governments, and the ease with which the 1979 Conservative administration destroyed regional frameworks for a decade tells quite another story. Until recently, to study regions in England was to be deliberately positioning oneself on the 'alternative' wing of a range of disciplines (with the possible exception of planning). After decades of this samizdat existence, the first Blair government, coming to power with a commitment to devolution, seemed to herald a new dawn for regional thinking in the UK. But now, only eight years after that bright May morning, the pendulum seems to have swung back once again, and devolution is being spoken of as being dead for a generation. It therefore hardly seems to be the time to be celebrating the 'rise of the English regions' in anything other than ironic tones.

However, the last seven years have revealed that there are considerable complementary strengths housed in the regions beyond London. Although British and English policy-making has remained heavily centralised, producing national solutions to problems of national importance, the regions have continued to thrive in their own ways. Despite the barriers to political devolution, to ignore the capacities and potentials lying idle in the English regions seems wilfully to neglect a huge array of talent and dynamism which could contribute to a transformation and modernisation of the UK. Likewise, focusing purely on national roles, on London as a world city, or the South East and East of England as London's hinterland, is to forget the proud heritage of Wessex, the long history of the East End of London as a haven for assimilating refugees and the continued importance of agriculture and regional produce to East Anglia. It seems the English debate somewhere lost sight of – or never really grasped – the value of regional diversity and difference. The abortive English devolution process of the last eight years appears to have revealed that these differences and diversity really do matter.

The Regional Studies Association has tried to be at the forefront of these debates and to provide a forum for discussions of regional devolution and development in England. However, it is an international organisation, and it has proved impossible to reflect in recent years the diversity we mention above. In earlier times, the Regional Studies Association published two studies of the British regions, but these were under quite different conditions. In the early 1980s, as regionalism really disappeared from the national policy agenda, Professor Peter Roberts (1983) led a team of branch members who provided an overview of each region, to try to keep some kind of spotlight on regional differences in economic development debates. A more ambitious programme of activity was undertaken by Professors Townroe and Martin in 1992. Alongside a selection of regional chapters, they presented a set of thematic chapters, highlighting the importance of regional variations in innovation, education and inward investment. In this book, we attempt to revive some of the spirit of those days, and to disentangle our own avowed enthusiasm for regions as sites of economic development and social wellbeing from its connection to any one particular form of political decentralisation.

Our response in this book has therefore been to try to make sense, in the light of the failure of this latest political experiment, of the other dimensions of regional uniqueness and diversity which contribute to broader processes of national change. The UK still suffers from its excessive and implicit centralism, and the theme of this book is that there are huge latent powers within the regions that have the potential to be tapped for the benefit and growth of the nation as a whole. In this chapter, we are setting the scene for conceptualising *why* regions matter, to lead into a more detailed theoretical discussion of the importance of regions, regional institutions and regional culture. There then follows a set of regional chapters, which are explored through the theoretical lens already developed, to gauge the significance of the regional evolutionary process, and whether what has taken place can be regarded as a 'rise'. The book has two main elements. In the first part, we provide some theoretical and background context for the re-emergence of regions as significant actors in economic development. In the second part, we then present a portrait of how each region has been shaped by, and responded to, these challenges, which offers some interesting insights for how a more general process of 'regional rising' is taking place in England. In the final concluding chapter, we turn to reconsider how England can be theorised as a coherent and vibrant nation, recognising the strengths and opportunities that lie within the diversity and dynamism of its constituent regions. In this chapter, we set the context for these discussions by setting out why regions have become more important, what can be learned from elsewhere, and how the current regional rise differs from previous incarnations of regional change.

# Theorising the region

It is necessary at the outset to explain what is meant by a region. Despite its rather abstract idiom, in this book we use a version of the concept that is imbued with a particular set of meanings; as an academic concept, it came back into vogue in the 1970s and 1980s. The recent rising academic interest in concepts of regions has been heavily motivated by its increasing importance to understanding economic development. However, 'English regions' are somewhat *sui generis*; and in the particular language of English governance the phrase refers to a particular division of England into nine parts for the purposes of central administration. It is much easier to conceptualise both the UK government's understanding of regions and why they have in reality become increasingly important through explaining the curious way in which 'regions' and regional institutions have become seen almost exclusively in some circles as a mechanism for promoting innovation, and hence pursuing a particular kind of neo-liberal agenda.

The notion that particular locations, such as cities or regions, can become centres of specialisation is not new. Marshall wrote in 1890 that differential spatial distribution of raw materials led to an 'elementary localisation of industry' (p. 268), but with industrialisation the localisation of industry arose from the 'groups of skilled workers who are gathered within the narrow boundaries of a manufacturing town or a thickly peopled industrial district' (p. 271). Much reference is made to the existence of 'something in the air' in such places, unique advantages which cannot be repeated elsewhere. It is undeniably true that industrialisation never repeated its history precisely in different places (Wennekes, 1993). The successive rise of textiles in Manchester, Flanders, Twente and Münsterland followed very different trajectories shaped by the dominant technological-organisational forms prevalent in each region at each time of take-off. However, in the case of textiles, it is true to say that the poverty associated with industrialisation provoked very regionally specific forms of collective response; however, these responses were shaped by other local factors, and ranged from anti-technology vandalism, garden cities, trade unions and cooperative movements (see Engels, 1851; Howard, 1890). Such early experiences demonstrate the complex interrelation and evolution between economy, place and people, which gave similar arrangements very place-specific features. Understanding the form of those places requires understanding the regional specificities, the general trends, and the outcomes of the interplay of those two factors.

Through the late nineteenth and early twentieth centuries, interest in 'regional studies' in a variety of forms grew. A significant element of this was the work of German economists, notably von Thünen, Weber and Christaller, who developed their theories of systematic place organisation in specific reaction to the universalist ontologies of British classical economists, notably Ricardo and Smith (Hospers, 2004). The French school, and in particular de la Blache, had a strong interest in understanding the causes of regional geographical particularities. The concept of *territoire* was articulated as a way to explain the complex relationship between physical environment, patterns of land use, agricultural practices and social formations. Associated with the study of these concepts came an increasing recognition of their potential value, although de la Blache could arguably be said to have been reflecting, rather than reimagining, traditional localist values which Jacobinist and republican France had strained to eliminate. Similarly, in the UK, Mandrell (2003) highlights the linkages between de la Blache's work on *pays* and the researches of Herbertson and Fleure linking climate, vegetation and society in the UK. She cites Archer's (1993) rather apposite description of these relationships as being Lamarckian – that is, probabilistic and continually evolving – rather than deterministic and complete.

Despite this proliferation of regional studies in the first half of the twentieth century, from the 1930s onwards there was a steady decline in the importance of 'the region' as a unit of economic organisation (Lawton, 1983). Hartshorne (1939) noted that regional geographies made sense only when the region was contextualised in terms of its linkages with the outside world. In the 1950s and 1960s, advances in science in general and computing power in particular seemed to offer the prospect for mapping, describing, analysing and ultimately understanding geographical phenomena, and, more contentiously, producing a more 'scientific' version of geography (Berry and Marble, 1968). This in turn raised hopes that it might be possible to generate a scientific 'grand theory' of activity location by simply putting enough of the right kinds of data into increasingly complex calculative frameworks. Consequently, academic interest in research into the concrete, dynamic meso-level lost much of its interest as an object of study (Schaefer, 1953). Clearly, such atemporal descriptions lacked the necessary rich detail to permit effective comparison across places, times and scales (Bird, 1981), making appropriate compensations for the significances of the differences and similarities between contexts (Sayer, 1989).

Of course, interest in the region never really disappeared; the work of Perroux (1955) dealing with growth poles was later to become revalued in the work of the GREMI school on innovative milieux. What did happen was that in the academic mainstream, ideographic–descriptive analysis was replaced with quantitative–numerical analysis. The work of Isard (*inter alia*, 1956) in establishing the disciplinary foundations of regional science played an important role in shaping the way that, even today, academics consider regions: that is, as linearly bounded spatial units with a limited number of interrelated characteristics.

The resurgence of interest in the region as an intrinsic object of study came at a time of much broader shifts in geography, and produced something of a schism between geographical and economic understandings of regions that have only recently begun to be reconciled. Harvey's (1973) seminal text *Social Justice and the City* was very much at the vanguard of those changes. The book itself charted the 'intellectual transformation' of one geographer from a philosophy of scientific geographical empiricism to a Marxist methodology, and presented a manifesto for change in the discipline. Harvey's previous work, *Explanation in Geography* (1969), was a handbook of empiricism and so his adoption of structural methods to address practical questions of social justice and economic change was highly influential, not least because it provided a rigorous framework to express dissatisfaction with geographical methodologies that were in danger of becoming overly self-referential, abstracting human experiences behind quantitative analyses. By emphasising the qualitative aspects of geography, an agenda was set within which regional difference became a legitimate object of enquiry. Within this intellectual trajectory of critical political economy, a range of concepts were developed to explain the economic importance of regions in terms of their capacity to deal better with the demands of a competitive global economy, from the flexible production system, learning regions, regional innovation systems to the recently ubiquitous clusters.

Although orthodox economics remained somewhat disdainful of regions as objects of enquiry rather than as data types, a number of key developments began to stimulate the development of regional economics back towards studies of particular regions. The new trade theory and geographical economics of Krugman and Venables intersected neatly with the 'new growth theory' of Romer and Solow, emphasising increasing returns to scale and the importance of knowledge as a factor of production. This seemed to suggest that particular places could achieve insurmountable economic advantages over other places, potentially creating a permanent disequilibrium and hence imperfections. The theoretical consequences of this are dealt with at greater length in Chapter 3, but suffice it to say here that when regions moved back into the popular mainstream in the 1990s, it was a lowest common denominator version of the dynamics and dynamism of regions. The version of the 'region' embedded in such an approach seems to suggest that economic development depends on dynamic local networks, channelling international investment into particular regions, exploiting existing unique industrial strengths, and laying the foundations for future productivity growth (Chapman *et al.*, 2004; Bathelt, 2005).

The problem with producing a widely acceptable view of the 'region', in this case as an innovative building-block of a competitive modern economy, is that the level of abstraction hides a number of contradictions in the commonsense concept of a region. The first is the importance of the national conditions which underpin particular regional success; despite the supposed hollowing-out of the nation-state (Scott, 1996), the state is still a particularly important source of regulation (Weiss, 1989). The second is the assumption that successful regions are a paradigm which less successful regions can aspire to rather than a particular outcome of the globalisation process (Amin and Robins, 1991; Gray *et al.*, 1996). Many regions have been successful not on the basis of manufacturing at all, but through agriculture or through the location of a city (Amin, 1993). A third critique of generalising from a few cases is that such generalisations can become politicised, and used to validate particular political projects, particularly in the 1990s, when the Maastricht criteria forced many Western European countries to slash their budgets. Regional institutional innovation can be regarded as a particular organisational response to a collapse of national-level capital–labour agreements (a shift to so-called post-Fordism), of benefit to only a very few regions, and there are a long tail of regions for which flexible specialisation has been a rather negative and unpleasant experience (Hudson, 1989; Kitson and Michie, 1996).

This view of the region, as an innovative building-block of a competitive modern economy, is the point of departure for this book. We would argue that this view of the region embodies a very deterministic and neo-Darwinian view of regional economic development, and we instead wish to use some of the insights of former Lamarckian approaches outlined above (see Mandrell, 2003). Rather than beginning with the rather theoretically limited view of considering how particular regional institutions and activities promote innovation and learning activities, our basis draws on Keating *et al.*'s approach (2003). We argue that beginning from the characteristics of those different places seems a rational point from which to commence a study of how things like trust, culture, reciprocity and associationalism – characteristics which are said to be central to the new regionalism – play out in particular places. Those factors which are often seen as functional or peripheral, such as socio-cultural norms and values, and institutions, can be explored in more detail for their influence in shaping eventual developmental outcomes. This provides the basis for beginning to sharpen the research question, to bring a coherence and structure to the diversity of contributions that the various English regions make to the overall 'national' project.

This task is made doubly difficult by the fact that there is a tendency towards exceptionalism in understanding the British polity which hinders structuring understandings in terms of similarities across different regions. The English regional situation is so self-evidently different from many other countries' that this rather begs the question of what can be learned from those places. But we are proposing something quite radical in this book – understanding an England of organic and interrelated regions – and drawing coherence and similarity between English regions could equally benefit from a wider contextualisation in the experiences of devolution in other European countries. It is to this issue that this chapter now turns.

## Coherence in diversity: lessons from 'overseas'

Contemporaneous regional debates in England now take place against a discouraging background, something that hints that such discussions are at best academic, and at worst futile. On 4 November 2004, around 500,000 voters in the North East of England ended the government's proposals to bring a new form of devolution to the fifty million residents of England. This vote by around 1 per cent of the total population of England seems to bring to a close a process which had slowly built momentum over the previous decade for a formal recognition of the regions of England. In that decade, three successive governments

(Major, Blair I and Blair II) had slowly moved towards having a solid regional tier of government, and elected regional assemblies for some regions were to be the next step in that process.

At every stage, representing the apparent interest in regions and region-alisation, a forensic eye has been passed over each and every proposal, and a huge volume of ink has been spilt in the interests of mapping the early stages of what was anticipated to be a full-blown 'rise of the English regions'. But now all those plans are in tatters; the destination, the journey and even the starting point are overcast with uncertainty and the voluminous and detailed arguments and justifications developed for English elected regional assemblies lie gather-ing dust. The idea that the English regions were, *pace* Harvie (1994), about to bark seems to have given way to the idea that they are best ignored, to be left to lie.

Of course, the referendum in the North East was not the only vote for regional devolution in England. In 2000, the Labour government devolved power in London to an elected Mayor and a new strategic authority, the Greater London Authority (GLA), consisting of twenty-five elected members. Londoners had been asked to vote on whether the elected Mayor and the GLA should be established, in a referendum held in 1998. In contrast to the vote in the North East, the turnout was 34 per cent of the electorate, of which 72 per cent were in favour.

The North East referendum seems an appropriate juncture at which to take stock, to distinguish between the changes and processes contingent on a national political process creating a particular set of regional institutions and a parallel regional process in which the regions have been emerging as increasingly impor-tant actors in their own right. In the 1990s, Leeds, Manchester and Birmingham all blazed trails in building dense agglomerations of knowledge-intensive service industries which formed the basis for a broader urban revitalisation. And yet, despite all the apparent economic potential in these places, their urban and regional revitalisations are too often overshadowed by London's continuing rapacious capacity for seemingly unbounded growth (and a city-region with an elected Mayor!). And whilst the success of London is seen as a *sine qua non* for national success, the relationship between these outlying metropolitan dynamos and the national economy has been only very weakly considered (see Amin *et al.*, 2003).

The historical processes through which England emerged have produced London as the dominant national economic force, which has left outlying places to be regarded as challengers to, rather than complementary with, the capital. If, as we argue, regions are, for a variety of theoretical and empirical reasons, becoming more important, then an understanding of England believed to be dependent on the fortunes of London ignores the reality of an increasingly complex, diverse and heterogeneous nation. It is this oversight which we seek to chart in this book, to tell a story of how the regions have emerged from the shadows cast by London, in a way that strengthens the vitality of the whole nation, including London itself.

One of the oddities of the North East referendum was that the 'no' campaign did not make any specific counter-proposals (Benneworth, 2005; Tickell and Musson, 2005). Nevertheless, the 'no' campaign was able to exploit every shortcoming and weakness of the draft bill, so what made for a very good piece of politics made for a very bad piece of governance. There is an intellectual and conceptual vacuum at the heart of current thinking about the English – there is no longer a strong narrative as to why 'regions' matter for England. And yet, we as editors believe that this is profoundly unsatisfactory, and moreover that the English regions do matter. There is evidence that the historical differences between the regions have become manifested in very different regional styles, offering complementary niches and opportunities to the overall national benefit. We do not conceptualise these contributions in purely economic terms: the life of the nation requires continual revitalisation, and revitalisation driven from across the country is conducive to social inclusion and sustainable development and environmental protection. One important problem is that the collapse of the political-democratic case for regions makes it more difficult to conceptualise their importance beyond a fairly naïve version of new regionalism so robustly critiqued by (*inter alia*) Lovering (2001), cataloguing regional events and activities and assuming their summation into a successful regional whole. In this book, therefore, we seek to develop an alternative (somewhat neo-Lamarckian) framework for understanding regional success, and use this framework to explore each of the regions in some detail. This is possibly best illustrated by reference to a series of international examples of how local context and general factors can interplay to produce unique, but cognate, regional outcomes. The processes through which those outcomes are produced can be regarded as drivers of this 'regional rise', and produce a lens through which to render the English case studies less exceptional.

## International comparisons

The regional dimension in England has historically followed a somewhat peculiar trajectory, a consequence of the denuded sense of what precisely is Englishness. Much has been written about the history of England and the idea of Englishness (*inter alia* Elton, 1992; Easthope, 1999), but what is absent from much of this thinking is the role of heterogeneity within the concept. This arises as a consequence of the elusiveness of the concept of Englishness. Taylor (1991), citing Newman (1987) and Smith (1988), argues that the English are 'a curiously mysterious, elusive and little understood people'. The curiously under-developed nature of the way that Englishness has been conceptualised has left it relatively impermeable to external influences, most notably in articulating effectively regional differences within a broader national consciousness.

## Background

The idea of England was not formed to realise a shared cultural goal of 'the English people', in contrast to what happened in Germany, the Low Countries and Italy, all of which were driven by elite nationalist movements able to mobilise popular sentiments. Rather, Englishness appeared as a political expression of a territory governed from London, which hosted a set of political institutions which themselves exerted control over a series of conquered territories, manifesting itself, as Taylor (1991) argues, through 'patriotism', a personal ethic, rather than a variant of 'nationalism' enforced through a collective structure. The net effect of this has arguably been to imbue Englishness with a character somewhat detached from its territorial origins; although it could be thought to be made in particular places, nowhere can the characteristics of 'the English' be seen (Paxman, 1999).

As a consequence of lacking strong connections to a *Heimat* (homeland), the concept of Englishness is somewhat fragile and one-dimensional, and in some senses is an atemporal and aspatial amalgam of the residual characteristics of those contemporaneous inhabitants of its territory. Certainly, in the 1980s there was a shrinking of the concept of Englishness to 'Middle England', a group which lacked any common defining elements, such as language, culture or identity. The fragility of the idea has left it unable to harness the undoubted regional strengths within England into a coherent social, cultural and economic national project (Newman, 1987). Of course, this has also enabled a significant and valuable cultural assimilation, which has meant that the English electorate has been largely immune to the dubious charms of charismatic 'nationalist' right-wing parties more common in continental Europe (Dodd, 1995).

In this book, we are interested in the potential of decentralisation to harness regional energies towards producing a nation-state better posed to compete and thrive in the new knowledge economy. Although this knowledge economy might appear to be a homogeneous mass, in reality R&D activities, knowledge-intensive business services and value-added engineering operate in hugely functionally differentiated market segments. A successful country needs to have competitive activities across extensive technological, knowledge and commercial fronts. Moreover, competitive economic strengths require a social contract that underpins this economic success with widespread social inclusion, generational justice and the absence of discrimination. Overlooking the diversity and knowledge base in the English regions seems therefore to forgo a set of opportunities for economic development, and, more worryingly, to fail to deal with the considerable social and environmental tensions which are engendered through London-centric economic growth. And yet the problem remains that there is no framework to step outside the self-referential and narcoleptic English regional debates because of assumptions of English exceptionalism, a shortcoming which we seek to address here.

A further consequence of this is that England and the English situation are regarded as being unique, and in attempting to make sense of the English situation, and the relationship between England and its regions, there has been a curious reluctance to draw lessons from other situations. English political discourse, as befits a country with fixed borders and an evolutionary and unwritten constitution, has a peculiarly evolutionary character. Its apparent dependence on present context means that external institutional arrangements appear to have little salience *for* England, because their own contexts differ so widely from those currently prevailing *in* England. At first glance, it is easy to dismiss the value of comparisons because of the seeming difference between the English unitary situation from examples elsewhere (Allum, 1995), where regional decentralisation has released the growth potential of outlying regions.

Indeed, a comparative study in 2000 of regional governance by the UK government (Russell-Barter, 2000: 15) made precisely this point:

> There is [on account of significant national differences] no norm to which the UK is an exception, and no agreement on what regional tiers should look like or how they should operate. There is no common pattern in their size, the functions they command, the source of their origins, their rights of representation at the centre and their control over local government. Rather there is a continuum. The implication of this in the English context is that current practice cannot provide a 'blueprint'.

Federalism is not entirely alien to British thinking: for example, the British government contemplated the need for a federal arrangement during the Cold War. Emergency draft legislation would have created a system of regional commissioners, to be appointed in the event of a full-scale nuclear strike disabling national command and control systems (Hennessey, 2002). Whilst we are of course not arguing that regional disparities and tensions in England are in any way comparable to a war, it is somewhat disingenuous glibly to dismiss what can be learned from elsewhere under all circumstances.

Since the abandonment of the latest regional project in England in the wake of the North East 'no' vote, it is easy to dismiss the English regions as artificial constructs. But what emerges very clearly in the second half of this book is that there are huge real differences between the regions, in terms of what makes them regions internally, and what sets them apart from other places. Looking at different places, we can learn the defining characteristics of the regional mobilisations; that is, we can identify what has led to the adoption of political changes that have altered the way government relationships are undertaken.

We shall now look at how regions have 'risen' elsewhere in Europe, in terms of what leads governments to give greater political recognition to regional interests, and how that in turn shapes localities in ways that produce distinctive regional forms. What is it that legitimates those interests, and can those features and characteristics be identified in the English regions? This allows us to say with more confidence that regional mobilisations have a broader significance, that a set of events is representative of the emergence of regions-in-themselves, which may form the basis for a reworking of the internal cultural, social and economic dynamics of the hollow English state.

## Regions as an outlet for divergent interests: lessons from federal systems

At first sight, formal federations seem very different from England and the UK. Clearly, neither the UK nor England is federal in any way, and the UK has not witnessed anything akin to a formal federal event in which state–nation relationships have formally been defined, such as occurred in the USA (1777), Australia (1901) and Germany (1948). However, the notion that federal relations are frozen in the time when elites decide to federate overlooks the rather obvious point that all real-world federations are themselves continually evolving, with the case of America showing how states can be added and constitutions amended over the centuries of a nation's life. From our perspective, it is interesting when those federal structures evolve to meet the aspirations of a particular shared national prospect because current structures prove inadequate to express changes in shared social and cultural norms and values.

One case in point would be Belgium, which emerged from the United Kingdom of the Netherlands from 1830 to 1839, and has since evolved a peculiar and distinct form of governance. The Brussels uprising against Willem I was inspired by the domination of the smaller Calvinist–Dutch northern provinces over the Catholic–French communities of the south (Wennekes, 1993). Empire and the depradations of Emperor Leopold III made Brussels the centre of a Belgian government ruled by French elites, making the northern Flemish minority (Catholic but Dutch speaking) something of a junior partner. The economic decline of Wallonia after the Second World War created tensions between the cultural groups, which required a rebalancing of power relationships, leading to the creation of the new federal state in 1980. The aim of creating a federal state was to balance these communal tensions, and allow for some agreement on national unity, preventing every tension reaching a crisis situation in which 'Every move by Flanders is seen as an attempt to break the national solidarity. Every reluctant reaction from Wallonia is seen by Flanders as the proof that Wallonia wants to live on Flemish subsidies' (Keating *et al.*, 2003: 106). The resultant situation is almost indescribably complicated, involving a twofold form of decentralisation to territorial regions and cultural-based communities, a euphemism for a regional government with competencies limited to the personal sphere of cultural and educational services. This situation is further complicated by the fact that the entity known as 'Flanders' has competencies as both a territorial region and a cultural-based community.[1] Conversely, Wallonia is only a territorial region. Brussels is also a territorial region, fully bilingual, and host to the francophone 'community' (Hendricks, 2001). To the east, a minority German-speaking group numbering some 71,000, inherited as a consequence of boundary changes after the First World War, has its own linguistic community. In the 1960s, when the linguistic communities were being established to alleviate Fleming–Walloon tensions, there was no rational reason not to establish a parallel authority for Germans.

In Germany itself, the Basic Law (*Grundgesetz*) of 1948 was drafted in a legal *terra nulla* to prevent the future domination of a unified Germany by any single state, as had been the case with Prussia from the 1850s onwards. An important part of this was the principle of *Finanzausgleich*, financial equalisation between the *Länder*, building a strong unitary welfare state within the federal system. However, in 1991 Germany experienced economic, monetary and social union with its eastern territories, separately established as the German Democratic Republic, whose wealth was substantially lower than that of the western *Länder* buoyed by the 1950s and 1960s *Wirtschaftswunder*. A supposed founding principle of centre–regional relations was amended specifically to take into account the overwhelming desire at the time of Germans for the formation of a unified German state.

Of course, these two countries are not examples of federalism providing perfect solutions to regional disparities and tensions. Flemish nationalism does still threaten – at some level – the integrity of the Belgian state. The recent phenomenon of '*Ostalgia*' in Germany, harking back to the certainties of the planned economy and its attendant full employment, highlights the transitory political windows of opportunity within which large constitutional changes can be made. However, the cases of Germany and Belgium do show the value of addressing these disparities to provide outlets for tensions which threaten the overall territorial integrity of the state.

Rather than simply arguing that England's unwritten constitution makes a federal approach irrelevant, Belgium and Germany suggest that federal structures can provide the basis to deal flexibly with divergent regions to which a unitary state is unresponsive. Clearly, in England one of the reasons for recent interest in regions is the growing divergence between rich and poor regions. It is perhaps unsurprising that more cognisance has not been taken of how 'spatial fixes' within federal systems have been used to provide routes for the expression of regional interests at the national level.

This provides us with the first element of the 'regional rise', where in the English regions we have seen socio-economic changes which have increased the levels of particular tensions, and crystallised tensions that were previously regarded as unimportant. Certainly, in the North East of England, although the existence of a distinct and singular identity has been widely disputed by some, there is clearly a common manufacturing-based culture prevalent from the Tees in the south to the Wansbeck in the north. The failure of central politicians to do much more than manage the decline of manufacturing has solidified this identity. And although this regional identity distinctiveness was not enough to force a 'yes' vote in the regional referendum, in Byrne and Benneworth's chapter (Chapter 6) it is argued that there is a definite coherence to the North East which suggests a region on the rise.

## Regional disparities and unequal geometries

In the German and Belgian cases, a federal system was amended at particular times to incorporate the needs of specific territorial and cultural interests along specific binary divides, Flemish/Walloon or *Wessi/Ossi*. In England, as was noted earlier, it is almost as if England's regions are 'little nations' themselves, with different characteristics and different defining features, so there is no simple binary divide to be addressed.

Whilst bespoke federal solutions are clearly impossible under the current British arrangements, other non-federal countries have introduced a range of political structures to differentiate between the needs of particular places. Formal maps of the EU always include pull-out boxes showing territories which are politically part of the European Union, including Martinique, Réunion, Guyana, the Azores and the Canaries. France in particular recognises the special status of *départements outre mer*, notionally identical to the mainland departments, but separated from France by more than the ocean. Likewise, the devolution to the Saami autonomous community in Norway is permitted precisely because it is a one-off distinction between two groups, rather than a more comprehensive settlement for a range of competing interests.

Spain is a very good example of a country that has introduced a more general differentiation of its regions, granting various levels of autonomy to regions depending on their overall coherence and need. The devolution process in Spain began immediately after the end of dictatorship, as part of the preparation for membership of the European Community, developing a new constitution with an abundance of checks and balances, including the autonomous communities (ACs). Despite the common nomenclature, the powers enjoyed by the ACs vary widely. The Basque Country in particular benefits from full fiscal federalism, under a statute in which its government is the primary taxing authority, paying a share to Madrid, unlike the other ACs, which are reliant on redistribution from the centre for their transfer payments. This high degree of autonomy at times does not appear sufficient to bind the Basque Country to Spain, and it could be compared to the devolution situation of Northern Ireland in the UK. Other Spanish regions have proceeded at different paces – there is not a simple Basque exceptionalism. Language is not the sole defining feature of devolution: whilst Catalonia enjoys a relatively high degree of autonomy within a unitary state, Galicia, despite having a language as distinct from Castilian as is Catalan, has a much weaker set of institutions. Keating *et al.* (2003) argue that this is a consequence more of the way powers have been used rather than formal institutional networks, with Catalan nationalists keen to demonstrate their difference from central politicians, whilst Galicia has been dominated by the national centre-right party, which is determined to maintain traditional patronage-based governance structures. And whilst Catalonia has powered forward in terms of its wealth levels, Galicia languishes as a backward region largely disregarded by the Spanish state.

There are by contrast not such sharp divisions in the English regions: a few regional languages are now entirely dead (the most politically salient of which is Cornish), and Taylor (1991) argues that the strongest real cleavage is between a 'Crown Heartland', the so-called Home Counties, and what he terms 'Upper England'. However, even within these two areas there are strong divisions (Fawcett, 1919), interrelated with the different roles played by the dominant urban and industrial places in each region. Such differences are qualitatively hard to discern; there are not, in marked contrast with the west coast of Scotland, strong communal divisions along religious lines. But the fact that the English situation is regarded as homogeneous arises because there is little capacity within central government to deal with those differences beyond bilateral discussions and the occasional symbolic multilateral gesture such as the ill-fated 'Council of the Isles' (the British–Irish Council). Leaving aside the recent rhetorical flushes associated with *Northern Way* and *Midland Way*, it must be acknowledged that government, even those elements nominally responsible for spatial policy, are incapable of making sensible distinctions between those regions.

In the absence of strong distinctions, this further problematises the English question; as in the case of Galicia, politicians in peripheral English regions have difficulties in capturing the national political imagination, and making a place for themselves in the overall national project. This is a huge waste of the potential human resources of those places, and undermines their contribution to national growth and development. But the story is not that political structures *always* produce these beneficial effects: indeed, the apparent failure of Galicia to use language as the basis to create structures for economic development makes that clear. In Part II of this book, we see some examples of apparently spontaneous mobilisations where regional coalitions have come together to try to raise their profile nationally, to rework the sense of Englishness in ways that allow for regional differences and recognise the particular strengths of different regions. This is the second element of the regional rise with which we are concerned: the emergence of local and regional capacity to exploit whatever political structures exist, to make the case for that region at a higher political level.

## Autonomous actors in unitary states

One defining feature of England and Englishness that we have already noted is the dominance of London, with the interests of England being assumed to be synonymous with those of the capital and the rump of prosperous localities lying in its orbit. There are other countries with similar problems, and France is often cited as one example of a unitary state with a primate city most analogous to the UK's. Balogh (2004) argues that this is also true in Central and Eastern Europe. Relatively evenly balanced economies have been greatly distorted in recent years by divergent levels of growth within capital regions, diverting investment and regeneration from those outlying areas in greatest need of restructuring.

In the case of France, its modernist founding fathers bequeathed a state so founded on the principles of equality that its counties were numbered in strict alphabetical order, as a means of facilitating central political control. However, from the 1950s onwards, serious efforts were made to devolve and decentralise powers, and in particular to ensure the growth of alternative economic and political powerhouses outside Paris and the Île-de-France. The regions of Rhône-Alpes and Provence-Alpes-Côte d'Azur (PACA) emerged as alternative economic engines for the national economy. PACA was strengthened with the creation of a new science city in the south, Sophia-Antipolis, and although this was imagined as a purely economic device, its success in wealth generation has led to the formation of a regional authority, taking powers away from communes the better to manage and plan its future prospects.

Much is made of the formal decentralisation which led Jacques Chirac to declare in 2002 that France was a devolved state. This process of devolution or decentralisation has been slowly emerging since the 1950s, with the creation of appointed regional prefectures, the *conseils régionaux*, in the 1970s and direct elections to them from 1986. Although their powers vary, and are certainly limited, their importance to the national state was demonstrated in March 2004 when the national administration of the day was hamstrung by regional elections which voted overwhelmingly against the policies and personalities of the central state. The bodies have begun in many cases to incorporate regional character-istics, dealing with such issues as minority languages (Breton, Occitan and Catalan), but also entering into cross-border partnerships with regional bodies in other countries, with the regional authorities active in a range of INTERREG and EUREGIO projects.

The lesson from France is not that devolution or flexible decentralisation produces economic growth, although there is certainly a relationship of indeter-minate directionality. The key point is that an indicator of emergent regions is the production of significant new political forms which are not necessarily mandated from the centre, but which provide a means to assimilate shared local characteristics and articulate local interests at a broader level, with both other regions and the nation-state. Clearly, in this sense the recent emergence of *Northern Way* and *Midland Way* in England is one such spontaneous mobilisation, although there are seemingly precious few other notable examples. The third feature of rising regions is therefore the emergence of endogenous political structures, legitimate in their own right, but which become mechanisms for expressing a broader set of sentiments and interests.

## The 'rise of the English regions'?

Regionalisation processes clearly operate independently of the political systems in which they take root, and all are to some extent unique. However, there are some parallels which can be drawn in terms of trying to make sense of the otherwise incomprehensible English regional question. Whilst no other state has the complexities of the Belgian situation, with its two parallel and over-lain forms of devolution, territorial governments and cultural communities, Belgium's problems with respect to defusing tensions of largely spatially distinct communities with divergent cultural aspirations are seen elsewhere.

Language/culture-based regionalism has been a driving force in many regional movements. Arguably, Brittany, Galicia, Flanders, Catalonia, Åland and Wales' devolution and regionalisation processes have far more in common in terms of the role played by language than in the similarities of the institutional frameworks which have emerged in each region. In this book, we seek to identify such commonalities in the English regions in terms of the significant mobilisation elements, significance being regarded in terms of the European regions cited above. One of the strengths of the South West, for example, is the extent to which Cornish nationalism has thrived despite an official insistence that Cornwall is not a region.

There is clearly a complexity in the interrelation between political representation and the 'region-in-itself'. The Spanish autonomous communities were not simply functional creations of Spanish elites to gain access to European markets by presenting a devolved and democratic constitution. In Belgium, constitutional change is being driven to meet the demands of conflicting communities. In the Netherlands, a proposed novel form of urban government which was claimed to be ideal for meeting the needs of city-regions, the urban province, was defeated in parliament in the 1980s because of fears among smaller urban local authorities that these new provinces would be dominated by the largest cities. Although in England there might not be political representation for our regions, Part II of this book demonstrates the extent to which the regions function in themselves. The question to answer then becomes: how can these regional assets and energies be productively employed in the furtherance of a broader 'national' project?

It is not for this book to speculate on whether the recent failure of the English regional project occurred because of a mismatch of the political structures on offer and the aspirations of the regional communities of England. However, a simple reading of the situation, that the North East referendum in 2004 reflected a lack of interest in regions, captures the complexity of the different constellations of interests, cultures and similarities in evidence in the regions of England. In Part II, we look in detail at the English regions, to highlight some similarities in the way in which they have started to assert themselves autonomously. This forms the basis for our concluding discussion concerning how these disparate elements and strengths might potentially cohere into a new form of Englishness more substantial than the currently rather one-dimensional post-imperial nationhood.

The message from this book that we, as editors, return to in the concluding chapter is that the fates of the English regions *are* bound together through collective national destiny. The national level, despite talk of hollowing-out by supra-national institutions, remains highly important for all the regions. That much is already understood, and is indeed a centrepiece of the *Weltanschauung* of the British polity. What seems less appreciated is the fact that the regions remain highly important for the centre. Although it is understood economically, in terms of the much-referenced (by HM Treasury) £39 billion productivity gap, the other benefits of strong regions for a more coherent and more dynamic centre do not appear entirely clear. The case of London winning the Olympics bid may be a little trite, but the support by the regions for the capital seems a neat metaphor for what this 'rise of the regions' means in practical terms. Each region brings very different and complementary facilities, and a pleasant

consequence is that a poor suburb of London is intensively developed, transport links improved and urban sprawl limited. Of course, the British polity is capable of evolving unpredictably in response to all kinds of problems and opportunities and the regional agenda is by no means compelling. However, if the UK is to revitalise itself in the twenty-first century, harnessing the potential of all its regions is clearly an imperative demanding further attention.

## Note

1   The Flemish authorities defend this situation aggressively, and as Brussels has grown, and francophone communities have been established in Flemish territories, there have been hostile stand-offs in campaigns for formal recognition of bilingualism, notably in the municipality of Brussels-Halle-Vilvoorde.

## References

Allum, P. (1995) *State and Society in Western Europe*, Oxford: Basil Blackwell.

Amin, A. (1993) 'The globalisation of the economy – an erosion of regional networks?', in G. Grabher (ed.), *The Embedded Firm – on the Socioeconomics of Industrial Networks*, London: Routledge.

Amin, A. and Robins, K. (1991) 'These are not Marshallian times', in R. Camagni (ed.), *Innovation Networks: Spatial Perspectives*, London: Belhaven.

Amin, A., Massey, D. and Thrift, N. J. (2003) *Decentering the Nation: A Radical Approach to Regional Inequality*, London: Catalyst.

Balogh, Z. (2004) 'The new regionalism in the Central and Eastern European countries: lessons for dealing with peripherality in the new European Union', *Regions*, 256: 10–15.

Bathelt, H. (2005) 'Cluster relations in the media industry: exploring the "distanced neighbour" paradox in Leipzig', *Regional Studies*, 39: 105–28.

Benneworth, P.S. (2005) 'What happened in the North East? Where do we go from here', paper presented to Regions after the Referendum – the End of a Dream?, QMW seminar, London, 12 January.

Berry, B. and Marble, D. (eds) (1968) *Spatial Analysis*, Englewood Cliffs, NJ: Prentice-Hall.

Bird, J. (1981) 'The target of space and the arrow of time', *Transactions of the Institute of British Geographers*, 6(2): 129–51.

Chapman, K., MacKinnon, D. and Cumbers, A. (2004) 'Adjustment or renewal in regional clusters? A study of diversification amongst SMEs in the Aberdeen oil complex', *Transactions of the Institute of British Geographers*, 29: 382–94.

Dodd, P. (1995) *The Battle over Britain*, London: Demos.

Easthope, A. (1999) *Englishness and National Culture*, London: Routledge.

Elton, G. (1992) *The Peoples of Europe: The English*, Oxford: Blackwell.

Engels, F. (1851) *The Condition of the Working Class in England*, London: Penguin.

Fawcett, C.B. (1919) *Provinces of England: A Study of Some Geographical Aspects of Devolution*, London: Hutchison.

Gray, M., Golob, E. and Markusen, A. (1996) 'Big firms, long arms, wide shoulders: the "hub-and-spoke" industrial district in the Seattle region', *Regional Studies* 30(7): 651–66.

Hartshorne, T. (1939) *The Nature of Geography: A Critical Survey of Current Thought in the Light of the Past*, Lancaster, PA: Geographical Association.

Harvey, D. (1969) *Explanation in Geography*, London: Edward Arnold.

—— (1973) *Social Justice and the City*, Oxford: Basil Blackwell.

Harvie, C. (1994) *The Rise of Regional Europe*, London: Routledge.

Hendricks, F. (2001) 'Belgium: federalism and subnational government in a divided country', in J. Loughlin (ed.), *Subnational Democracy in the European Union: Challenges and Opportunities*, Oxford: Oxford University Press.

Hennessey, P. (2002) *The Secret State: Whitehall and the Cold War*, Harmondsworth: Allen Lane, the Penguin Press.

Hospers, G.J. (2004) *Regional Economic Change in Europe: A Neo-Schumpeterian Vision*, Münster/London: LIT-Verlag.

Howard, E. (1890) *Garden Cities of Tomorrow*, Welwyn Garden City: Atlas Books.

Hudson, R. (1989) *Wrecking a Region – State Policies, Party Politics and Regional Change in North East England*, London: Pion.

Isard, W. (1956) *Location and Space Economy*, Cambridge, MA: MIT Press.

Keating, M., Loughlin, J. and Deschouwer, K. (2003) *Culture, Institutions and Economic Development: A Study of Eight European Regions*, Cheltenham: Edward Elgar.

Kitson, M. and Michie, J. (1996) 'Manufacturing capacity, investment and employment', in J. Michie and J. Grieve Smith (eds), *Creating Industrial Capacity – Towards Full Employment*, Oxford: Oxford University Press.

Lawton, R. (1983) 'Space, place and time', *Geography*, 68(3): 193–207.

Lovering, J. (2001) 'The coming regional crisis (and how to avoid it)', *Regional Studies*, 35(4): 349–54.

Mandrell, A. (2003) 'Hilda Ormsby: negotiating the "ordinary" region and "normal" geographical enquiry 1918–1939', paper presented to 'Geography, Serving Society and the Environment', RGS/IBG International Annual Conference, 3–5 September.

Marshall, A. (1890) *Principles of Economics*, London: Macmillan.

Newman, G. (1987) *The Rise of English Nationalism*, London: Weidenfeld & Nicolson.

Paxman, J. (1999) *The English: A Portrait of a People*, London: Penguin.

Perroux, F. (1955) 'La notion de pôle de croissance', in *idem* (1969) *L'Économie du XXe siècle*, revised third edition, Paris: Presses Universitaires de France.

Roberts, P. (1983) *Report of an Inquiry into Regional Problems in the UK*, Norwich: Geo Books.

Russell Barter, W. (2000) *Regional Government in England – a Preliminary Review of Literature and Research Findings*, London: DETR.

Sayer, A. (1989) 'The "new" regional geography and problems of narrative', *Environment and Planning D: Society and Space*, 7(2): 253–76.

Schaefer, F.K. (1953) 'Exceptionalism in geography: a methodological examination', *Annals of the American Society of Geographers*, 64: 189–92.

Scott, A.J. (1996) 'Regional motors of the global economy', *Futures*, 28(5): 391–411.

Smith, G. (1988) *The English Reader: An Anthology*, London: Pavilion.

Taylor, P.J. (1991) 'The English and their Englishness: a curiously mysterious, elusive and little understood people', *Scottish Geographical Magazine*, 107(3): 146–61.

Tickell, A. and Musson, S. (2005) 'The referendum campaign: issues and turning points in the North East', ESRC Devolution and Constitutional Change Briefing No. 20, Swindon: ESRC.

Townroe, P. and Martin, R. (eds) (1992) *Regional Development in the 1990s: The UK in Transition*, London: Jessica Kingsley.

Weiss, L. (1989) 'Regional economic policy in Italy', in C. Crouch and D. Marquand (eds), *The New Centralism: Britain out of Step in Europe*, Oxford: Blackwell.

Wennekes, W. (1993) *De Aartsvaders: Grondleggers van het Nederlandse Bedrijfsleven*, Amsterdam: Atlas.

# 2 Regions and regional identity

*Peter Roberts and Mark Baker*

## Introduction: the fall and rise of the region

It is somewhat ironic that as globalisation extends its web of economic uniformity and ever-increasing cultural blandness, the importance of place and regional identity has increased. This phenomenon can be seen at various levels: the European Spatial Development Perspective (ESDP) (Commission of the European Communities, 1999) has emphasized the need to respect and reinforce the distinctiveness of place, devolution to the Celtic nations and the Greater London region of England is a reflection of the political importance attached to place-based and national or regional politics, whilst the increased attention paid to regions, sub-regions and city-regions as key spatial components for the planning and development of England is evident in a number of recent governmental and academic studies (DTLR, 2002; ODPM, 2004; Roberts and Baker, 2004).

Despite the renewed attention which is paid to issues of regional identity, definition, planning and governance, the most noticeable feature of the broad regional debate over the past six decades is its rollercoaster nature. This uneven history applies equally to both the theory and the implementation of the regional concept. Given that the regional debate has its origins in long-standing concerns about the nature, definition and practical implementation of territorial units that can be used for various purposes, it is hardly surprising that the notion and application of the region have been subject to considerable dispute. As is evident in daily press reports, the term 'region' is defined and utilized in many ways, some of which contradict the implicit assumptions which underpin the use made of the word elsewhere in this book: that is, that the region is a territorial unit smaller in physical extent and political significance than the nation-state. Politicians and other commentators commonly refer to transnational regions, such as the Middle East or Central America, reflecting their geopolitical perceptions and agendas. Whilst this usage may contrast with the dominant application of 'region', it does reflect two defining characteristics of the region which are discussed later in this chapter: the elements of territorial commonality and relative homogeneity. Although these difficulties of definition and application have constantly created confusion in the minds of certain analysts and politicians, the cause of the uneven progress of the regional idea lies not so much in disputes over definition, but rather in the ways in which the regional concept has been applied. Wannop (1995) and others have referred to the pattern of decline and fall of the regional idea, in particular in circumstances when the region has been used as a vehicle for planning or development. However, despite the 'mercurial' (Wannop, 1995) nature of the regional debate and its application in practice, the fact remains that regions in their varying guises are enduring elements of the geographical, planning and political landscape of England.

However, within the general debate on the definition and identity of the region, with regard to the situation in England it is also necessary to consider the special question of the constitutional position of sub-national government. Unlike other member states of the European Union, the United Kingdom lacks a written constitution which sets out and guarantees the powers, duties and responsibilities of the various tiers of government. This arrangement creates both problems and opportunities. In the past it has resulted, for example, in the abolition of regional-level metropolitan government when the metropolitan county councils and the Greater London Council were swept away, but it has also enabled the establishment of regional-level agencies and institutions for special purposes without the need for wholesale constitutional and administrative change. Irrespective of the merits or demerits of the particular constitutional arrangements which exist in the United Kingdom – a topic to which this chapter will return later – the politics of sub-national government and governance would appear to exert a significant influence over the nature and application of the regional model: without political capacity and capability even the best regional plans and programmes are likely to lack the powers which are necessary in order to ensure that they are implemented in full.

A final point of introduction links the two preceding issues – the relatively 'mercurial' nature of the regional model and the absence of a constitutional system which might help to nurture embryonic regional arrangements – and also reflects the importance which is attached to the governance of regions. In using the term 'governance' rather than 'government', the intention is to widen the scope of the debate on the effective management of regional space (Roberts, 2000). This wider-than-government approach also represents an attempt to link 'process' with 'product' in terms of the nature and quality of territorial governance: such an approach suggests that the region is more than an administrative convenience or an ephemeral political unit. Rather, the region or sub-region can be seen to represent a relatively permanent feature in the socio-political landscape. Whatever local government arrangements may come or go, the broad regional structure of England has proved to be remarkably enduring. Equally, the sub-regional units and organizations – be they formal or informal – provide a degree of continuity in a kaleidoscopic pattern of local government areas. These enduring characteristics of the regional and sub-regional territories of England have been said by some commentators to reflect the inherent qualities of this level of governance – strong identity and inherent functionality – whilst others have argued that the absence of formal government arrangements offers the possibility of providing operational flexibility for the management of space. Despite the rejection of the devolution package which was offered to the electorate of North East England, principally on the grounds that it contained too few powers, it is evident that a strong North East identity remains. Using Scotland as a mirror to reflect the English regions, it has long been possible to argue that the region can be regarded as a 'reality in popular consciousness' (Royal Commission on Local Government in Scotland, 1969: 167).

The following sections of this chapter offer a series of reflections on various aspects of the regional (and sub-regional) debate, and especially in relation to the questions of what is a region, what is the nature of the regional 'problem', what is the scope and content of regional analysis, planning and programming, what is the role of regional identity and consciousness in the governance of regional space, and what potential does the region offer as a common 'vehicle' for the delivery of a range of policy objectives? Although in this chapter 'region' is chiefly used in the generally accepted formal sense of the 'standard' region – that is, the Government Office region, of which there are nine in England – it is also used in a more generic manner in order to reflect the full range of alternative definitions and applications. As will become evident, concept and definition are two sides of the same coin in matters related to territorial analysis, whilst in operational terms it is often helpful to regard precise boundaries as barriers to clear strategic vision, understanding and planning. Patrick Abercrombie (1937) offered sage advice to the would-be regional analyst or planner when he advocated ignoring administrative boundaries as an aid to clear strategic thinking and action. This advice is sometimes heeded, but more frequently it is ignored in the majority of regional planning and development exercises.

## Defining the region

The region is an ancient administrative unit, used either to define and delimit a territory smaller than the nation–state or, as was noted in the preceding section, to describe a unit of territory at a sub–global scale. Political scientists, planners, geographers, historians, students of public administration and, more occasionally, sociologists, psychologists and philosophers, have all grappled with the task of providing an authoritative and universally applicable definition of the region, but without total success. This lack of success in developing a universal concept and method of application is not, however, a problem; rather it indicates the inherent flexibility and value of the region as a territorial concept and as a formal or informal unit of analysis and administration. It also reflects the different constitutional position of regions in the UK and elsewhere in the European Union (Committee of the Regions, 2001).

Grieve (1964: 18) hints at the ubiquity and essential robustness of the regional concept and the region when he describes the evolution of regional planning in France. He argues that (rational) economic planning is not enough, and that the formulation and implementation of regional policy need to go beyond the recognition of 'importance not only in the material senses but in the social and aesthetic senses'. This view of the region as more than an area of land or an economic object is one to which this chapter will return, but at this juncture it is sufficient to indicate that in some cases a region can and does extend beyond the national territory in order to express the commonality of a culture or a social system. Whilst such a view may not appear to be directly acknowledged or applicable in England – at least, in the sense that it is evident and accepted in the wider 'hidden' or 'stateless' nation (beyond Spain and into France) of Catalonia or in the use of 'region' to describe and implement a number of transfrontier exercises elsewhere in mainland Europe – it is increasingly evident that the region is a unit of territory to which the residents of such an area feel a sense of attachment and/or loyalty. Although this aspect of the regional concept may not be as explicitly evident in England, it is possible to point to the undertones of social attachment and regional loyalty which were evident in the concerns expressed about the transfer of areas of Yorkshire (part of the then Yorkshire and Humberside standard region) to Greater Manchester and Lancashire (part of the North West region) as a consequence of the local government reorganization of 1974; these concerns were, in part, the result of the strict rule in force at the time regarding the eligibility of persons to play cricket for Yorkshire. So even in England regional attachment is not just about economic logic and resource allocation.

The above discussion of the primary distinction between the region as an economic unit and as a socio-cultural and political territory opens up a further debate on the fundamental nature of territory and space. Once again, it is evident that this second distinction is not new. Boudeville, for example, distinguishes between space and the region; for him, an 'economic region is a continuous and localized area' whilst an 'economic space is not' (Boudeville, 1966: 3). By distinguishing between space and territory – something which few English analysts in recent years have attempted to do – Boudeville provides a point of entry into the wider debate on the typology of regions. This entry point is important because it allows the analyst to distinguish between the non-spatial notion of economic or mathematical space, which could be used anywhere, and geographical space, which has the role of fixing or applying the economic or mathematical variables in a locational sense. The importance of this 'transformation' is seen by Boudeville to be central to any attempt to build a typology: space in this sense can be defined 'in terms of homogeneity, polarization, or finality' (Boudeville, 1966: 2). In searching for the underlying logic of the ESDP and the various manifestations of its understanding of the drivers of change at work in the European spatial system, a sensible point of origin would appear to be the contribution made by the French school of regional analysis and planning during the late 1950s and 1960s. By emphasizing the importance of identifying and analysing the strengths and weaknesses evident in a given regional structure, they established a number of the fundamental mea-surements currently used to assess the coherence and potential for application of regional units of territory. This approach can still be seen to be valued as a means of assessing the logic of regional and sub-regional operational structures, as is evident in the recent French initiative on co-operation in metropolitan regions (DATAR, 2004).

These fundamental distinctions between territory and space, including the importance of identifying the essential characteristics of operational regions, are of considerable significance in the current regional debate in England. It is apparent, for example, that some of the Regional Economic Strategies prepared by the Regional Development Agencies (RDAs) focus on issues in economic space that are strictly speaking outwith their ability to control or influence. In one sense, responsibility for the planning and development of an individual region could be seen to have been transferred to the relatively amorphous zone of the global economy; this is an economic space over which an individual region exercises little or no control and this is likely to cause the replication of a number of the problems which have traditionally been associated with the 'branch plant economy'. Although such problems continue to beset regional agencies, in reality they reflect the enduring distinction which was identified by Boudeville in 1966. As such, it is surely better to acknowledge the differences between the various regional types, and seek to accommodate these differences in regional operational models, than to attempt to superimpose an unrealistic regional universal model on an increasingly 'open' and fragmented regional space.

A further dimension of the territory and space debate has significant implications for the practical application of the regional model. This reflects the desirability or otherwise of regional self-containment. As has been argued by many observers over the years, whilst regional uniqueness may prove to be a desirable attribute for the purposes of study, it does not always prove helpful when the region in question is chiefly considered to be a means of ensuring equality in service delivery or providing a basis for administration. In this context the determination of self-containment can only be considered to be a relative measure of the extent to which a region is unique and, as such, it is important to remind ourselves of the warning given by W.G. East that 'regions are often conceptual – creations of the geographer's mind – rather than intrinsic and evident realities of the landscape' (East, 1967: 9). This warning is all the more stark when it is acknowledged that the boundaries of the standard regions of England have been adjusted by successive governments without recourse to any formal committee of inquiry or detailed research study. Regions for most political and service delivery purposes would appear to be useful as long as they don't present an inconvenient barrier to the implementation of a preferred policy or the achievement of a specified target.

Much of the preceding discussion represents a variation on the theme of the relationship between territory and space, rather than offering a basic assessment of the fundamental characteristics of the region. In this context it is valuable to consider the nature of the national–regional interface, especially in the determination of what are the primary purposes and functions of each of these spatial levels. This is an issue of long standing, with no clear agreement emerging despite decades of debate. Strassoldo's definitions based on the semantic content of the two words 'nation' and 'region' represent a summary of the debate: 'the nation involves the idea of biological community, of blood (nation from nasci, to be born); the region, on the contrary, conveys the meaning of rational organisation ("regio" from "regere", "to govern") [and] historically the nation has concerned itself mainly with self-assertion, armed forces and war, while the region strives for co-operation, administration and planning' (Strassoldo, quoted in European Conference of Ministers Responsible for Regional Planning, 1973: 3).

Although Strassoldo's definitions help to clarify the theoretical purposes and functions of the nation and the region, the reality, as will be discussed in greater detail later, is that in England government and governance have long been dominated by national and local institutions. However, if the three Celtic nations of the UK are also considered, it can be seen that the sub-nation-state level of governance, which in these cases is coincident with what have previously been described as 'hidden' or 'stateless' nations (Balcells, 1996; Ventura, 1963), has existed for many years. The former governmental arrangements discharged by the Scottish, Welsh and Northern Ireland Offices reflect the enduring validity and viability of the small nation–cum–region, even though it has been observed by some researchers that the powers of these territorial administrations were somewhat circumscribed by the imposition of controls from the central state. As has been noted, in Scotland and Wales prior to devolution, territorial management was constrained by strict conditions which precluded 'significant variations in policy implementation if the Imperial core is not prepared to countenance such variations' (Goldsmith, 1986: 167).

What the Celtic nation model demonstrates, however, is that territory, culture and the socio-political 'natural' small nation–cum–region are enduring features of government and governance. One example of the survival of a socio-political 'natural' region in England can be seen in the continued presence of government for the London region. Despite a number of attempts to restrict or destroy regional government for London, this 'natural' socio-political region has survived: the London County Council became the Greater London Council, and the presence of London-wide government now continues in the form of the Greater London Authority. One explanation for the survival of such regional units is provided by the presence of certain bonds of economy, society and culture, or the influence imposed by the presence of controls associated with the capacity of the natural environment, or both, which require that a territory is governed at a specific spatial level. These ideas can be traced back to the work of de Tocqueville, Ruskin, Comte and Geddes, who argued in favour of the somewhat elusive 'natural', ecological or bio-region (Harvie, 1994). Such ideas survive to the present day and offer evidence of the inherent value of sub-nation-state arrangements for government and governance. A second explanation for the presence of 'natural' regional units is the inevitable tendency to default to such a territorial arrangement in the absence of a viable alternative. In part, the recent emergence of city-regions, sub-regions and core (big) cities is testimony to the inherent usefulness of these spatial units, which can best be considered as territories of identity and allegiance. A third and final explanation reflects the simple fact that the 'natural' region has frequently been reinforced by successive rounds of infrastructure investment. As a consequence, although local government boundaries may be adjusted or radically altered, 'central city' remains at the hub of the transport system and this, in turn, defines the region.

Such ideas are not new. Indeed, Geddes (1915) was describing the city-region and the conurbation as reflections and physical manifestations of the functional evolution of a natural region over ninety years ago. This relationship between the region as an object of study and as a natural reality introduces the second element of this section of the chapter: the definition of the region.

Once again, the origins and substance of the modern regional concept can be traced back to the work of early twentieth-century planners, geographers and political scientists. As Glasson (1974: 18) notes, whilst the fundamental elements of the debate on the nature and form of the region have existed for well over a century, the 'idea of the region has been much used and abused over the years and there have been numerous controversies and disagreements over its meaning'. This history of disagreement is not uniquely English; rather it reflects a wider debate which would appear, quite appropriately, to transcend national interests and perceptions. Most important among the basic distinctions is the division between formal and functional regions. Although various elaborations and systems of classification have extended and complicated this simple distinction, the formal–functional divide is still helpful. Put simply, the formal region is an area which is uniform or homogeneous in relation to certain specified criteria, be the criteria physical, social, economic or a reflection of some other characteristic. By way of contrast, the functional region has been described as 'a classic example of unity in diversity' (Minshull, 1967: 40); an area which in terms of the defining characteristics of a formal region would be considered diverse, but also an area which displays an essential unity in relation to a range of activities. Such functional relationships include activities such as journey-to-work, the retail catchment of a single urban centre or a group of urban centres, or the area of influence associated with some other type of service provision or function.

Whilst traditionally geographers and planners have devoted considerable time and effort to the development of an ever more complex and sophisticated analysis of formal and functional regions, including the elaboration of the functional region model to incorporate functional relationships between areas which are spatially separate and connected only by functional bonds such as trade routes, the reality of modern regional analysis suggests that the formal and the functional are now often intermeshed. In one sense this is not a new phenomenon. Geddes (1915), in developing his classic valley section and bioregional model, made reference to what in strict terms could be considered to be both the formal and the functional characteristics of a region. By linking the formal and the functional characteristics, Geddes argued in favour of treating the region as an entity within which evolving activities could and should be related to the relatively more fixed features or factors which traditionally have been used to determine and delimit a region. In such an arrangement a river basin region would reflect and combine the natural elements of drainage and water supply, on the one hand, with socio-economic characteristics, such as journey-to-work patterns and retail zones of influence, on the other hand. Modern regional arrangements in England also reflect this blend of the formal and the functional with, for example, private sector regional water companies interacting with a range of multipurpose regional agencies that operate within the nine 'standard' regions. A further elaboration of this formal–functional interrelationship can be seen in the designation of special-purpose operational regions, such as the Thames Gateway, which demonstrate formal unity and homogeneity through the perception that they represent areas that have common problems and opportunities combined with functional relevance in terms of a range of socio-economic characteristics.

Above and beyond the distinctions between formal and functional regions, and between natural regions – however defined – and regions as objects of study, there are other questions of definition that must be addressed. Chief among these questions are matters of purpose and policy relevance: what, for example, is a planning or programming region and how can it be defined and utilized in practice? Such questions demonstrate the enduring importance of Glasson's warning that 'regions are a means to an end, rather than ends in themselves' (Glasson, 1974: 22), a point of considerable significance which was made by the current government in presenting the initial case in support of the creation of Regional Development Agencies (DETR, 1997). In this case, the previous regional arrangements were adjusted in order to allow for the establishment of regions which were seen to be better suited to the requirements of regional planning, programming and development, including the creation of a new East of England region from the old East Anglia region plus three of the counties of the former, larger, South East region. A further matter of purpose and policy relevance is the issue of democratic legitimacy, especially in relation to the scrutiny and auditing of regional policies and their implementation. It has been argued that some of the English regions are too large to be suitable units for the purpose of directly elected regional government, whilst others lack a clear regional identity or image. Whilst all of these considerations are matters of judgement, it is the case that one of the largest regions in terms of its population size – London – has seen the establishment of limited regional government, whilst one of the smallest – the North East – has recently rejected the opportunity to create an elected regional assembly. Although these issues are discussed at greater length elsewhere in this chapter and in other chapters of this book, it is instructive to consider purpose and policy relevance as prime determinants of regional structures.

A final topic associated with the consideration of regional definition is the delimitation of regions. By selecting the characteristics or features that are seen as desirable attributes of a region, the issue of delimitation is almost inevitably involved, for the simple reason that the factors which provide the basis for analysis and identity also offer the foundations for determining patterns of activity within (or between) regions and, as a consequence, the boundaries of regions themselves. This means that patterns of activity and distribution should be seen as the determinants of regional spaces. An early attempt to use the distribution and pattern of activity as a means of delimiting regions can be seen in the notions of polarization and aggregation. By implication, polarization represents the outcome of an evolving process of activity formation, with the product of such a process of evolution emerging as a network of settlements. This network may take the form of a hierarchy of settlements and each element within the hierarchy may develop a series of interactions with other settlements. The end product is a pattern of networks with flows and links between the component settlements; interdependence is a key analytical concept within the polarized region, and this allows for delimitation of regional or sub-regional space. Boudeville (1966) places particular emphasis on the notion of polarization and notes that it provides the basis for the spatial analysis of activity flows, including the analysis of poles of development – an important antecedent of cluster analysis.

The foregoing discussion provides the foundation for subsequent sections of this chapter. The debate which has been presented herein represents a brief summary of a wide and complex literature and body of theory. For a fuller and wider discussion the reader is directed towards a number of sources, including those referred to in the text and to Casati and Varzi (1999), Johnston (1991), Blomley (1994) and, for a discussion of certain practical consequences of regional and city-regional definition, Herrschel and Newman (2002).

## The regional 'problem'

There is no single regional 'problem'. Rather, it has become increasingly evident that a complex and often confused web of spatial problems and opportunities has emerged and evolved over the past century and more. It was a relatively easy matter to identify and determine the major features of the classic regional problem in the 1930s – a problem described by Wal Hannington (1937) as 'the gravest in the social, political and economic life of this country' and one which implied that a 'means of restoring economic life' must be found and applied as a matter of urgency.

The regional problem which currently prevails, however, is the product of the conflation of a succession of changes in the social, environmental, political and economic geographies of England's regions. As a consequence, it is no longer possible to regard the regional problem as synonymous with the difficulties encountered in managing the spatial concentration of declining or expanding economic activities; rather it is a problem which has a number of sectoral and non-sectoral dimensions. Although the regional economic problem endures, increasingly it is accompanied by problems of social exclusion and deprivation, a range of environmental challenges, disparities in terms of both access to and quality of infrastructure, a significant imbalance in the availability and quality of housing, a number of difficulties with regard to access to services, and a range of operational problems associated with the planning, management and governance of regions. This suggests that the modern regional 'problem' is the consequence of the coincidence of a series of spatial disparities and difficulties combined, in some cases, with disputes as to the suitability of 'standard' regions as units of territory to deal with particular spatial management challenges. It is, in short, now acknowledged that 'regional experiences are diverse and the general questions have a different purchase in each case' (Tomaney, 2002a: 4).

Given the combinatorial nature of the contemporary regional problem, the remainder of this section briefly reviews each of the major elements. In conducting these reviews the intention is to demonstrate the interconnected and enduring character of the regional problem or, to be more precise, the set of related problems. Each of these interconnected problems acts both as an issue to be resolved in its own right and as a potential stimulus, solution or cause of other associated problems. This has always been the case, although the concentration on regional economic problems has tended either to mask other issues or to dominate the political response. Whilst the multi-causal origins and outcomes of the regional problem are not in doubt – the Barlow Report (Royal Commission on the Distribution of the Industrial Population, 1940) identified the interrelationship between regional disparities, economic performance and the associated rapid growth of the population and built-up area of Greater London during the 1930s, for example – the real difficulty is that many elements of the regional problem have been analysed and treated as separate issues. The so-called 'silo syndrome', which is evident in the way in which large public and private organizations separate functions from each other and, as a consequence, fail to deliver an integrated or co-ordinated service, is also present in much academic analysis, and especially in the economic literature. In the absence of a comprehensive analysis and approach to policy, it is unlikely that the true nature and outcomes of the regional problem or problems can be understood.

Although the overemphasis on the economic component of the entire set of issues that make up the regional problem can readily be understood, it has also been the subject of a series of major disagreements over the past eight decades. These disagreements continue to the present day, with a range of views displayed regarding the causes of, consequences of and remedies suitable to treat the regional (economic) problem. Taylor and Wren (1997) have summarized the key elements of the debate: they identify and analyse the origin and progress of the spatial and sectoral disparities evident in the UK regions and assess the case for, and benefits of, selective intervention policy. In addition, they point to the range of associated benefits that accompany the reduction of regional economic disparities, including 'the real output gains from a more balanced demand for labour . . . since the economy would not run into inflationary bottlenecks so quickly during periods of expansion' (Taylor and Wren, 1997: 837), and the avoidance of unnecessary and undesirable migration, especially to South East England. Despite the fact that regional disparities in unemployment virtually disappeared during the 1990s, it is also evident that other regional economic disparities have persisted, especially differences in prosperity, productivity and the structure of economic activity (Tomaney, 2002a). Indeed, as MacKay (2003) has demonstrated, the reality is that whilst a general pattern of convergence could be observed in the period up to the mid-1970s, since then regional inequalities have become more substantial. The most significant element of this growing divergence, and one which much of current government policy seeks to address, is what MacKay describes as the 'major prosperity gap between the Inner Region Core (London, South East and East) and Wales and North, the least prosperous parts of Britain' (MacKay, 2003: 315). However, the prosperity gap is not the only element of economic divergence which is of concern to analysts; other elements of regional economic inequality, such as the costs associated with growing congestion in MacKay's Inner Regions Core, add to the divergence. In short, the potent combination of regional differences in economic activity, employment, income, inflation and congestion, which were noted in the Barlow Report and other documents written during the 1930s and 1940s, continue to present a significant, but not insurmountable, regional economic problem. What is different now is that a substantial component of the solution is seen to rest with the establishment and operation of 'bottom-up' initiatives, such as the work undertaken by the RDAs. This new model of economic policy-making and implementation is closer to Stöhr's (1990) development-from-above and development-from-below model, which emphasizes the need for simultaneous 'top-down' and 'bottom-up' intervention.

Although readers may regard the above discussion of the regional economic problem as somewhat cursory, the following discussions are even briefer. In addition to the classical economic problem, McCrone (1969) identifies the social and political problems encountered in dealing with regional analysis and policy; with the analysis of regional social problems consistently focused on the causes and consequences of what has been described as a 'vicious circle, a downward stagnation spiral' (Glasson, 1974: 174). Other commentators emphasize the need 'to link the goals of social justice and economic efficiency' (Byers quoted in Tomaney, 2002b: 28). The social justice dimension of the regional problem has frequently received insufficient attention, especially during periods when regional and local priorities have been regarded as subservient to the goal of promoting national economic growth, but in recent years this neglect has been redressed as a consequence of the general adoption of the sustainable development model with its advocacy of the simultaneous promotion of responsible economic progress, enhanced social justice and improved environmental management. A particular point of emphasis with regard to the social justice element of sustainable development is the identification of spatial priorities and appropriate mechanisms for their delivery (Roberts, 2003); this offers a direct link to the current debate on the most effective way of introducing a stronger social component in regional policy.

Moving to the political dimension of the regional problem, the difficulty of disconnecting the substance of regional analysis from the design and delivery of policy is immediately apparent. Grant (1982: 57) discussed the inherently political nature of regional policy some years ago, when he observed that 'regional aid is a highly evident form of location-specific benefit'. However, the regional political sword has two cutting edges: whilst political benefits may be associated with policy successes, equally, political problems may result from policy failures. These political issues are of long standing, with McCrone (1969) noting, for example, the pronounced anti-government swing in 1959 in areas experiencing regional difficulties and, more recently, Herrschel and Newman (2002) pointing to the growth of new political coalitions in order to promote the needs of lagging or overheated regions and city-regions. Much of the politics of devolution since 1997 represents recognition of the above issues, with the establishment of elected governments in the Celtic nations setting the pace for the English regions. However, even in the absence of elected regional government in the eight English regions outwith Greater London, it is evident that a new regional politics has emerged as a key component of the broader spatial governance agenda. This new regional politics takes a number of forms: non-elected regional assemblies, strengthened Government Offices, RDAs and a new commitment to sub-regional working through both the establishment of formal sub-regional arrangements and the creation of city-regional partnerships. Once again, the political 'problem' encountered in the English regions is a complex and difficult matter which is considered more fully elsewhere in the present volume.

In addition to McCrone's (1969) classic triad of regional problems – economic, social and political – an extra element has risen to prominence in recent years. This is the regional environmental problem, which in reality reflects a series of problems related to matters such as the degradation of the natural environment due to excessive or poorly planned urbanisation and industrialisation, the overprovision of certain forms of environmentally damaging infrastructure and the underprovision of more environmentally benign infrastructure – what has been described by one analyst as a 'tonnage ideology' approach to regional infrastructure development (Simonis, 1993) – and the difficulties encountered due to a rising level of demand for housing and other urban provision in the greater South East region. One of the major difficulties associated with the regional environmental problem has been identified as a lack of knowledge and understanding of the consequences of growth which is not in accord with the principles of sustainable development – although this frequently appears to be an excuse rather than a reason for the lack of attention paid to the environmental dimension of sustainable regional development. As has been demonstrated by a succession of researchers, the environmental component of responsible, balanced or sustainable regional development has been well understood for more than a century (Geddes, 1915; Friedman and Weaver, 1979). The real problem regarding the management of the environmental dimension of regional analysis, planning and development would appear to be a product of the somewhat fragmented nature of our collective understanding and policy capacity, rather than a lack of technical knowledge. This difficulty could be considered to be illustrative of the wider problems associated with the absence of a capacity for the effective comprehensive management and governance of the English regions; this is a matter which may not now be addressed in the near future.

The above comment links this section of the chapter to the next. The nature and outcomes associated with the problem (or problems) evident in the English regions can no longer be stated to be the consequence of a single event or cause. Rather, the regional problem is now acknowledged to be multi-causal and highly varied in terms of its form and intensity between and within regions. If a single all-embracing problem has to be identified, it would probably be associated with the difficulties encountered in attempting to provide a comprehensive and integrated planning and management regime in each region, together with the desirability of introducing a more effective system of regional governance. This discussion is linked inextricably to the consideration of the scope and content of regional analysis, planning and programming.

## The scope, content and governance of regional analysis, planning and programming

Although much has been written on the first two topics discussed in this chapter, the question of how best to define and develop the scope and content of regional activities has largely been ignored. This is regrettable, because although issues related to the definition of the region and the nature of the regional problem are academically interesting, they do not in themselves provide a basis for the effective planning, development and management of a region. Most importantly, it is also possible to argue that the search for the solution to the 'real' regional problem – how to provide a comprehensive and integrated planning, management and governance regime in each region – can best be conducted through a consideration of the scope and context of regional analysis, planning and programming.

Rather than searching for solutions to this 'real' regional problem, a substantial part of the published literature reports the findings of investigations of the individual components of the overall problem. Whilst these contributions are helpful, they sometimes fail to make the essential connections between the three linked elements of a viable system of regional (or more general) planning, management and governance: comprehensive policy based on clear analysis, an integrated toolkit of instruments or 'products' that can be applied to the problems that need to be addressed, and a clearly defined process or processes that can help to ensure the effective implementation of policy. This policy–product–process relationship is important, and it reflects the desirability of analysing and managing regional affairs as an entity. This approach to territorial strategic planning and management both reflects the established generic principles of good strategic management (So, 1984; Sorkin, Ferris and Hudak, 1984) and responds to the weaknesses identified by successive rounds of research, especially related to the division of functions into separate policy 'silos' (Mawson, 1999) and the fragmentation of responsibility for regional matters leading to contestation and conflict on an increasingly congested regional institutional platform (Murdoch and Tewdwr-Jones, 1999). It is also seen to be essential to base any analysis and assessment of the desirability of providing effective territorial governance and spatial planning at the regional level (Shaw and Sykes, 2005).

Probably the most insightful analysis of the subjects and policy areas contained within the regional portfolio was provided by Breheny (1996). In defining the scope and content of regional planning and associated policy areas – a task which is as difficult and potentially contentious as attempting to define or delimit regions – Breheny was seeking to inject clarity and reality into a somewhat confused and sometimes ill-tempered debate. It has been argued that the so-called 'turf wars' between and within national, regional and local organizations and agencies result in part from a lack of clarity regarding the various functions to be discharged and the assignment of responsibilities to individual actors. However, it is also the case that these conflicts of perception and purpose reflect disputes over the control of resources between departments within central government (and their regional and local counterparts) and between central, regional and local institutions (Adams, Lee and Tomaney, 2002). More disturbingly, the absence of clarity regarding the design and delivery of local and regional functions and services has been identified as a potentially serious problem in the operation of area-based initiatives, with concerns surfacing about a lack of integration between initiatives and the possible duplication of activities (Regional Co-ordination Unit, 2002). By providing clarity and reality regarding the total span of regional activities and functions, the intended output is a more explicit definition of the responsibilities, although this then begs the question: are appropriate governance arrangements in place to allow for these responsibilities to be discharged?

Breheny (1996: 1) echoes earlier writers on the subject of the scope and content of the regional portfolio when he makes reference to the absence of any real debate on the subject: 'while issues of why?, where?, and how? have received considerable attention, the question of what? has remained strangely neglected'. So it would appear that whilst the policy and process elements of the regional portfolio have been the subject of considerable attention, the product element has been neglected or, as Breheny observes, 'taken for granted'. This explanation is most telling: it suggests that either research interest has been directed towards the 'shell' of regional analysis, planning and management activity because it is considered to be essential to establish a clear context for the delivery of a regional product, or attention has been focused on the 'shell' matters of policy and process because dealing with the inner core of product is too difficult. As noted earlier, one of the possible causes of neglect or the lack of interest in matters of content could be the presence of 'turf wars' between central government departments regarding responsibility for matters within the regional portfolio. Equally, regional and local institutions contest control of the matters within the portfolio and, to a certain extent, such institutions also dispute ownership and control with the departments of central government. In such a situation it could be considered to be convenient to leave the definition of scope and content as fuzzy as possible.

A problem in the case of the English regions outwith London is the absence of any meaningful precedent for the establishment of a comprehensive and fully accountable integrated regional portfolio. The models of scope and content available from the devolved nations – Wales, Scotland and Northern Ireland – and the Greater London region are only partly appropriate because they were established on the basis of either a long-term division of functions and responsibilities or an established tradition of local and regional governance (McQuail and Sandford, 2002). The Welsh, Scottish and Northern Ireland Offices already had responsibility for most 'home' functions and discharged these responsibilities through a specific structure of government and agencies. Although the chain of continuity of formal government for the Greater London region was severely tested during the 1980s, general agreement existed on the content of the list of the key strategic matters of scope and responsibility prior to the establishment of the devolved Greater London Authority. In the absence of prior region-wide governance arrangements in the other eight English regions – although successful governance arrangements for the metropolitan regions did exist for a number of years prior to the abolition of the metropolitan county councils in the mid-1980s (Roberts, Thomas and Williams, 1999) – it is not surprising that matters of scope and content have belatedly become matters of intense debate.

Following Breheny's (1996) assessment of the scope of regional planning, which in reality extended by implication to a range of associated aspects of regional policy, it is evident that in the past the definition of the various fields of activity within the regional portfolio has sometimes been neglected or regarded as a secondary matter. As noted above, one consequence of this neglect has been to generate confusion or even conflict regarding the scope and responsibility for particular aspects of policy, whilst another outcome has been a lack of adequate co-ordination or integration between policy areas. By defining the scope, content and responsibilities for the various aspects of policy within the regional portfolio, Breheny (1996) also attempted to identify the relationships between the various organizations and agencies that are involved in the design and delivery of individual aspects of policy. In order to determine the scope and coverage of the individual policy fields, two issues were addressed:

- the degree of coverage – the substantive areas addressed by each policy field; and
- the responsibility for activities – the powers available to agencies to address the substantive matters.

As Breheny (1996: 5) notes, 'there is a close link between degrees of coverage and responsibility, particularly because the latter will inevitably constrain the former'. Extending Breheny's discussion of regional planning, Roberts (2006) has applied the analysis of coverage and responsibility to a number of other policy 'sets' within the regional portfolio. This extended analysis indicates, first, the considerable extent of the list of substantive areas covered, especially if the former Scottish Office definition of 'home' areas is used to determine the content of a model regional portfolio, and, second, the considerable scope for the provision of a more co-ordinated approach to the management of the various aspects of the portfolio.

This body of research evidence was generally accepted in the proposal made for the establishment of elected regional assemblies in the eight English regions outwith London (DTLR, 2002). This proposal pointed to the desirability of encouraging greater co-ordination between the plethora of regional strategic exercises and activities. Although at present it is unlikely that the creation of elected regional assemblies will proceed, a number of the suggested reforms have subsequently been incorporated in other pieces of legalization and in the various guidance issued to regional stakeholders. One example of the search for greater co-ordination and coherence in regional policy-making and implementation can be seen in the guidance provided for the formulation of Regional Spatial Strategy (RSS), which should aim to ensure 'greater integration of the RSS with other regional strategies' (ODPM, 2004: 1). By encouraging greater co-ordination and integration through the medium of a common spatial perspective, the intention is to promote the introduction of a more coherent regional portfolio of activities within each region. It is argued that this more coherent package of activities will enable greater efficiency in the use of resources and the more effective operation of individual aspects of policy. This suggests that the governance of the regional portfolio is about more than the electoral politics of regionalism.

The final element to be discussed in this section is the governance of regions and the relationship between regional identity and the structure of the regional governance map of England. Territorial governance implies more than simply the presence of an elected tier of government; in Healey's view it reflects the ways in which 'business groups, environmental groups, neighbourhood groups and amenity societies interlink with formal government and in that way manage aspects of the collective affairs or public realm' (Healey, 1997: 8). Contrary to much of the anecdotal evidence, there would appear to be a relatively strong public identification with the regional scale of organization and administration, although the strength of this identification, and therefore the likelihood of ensuring that regional governance is based on a strong partnership, varies from region to region. A survey conducted by MORI and *The Economist* in 1999 demonstrated the relative strength of regional identity when compared with other spatial levels, with:

- 50 per cent of respondents identifying most with their region;
- 41 per cent of respondents identifying most with their locality;
- 45 per cent of respondents identifying most with England/Scotland/Wales; and
- 40 per cent of respondents identifying most with Britain.

In this survey respondents were asked to indicate which two or three spatial levels they most identified with. Considerable regional variation existed in terms of the level of regional identification, with 83 per cent identifying with the 'standard' Government Office region in the North East, but only 17 per cent in the East of England. Other English regions scoring above the national average of 50 per cent included the North West, South West, West Midlands and Yorkshire and Humberside. This evidence is of considerable interest because it indicates a generally high level of attachment to the region, which is a spatial level which lacks formal directly elected regional government. As a consequence of the absence of directly elected regional government, the only effective method of governance is through the establishment of a strong regional partnership (Roberts, 2000), an approach which is most likely to be successful in circumstances where a high level of regional identification and attachment exists.

A remaining issue related to the governance of the English regions reflects both the reality of the varying levels of regional attachment and the relative strengths of the current regional arrangements. Whilst it may appear to be counter to the expected position, in some regions a relatively weak tradition of regional working and a below-average level of attachment to the region have helped rather than hindered the development of regional governance. This could appear to be the case, for example, in the East Midlands, where an Integrated Regional Strategy was published by the East Midlands Regional Assembly in June 2001. Although the East Midlands region had a relatively weak tradition of regional working, it quickly became apparent in the late 1990s that the adoption of an integrated approach to spatial strategy preparation would be beneficial for a range of organizations and agencies. As a result of the acknowledgement of the merits of adopting an integrated approach, the newly established regional assembly, which was not an elected regional government, 'believed that it could perform a valuable function in bringing together the key regional policy and decision-makers, on a voluntary basis, to try and secure a more integrated and coherent approach to the "new" regional policy agenda' (Aitchison, 2002: 167). As this case demonstrates, the quality and extent of regional governance are not always determined or circumscribed by the strength of regional identity. However, as a number of studies have demonstrated, strong partnership working does take time to establish at a regional or sub-regional level (Roberts and Baker, 2004) and, as a consequence, the creation of an effective system of integrated territorial governance is not likely to be achieved quickly.

## Delivering policies and programmes at regional level

The final section of this chapter provides a brief assessment of the potential offered by regional arrangements for the delivery of a range of functions. This section also offers some conclusions. Although certain regional administrative arrangements in England have been in place since the 1930s, it is only during the last decade that the region has emerged as a significant and extensive level of policy delivery and governance. In part this rise to prominence is a result of evolution – the present Government Office arrangements, for example, have evolved from the previous regional arrangements for the discharge of central government functions in the regions – and in part it is a consequence of the introduction of a more extensive regional agenda following the election of a Labour government in 1997. Although the establishment of directly elected regional government has so far taken place only in the Greater London region, the creation of a range of regional organizations and agencies, such as the RDAs, has stimulated the introduction of a number of other regional institutions, especially the non-elected regional assemblies, which now receive central government funding.

Whilst the provision and structure of regional governance are discussed at greater length elsewhere within this volume, three points are of particular significance here: the appropriateness of the region as a spatial level for the design of policy and service delivery, the co-ordination of regional functions, and the difficult question of how best to ensure accountability and effective governance.

The first issue has been hinted at in a number of sections of the chapter. Ideas related to functional definition, to the characteristics of formal regions, to the concept of polarization and to the enduring importance of the 'natural' region – however defined – provide clues as to the potential and actual significance of the region as a spatial level at which a range of policies and functions can best be developed and discharged. The boundaries of 'standard' regions have varied considerably over time, and different organizations have used, and continue to use, a variety of different regional definitions and areas – indeed, according to Hogwood (1996), nearly 100 regional administrative structures existed in Britain in the mid-1990s. Nevertheless, there are a number of generally agreed core regional designations and definitions. The emergence of the more extensive regional agenda over the past eight years has been accompanied by a period of stability in terms of the regions defined for general purposes – the extensive reformulation of 'standard' regions has been avoided because such an exercise would take a considerable period of time and would be extremely disruptive. As a consequence, there is now in place a generally accepted and widely utilized regional map. Reinforced by governance arrangements through the non-elected regional assemblies, regional partnership working has extended to a wide range of functions (Bridges *et al.*, 2001) and offers the potential to provide greater efficiency in the design and delivery of services. This was recognized in the proposals made for the establishment of elected regional assemblies (DTLR, 2002) and is further reflected in the continuous strengthening and extension of the role of the Government Office in the nine English regions.

A further refinement of the role of the regions has seen the introduction of more powerful and statutory regional planning in the form of Regional Spatial Strategy (ODPM, 2004) with the intention of providing a common spatial platform that can be used for the design and delivery of a wide range of functions and services. Building on the experience of the three Celtic nations and Greater London, it is evident that the presence of an agreed spatial strategy is a fundamental prerequisite for the development of a single, common regional policy vehicle responsible for the co-ordinated delivery of a range of services (Roberts and Sykes, 2005). Equally, it is evident that such a common policy vehicle offers the potential to avoid the complexities and inefficiencies that accompany the multiple delivery of a range of overlapping area-based services (Regional Co-ordination Unit, 2002).

This takes the discussion to a consideration of the merits of the co-ordination or integration of regional function and services. Although most commonly discussed in terms of the horizontal co-ordination of functions at regional level, increasingly the vertical co-ordination of activities – from local to regional and national levels – is equally important. As was mentioned earlier, the value of the regional model, be it a large 'standard' region, a city-region or some other arrangement, is best reflected in the strength of the relationships which it can establish between the spatial tiers within and outwith the region. Building on Breheny's (1996) analysis, the co-ordination function of regional (or sub-regional) governance can best be considered in terms of a matrix, with the spatial levels of activity along the horizontal axis and the functional responsibilities on the vertical axis. Different sets of functional responsibilities may be discharged in different ways in individual regions. An equally important consideration in contemporary regional governance is the role performed by sub-regional arrangements (Roberts and Baker, 2004). As with the various functions, it is essential that the roles of the lower-tier spatial units are agreed at the outset and are subject to regular review. Under such an arrangement – normally enabled through some sort of partnership structure which attempts to establish 'meta-governance' across a given territory (Whitehead, 2003) – the spatial co-ordination of service design and delivery can be improved and the possibility of inter-regional working can be introduced through special sub-regional arrangements, such as that for the Tees Valley. A further recent refinement of spatial co-ordination has seen the introduction of general-purpose inter-regional strategic planning and management through the Northern Way (Northern Way Steering Group, 2005) and other initiatives.

A final matter to be considered, and one which is more about the future governance prospects for the English regions, is the issue of accountability and democratic control. This is a single issue, or at least has been considered to be so in much of the literature (Harman, 1998), and it is representative of the dilemma which has confounded the regions of England for many decades: in the absence of real powers and mechanisms for the effective implementation of regional strategies, how can the intentions of such strategies fully be realized? Much of the case against the creation of regional institutions has rested on the assertion that past initiatives have not been delivered, but this case can be refuted on the grounds that regional strategies have never been fully or correctly implemented (RTPI, 1986). Equally, the recent rejection of the elected regional assembly model in North East England owes more to the absence of substantial powers for the proposed assembly than to any rejection of the fundamental principles of the regional model itself. With powers – and powers there must be in order for any level of government to be effective – comes accountability, and accountability is generally best achieved through the presence of a directly elected body.

So, turning full circle, the fall of the region from the 1970s onwards as a level of analysis, policy-making and implementation was chiefly a consequence of the absence of a formal tier of regional government. Whilst the recent resurgence of the region as a level of analysis and action is most welcome, history tells us that such an arrangement may prove to be temporary in the absence of adequate constitutional and governance arrangements. For the region to become a permanent and meaningful feature of the political landscape of England it is necessary to go beyond the present 'unstable' arrangements (Morgan, 1999). This implies the direct election of regional assemblies which can work in concert with other actors and stakeholders in order to establish complete regional governance.

## References

Abercrombie, P. (1937) *Planning in Town and Country – Difficulties and Possibilities*, University of Liverpool Press, Liverpool

Adams, J., Lee, S. and Tomaney, J. (2002) 'Conclusions: prospects for regionalism'. In J. Tomaney and J. Mawson (eds) *England: The State of the Regions*, Policy Press, Bristol

Aitchison, T. (2002) 'Integrated policy development at the regional level'. In T. Marshall, J. Glasson and P. Headicar (eds) *Contemporary Issues in Regional Planning*, Ashgate, Aldershot

Balcells, A. (ed.) (1996) *Catalan Nationalism*, Macmillan, Basingstoke

Blomley, N. (1994) *Law, Space and the Geographies of Power*, Guilford Press, New York

Boudeville, J.-R. (1966) *Problems of Regional Economic Planning*, Edinburgh University Press, Edinburgh

Breheny, M. (1996) 'The scope of regional planning'. Paper presented at the RGS–IBG Conference, Glasgow, January 1996

Bridges, T., Edwards, D., Mawson, J. and Tunnell, C. (2001) *Strategy Development and Partnership Working in the Regional Development Agencies*, DETR, London

Casati, R. and Varzi, A. (1999) *Parts and Places*, MIT Press, Cambridge, MA

Commission of the European Communities (1999) *The European Spatial Development Perspective*, Office for Official Publications of the European Communities, Luxembourg

Committee of the Regions (2001) *Regional and Local Government in the European Union*, Office for Official Publications of the European Communities, Luxembourg

Délégation à l'Aménagement du Territoire et à l'Action Régionale (DATAR) (2004) *Appel à Coopération Metropolitaine*, DATAR, Paris

Department for the Environment, Transport and the Regions (DETR) (1997) *Building Partnerships for Prosperity*, The Stationery Office, London

Department for Transport, Local Government and the Regions (DTLR) (2002) *Your Region, Your Choice*, The Stationery Office, London

East, W.G. (1967) 'Editorial preface'. In R. Minshull, *Regional Geography*, Hutchinson, London

European Conference of Ministers Responsible for Regional Planning (1973) *Frontier Regions and Regional Planning*, Council of Europe, Strasbourg

Friedman, J. and Weaver, C. (1979) *Territory and Function*, Arnold, London

Geddes, P. (1915) *Cities in Evolution*, Williams and Norgate, London

Glasson, J. (1974) *An Introduction to Regional Planning*, Hutchinson, London

Goldsmith, M. (1986) 'Managing the periphery in a period of fiscal stress'. In M. Goldsmith (ed.) *New Research in Central–Local Relations*, Gower, Aldershot

Grant, W. (1982) *The Political Economy of Industrial Policy*, Butterworths, London

Grieve, R. (1964) 'The region'. In R. Grieve and D. Robertson, *The City and the Region*, Oliver and Boyd, Edinburgh

Hannington, W. (1937) *The Problem of the Distressed Areas*, Gollancz, London

Harman, J. (1998) 'Regional development agencies: not the final frontier', *Land Economy*, 13, 194–7

Harvie, C. (1994) *The Rise of Regional Europe*, Routledge, London

Healey, P. (1997) 'The revival of spatial planning in Europe'. In P. Healey, A. Khakee, A. Motte and B. Needham (eds) *Making Strategic Spatial Plans*, UCL Press, London

Herrschel, T. and Newman, P. (2002) *Governance of Europe's City Regions*, Routledge, London

Hogwood, B. (1996) *Mapping the Regions: Boundaries, Coordination and Government*, Policy Press, Bristol

Johnston, R. (1991) *A Question of Place*, Blackwell, Oxford

McCrone, G. (1969) *Regional Policy in Britain*, Unwin, London

MacKay, R. (2003) 'Twenty-five years of regional development', *Regional Studies*, 37, 303–17

McQuail, P. and Sandford, M. (2002) 'Elected regional government: the issues'. In J. Tomaney and J. Mawson (eds) *England: The State of the Regions*, Policy Press, Bristol

Mawson, J. (1999) 'Devolution – the English regions and the challenges of regional governance'. In M. del Pilar Gardner, S. Hardy and A. Pike (eds) *New Regional Strategies: Evolution, RDAs and Regional Chambers*, Regional Studies Association, London

Minshull, R. (1967) *Regional Geography*, Hutchinson, London

Morgan, K. (1999) 'England's unstable equilibrium: the challenges of the RDAs', *Environment and Planning C*, 17, 663–7

Murdoch, J. and Tewdwr-Jones, M. (1999) 'Planning and the English regions: conflict and convergence amongst the institutions of regional governance', *Environment and Planning C*, 17, 715–29

Northern Way Steering Group (2005), *Moving Forward: The Northern Way*, Northern Way Steering Group, Newcastle upon Tyne

Office of the Deputy Prime Minister (ODPM) (2004) *Planning Policy Statement (PPS) 11: Regional Spatial Strategies*, The Stationery Office, London

Regional Co-ordination Unit (2002) *Review of Area Based Initiatives*, Regional Co-ordination Unit, London

Roberts, P. (2000) *The New Territorial Governance*, Town and Country Planning Association, London

—— (2003) 'Sustainable development and social justice: spatial priorities and mechanisms for delivery', *Sociological Inquiry*, 73, 228–44

—— (2006) 'Regional economic planning and development: policies and spatial implications'. In H. Dimitriou and R. Thompson (eds) *Strategic and Regional Planning in the UK*, Spon, London

Roberts, P. and Baker, M. (2004) 'Sub-regional planning in England', *Town Planning Review*, 75, 265–86

Roberts, P. and Sykes, O. (2005) *Regional Spatial Strategy for the North West: Learning the Lessons from Elsewhere*, North West Regional Assembly, Wigan

Roberts, P., Thomas, K. and Williams, G. (eds) (1999) *Metropolitan Planning in Britain*, Jessica Kingsley, London

Royal Commission on Local Government in Scotland (1969) *Report of the Royal Commission on Local Government in Scotland*, Cmnd 4150, HMSO, London

Royal Commission on the Distribution of the Industrial Population (1940) *Report of the Royal Commission on the Distribution of the Industrial Population (Barlow Report)*, Cmd 6153, HMSO, London

Royal Town Planning Institute (RTPI) (1986) *Strategic Planning for Regional Potential*, RTPI, London

Shaw, D. and Sykes, O. (2005) 'Addressing connectivity in spatial planning', *Planning Theory and Practice*, 6, 11–33

Simonis, U. (1993) 'Industrial restructuring: does it have to be jobs versus trees?', *Work in Progress of the United Nations University*, 14, 6–7

So, F. (1984) Strategic planning: reinventing the wheel?', *Planning*, 50, 16–21

Sorkin, D., Ferris, N. and Hudak, J. (1984) *Strategies for Cities and Counties*, Public Technology Inc., Washington, DC

Stöhr, W. (1990) 'Introduction'. In W. Stöhr (ed.) *Global Challenge and Local Response*, Mansell, London

Taylor, J. and Wren, C. (1997) 'UK regional policy: an evaluation', *Regional Studies*, 31, 835–48

Tomaney, J. (2002a) 'Introduction'. In J. Tomaney and J. Mawson (eds) *England: The State of the Regions*, Policy Press, Bristol

—— (2002b) 'New Labour and the evolution of regionalism in England'. In J. Tomaney and J. Mawson (eds) *England: The State of the Regions*, Policy Press, Bristol

Ventura, J. (1963) *Les Llengues Europeen*, Edicons D'Abortacio Catalana, Barcelona

Wannop, U. (1995) *The Regional Imperative*, Jessica Kingsley, London

Whitehead, M. (2003) 'In the shadow of hierarchy: meta-governance, policy reform and urban regeneration in the West Midlands', *Area*, 35, 6–14

# 3 The 'rise' of the region

## The English context to the raging academic debates

*Paul Benneworth*

## Introduction

It is all too easy to think of the latest programme of English regional devolution as an exceptional entity, a modern contrivance with no historical or political roots in the life of the nation. Indeed, many of the critiques of English regional devolution make precisely that point, and at the most extreme end blur into conspiracy theories concerning the supposed break-up of the United Kingdom. However, the United Kingdom itself is a country with a profoundly uneven political geometry, having evolved over the course of several centuries, and with an informal constitution that attempts to make a country comprising distinctive political entities and cultures function effectively (Bogdanor, 1999). And the 'elephant in the corner' of devolution, wordlessly dominating the debate, is the role of England in the UK. Just as Prussia unhealthily dominated the German federation from the 1860s to 1933, so England would dominate any kind of federal arrangement for the UK which gave a status to England which enjoyed legal parity with the other national territories (Fawcett, 1921). The solution to date has largely been through a resort to informal arrangements mediated through a national parliament, Westminster, in which the smaller (non-English) territories have been over-represented with respect to their national populations.

The devolution project since 1997 can be merely regarded as an attempt to make this ad hoc arrangement more rational, more fit for purpose, and ultimately more formal. Thus far it has involved giving the various (non-English) nations in the United Kingdom more autonomy over decision-making processes for policies affecting themselves. However, the problem of the UK's unwritten constitution, and the imbalance and imperfections in mediating between the different nations, has persisted since the United Kingdom formally came into existence. The latest round of changes can be regarded as merely the most comprehensive step in attempting to disentangle the complex historical legacy of a state which emerged from feudal antecedents into a modern democracy without the benefits of a revolution or constitutional convention to jettison those unhelpful and outdated elements.

In this chapter, I begin by placing the current round of devolution into its historical perspective, and observe that there was a renewed impulse to English *regional* devolution from the 1970s on primarily economic rather than political grounds. From this, I go on to question the necessity of a link between political devolution and regional economic mobilisations, the idea which is repeatedly referred to in this book as the 'regional rise'. I then turn to consider a range of different literatures that discuss economic regionalisation and its interrelationship with political expression and socio-cultural coherence. In this discussion, whilst it is clear that there are a number of theoretical economic rationales under-pinning the idea of a regional rise, what is not clear is how these theories, and the kinds of activities they see as significant, hang together in concrete ways in particular places. In the final section, I therefore briefly consider how these literature discussions can be used to create a conceptual framework to analyse the significance of change in the English regions, despite the unlikelihood of political devolution in the medium term.

## Historical perspectives

There are long historical antecedents to devolution in England: William Gladstone, a Liberal prime minister well known for his commitment to home rule in Ireland, was, according to the Churchill papers, considering devolution to all English regions as early as 1866 (CHAR 2/60/56). Churchill himself was during his Liberal period also intellectually engaged with ideas of English devolution, and although it was a primarily Liberal concern during this period, Morton (2003) points out that many home rule bills were placed before Parliament during the period 1910–1929, a time when all three major parties enjoyed time in power. One of the greatest proponents for English devolution in this period, C.B. Fawcett, noted that he personally had first heard the call of 'Home Rule for All', including England, in 1909. His proposal, published in 1921, was to divide England into a number of 'provinces', whose boundaries he proposed on the basis of a 'best fit' to a spectrum of commonalities, of indus-trial structure and culture, but which also had sufficient population, transport links, natural capital cities and universities to be a naturally self-sufficient unit. This of course was influenced by Irish home rule (and formal independence) – when the North and South of Ireland were both granted varieties of home rule.

In concert with Scottish and Welsh nationalists calling for devolution to their nations at that time, the 1920s and 1930s were clearly a fertile time to be thinking about home rule within England. Interest in the idea was expressed across the political spectrum: by the 1930s, Tomaney (2003) points out, Lord Percy, a Tory (aristocratic, right-of-centre) peer from Northumberland, was calling for devolution to the North of England. There were a variety of moti-vations behind these various proposals. It needs to be remembered that at this time the United Kingdom was still a significant imperial power, although that power was slowly unravelling. During this period, the so-called Dominions (Australia, Canada, New Zealand) were being granted their own parliaments, to be subordinate to – but nevertheless associated with – the Westminster

Parliament. This early devolution project was part of a rebalancing of imperial power in an attempt to prolong the life of the empire by meeting the emerging aspirations of its constituent territories.

From the 1940s to the 1970s, as the notion of 'imperial Britain' was gradually replaced by a more 'European Britain', the English 'regional project' veered sharply away from this politically motivated process of meeting the demands of sub-national groups. However, it was at this time that the regions with which readers of this book will be familiar slowly came into being through a gradual administrative process. This had the effect of solidifying regional boundaries at that time, and they have since diverged from the evolving social, political and cultural territories with which cultural communities identify at a particular time. The Barlow Report on the location of industrial activity, published in 1940, but only implemented after the end of the Second World War, envisaged a regional dimension to the new spatial planning regime, but of a primarily technical rather than political or administrative nature. It is these regional boundaries (the so-called 'Standard Region') on which the current English ('Government Office') regions are largely based, although they were adjusted in the 1990s as part of the process of forming GORs. In the 1950s and 1960s, the Civil Defence regions developed during the Second World War were also secretly adopted as the basis for regional government during a nuclear war; legislation was planned which could quickly be enacted which – in the case of nuclear devastation – would have passed the responsibility for Her Majesty's Government to Regional Commissioners, with powers of life and death to enable them to prevent looting, restore law and order, undertake evacuations and rapidly dispose of corpses (Hennessey, 2002).

Interest in the political rather than the administrative dimensions of devolution really returned to the agenda in the late 1960s, when two Royal Commissions were established. These were to become known as the Redcliffe-Maude and the Kilbrandon Commissions, one dealing with reform of local government, and the other with regional devolution. The Kilbrandon Commission, which reported in 1973 (Alden, 2001), put forward a set of proposals for devolution to English regions in both the main report and the memorandum of dissent. However, the government of the day under Heath chose to defer implementing these regional devolution proposals until the reforms to local government to be contained in the Redcliffe-Maude Report had successfully been implemented. The government chose to reorganise local government along a two-tier route (Cullingworth, 1982). This reorganisation has since proven an insuperable barrier to devolution, because of the commonsense principle, first articulated in England by Fawcett in 1921, that regional government in England also requires a form of unitary local government. Consequently, although the Kilbrandon Report was very well received, it was never implemented. Although a Green (discussion) Paper on English devolution was published by the next (Labour) government of Wilson (OLPC, 1976), it was never followed up with more tangible proposals for English devolution in the form of a White (policy) Paper (Benneworth & McInroy, 2002). With the fall of Wilson's Labour successor, Callaghan, in 1979, and the election of the Conservatives under Thatcher espousing a philosophy profoundly opposed to devolution, the idea moved to the political sidelines, where, away from its natural opponents, the ideas slowly emerged that were to be proposed in England in 2002. During the following eighteen years in opposition, the Labour Party provided fertile ground for the development of ideas around English devolution. The Parliamentary Spokesman's Working Group published a report, the *Alternative Regional Strategy* (1982), which – although it achieved little of substance in an anti-regional age – provided the foundation for the formation of a devolutionary cadre around John Prescott, the politician perhaps most closely associated with the proposals for English regional assemblies which emerged in 2002.

In the 1992 Labour manifesto, there was a firm commitment to an extensive programme of devolution to Scotland, Wales and the English regions. Even by 1996, at the height of the Blair transformation of the Labour Party and its abandonment of many of its former shibboleths, proposals for Regional Development and Regional Skills Agencies were published, envisaging the regionalisation of some powers delegated to non-departmental public bodies (quangos), as an administrative precursor to (later) full political devolution to the English regions (Regional Policy Commission, 1996). Although the proposals for English devolution in the 1997 manifesto were less explicit than in 1992, New Labour was elected with a mandate at least to examine and bring forward substantive proposals to devolve power to the English regions. Some of these proposals have moved forwards, but it cannot be denied that since the referendum of 4 November 2004 in the North East, they appear to have been prematurely curtailed.

It is possible to characterise the current English devolution programme, which has emerged since 1997, according to a number of its distinctive features. One feature has been that it has evolved by a series of rapid steps, from Regional Development Agencies to a referendum on elected regional assembly in the North East of England. Each step has been successful, and has led naturally to the subsequent step. This process has been successfully followed in the case of the London Assembly and Mayor. The idea was originally floated for a 'joining-up' Mayor, taking over powers from a number of London-based bodies (fire and political services and transport), along with an economic development body (the London Development Agency). However, when the government became convinced that the idea was successful, and Mayor Livingstone introduced a hugely successful road-pricing scheme, the government became keen to devolve further powers to the Mayor and the Greater London Authority.

That is why the 'no' vote in November 2004 was seen as so catastrophic, because it removed all sense of momentum, continuity and progress from what was envisaged as a very long journey. A second feature is that – in reality – democratic considerations have not played a significant role in rationalising and justifying these changes. In the cases of the Scottish and Welsh devolved territories, such institutional and political concerns about democratic legitimacy were at the forefront of making the case for the political pressure necessary to realise devolution. However, in the case of England, it has been much more the case recently (since 1997) that economic considerations, and in particular a desire for less successful regions to close the productivity gap with the most successful regions, have been the prime motivations for concerted efforts for regionalisation and devolution. The enthusiasm for regions as spaces of economic development is based on the fact that there is increasing recognition that 'regions' matter to economic development, and that the UK (and England) cannot hope to succeed unless they are allowed to realise their full potential.

## Economic and political arguments in the latest devolution debates

Scotland and Wales were granted devolution through Acts of Parliament introduced immediately following the 1997 election of a Labour government. The political commitment to the institutional settlements was inherited from the previous – failed – attempts to create devolved legislatures in the late 1970s. The 'spirit of devolution' had been fanned in Scotland by the work of the Scottish Constitutional Convention from 1989 onwards, and Wales followed suit with its own Convention, which argued very effectively in 1997 for genuine secondary legislative powers to shape parliamentary legislation. In Northern Ireland, devolution represented the restoration and overhaul of the (flawed) partial enfranchisement provided by the Unionist-dominated Stormont Parliament, which the UK Prime Minister Edward Heath only prorogued in 1972 (Bogdanor, 1999). Although subsequently the institutions in each territory to some extent became bogged down in scandals over new buildings or suspensions over power-sharing arrangements, they were in all three nations introduced with great fanfare as meeting these new nations' democratic aspirations. Both Scotland's and Wales' new legislatures used their powers to set out plans for the cultural and social rebirth of the nations, harnessing the new democratic legitimacy to reinvigorate languishing national development projects.

By contrast, these ideas and discourses of legitimacy, renewal and nation-building have been greatly underplayed in the parliamentary and associated debates about English regional institutions. Indeed, arguments about democratic legitimacy were initially used to make the case *against* regionalisation in England, arguing that constructs like the unelected Regional Chambers of stakeholders removed the voice of democratically elected MPs and councillors and replaced them with a more corporatist and consensual (and by implication illegitimate) set of voices. Speaking in a debate over the creation of the Regional Development Agencies, Sir Norman Fowler noted that 'The Minister does not believe – and certainly no one in the west midlands believes – that the [West Midlands Regional Economic Consortium] remotely speaks for the west midlands. To suggest otherwise is nonsense. It is elected people such as councillors and hon. Members who speak for the area' (Hansard, 14 January 1998, Col. 343). Angela Eagle replied by indicating that the primary purpose of the RDAs, and by implication the new regional arrangements, was not democratic, but precisely about increasing the efficiency of government in the regions to improve their economic prospects:

> The Bill is essentially evolutionary. It is not the final say on regional government; it is the beginning of what we hope will be an evolutionary process that will lead to the creation of regional government that will make our regional economies more focused strategically and more able to act efficiently, thereby giving to the people of the regions the higher living standards that this Government believe they deserve . . . The Bill is about baking a bigger cake so that we can better distribute and increase prosperity . . . We recognise the democratic deficit argument, but the Bill is evolutionary. It is the first stage and, with the consent of those at regional level, we hope to pursue the accountability argument and, where the regional electorate wants it, create directly elected chambers.
>
> (Hansard, 14 January 1998, Col. 448)

It is almost possible to believe that the case was made as a consequence of the fact that the bodies then under discussion, the RDAs, were primarily agents of regional economic development. However, it remains undeniable that even in the later stages of the debate around English regional assemblies, this economic rationale remained dominant. There was a problem for UK policy-makers in that their initial perspective was that they believed that decentralisation helped to address local market failures. However, a market-failure perspective has difficulty in articulating why such failures need addressing locally with a regional political fix, particularly in large, relatively closed economies such as the UK in which the major structural determinants are national. Consequently, it was difficult for the government to make a compelling case for elected regional assemblies as vital for economic development, leaving them open to criticism that they would undermine regional economic performance by increasing regulation and raising the tax burden (Knowles, 2002).

The need to frame the need for assemblies in the language of cost/benefit analyses and the neo-classical economics favoured by the Treasury in the late 1990s culminated in this most curious of statements in the 2002 White Paper on Regions, *Your Region, Your Choice*: 'Of course, one of the main reasons why the Government wants to establish elected regional assemblies is our wish to increase democratic accountability over decisions taken at the regional level. It is clearly not possible to quantify the benefits of greater democracy' (ODPM, 2002: 55).

Accepting that local market failures may have local origins requires in turn a language to articulate how local contextual differences can produce localised failures to which devolution and local solutions are the best 'technical' solution. Indeed, the Treasury published two papers (2001, 2003) setting out its view of how local and regional decentralisation could increase UK productivity. However, such arguments are necessarily technical and not readily amenable to heated political debate, certainly in comparison with approaches that appeal to emotions such as national pride. It is possible that the government reaped the whirlwind from choosing to emphasise the economic, technocratic and managerial benefits of devolution in the North East referendum on 4 November 2004. A turnout of fully half the eligible electorate saw 78 per cent voting against the government's proposals, the result of that election suspending all plans for regional devolution in the foreseeable future. The North East result was arguably a consequence of the very limited range of powers being proposed (essentially an overseeing of a number of strategies) against the very deep-seated problems faced in that region (Tickell *et al.*, 2005).

As Byrne and Benneworth show in Chapter 6, the way in which UK politicians have chosen to manage the decline of the old industries in the North East has provided the foundation on which the regional identity is based, and has created a public scepticism towards politicians and a belief that their interests are not congruent with those of the North East. The dilemma is that the regions in England have begun to develop their own economic trajectories as continuations of their historical trajectories. Regional traditions and economic strengths are becoming increasingly important in the modern global economy. Understanding the prospects for regions to emerge with their own self-confidence and dynamism in turn requires understanding why 'regions' have become increasingly important as an object of study. The editors' argument in this book is that despite the failure of the referendum, regions have developed a greater political, economic and social coherence, and are developing along divergent, if complementary, paths. These divergent developments can contribute collectively to a national development project, but they are currently constrained by central government's rather simplistic and singular vision for English economic development.

The argument is therefore that this economic imperative can support existing cultural and political mobilisations on the regional scale, and understanding the regional economic benefits can provide greater insights into understanding national development processes. I now turn to look at why this regional scale has become important to contemporary understandings of economic development. It is possible to identify a wide variety of literatures in which the notion of the regional scale and the regional actor has become conceptually significant. However, the problem is that these various theoretical frameworks are not easy to reconcile at the empirical scale, which raises difficulties in using these literatures to analyse the rise of the English regions. The intention in the empirical chapters in the second half of the book is to try to unite these various theoretical frameworks at the concrete/practical scale, identifying how various factors have come together to create place-specific but more widely beneficial environments in the English regions.

## The rise of the regions from a historiographical perspective

Despite the rather abstract idiom of the word 'region', it is a concept that is imbued with a particular recent meaning in the English context. Indeed, a number of the regional chapters do discuss their own distinct definitions of a region, reflecting the different meanings that the concept has taken on in different parts of the country. Moreover, as an academic concept, it came back into vogue in the 1970s and 1980s (the 'rise of the region' alluded to above, and in Chapter 1). The notion that particular locations can become centres of specialisation is of course not new, and indeed was a key element of the emergence of industrial location theory in the first half of the twentieth century, something dealt with in more detail in Chapter 1. However, although the region emerged as a significant object of study in this period, a number of parallel currents in the 1950s and 1960s – the rising dominance of neo-classical economics, increasing applications of computing power – led to a falling interest in the importance of the region in understanding processes of economic change (see also Chapter 1). More recently, there has been renewed interest in the dynamics of place-specific economic advantages, and the fact that different places have advantages that are not easily reproducible. We highlight four different sets of theoretical debates in which 'regions' have become increasingly important in a variety of ways: as a new scale, as a container for new types of activities, as spaces where particular types of (knowledge-based) capital are most easily created and exchanged, and as the units at which comparative advantages are increasingly becoming expressed. However, there has never really been a fair reconciliation of the tensions which exist between various processes and mechanisms, particularly between territorial/economic as well as regional/global. To address this shortcoming, four separate debates are explored to give a variety of fragmentary insights into how a regional rise might be conceptualised through an intuitive overview of these debates.

### Radical geography and regional political economy

It has already been pointed out in Chapter 1 that the resurgence of interest in the region in the 1970s came at a time of much broader shifts in the academy. Harvey's (1973) seminal text *Social Justice and the City* was very much at the vanguard of those changes in the field of geographers and urban sociologists, although the renewed interest in regional economics was to re-emerge somewhat later. The book itself charted the 'intellectual transformation' of one geographer from a philosophy of scientific geographical empiricism to a Marxist methodology, and presented a manifesto for change in the discipline. His previous work, *Explanation in Geography* (1969), was a handbook of empiricism and so his adoption of structural methods to address practical questions of social justice and economic change was highly influential, not least because it provided a rigorous framework to express dissatisfaction with quantitative geographical methodologies that were in danger of becoming overly self-referential, abstracting human experiences behind numerical analyses. By emphasising the qualitative aspects of geography, this set an agenda within which regional difference became a legitimate object of enquiry. However, it also signified a detachment of much of the regional geography from formal economic methods, a problem which would only be corrected with the emergence of the new economic geography.

Consequently, this work laid the foundation for much of the application of the emergent structural and radical analyses to the field of geography, contextualising the objects of study into the condition of their social production. Geography was privileged in this system of analysis, as much emphasis was placed on the way structures encouraged actors in ways that created regional specificities (Lefebvre, 1974). Many authors have developed this into a full system of Marxian economic geography (*inter alia* Moulaert & Swyngedouw, 1991; Diogiovanna, 1996). This broke the link between geography and empirical but non-quantitative approaches to the discipline of geography emerging in radical journals such as *Antipode* and in the works of (*inter alia*) Bunge (1971) and Peet (1977).

Although Harvey was strongly influenced by the writings of Marx and later Marxian writers such as Dobb (1971), his overwhelming interest throughout this period was the theorisation of a historical geographical materialism and understanding the interrelation between space and social processes as a foundation for the understanding of uneven geographical development. Following his lead, neo-Marxian writings in the 1970s and 1980s moved to reassert the importance of the notion of 'region' within geography. Of particular importance were Massey's writings (particularly 1984) in terms of the explanation of this through the spatial division of labour within capitalist economies. An interesting development was made by Massey in dealing with the importance of the role of gender as a dialectic agent in regional development processes (see Chapter 5). In a fascinating chapter written with Linda McDowell (1984), they chart the way that the different tensions within gender dialectics were intimately involved in the making of four very different industrial cultures in four English localities, tensions whose imprint can still be felt when reading the regional chapters in the second half of this book.

In parallel with this, it is worth mentioning the importance of Swyngedouw's contribution to the debate. Although he first coined the term 'glocalisation' in the low-key environs of a book chapter (1992), since then the concept has been developed and worked through to a much more complete extent (see Swyngedouw (2005) for a complete discussion). His argument is that regional space has been produced as part of strategies of particular elite actors (corporations and state bodies) in their struggles for shares of the surplus of production. The production of the regional scale, and indeed the production of 'regions', cannot be understood as separate from the broader class conflict and shifting relationships of production within capitalism. These struggles produce what Swyngedouw terms a new spatial 'gestalt': that is to say, there is acceptance by economic actors that the 'region matters' as a scale, and this acceptance affects the strategies that particular actors pursue in their class struggles. In this conceptualisation, this regional scale is real, but has been produced through a series of struggles between actors whose primary concern is not necessarily those regional spaces which nonetheless arise as a by-product of the conflict.

A particularly neatly grounded example of this is provided in Swyngedouw & Baeten (2001) in the case of Brussels, where there are a range of struggles taking place which shape the physical fabric and urban form of the city. However, these struggles are between actors competing over a much more geographically diverse set of interests, such as European financial systems, the political economy of NATO or Belgian Flemish/French/Walloon cultural interrelations. In the case of the English regions, possibly the most notable exemplar of this is London, a city comprising many small and highly specialised districts, such as Soho and the City, each dominating their own global verticals but which come together to produce a highly competitive world environment at the global scale (Gordon & McCann, 2000; Keeble & Nachum, 2002). Likewise, the architectures of Northern cities such as Liverpool, Manchester and Leeds are strongly influenced by their dominance of global trade and industry flows in the pre-industrial and industrial ages. In this first conception of regions, the regional rise is a consequence of the production of regions through conflict, then the regional scale being deemed as significant by key actors in what Swyngedouw terms 'the new scalar gestalt'.

## Exemplar regions, new institutionalism and the conditions for economic success

A second strand of analysis of regions emerged in which the key analytic subject was the regions themselves, and in particular the intrinsic features of regions which would lead to improved regional success. There were a number of important success stories which had already hinted that 'regions' as an abstract concept might have increased appropriateness for understanding the drivers of regional economic development. Considering the 'new regionalism' retrospectively, it is easy to overlook the historicity of the evolution of the ideas. The first of the seminal 'new regional' studies to attract the interest of academe was Bagnasco's (1977) tract *Tre Italie: La Problematica Territoriale dello Sviluppo Italiano*, which outlined the economic rise of an industrial region in a part of Italy without any particular history of industrialisation, Emilia-Romagna.

Uptake of the ideas contained in the work was relatively slow (in part because of language barriers), but they resurfaced in *The Second Industrial Divide*, by Piore & Sabel (1984). A number of regions have since become identified as exemplars, and their status has been stabilised by a general academic acceptance of their success in exemplarity discourses, making them what Armstrong (2001: 526) terms 'the totemic sites of the new economy'. Baden-Württemberg's status as an exemplar originated with Sabel's own work (1994), whilst the later Silicon Valley example was a much more synthetic construct assembled by writers looking for new exemplar regions. Indeed, much of current understanding of these three regions was heavily influenced by the later synthetic work of Scott (1996) and Storper (1995) (also Storper & Scott, 1995), which had the effect of decontextualising the case studies away from the very particular political economies within which those regions were successful (Lovering, 1999).

Although Emilia-Romagna and Baden-Württemberg were identified to a degree *ex post* as exemplar regions, the process of theorisation of the conditions of success was then interwoven into the identification of new exemplar regions. As I have said, the idea of Silicon Valley as a 'new region' is largely a synthetic construct, an *ex post* rationalisation of a very successful region. Indeed, it is almost true to ask, when learning from Silicon Valley, which Silicon Valley is meant, the bucolic rural idyll of Hall & Markusen (1985) or the sprawling and somewhat dystopian suburban ant-hill of Lee *et al.* (2000). Bathelt (2001) demonstrated in the equally totemic site of Route 128 in Massachusetts that there were several distinct regional knowledge economies that overlapped and reinforced one another, and that attempts to distil singular territorial accounts for that success were forced to overlook this very important place complementarity.

One of the factors underlying the success of these case studies with academics was that they fitted neatly with broader macro-economic analyses that had suggested that there was a deep shift under way in the nature of economic production. These changes in the nature of economic activity had made what was called 'knowledge' capital increasingly important as a factor of production (Romer, 1994; Solow, 1994). Unlike more traditional production factors, knowledge capital was found to have increasing returns to scale (Temple, 1998), which in turn implies a continual agglomeration of knowledge in a decreasing number of global places. These explanations of the success of particular places, such as Silicon Valley and London, fitted neatly with these macro-models of knowledge-based development, providing an insight into some of the mechanisms which might be underpinning the increasingly important knowledge capital of the most successful economies. And if the growth in knowledge capital in developed economies was being led by a limited number of highly specialised regions, and these regions were a cause rather than a consequence of success, this suggested in turn that regions were an increasingly important anchor and motor of this new knowledge economy.

Because of the obvious differences between the various totemic regions, the next stage of the intellectual agenda involved a series of attempts to identify the commonalities across the regions, those features which were responsible for their continuing economic success. Storper (1993) produced a rather neat retrospective of the new regionalism, in which he characterised a number of particular regions (including these three examplars) as 'worlds of production'. By this he meant those regions whose internal political, economic and socio-cultural systems strongly supported their companies' global competitiveness. Storper's analysis was predicated upon the assumption that continuous technological change was necessary for effective global competition. He argued that there was a consensus that the exemplar regions included Baden-Württemberg, Emilia-Romagna, Silicon Valley and Paris, without adequately acknowledging their privileged positions in political and economic production structures. The history of these regions was stripped of all agency, and reduced to a supposed lumpen socio-history for successful regions, which were assumed to have evolved an institutional structure in which supposedly competing businesses came together mutually to support each other; the critical feature for these analysts was the institutional structure rather than its historical conditions of production (Markusen, 1999).

The key features of the new regionalism were that it identified the region as the optimum space or scale for the kind of mobilisations and activities which could improve the position of less successful regions. In particular, in the ideas of the 'new institutionalism' associated with Amin & Thrift (1994), it was argued that regional institutions were becoming increasingly important for co-ordinating economic activities in ways that produced tangible competitive advantages and economic benefits. The definition of 'institution' covered both formal organisations, such as the collection of subscriptions for training and technological development, and behavioural routines, such as capacity sharing and family-based survival strategies. Amin & Thrift (1994) attempted to give some meaning to institutional strength in developing the concept of institutional thickness to describe what it was that characterised places with such successful institutional bases. This approach was critical to the emergence of what Lovering (1999) termed 'new regionalism', in that it stressed the particularism and contingency of economic success. Although later writers would emphasise the conditionality of regional success in terms of a division of labour within global capitalism (first identified by Amin & Robins, 1991; Thrift, 1991), it stressed the interdependency within economic success of non-economic and, in particular, cultural factors. From this perspective, the rise of the English regions would be associated with the development of particular new types of institution, such as Regional Development Agencies, and regional networking organisations and regional political representative organisations which helped to promote the local features identified as necessary for global competition, such as innovation and flexibility.

### Regional learning as an interactive process

A third set of debates emerged which focused more clearly on the nature of the activities supposedly stimulated by regional institutions, and what emerged was the importance of those institutions which had some capacity to promote learning as an interactive process (Hassink & Lagendijk, 2001). In these debates, 'regions' have been conceptualised as hosting institutions which played one or more roles in facilitating interaction and knowledge development between various knowledge actors. In the course of these debates, it became clear that a range of cognate but not identical conceptual frameworks had been developed to explain why the region was so important in explaining innovation-driven economic development. This point was made explicitly by Moulaert & Sekia (2003) in their attempts to map the intellectual pedigree of the 'Territorial

Innovation Models' approach to economic development. What differentiates those concepts of 'territorial innovation' identified by Hassink & Lagendijk is their concentration on activities which have taken place within particular regions but have become conceptualised in ways that imbue them with a *faux* generalism. They highlighted three families of theoretical constructs which failed to take account of this feature, namely regional innovation systems, learning regions and institutional thickness.

A good example of the issues raised in trying to develop a regional/territorial innovation model can be shown in the case of the learning regions concept. The notion of a learning organisation had emerged in the management literature, as one in which the free flow of information encouraged learning activities and improved competitiveness, underpinned by supporting organisational arrangements (Pedler *et al.*, 1991; Garvin, 1993). This linked with empirical observation in a number of regions across Europe which noted that several of the most successful regions had in place a strong regional innovation system to encourage endogenously driven growth (Lundvall, 1988; Lundvall & Johnson, 1994; Asheim, 1996). The regional dimension was introduced through the means of the concept of 'tacit knowledge' (Nonaka & Takeuchi, 1995). Tacit knowledge is knowledge which is not easily codified, and is transmitted primarily by face-to-face contact. This implied a link between economic success, the presence of particular forms of tacit knowledge, and the formal and informal institutional mechanisms (such as governmental agencies and cultural agencies) which encouraged and facilitated the exchange of tacit knowledge in particular places (Lorenz, 1999), what Cumbers *et al.* (2003) refer to as the institutional turn in new economic geography. This in turn suggested a geography in which pools of tacit knowledge would accumulate in particular places as a precondition for economic success, and the region was an important scale at which these knowledge pools could exist (Maskell & Malmberg, 1999).

Within regions previously identified as successful, firms were active participants in a networked form of learning that transcended traditional organisational boundaries (Johnson & Gregersen, 1995; Edquist, 1997). This suggested that there was a natural junction between the previously identified institutional frameworks and this inter-agent learning, the 'learning region' (Florida, 1995). A successful regional innovation system was one which encouraged learning activities at all levels of economic behaviour (Cooke, 1998). Indeed, evolutionary, institutional and regional economics all provided particular geographically informed insights into the relationship between territory, learning and development (*inter alia* Lorenz, 1999; Maskell & Malmberg, 1999). Cooke & Morgan (1998) argued from the concept of the learning region to the idea of the associational economy, in which a capacity to build linkages to, and exchange tacit knowledge with, other partners was a key foundation for economic development.

An alternative conceptualisation of the learning region is as a set of institutions which underpin a context of social relations which encourage learning activities and innovative behaviour (Pratt, 1997). However, Simmie (1997: 236) notes that this definition obscures an explanation for the poor performance of regions, which is that, rather than the absence of institutions, the '[e]xisting relations are often those that have generated uneven economic development in the first place. The development of local supply networks needs to beware [*sic*] of re-inventing these relationships with respect to new industries'. This neatly casts the problem of peripheral regions from a new perspective, that is to say modernisation is the transformation of a set of relations engendered by a particular institutional framework to improve the overall economic performance of the region. Cumbers *et al.* (2003: 331) argue that this perspective treats regions as strategic actors in ways that are not necessarily justified, beginning from 'rather underdeveloped conceptions of institutions, space and power', which fits with Lagendijk & Oinas's (2005: 7) critique:

> Economic development and success thus seems to be engendered by what can be described as 'happy regions', through harmonious collaboration between a range of firms, authorities and other organisations . . . Yet on closer examination, it is not always clear-cut what the competing agent in this literature is, the firm or the region as some kind of collective agent.

Hassink & Lagendijk (2001) note that the purpose of such theories is to try to make sense of the fact that economic success is geographically situated, and less successful regions want to draw lessons from those places that have already succeeded. In understanding the conceptual position of theories in the TIM family, it is important to appreciate precisely this fact: that they are also attempts to make sense of place particularities, rather than a set of recipes for economic success under the new conditions of production. In this perspective, the rise of the regions reflects the fact that territorial economic success has become increasingly dependent on innovative capacity, and so those regions which have had the greatest economic success are seen to be those that have mobilised their cultural and social assets most effectively to promote recurrent, systemic and engendered innovation which is not easily copied or transmitted.

### Regional science in new bottles: the so-called 'new economic geography'

In this chapter, it has been noted that the emergence of the regional agenda in the 1970s was associated with a schism between geographers and economists arising from a dispute over the ontological foundations of the so-called quantitative revolution. However, more recently, orthodox economics has rediscovered an interest in explaining space through economic mechanisms, leading to the emergence of the so-called 'new economic geography'. There has of course been a long-standing interest – in some areas of economics – in the analysis of regional issues, dating to the work of Isard at the University of Pennsylvania. Scott (2000: 21) notes that the interest in regional science arose from disquiet in the 1950s that orthodox economics seemed to lack the tools to deal with a spatial dimension, giving rise to the discipline of regional science: 'The central objective of this hybrid *regional science* . . . was to rewrite neo-classical competitive equilibrium theory in terms of spatial co-ordinates so that all demands, supplies and price variables could be expressed as an explicit function of location.'

Glaeser (2000) argues that this intellectual programme was successful in contributing a set of stylised facts about the nature of urban and regional growth upon which other spatial scientists could draw in their own analyses. At its heart, the regional science research programme was a cumulative and multi-disciplinary innovative frontier in which earlier classical location models were stimulated and improved through the application of then-novel neo-classical approaches (McCann & Sheppard, 2003). However, the effect was that regional science emerged as a discipline closer to planning and geography rather than orthodox economics thinking.

Although this discipline of regional science built up an impressive infrastructure of learned societies, respected journals, academic departments and graduate programmes, in this early period it never successfully achieved its objectives of reinserting space into the economic mainstream (Brakman & Garretsen, 2003). In the 1970s, the Marxian turn typified by Harvey (1973) in *Social Justice and the City* denuded the discipline of regional science of some of its most dynamic thinkers. In the 1980s, however, orthodox economic thinking provided a new inspiration to regional scientists because of the increasing importance of knowledge as a factor of capital, and its unusual spatial behaviour, namely its tendency to agglomeration because of its increasing returns to scale. An increasing volume of work from, *inter alia*, Romer (1994) and Solow (1994) was beginning to demonstrate that productivity growth was becoming increasingly detached from investment levels, if investment was measured purely in the standard terms of land, labour and machinery. This residual amount through which the growth was accounted for was termed Total Factor Productivity (TFP), and further analysis and explanation deemed this TFP to correspond to investments in knowledge capital and learning (see Temple, 1998). A key feature of this knowledge capital was its increasing returns to scale: that is, that the marginal return on an additional unit of investment increased endlessly, unlike investments in more traditional forms of capital, which beyond a certain point experienced diminishing returns.

The increasing returns functioned through the putative process of positive externalities, knowledge spill-overs, which were a form of agglomeration economy already well known to scholars of location theory (Oort, 2004). The critical issue for the 'rise of the regions' was that it had been well established that knowledge was heavily dependent on place. Neo-classical economics tended to assume perfect knowledge best allocated by markets, which would necessarily imply that place was not important; crudely, that perspective could be characterised by assuming that either knowledge was immediately ubiquitously available or that the market mechanism would move to iron out any short-term imperfections in the knowledge market. However, this suggested that there were no long-run consequences of imbalances in the allocation of knowledge capital, because in the long run it was perfectly transferable.

This ran contrary to what was already known in evolutionary economics, and it had previously been demonstrated that knowledge markets did not function freely because of the dissociation between investment and ownership; Williamson (1975) demonstrated that these imperfections led to the adoption of hierarchy and network forms of organisation to ensure that there was exchange where knowledge capital was important. This in turn intuitively helped to explain why regional institutions were important – regional institutional arrangements could ensure localised flows of knowledge, underpinned by features such as trust and culture, which meant that these places enjoyed unique and irreplaceable advantages, and that knowledge investments in those places enjoyed enduring higher returns than elsewhere. The overall corollary of these various research programmes was the implication that knowledge capital would become increasingly concentrated in successful places, and that the market mechanism could not be relied upon to iron out any unevenness. This in turn led to an increasing interest in explaining these new locational advantages, and the regional scale seemed the most appropriate at which to understand these advantages.

What really sealed the intellectual emergence of the 'new economic geography' – in which regions, and space more generally, are important – was an infusion of concepts from trade theory (Fujita et al., 1999). A key element of this was that it introduced as the main model of economic behaviour a framework based on monopolistic competition rather than of perfect competition, the so-called Dixit–Stieglitz formulation (Rice & Venables, 2003; Oort, 2004). This was very useful in helping to provide a framework to deal with the imperfect mobility and transferability of knowledge. However, the fact that this model was drawn from economics had the unforeseen and somewhat unintended consequence of creating entirely new economistic models to explain well-understood and well-analysed subjects in regional science and geography. The overall effect of this was to ensure that the dialogue between economic geographers and geographical economists was somewhat weak. As Brakman & Garretsen (2003: 640) noted, central to new economic geography was a particular assumption and belief in general equilibrium, which, whilst uncontroversial to economists in general, would prove anathemic to many geographers now concerned with regional studies: 'The core model [of the new economic geography] is a general equilibrium model with a market structure that is consistent with increasing returns-to-scale, and furthermore, explicitly includes transportation costs and the location decisions of mobile factors of production.'

The concept of the region does emerge very strongly in these analyses, although precisely what is meant by a 'region' varies widely (Scott, 2000; Oort, 2004). The essence of this approach is focusing on economic processes through which the mechanisms of knowledge overspill and agglomeration economies operate. However, as Gordon & McCann (2000) indicate, in particular regions there may be a range of different processes under way which work in parallel or interfere with one another to make places more or less attractive for the location of economic activities. Parr (2002: 727) goes so far as to argue that these agglomeration economies cannot be understood as independent from more general processes of regional economic development, making them dependent on the emergence of what he terms 'regional space'.

This new economic geography has become politically important, and endogenous regional growth has emerged as a political as well as an academic interest. During the Clinton years in America (1992–2000), Paul Krugman achieved a high political as well as academic profile as a number of his papers and analyses played a role in shaping policy, as well as stimulating a coherent research programme. More recently, there has also been an interest in the UK government in using the insights from new economic geography to explain, and deal with, the relatively poor productivity performance of the country as a whole, including involving Michael Porter extensively in the development of cluster approaches to regional economic development (Porter & Ketels, 2003). Rice & Venables (2003) used the new economic geography framework to analyse persistent regional disparities in the UK, with some rather interesting insights on producing a balanced urban hierarchy, in particular that there needed to be explicit policies to target transport and other infrastructure investments outside London to realise considerable potential knowledge spill-overs in the larger provincial centres.

The consequences of the new economic geography for understanding the importance of regions are possibly somewhat underappreciated because of the as-yet unhealed schism between spatial economics and economic geography. The new economic geography has provided compelling evidence of what can be conceptualised ideographically as sticky knowledge pools in successful areas, but also the fact that even in less successful areas, knowledge is perhaps more sticky than might be expected under a political-economic core–periphery dichotomy. At their best, these studies have helped to demonstrate the complex ways in which multiple sets of variables lock success into particular places, and make nonsense of the idea that simple institutional borrowing can result in 'regional catch-up'.

## Towards a new paradigm? A concluding discussion

Reviewing these various debates in which the 'region', and indeed a particular type of 'region', appears to have emerged as an important explanatory variable and political actor suggests that there might be a heuristic framework in which insights from these various elements can be coupled to provide a more general indication of the significance and meaning of this new regional scale. Despite the fact that these various concepts did not lend themselves to immediate broader theorisation, there did seem to be the indication that something was happening at the regional scale which implied that regions were in some way significant, and were becoming more significant, in determining the geographies of growth and uneven economic development. If historical antecedents are critical to current economic success, what is it that leads to the shifting of positions of regions within broader systems of political economy? In the formulations of new economic geography, how do some places build up monopolistic control over knowledge resources?

The common theme running through these debates is the importance of knowledge, and in particular the idea that successful regions are, for some reason, better configured to circulate, exploit and profit from knowledge capital than other regions. The TIM model family suggests that this is because such regions have institutional arrangements more conducive to the promotion of innovation. New economic geography suggests that these systems which promote innovation help to improve the competitiveness of businesses and sectors located in these places. More structuralist analyses in turn suggest that what we currently understand as 'regions' have been actively constructed by firms that have tried to use the regional scale to improve their competitiveness and productivity (and of course profitability). It seems intuitively possible to construct a heuristic understanding from the various literatures above to explain how several very different regional production systems have each managed to achieve success. Within such a framework, it is possible then to determine common characteristics of those successful regions (Harrison, 1992; Storper, 1995; Garnsey & Longhi, 1997). However, this still does not provide a rigorous intellectual framework which explains what it is about those regions which is significant, or how the various disciplines might begin to interrelate in what we might facetiously describe as a 'Grand Theory of the Regions'.

Whilst it is perhaps unfair to describe this as a new paradigm, it is clear that there is a huge amount of work all pointing towards the importance of the 'region' to processes of economic development. The fundamental heuristic seems to be that in the new economy, as knowledge capital has become increasingly important to economic growth, so regions have become increasingly important as sites within which knowledge capital accumulates. There are various reasons which mean that particular regions hold privileged positions in those systems, and often these arise from a confluence of actions at multiple scales, local culture and institutions, reinforcing and benefiting from national and supra-national policy and investment decisions. Gray *et al.* (1996) identify four different configurations which can give such places this regional advantage, including those that have a leading industrial employer, and the more classical industrial district model. From such classifications, and indeed there are others, it seems intuitively right that regions are a key spatial scale in understanding patterns of uneven economic development. From the perspective of a narrative for the 'rise of the regions' the synthetic approach seems to begin to provide a conceptual framework from which sense can be made of particular concrete situations, to understand and indeed theorise further on the basis of the economic, political and social changes under way in England in recent decades.

However, there remain a number of key tensions within this broad agreement: tensions between different disciplinary positions, but also within particular theories. Indeed, the notion of a region can be regarded as particularly problematic, because of the inconsistencies between precisely what people refer to when talking about regions. It is very difficult in many cases to disentangle the various phenomena, and also their interaction and evolution. Swyngedouw (2005), for example, regards regions as a newly produced scale arising from the struggles between different actors within capitalism, and the new regions are a reality which has been socially produced, but nonetheless are a reality for those living within that particular space, and which conditions the future nature of those struggles. Such a notion of the region is particularly slippery, as the 'region' continually evolves through active and dynamic struggles between different capitalist actors. Regional boundaries are continually shifting, and the meaning and value of particular regional characteristics continually change as they are enrolled, consumed and transformed in this much broader process of regional development.

A further tension is between the different commonalities which provide the regional glue which gives the activities a cohesion and stickiness in particular places. Keating *et al.* (2003) demonstrate in great detail how even in regions that are perceived as successful and coherent, the attributes and paraphernalia of regionality do not always cover a common territory. Their clearest example is of language, with Catalan spoken in both the 'strong' region of Catalonia and the 'weak' region of Languedoc-Roussillon in France. Even in apparently successful regions, the political, linguistic and social boundaries of communities overlap in heavily complex ways. Over time, political boundaries can evolve to change linguistic and social realities, and yet those cultural variables are themselves dependent on complex political processes. This complexity of what it is that 'makes' a region, what are its assets and capacity for action and how regional boundaries are defined, makes it very difficult to transfer lessons between places. This complexity is intuitively unsatisfying because it suggests that a more general theory of the regions and economic development is unreasonable to develop. This sits uneasily with analyses such as Keating *et al.*'s which hint at such commonalities in what gives regions their capacity, but suggests a need for a much deeper level of understanding in drawing comparisons between places. Added to the importance of national and international dimensions in affecting the economic capacity and asset base of regions, there seem to be profound difficulties in isolating the essence of regional success in ways which support the development of new institutional arrangements to support that economic success.

Even within more intuitive and naturalistic perspectives on the extent of region, Lagendijk & Oinas (2005) identify a tension between different classes of actors within a region, noting that much new regionalism assumes that tension between actors reduces the economic development potential and place competitiveness rather than stimulating complementary growth sources. The basis within new institutionalism on what Cumbers *et al.* (2003) argue are very poorly developed models of institutions means that there is little exploration of how institutions produce particular successes. There is evidence that some regional institutional frameworks have encouraged myopia and lock-in amongst the participants, leading to economic decline in places that appear at first glance to be institutionally thick (Fuchs & Wolf, 1997). By assuming that places need to conform to a particular neo-liberal and competitive prescription to realise their economic potential, such coalitions can actually be anti-emancipatory and reduce the potential and autonomy of the region to reposition itself within the knowledge economy.

The editors deal with these tensions in this book by refusing to overdetermine what is responsible for the economic success of those particular places, and instead beginning from concrete regional examples to illustrate and illuminate the complementary frameworks presented above. By contrasting the institutional trajectories and economic fortunes of a range of English regions over the longer term, it should be possible to identify more specifically, and less generically, precisely which regional mobilisations have been able to produce a beneficial regional effect and how the various key factors identified in the dominant regional debates interrelate in particular concrete contexts. This is the first step towards developing a more rigorous conceptual and ultimately theoretical understanding of the rise of the English regions.

This provides a framework – and also raises a challenge – for the later regional chapters within this book in seeking to account for, conceptualise and gain a sense of perspective of the rise of the English regions. In Chapter 1, the editors noted that it appears that the English regions have once more become significant players in economic development, and, critically, have significant untapped economic and political potential which they could apply to a broader national development project. However, from this theoretical discussion of the rise of the regions, it is now clear that there is no magic recipe for a 'regional rise', a particular institutional fix or industrial policy which can give regions a 'stickiness in slippery space'. The empirical chapters of this book focus on the ways in which the different elements identified in these key debates hang together in particular regional contexts and trajectories. This provides the basis for a more general conceptual analysis of regions, regional development and the rise of the English regions in Chapter 13.

In this chapter, the theoretical debates which have to a greater or lesser extent placed emphasis upon the role of capital in economic growth and business have been highlighted. As a complement to this, in the next chapter we focus on the role of business interests and organisations within the devolution process, examining the political representation of business interests. This is then followed in Chapter 5 by a study of the importance of the role of gender as a dialectic agent in regional development processes which builds on the work of Massey & McDowell (1984).

## References

Alden, J. (2001) 'Devolution since Kilbrandon and scenarios for the future of spatial planning in the United Kingdom and European Union', *International Planning Studies* 6(2), pp. 117–32

Amin, A. & Robins, K. (1991) 'These are not Marshallian times', in R. Camagni (ed.), *Innovation Networks: Spatial Perspectives*, London: Belhaven

Amin, A. & Thrift, N. (1994) 'Living in the global', in A. Amin & N. Thrift (eds), *Globalisation, Institutions, and Regional Development in Europe*, Oxford: Oxford University Press

Armstrong, P. (2001) 'Science, enterprise and profit: ideology in the knowledge-driven economy', *Economy & Society* 30(4), pp. 524–52

Asheim, B.T. (1996) 'Industrial districts as "learning regions": a condition for prosperity', *European Planning Studies* 4(4), pp. 379–400

Bagnasco, A. (1977) *Tre Italie: La Problematica Territoriale dello Sviluppo Italiano*, Milan: Il Mulino

Bathelt, H. (2001) 'Regional competence and economic recovery: divergent growth paths in Boston's high technology economy', *Entrepreneurship and Regional Development* 13, pp. 287–314

Benneworth, P. & McInroy, N. (2002) 'Introduction: our regions, our choices', in P. Benneworth & N. McInroy (eds), 'Our regions, our choices: debating the future for the English regions', CLES Policy Paper, Manchester: Centre for Local Economic Strategies

Bogdanor, V. (1999) *Devolution in the United Kingdom*, Oxford: OPUS

Brakman, S. & Garretsen, H. (2003) 'Rethinking the "new" geographical economics', *Regional Studies* 37(6/7), pp. 637–48

Bunge, W. (1971) *Fitzgerald: Geography of a Revolution*, Cambridge, MA: Shenkman

Cooke, P. (1998) 'Regional innovation systems – origins of the concept', in H.-J. Brazyck, P. Cooke & M. Heidenreich (eds), *Regional Innovations Systems – the Rôle of Governances in a Globalised World*, London: UCL Press

Cooke, P. & Morgan, K. (eds) (1998) *The Associational Economy: Firms, Regions and Innovation*, Oxford: Oxford University Press

Cooke, P. N. (1995) 'Keeping to the high-road: learning, reflexivity and associational governance in regional economic development', in P. N. Cooke (ed.), *The Rise of the Rustbelt*, London: ICL Press

Cullingworth, R. (1982) *Town and Country Planning in Britain*, London: George Allen & Unwin

Cumbers, A., MacKinnon, D. & McMaster, R. (2003) 'Institutions, power and space: assessing the limits to institutionalism in economic geography', *European Urban and Regional Studies* 10(4), pp. 327–44

Diogiovanna, S. (1996) 'Industrial districts and regional economic development: a regulation approach', *Regional Studies* 30(4), pp. 373–86

Dobb, M. (1971) *Theories of Value and Distribution*, Cambridge: Cambridge University Press

Edquist, C. (ed.) (1997) *Systems of Innovation: Technologies, Institutions, and Organizations*, London: Pinter

Fawcett, Charles Bungay (1921) *The Provinces of England: A Study of Some Geographical Aspects of Devolution*, London: Hutchinson University Library (revised edition, 1961)

Florida, R. (1995) 'Towards the learning region', *Futures* 27(5), pp. 527–36

Fuchs, G. & Wolf, H.G. (1997) 'Regional economies, interactive television and inter-organisational networks – a case study of an innovation network in Baden-Württemberg', paper presented to 2nd International Conference on Industry, Innovation and Territory, University of Lisbon, Portugal, 20–22 March

Fujita, M., Krugman, P.R. and Venables, A. (1999) *The Spatial Economy: Cities, Regions, and International Trade*, Cambridge, MA: MIT Press

Garnsey, E. & Longhi, C. (1997) 'Converse paths, constricting taxonomies: a study of high-technology locations', paper presented to 2nd International Conference on Industry, Innovation and Territory, University of Lisbon, Portugal, 20–22 March

Garvin, D.A. (1993) 'Building a learning organisation', *Harvard Business Review* July–August, pp. 78–91

Glaeser, E. (2000) 'The new economics of urban and regional growth', in G. L. Clark, M.P. Feldman & M.S. Gertler (eds), *The Oxford Handbook of Economic Geography*, Oxford: Oxford University Press

Gordon, I.R. and McCann, P. (2000) 'Industrial clusters: complexes, agglomeration and/or social networks?', *Urban Studies* 37, pp. 513–32

Gray, M., Golob, E. & Markusen, A. (1996) 'Big firms, long arms, wide shoulders: the "hub-and-spoke" industrial district in the Seattle region', *Regional Studies* 30(7), pp. 651–66

Hall, P. & Markusen, A. (1985) *Silicon Landscapes*, Boston, MA: Allen & Unwin

Harrison, B. (1992) 'Industrial districts: old wine in new bottles?', *Regional Studies* 26(5), pp. 469–83

Harvey, D. (1969) *Explanation in Geography*, London: Edward Arnold.

—— (1973) *Social Justice and the City*, Oxford: Basil Blackwell

Hassink, R. & Lagendijk, A. (2001) 'The dilemma of inter-regional institutional learning', *Environment and Planning C: Government and Policy* 19, pp. 65–84

Hennessey, P. (2002) *The Secret State: Whitehall and the Cold War*, Harmondsworth: Allen Lane, Penguin Press

HM Treasury (2001) *Productivity in the UK 3: The Regional Dimension*, London: HMSO

—— (2003) *Productivity in the UK 4: The Local Dimension*, London: HMSO

Johnson, B. & Gregersen, B. (1995) 'Systems of innovation and economic integration', *Journal of Industry Studies* 2(2), pp. 1–18

Keating, M., Loughlin, J. & Deschouwer, K. (2003) *Culture, Institutions and Economic Development: A Study of Eight European Regions*, Cheltenham: Edward Elgar

Keeble, D. & Nachum, L. (2002) 'Why do business service firms cluster? Small consultancies, clustering and decentralisation in London and southern England', *Transactions of the Institute of British Geographers* 27, pp. 67–90

Knowles, M. (2002) 'The business community', in P. Benneworth and N. McInroy (eds), 'Our regions, our choices: debating the future for the English regions', CLES Policy Paper, Manchester: Centre for Local Economic Strategies

Lagendijk, A. (2003) 'Towards conceptual quality in regional studies: the need for subtle critique – a response to Markusen', *Regional Studies* 37(6/7), pp. 719–27

Lagendijk, A. and Oinas, P. (2005) *Proximity, Distance and Diversity: Issues on Economic Interaction and Local Development*, Aldershot: Ashgate

Lee, C.M., Miller, W.F., Hancock, M.G. & Rowen, H.S. (eds) (2000) *The Silicon Valley Edge: A Habitat for Innovation and Entrepreneurship*, Stanford, CA: Stanford University Press

Lefebvre, H. (1974) *La Production de l'espace*, Paris: Edition Anthropos, and (1991) *The Production of Space* (trans. D. Nicholson-Smith), Oxford: Blackwell

Lorenz, E. (1999) 'Trust, contract and economic cooperation', *Cambridge Journal of Economics* 23, pp. 301–15

Lovering, J. (1999) 'Theory led by policy: the inadequacies of the "new regionalism" (illustrated from the case of Wales)', *International Journal of Urban and Regional Research* 23(2), pp. 379–95

Lundvall, B.-Å. (1988) 'Innovation as an interactive process: from user–producer interaction to the national system of innovation', in G. Dosi (ed.), *Technical Change and Economic Theory*, London: Pinter

Lundvall, B.-Å. & Johnson, B. (1994) 'The learning economy', *Journal of Industrial Studies* 1, pp. 23–42

McCann, P. & Sheppard, S. (2003) 'The rise, fall and rise again of industrial location theory', *Regional Studies* 37(6/7), pp. 649–64

Markusen, A.R. (1999) 'Fuzzy concepts, scanty evidence, policy distance: the case for rigour and policy relevance in critical regional studies', *Regional Studies* 33(9), pp. 869–84

Maskell, P. & Malmberg, P. (1999) 'Localised learning and industrial competitiveness', *Cambridge Journal of Economics* 23(1), pp. 167–85

Massey, D. (1984) *Spatial Divisions of Labour: Social Structures and the Geography of Production*, Basingstoke: Macmillan

Massey, D. & McDowell, L. (1984) 'A woman's place?', in J. Allen & D. Massey (eds), *Geography Matters: A Reader*, Cambridge: Cambridge University Press

Morton, R. (2003) 'Devolution: Scotland', in D. Loades (ed.), *The Reader's Guide to British History*, London: Fitzroy Dearborn

Moulaert, F. & Sekia, F. (2003) 'Territorial innovation models: a critical survey', *Regional Studies* 37(3), pp. 289–302

Moulaert, F. & Swyngedouw, E. (1991) 'Regional development and the geography of the flexible production system: theoretical arguments and empirical evidence', in U. Hilpert (ed.), *Regional Innovation and Decentralisation: High-tech Industry and Government Policy*, London: Routledge

Nonaka, I. & Takeuchi, H. (1995) *The Knowledge Creation Company: How Japanese Companies Create the Dynamics of Innovation*, Oxford: Oxford University Press

Office of the Deputy Prime Minister (ODPM) (2002) *Your Region, Your Choice: Revitalising the English Regions*, London: The Stationery Office

Office of the Lord President of the Council (OLPC) (1976) *Devolution: The English Dimension: A Consultative Document*, London: HMSO

Oort, F.G. van (2004) *Urban Growth and Innovation: Spatially Bounded Externalities in the Netherlands*, Aldershot: Ashgate

Parliamentary Spokesman's Working Group (1982) *Alternative Regional Strategy: A Framework for Discussion*, London: Labour Party

Parr, J.B. (2002) 'Agglomeration economies: ambiguities and confusions', *Environment and Planning A* 34(4), pp. 717–32

Pedler, M., Burgoyne, J. & Boydell, T. (1991) *Towards the Learning Company: Concepts and Practices*, London: McGraw-Hill

Peet, R. (1977) *Radical Geography: Alternative Viewpoints on Contemporary Social Issues*, London: Methuen

Piore, M.J. & Sabel, C.F. (1984) *The Second Industrial Divide*, New York: Basic Books

Porter, M. & Ketels, C. (2003) 'UK competitiveness: moving to the next stage', DTI Economics Paper No. 3, London: Department of Trade and Industry

Pratt, A. (1997) 'The emerging shape and form of innovation networks and institutions', in J. Simmie (ed.), *Innovation, Networks and Learning Regions*, London: Jessica Kingsley

Regional Policy Commission (1996) *Renewing the Regions – Strategies for Regional Economic Development*, Sheffield: Sheffield Hallam University

Rice, P. & Venables, A. (2003) 'Equilibrium regional disparities: theories and British evidence', *Regional Studies* 37(6/7), pp. 675–86

Romer, P.M. (1994) 'The origins of endogenous growth', *Journal of Economic Perspectives* 8, pp. 3–22

Sabel, C.F. (1994) 'Flexible specialisation and the re-emergence of regional economies', in A. Amin (ed.), *Post-Fordism: A Reader*, Oxford: Basil Blackwell

Scott, A. (2000) 'Economic geography: the great half century', in G.L. Clark, M.P. Feldman & M.S. Gertler (eds), *The Oxford Handbook of Economic Geography*, Oxford: Oxford University Press

Scott, A.J. (1996) 'Regional motors of the global economy', *Futures* 28(5), pp. 391–411

Simmie, J. (ed.) (1997) *Innovation, Networks and Learning Regions*, London: Jessica Kingsley

Solow, R. (1994) 'Perspectives on growth theory', *Journal of Economic Perspectives* 8, pp. 45–54

Storper, M. (1993) 'Regional "worlds" of production: learning and innovation in the technology districts of France, Italy and the USA', *Regional Studies* 27(5), pp. 433–55

—— (1995) 'The resurgence of regional economies ten years later: the region as a nexus of untraded interdependencies', *European Urban and Regional Studies* 2(3), pp. 191–221

Storper, M. & Scott, A.J. (1995) 'The wealth of regions: market forces and policy imperatives in local and global context', *Futures* 27(5), pp. 505–26

Swyngedouw, E. (1992) 'The mammon quest: "globalisation", interspatial competition and the monetary order: the construction of new scales', in M. Dunford and G. Kafkalis (eds), *Cities and Regions in the New Europe*, London: Belhaven Books

—— (2005) 'Governance, innovation and the citizen: the Janus face of governance-beyond-the-state', *Urban Studies* 42(11), pp. 1991–2006

Swyngedouw, E. & Baeten, G. (2001) 'Scaling the city: the political economy of "Glocal Development – Brussels" Conundrum', *European Planning Studies* 9(7), pp. 827–49

Temple, J. (1998) 'The new growth evidence', *Journal of Economic Literature* 37(1), pp. 112–56

Thrift, N. (1991) 'For a new regional geography', *Progress in Human Geography* 15, pp. 456–65

Tickell, A., Musson, S. & John, P. (2005) 'The referendum campaign: issues and turning points in the North East', Devolution Briefing No. 20, ESRC Devolution & Constitutional Change Programme, Swindon: ESRC

Tomaney, J. (2003), 'Governing the region past, present and future', inaugural lecture, Newcastle upon Tyne, University of Newcastle/Centre for Urban and Regional Development Studies

Williamson, O.E. (1975) *Markets and Hierarchies: Analysis and Antitrust Implications*, New York: The Free Press

# 4   The limits to devolution

*Andrew Wood, David Valler, Nick Phelps,*
*Mike Raco and Pete Shirlow*

## Introduction

A recurring theme within this book thus far has been the 'watershed effect' of the devolution referendum in the North East of England. With an over-whelming 'no' vote on 4 November 2004 the regional electorate sent out a very clear message to those advocating the greater devolution of power and decision-making to the English regions. In various ways it was a quite remarkable result. Campaigners for an elected regional assembly had outspent their opponents by a wide margin;[1] central government and the Labour Party appeared committed to an elected assembly; and informed opinion was that the move to elected regional assemblies had built significant momentum. All signs indicated a 'yes' vote, and even when private polling before the election indicated a victory for the 'no' camp, most regional commentators assumed it would be close. However, despite the 'no' campaign being under-resourced and lacking in significant visible support from politicians, not a single local authority district registered less than a 70 per cent 'no' vote, as the overall electorate voted by a more than 3:1 margin against an elected regional assembly (Rallings and Thrasher, 2005).

The 'yes' campaign in the North East, like similar campaigns in a number of other English regions, counted a wide array of politicians, celebrities, academics and civic organizations – including voluntary and labour groups – amongst its most vocal supporters. Conspicuous by their absence were official representatives of the business community.[2] Paul Benneworth, in the previous chapter, noted that an increasing rationale for devolution has been its economic, growth-boosting, rather than democratic, legitimacy-boosting, effects. If businesses – as representatives of the economic interest – cannot be convinced of the value of devolution for economic growth, this raises significant questions for the potential for a 'regional rise' in England involving building broad-based regional coalitions to mobilize place-specific assets to build competitive and socially inclusive regions across England.

We therefore seek to use this chapter to explore this interesting conundrum as a means of shedding further light on the context and the process of the English regional rise. We further explore the role of business interests and organizations within the devolution process, focusing on the political representation of business interests. The chapter draws on a larger research project designed to examine the involvement of formal business organizations in the devolutionary process in Scotland, Wales, Northern Ireland and England (see Valler *et al.*, 2004; Wood *et al.*, 2005).[3] Here we narrow the focus to England alone and argue that business interests have adopted a stance that expresses, for want of a better phrase, a 'deep ambivalence' towards the devolution process, which desires the limited decentralization of certain powers and responsibilities, but is profoundly hostile to the democratization of the institutions responsible for economic governance.

The structure of the chapter is as follows. In the following section we provide a brief review of business–state relations in the UK, focusing on business representation at the sub-national scale. Here we argue that business representation has been historically weak and subject to the same centralizing tendencies that affect the UK economy and polity more broadly. In the next section we describe the response of business organizations to the devolution process, emphasizing the cautious nature of business engagement with the new regional institutions in England. Then we seek to account for this pattern. Rather than focusing on the political strategies of particular government administrations, we suggest that examining the dynamics of political and economic change over the longer term licenses a rather different view of the devolution process. Here we argue that the centralism of business representation reflects an underlying centralization of capital, echoing the 'colonial nature' of political institutions to which the editors of this book allude in the introductory chapter. This has in turn been an important element in progressively undermining a social base for regional forms of economic governance within the business class. This is a structural dynamic that is difficult to dislodge through appeals to the cultural or political specificity of the English regions or indeed to the notion of a 'regional economic interest'. In the concluding section we suggest that a critical view of the dynamics of the devolution process in England provides some salutary lessons for the future of democratic regionalism and, moreover, places limits on the ambitions which should be held for any putative English 'regional rise'.

## Business–state relations

Accounts of regionalization and devolution in England have tended to overlook the role of business interests and organizations. Our previous work has sought to fill this gap by exploring the role of business organizations in shaping the devolution process in the UK as a whole. In this chapter we try to restrict our empirical materials to England and the English regions although with an understanding that the dynamics of business–state relations cannot ignore developments in the historic nations of Scotland and Wales nor indeed at the overall UK scale. Our interest in business organizations is founded in the view that business interests occupy a powerful and privileged position within capitalist society. The 'structural' power of capital and the asymmetric nature of the relationship between capital and both labour and the state ensure that states, whatever their geographic scale, are keen to secure the cooperation of business interests and actors. The globalization of capital and the development of increasingly neo-liberal forms of economic regulation have only served to enhance the central significance of the business–state relationship. As Offe (1985: 191) suggests, governments are under considerable pressure to 'pay special attention to what businessmen [*sic*] have to communicate either individually or through their associations'. The processes by which capital and labour collectively represent their interests are also seen as quite different, with capital exercising a structural power independent of its ability to organize collectively. A structural reading of this form serves to counter an interpretation of political activity in terms of 'interest groups', where political success is much more dependent upon the ability to organize collectively and establish a shared set of objectives and goals. In this sense an interpretation of the devolution process that sees business as merely one among a number of equivalent 'interest groups' or regional 'stakeholders' represents a very different reading to the one we adopt here.

Yet a strictly structuralist account fails to provide much in the way of further insight into the role of collective business organizations within the political process.[4] In order to generate further analytical leverage we need to come to terms with the variable and contested nature of capitalist interests. As Jessop (1990: 159) argues:

> the collective interests of capital are not reducible to the various interests that capitals happen to have in common. Far from these collective interests comprising the lowest common denominator of shared interests in the reproduction of the general external conditions of the circuit of capital . . . they are not wholly pre-given and must be articulated in, and through, specific accumulation strategies which establish a contingent community of interest among particular capitals.

A focus on strategies licenses a much more significant role for business agents and organizations in the political process. Rather than reducing representation to an expression of the structural power of capital, Jessop calls for an alternative strategic-relational approach (SRA) which recognizes that agents can influence structural conditions but that their ability to do so is uneven or 'selective', given that structures privilege certain forms of agency by reinforcing certain actions while discouraging others. In its broadest terms the SRA seeks to 'examine structure in relation to action and action in relation to structure, rather than bracketing out one of them' (Jessop, 2001: 1223). Adopting a strategic-relational account to business representation encourages us to focus on the ideas and discourses that animate business actors and organizations, while always recognizing the privileged position of these actors within the context of devolution and regionalization.

This foundational perspective provides the basis for our examination of the role of business organizations in shaping and responding to the devolution process in England. Again we emphasize that business is more than simply another stakeholder whose views factor into the devolution process. Neither is this privileging of the role of business a normative claim; instead it stems from the structural power of business within the political economy of the UK. As Peck (1995: 26) argues, 'analysis of business elites needs to be set within a structural context: business leaders must not be seen as completely autonomous social actors, but as agents operating within a particular institutional context'.

At the most abstract level the context of interest here is clearly a capitalist one. In more concrete terms the post-1997 devolution process in England might be interpreted as a shift in the institutional context within which business organizations operate. Yet clearly there are a number of longer-term continuities that are important in examining the business role within the new institutions of governance. Changes in the nature of business–state relations at the national level have been subject to a number of detailed and insightful treatments (Boswell and Peters, 1997; Blank, 1973; Grant, 1993). In contrast, studies of business–state relations at the local and regional scale are much less common. It is clear that business involvement in sub-national economic governance has been patchy – although historically the Conservative Party has provided an important link between business and government in certain localities and regions (see, for example, Saunders, 1979). The push for a more sustained and systematic role for business is largely a product of Thatcherism, although the rhetoric itself harks back to a Victorian 'golden age' in which local businesspeople were prominent in civic affairs. As Conservative governments after 1979 introduced a patchwork of different initiatives, Harding (1990: 108) argues that 'the one clear thread which runs through post-1979 central government attempts to promote programmes which aim to tackle the problems of urban economic decline and employment loss . . . is the desire to involve the private sector more fully in the policy process and in substantive programmes'. Given the link to Thatcherism, the push for business involvement provides one of the key continuities between New Labour and the Conservative regimes of the 1980s and 1990s.

It is important to note that attempts to encourage greater 'business engage-ment' at the local and regional scales have taken place against a long-term historical pattern of relatively weak institutional representation of business interests in the UK. This is particularly evident at sub-national scales. As Grant indicates, and as we have discussed elsewhere (Grant, 1993; Valler *et al.*, 2004; Wood *et al.*, 2005; Valler and Wood, 2004), there are a number of reasons for this relative weakness of business representation compared to similar European and especially North American cases. While business organizations in the UK are fragmented along the traditional lines of size, sector and territory, the division between finance capital in London and the South East and industrial capital in the older industrial regions has hindered the development of effective political representation. Second, the voluntary nature of UK business organizations, in contrast to the German or Dutch examples, robs them of significant financial and political resources. Third, the UK's most prominent business organiza-tion – the Confederation of British Industry (CBI) – has been hampered by a generally reactive character as well as a breadth of membership that, according to Grant (1993), tends to generate a politics of the lowest common denominator.

Institutional weakness is particularly evident at the regional scale in England. Historically, business organizations in the UK have either been sub-regional in scale – such as local chambers of commerce or trade focused on individual towns and cities – or national in extent, as in the various trade and professional associations. Only the CBI has had a long-standing regional scale of representation with its regional network of offices dating back to 1946. However, policy-making capacity and resources remain concentrated in the CBI's national headquarters in London. We have described elsewhere the escalating demands placed on the regional branches of the CBI but in terms of policy and political representation the activities of these regional offices remain very largely steered by the centre (Wood *et al.*, 2005; Valler *et al.*, 2004).

Given the centrality of business interests to New Labour's political strategy, the historic weakness of business representation at the regional scale raises some challenging questions about the general efficacy of business engagement and the business role in the devolving context. Our view, which we shall expand on shortly, is that attempts to enable or enforce a 'regionalization' of business interests in England quickly run into an alternative logic that emphasizes the centralization of British capital and its associated structures of political representation. Just as the UK polity is very heavily centralized on London (see Chapters 1–3), and implicitly favours London in its decision-making, so business representation reflects this reality by focusing its engagement efforts on national – rather than regional or local – decision-makers. Active business engagement with the devolved institutions in England is thus subject to two hurdles. In the first instance, the structural power of capital ensures that business interests are taken into account irrespective of whether business is well organized and mobilized. Second, the geographic specificity of business interests exhibits a long-term drift away from the locality and the region towards more centralized forms. The logic for business representation and activity at the regional scale in England is a weak one at best.

So far we have sought to establish the significance of business interests on theoretical grounds and, more concretely, in terms of their prominence in UK government strategy after 1979. This centrality has continued under New Labour, and, indeed, been further deepened, for example through the Regional Development Agencies Act, which stipulated minimum proportions of board members with experience of running a business. While there has been considerable academic work detailing the new institutional arrangements that characterize local and regional governance, and especially the rise of public–private partnerships (Bailey, 1995), there have been far fewer attempts to problematize the form and character of private sector involvement. As we have argued previously, 'the nature of local business interests, their translation into and through specific discourses and institutional forms, and the motivations underlying particular patterns of business representation, remain largely neglected' (Wood *et al.*, 1998: 12). In the next section we examine the place of business interests and organizations in the devolution/regionalization process in England.

## Devolution and business representation

It is widely agreed that during the 1980s and early 1990s, Conservative administrations centralized power and authority, while also striving to change the nature of local government. The strategy was one of fostering business involvement on the one hand and disciplining and even abolishing local authorities that served as sources of opposition to the Thatcherite agenda on the other. By the late 1980s Labour administrations in a number of England's largest cities had moved from a hostile and acrimonious relationship with business to a much more accommodating one, often formally marked by the development of public–private partnerships of one kind or another. Sheffield is a particularly striking example (Lawless, 1994).

Yet while the municipal socialism of the early 1980s has effectively vanished, it is clear that attempts to incorporate business interests and organizations into governance and decision-making have met with mixed results. The territories of Scotland, Wales and Northern Ireland are different from England in this respect. In Scotland business organizations have expanded their activities and developed more collaborative forms or representation. However, as Raco (2003) indicates, the networks of influence in advancing a 'Scottish' business agenda continue to touch Whitehall and Brussels rather than ending at Holyrood. In Wales business organizations have attempted to engage with the new institutions, modifying their own structures and beginning to collaborate in order to do so. However, in essence, business organizations remain outsiders in the main strategic policy-making venues in the new institutional arrangements, and much of the business influence has occurred at an operational level in, for instance, Assembly Supported Public Bodies or regional economic fora (Phelps *et al.*, 2005; Valler *et al.*, 2004). In Northern Ireland business organizations have retained an important role, although the political dynamics in this case are shaped more by the peace process than by devolution *per se*. In contrast, the work of Peck and colleagues on business representation in the North West of England (Peck and Tickell, 1995; Tickell *et al.*, 1995), as well as a range of other studies that we shall discuss shortly, highlight the fragility of business representation and the obstacles to creating a coherent and compelling regional business voice in the English case.

The mobilization of the business community during the 1980s and early 1990s relied as much upon exhortation as any significant change in the incentive structure for involvement. The rallying cry centred on the economic and social costs of urban decay as well as economic malaise more generally. By the early 1990s the voluntarism of the Thatcher administrations had begun to give way to a strategy that mandated business involvement in agencies – such as Training and Enterprise Councils (TECs) – and required evidence of consultation with business on various local-government-led funding initiatives and programmes.

New Labour has extended this strategy via a statutory requirement to consult with business in the legislation establishing the Welsh Assembly (Section 115 of the Government of Wales Act) and through the creation of 'business-led' Regional Development Agencies (RDAs) in the English regions. The RDAs were established in April 1999 in eight of the English regions, with London's equivalent body following in July 2000, and are charged with coordinating and driving the economic development of their respective regions. Business involvement in the RDAs is secured through the requirement that their boards be business led, although businesspeople officially serve in an individual capacity rather than as formal representatives of business organizations. Analysis of the backgrounds of RDA board members indicates that the boards tend to be broadly similar in form, typically comprising thirteen or fourteen members. Individuals from a business background do indeed dominate the boards numerically, although the number of *currently* active businesspeople is usually no more than four to six individuals. As we have argued elsewhere, 'the extent to which RDAs and their boards act as a voice of business in the region is probably not as strong as was originally conceived' (Valler *et al.*, 2004: 101). Clearly there are limits to the extent to which a handful of individuals can represent business more broadly.

While the RDA structure ensures a degree of business representation, the results from our research indicate a certain distance between the RDAs and the business community in their respective regions. Indeed, this is corroborated by recent research from one such business representative organization, the Institute of Directors, which published a report in 2005, *Transforming England's Regions? A Business View of the Regional Development Agencies*, which criticized the limited scope of RDA–business engagement. Part of this stems from the lack of formal representation on the RDA boards but business representative groups as well as some RDA board members referenced a range of additional concerns. These included:

> a cultural distance between RDAs and private sector representatives, the 'instinctive' public sector ethos of RDAs, the frustrations of businesspeople in engaging with RDA processes, the dilution of business leadership on RDA boards, a perceived under-emphasis on policy outcomes, and the problematic relationships that have emerged in some regions with their respective regional assemblies and chambers.
>
> (Valler *et al.*, 2004: 101)

The regional assemblies or chambers also provide a vehicle through which a business voice is articulated (for a gender dimension, see Chapter 5). Regional chambers or assemblies were established to parallel the RDAs and provide some scrutiny of their operations. Representatives of local government dominate the assemblies, accounting for roughly two-thirds of assembly seats. However, at least 30 per cent of chamber seats are reserved for civil sector members, including businesspeople, along with trade unionists and religious leaders. Given that a number of key problems with the RDAs are seen to stem from their 'public sector' nature and ethos, it is little surprise that relations between business interests and the regional chambers have often been fractious. In the North West business representatives staged a walkout from the regional chamber, while problems are also apparent in the East of England and the West Midlands. We have a different perspective on Humphrey and Shaw's (2004) research on partners on the North East regional chamber to that expressed by Hardill *et al.* in the next chapter of this book. From our perspective, Humphrey and Shaw highlight general concerns about the 'representative' nature of business involvement in the North East Assembly as well as the overall coherence of a business voice. Yet they also suggest that the business sector as a whole was seen to have a 'rather limited level of interest in NEA affairs' (p. 2194). The general evidence accords with Adams and Robinson's (2002: 203) claim that, in contrast to other interests, business representatives have been 'less successful in engaging with the new structures'.

Although business interests are accorded a prominent role in relation to the RDAs, the allocation of a majority of board member seats to individuals with a 'business background' is not necessarily an indication of the power of business interests and organizations in setting the regional agenda. Instead, this attempt to 'lock in' business involvement might equally be seen as derived from continued recognition of the limited and partial nature of business activism, twinned with a perceived need on the part of the New Labour government to demonstrate its business-friendly credentials, especially in the context of devolution. Traditionally, business interests have viewed devolution with considerable scepticism, fearing left-leaning administrations in Scotland and Wales as well as inefficiencies associated with the duplication of state activities. With the election of a Labour administration in 1997, opposition and hostility to devolution became something of a moot issue and business organizations engaged in a tactical switch that focused on shaping the nature and extent of the devolution process. Lynch (1998), for example, attributes the circumscribed nature of the taxation powers of the Scottish Parliament to consultation between business interests and government.

A similar argument can be applied to the regionalization process in England. In the mid-1990s a number of business organizations offered measured support for the Conservative administration's regional agenda, conditional on business input into decision-making and the need to ensure coordinated policy-making (Mawson, 1997). In this sense business organizations have not simply responded to administrative devolution in England but also helped to shape its particular nature and form. Accordingly, and despite the problems listed above, the official response of business representative bodies to the RDAs has been broadly positive, although the CBI has repeatedly called for an even greater level of business presence on RDA boards. Business organizations have also maintained throughout that the RDAs should retain a tight focus on economic development matters. The August 2001 CBI response to the Department of Trade and Industry (DTI) review made this concern explicit, while also providing a signal of business attitudes to elected forms of regional government: 'The DTI should use its responsibility for regional development agencies (RDAs) to ensure that the regional policy agenda remains focused on economic development, rather than becoming diverted into a push for more regional governance' (CBI, 2001: 5).

The business response to what many saw as the natural next stage of the devolution process – the creation of elected regional assemblies – has been ambivalent at best. Digby Jones, the CBI's director-general, stated in January 2002 that business 'was deeply sceptical about government plans for elected Regional Assemblies'. Following a two-month consultation exercise the CBI stated that its members in the English regions had given a vote of 'no confidence' to the idea of regional assemblies. Assemblies would, according to Jones, serve as 'just another tier of bureaucracy on top of a plethora of decision-making bodies'. Furthermore, the CBI expressed considerable doubts about the 'quality' of politicians likely to serve on the new elected bodies: 'We have little confidence that elected assemblies would be best able to tackle the problems of economic growth and job creation or that they would attract good enough people to make a real difference' (Jones in Tomaney and Hetherington, 2003: 55).

Popular support for the idea of elected regional assemblies has been variable across the English regions, with figures tending to show a broad North–South gradient in terms of support, albeit with key anomalies such as Cornwall (see Chapter 12). We might anticipate that business attitudes would follow a similar pattern. John *et al.*'s (2002: 734) research on the South East of England indicates that 'elite networks rarely identify with the South East region, nor do they mobilize behind regional institutions'. But even in the North East of England – widely regarded, at least until November 2004, as England's poster-child for devolution – the business community has been sceptical at best about the promise of and prospects for democratic regional government (see Chapter 6).

## Explaining ambivalence

Advocates for devolution have tended either to underplay the role of business interests and organizations within the devolution debate or to assume that local and regional business organizations support the devolution of political power and authority in order to enable the better expression of a 'regional business interest'. While the regional institutions and their decision-making arrangements are not yet fully bedded in, our research on the representation of business interests indicates that even in the regions seen as most disposed to devolution, business engagement with the new institutions has generally been 'reactive' rather than proactive. In relation to the Northern regions we have argued that

> the development of activities in the North East, North West and Yorkshire and the Humber is best interpreted as a defensive response to devolution,

and the associated development of new channels of influence, rather than as a means of giving voice to regionally specific concerns and interests of individual members.

(Wood *et al.*, 2005: 312)

Our work on the role of business interests and organizations within the devolution and regionalization process has sought to interrogate the nature and expression of 'the regional business interest'. Academic work commonly makes reference to a 'regional elite' or a 'regional business community'. The terminology here is important for it marks a clear alternative to a more explicitly class-based reading of the process. Furthermore, the failure to problematize the nature of that 'community' or 'elite' parallels a wider issue of taking regions as given rather than investigating their discursive construction. As Paasi (2001: 16) indicates, regions 'are social constructs that are created in political, economic and administrative practices and discourses. Further, in these practices and discourses regions may become crucial instruments of power that manifest themselves in shaping the spaces of governance, economy and culture.' Accordingly, the notion of a regional business interest is one that deserves careful and critical scrutiny.

The parallel notions of 'a regional business community' and 'a regional business interest' tend to fuse the cultural, political and economic dimensions of regionalism, and hide key tensions within those problematic terms. The assumption is that firms and businesspeople with a particular attachment to the region – what we might term a local or regional business class – will readily and effectively represent the interests of the business community. While in the case of Scotland and Northern Ireland there is some basis for specifying an indigenous business class – with its roots in financial as well as industrial capital – the contemporary English regions (and arguably also contemporary Wales) provide a much less convincing set of cases. London might be a possible exception here, given the influence of the City on the one hand and its increasingly dominant role as a location for the head offices of the UK's largest corporations on the other. In the remaining English regions the contours of a regional business class are much harder to specify.

Again a longer-term historical perspective is useful in understanding the current pattern (Hannah and Kay, 1977; Law, 1980). Savage *et al.* (2001: 298) argue that

> [w]hereas, in the Victorian period, regional economies had a high degree of autonomy and could find most of the services they needed within their region, the development of large national and multinational firms steadily reduced the integrity of regional economies and led to them becoming increasingly dependent on services located in the South East.

Harvey (2003: 104–5) has also noted the importance of regions and regional economies to British politics, suggesting that the politics of state for Britain as a whole were captured by regional interests which were not necessarily those of the rest of the country . . . The axis that runs from London through Birmingham and the Midlands and up to the conurbations of Lancashire and Yorkshire dominated British politics for the best part of a century and still exerts enormous pull and power.

The centralization of the clearing banks and banking capital in London is one important change that has hollowed out local and regional business elites, although, as Savage *et al.* (2001) note, even bureaucratic organizations like Lloyds Bank sought to harness rather than simply eliminate the bank's embeddedness within local and regional economies.

In the older industrial regions the nationalization of key industries also removed an important fraction of the business class – via state control of the coal industry, for example – that had tended to play a prominent role in local civic affairs. In these regions the attraction of foreign direct investment in the form of branch plant facilities has been sought as a means of diversifying regional economies and compensating for job losses associated with the decline of traditional industries. While there have been a number of successes – such as the Nissan investment in the North East (Garrahan and Stewart, 1992) – the broader pattern is one of considerable volatility of investment and disinvestment (Bostock and Jones, 1994; MacKinnon and Phelps, 2001). Furthermore, while foreign direct investment has served to provide some stimulus to economic development in the older industrial regions, these firms and the businesspeople who run them are likely to express a set of interests that are trans-regional and often transnational in scope. The shift from an indigenous and politically powerful business class to a much more fragmentary and eclectic pattern of business ownership is particularly marked in the North East, where corporatist tripartite decision-making, involving business, government and the trade unions, had long been the dominant model (Shaw, 1993; see also Chapter 6, this volume).

The contrast between England and the United States on this question of the nature and coherence of sub-national business elites is particularly instructive. Over the last forty years scholars of US urban and regional politics have documented at length the presence and power of local business interests in animating local economic development and policies designed to stimulate economic development. From urban renewal to inward investment to infra-structure development to the more amorphous notion of a 'healthy business climate', business interests and organizations have served as a central social force in promoting economic development initiatives (Salisbury, 1964; Molotch, 1976; Logan and Molotch, 1987). The drive for local economic development is derived, in significant part, from the place-bound character of particular business interests. Cox and Mair (1989: 142) conceptualize these interests in terms of their local dependence, which they define as 'a relation to locality that results from the relative spatial immobility of some social relations'. These attachments may take the form of fixed assets, such as plant or land, or other sunk investments that would be difficult to reproduce elsewhere, such as the costs of training specialized labour, those associated with creating a favourable local reputation or those that serve to limit a firm's market and/or supply chain. The transfer of knowledge between firms, especially that of a tacit kind, can also serve to localize and fix economic activity. Consequently, locally dependent interests have a considerable stake in ensuring that investments are channelled through their particular 'space of dependence' (Cox, 1998).

The shared nature of these spaces provides a basis for more collective forms of activity. In pursuing local economic development, locally dependent business interests find a natural ally in local and state governments, given their heavy dependence on revenues derived from local sources. Cox and Townsend (2005: 550; original emphasis) make clear the stark differences between the US and the English contexts:

> Strong local business interests in the 'health' of local economies are present in the USA, and their activities are facilitated by a state form that fragments power territorially. At the same time, territorial fragmentation of power gives local governments reason to make common cause with those business interests. In England it is the reverse: little in the way of strong, place-specific interests on the part of business, and local governments that, in virtue of state structure, are *relatively* indifferent to local economic development.

The academic debate around regionalization in England has tended to focus on the 'appropriate' institutional architecture for expressing 'regional interests', culminating in the oceans of spilt ink alluded to by Benneworth *et al.* in their introductory chapter to this volume. Interrogating the nature of the social forces that provide the basis for that interest raises the possibility of a significant disjuncture between the geographies of interest and the territorial shape of the new institutions. As Cox and Townsend (2005: 552) suggest in the context of RDA-led efforts to attract inward investment, 'while there has been change in the institutional forms in England, in the absence of interests, whether corporate or otherwise, in the growth of particular local or regional economies, it seems unlikely that there will be further transformation in the same direction'. Cox and Townsend's sober assessment resonates well beyond their particular focus on the institutions that mediate inward investment. Indeed, a variety of studies of business involvement in local economic governance in Britain point to a similar absence of strong material stakes in the local economy that might serve as a driving force for business engagement (Rogerson and Boyle, 1998, 2000; Bassett, 1999; Ward, 2000, 2004; for a review, see Wood, 2004).

Our own previous work on business involvement in three economically distressed English localities indicated reasons for business involvement that extended well beyond a material stake in the health of the local economy, although this is not to deny that some businesspeople interpreted their activities in these terms (Wood *et al.*, 1998; Wood, 2004). However, other businesspeople explained their engagement in terms of a positive cultural attachment to the locality and/or an individual or corporate commitment to social responsibility. The diversity of reasons for participation and the absence of a significant group or class of businesspeople firmly dependent upon the local economy – or at least acting on that basis – translate into a relatively weak impulse for economic development and for a corresponding interest in economic governance and policy. We also found little evidence of a well-developed, singular and coherent 'business vision' or 'agenda' for the locality (see also Strange, 1997; Peck and Tickell, 1995). As we have argued elsewhere,

> While business interests claimed a significant role in generating local wealth and providing employment opportunities, there was little agreement as to the nature of the problems facing the locality, the appropriate strategy for addressing economic decline and thus no reasoned and consistent business agenda to provide the basis for a coherent and robust local coalition.
>
> (Wood, 2004: 2113)

The problem of specifying a 'local business interest' is one that also applies at the regional scale. In short, while the notion of a 'regional interest' may have historical resonance and certain rhetorical force, it fails to connect to a well-defined and relevant set of contemporary spaces of dependence. This is not to deny that certain firms – especially in the utilities and media sectors – are regionally based and indeed define their interests in such terms.[5] Nevertheless, the business interests that are active within the current institutions of regional economic governance represent a diverse and eclectic mix of firms with geographic interests that range from the highly localized to the transnational. The extent to which these firms constitute a coherent regional business community or class that, in turn, allows for the expression of a 'regional business interest' is decidedly limited.

One response of business organizations to the developing regional agenda in England has been to restructure organizational forms to match more closely the territorial ambit of the RDAs (see Valler *et al.*, 2004: 85–93). There are now regional organizations of chambers of commerce in each of the English regions, although some are little more than embryonic. Both the Institute of Directors (IoD) and the Federation of Small Businesses (FSB) have also established a regional network of offices and personnel that sit above the traditional branch (i.e. sub-regional) structure (Valler *et al.*, 2004). This organizational shift is designed to enable business interests and organizations to monitor and feed into regional-scale debates and decision-making. But again, this should not be taken as prima facie evidence of the expression of a new, or previously latent, set of regional concerns and issues. Indeed, despite the firmer institutionalization of a regional template, we remain somewhat sceptical of the variability of business concerns across the English regions.

The CBI's detailed regional surveys of economic trends enable comparison between English regions and thus provide a useful indicator of the extent of regional variability in business concerns. The latest survey results (June 2005 at the time of writing) reveal a very clear pattern in which more or less the same key issues animate firms irrespective of region (Table 4.1). Results indicate that in all nine English regions 'regulation/red tape' is seen as the most important factor 'inhibiting growth of the region'. In five of the nine regions 'inadequate business support from government' ranks as the second most important factor, while 'shortage of finance' also ranks as one of the top three concerns in five of the nine. Only Greater London, and to a lesser degree the East and South East, exhibit distinctive concerns centred on 'high unit labour costs' and difficulties 'attracting staff to the region'. Previous surveys have indicated a broadly similar pattern in which the dominant issues nationally are reproduced across the regions, albeit with slight variation in the rank ordering. Furthermore, it is difficult to cast the most important concerns as 'regional issues'. Given that the regional agenda rests on the need to develop tailored solutions to distinctive regional problems, the evidence from business surveys paints a rather awkward picture.

Only London provides a real and persistent exception to this pattern. As Sandford (2004: 162) claims, in focusing on transport issues the GLA has found 'the ideal politically-salient issue . . . because concern about it unites the electorate of London. It is hard to see a similar issue in the White Paper on regional government which could catch the "regional imagination".'[6] While some – not least the GLA itself – see London as the template for elected bodies in the other regions of England, its metropolitan status is always liable to generate a rather distinctive set of concerns. Indeed, whether the arrangements in London represent a devolved administration or a strategic form of local government is not entirely clear, although the Blair government and the civil service clearly regard it as the latter (see Pilkington, 2002: 179).

Harvey (2003: 103–4) suggests that while regional specialization is a 'fundamental feature of how capitalism works', the relationship between regions and political geographies of the state is such that they 'have nothing necessarily to do directly with one another'. Again a longer-term historical perspective is useful in understanding the current state of affairs in England. The current regional structure basically aligns with the administrative template put in place to manage the wartime economy and civil affairs. As was noted in the preceding two chapters, this geographical structure came to serve, with some modification, as a basis for administrative planning, especially after 1964. Regional structures that more often than not failed to align directly with the 'standard regions' were also used to coordinate and regulate the state provision of basic utilities such as water, gas and electricity. Ironically, then, while private sector interests are positioned as pivotal to the success of the new devolved and regionalized organizations, the structure, at least in terms of business representation, is much better suited to the 'mixed economy' of Fordism than it is to the new world of neo-liberalism and privatized service provision.

Table 4.1 Business response to 'What are the key factors inhibiting growth of the region?'

| East | East Midlands | Greater London | North East | North West | South East | South West | West Midlands | Yorkshire & Humber | Great Britain |
|---|---|---|---|---|---|---|---|---|---|
| Regulation/ red tape | Regulation/ red tape | Regulation/ red tape | Regulation/ red tape | Regulation/ red tape | Regulation/ red tape | Regulation/ red tape | Regulation/ red tape | Regulation/ red tape | Regulation/ red tape |
| Hard to attract staff to the region | Inadequate business support from government | High unit labour costs | Inadequate business support from government | Inadequate business support from government | High unit labour costs | Finance shortage | Inadequate business support from government | Inadequate business support from government | Finance shortage |
| Finance shortage | High unit labour costs | Transport costs | Finance shortage | Skills problems | Finance shortage | Hard to attract staff to the region | Hard to attract staff to the region | Finance shortage | Inadequate business support from government |

Source: CBI, 2005, A results overview of the Regional Survey of UK Economic Trends, June, Appendix A, Table 11

# Conclusion

John Tomaney, one of the principal advocates of devolution for the North East, argued in 2002 that 'the future of regionalism in England remains uncertain – although the pressures for greater devolution may be growing, the forces of centralization are massive' (Tomaney, 2002: 731). Clearly the dynamics of devolution are a complex affair encompassing cultural, political and economic dimensions. Yet in focusing on questions of governance and the appropriate institutional arrangements through which to enable effective regional-scale administration, academic analysis has tended to underplay longer-term, structural dynamics that bring into question the efficacy of the regional scale as a meaningful level of governance. We have argued in this chapter that an important aspect of the forces of centralization, albeit largely operating beneath the surface of the devolution debate, is the centralism of business representation.

In examining the debate on 'the English question' and its putative regional fix we need to examine carefully not just the nature of the claims that are made but also '*who* it is who effectively comes to express regional interests and concerns' (Gordon, 2002: 88; original emphasis). The RDAs and New Labour's regional agenda more broadly have positioned business interests as central to the success of the devolution project in England. Yet the construction of a 'regional business interest' and the efficacy of a regional business voice are fraught with contradiction in the face of powerful centralizing tendencies. We have argued in this chapter that these contradictions are grounded more in the changing political economy of the UK than they are in the 'control freakery' of Tony Blair or the avowed centralism of previous Tory administrations. Our goal has been to use the political representation of business interests as one particular barometer of the way in which, whether we like it or not, pressures for the devolution of political power in England encounter an alternative and compelling set of counter-tendencies. In the following chapter the issue of inclusion is explored through a gender lens.

Adams and Robinson (2002: 224) argue that 'British politics and governance still have a southern-centric axis'. The political representation of business interests clearly reflects and reinforces this particular geography. They go on to suggest that 'over time we can expect to see new centres of political powers in the English regions and further divergence in important areas of public policy' (*ibid*.). In England the failed referendum for an elected regional assembly in the North East points to the inherent dangers of such predictions. Tickell *et al.* (2005: 3) suggest that the vote has effectively 'derailed the policy of elected regional government proposed for England for a decade at least'. The arguments in this chapter suggest that there are good reasons to expect the derailment to be rather more permanent, at least shorn of a fundamental transformation of business–state relations.

## Notes

1 According to the Electoral Commission, Yes4theNorthEast spent £361,091 while North East Says No Ltd spent £145,008.
2 The 'yes' campaign in the North East could, however, count on the support of prominent *individuals* within the business community, such as John Hall and John Bridge.
3 The chapter draws on research undertaken as a project funded by the UK Economic and Social Research Council, 'Devolution and the Politics of Business Representation', as Project L219 25 2040, by the authors of this chapter. This project was part of the 'Devolution and Constitutional Change' programme managed by Professor Charlie Jeffery.
4 Indeed, such accounts are limited in explaining the very existence of collective business organizations.
5 These interests are not always advocates of the further devolution of power to the regional scale. The *Yorkshire Post* newspaper, for example, 'remained implacable in its opposition to a regional assembly' (Tomaney and Hetherington, 2004: 134).
6 Sandford (2004: 162) goes on to argue that 'It is hard to see a solution to this conundrum which does not involve giving substantial extra powers and/or money to the proposed elected assemblies.'

## References

Adams, J. and Robinson, P., 2002, Divergence and the center, in J. Adams and P. Robinson (eds) *Devolution in Practice: Public Policy Differences within the UK*, Institute for Public Policy Research, London, 198–227

Bailey, N., 1995, *Partnership Agencies in British Urban Policy*, UCL Press, London

Bassett, K., 1999, Growth coalitions in Britain's waning Sunbelt: some reflections, in A. Jonas and D. Wilson (eds) *The Urban Growth Machine*, State University of New York Press, Albany, 177–93

Blank, S., 1973, *Industry and Government in Britain: The Federation of British Industries in Politics 1945–65*, Saxon House, Farnborough

Bostock, F. and Jones, G., 1994, Foreign multinationals in British manufacturing, 1850–1962, *Business History*, 36, 89–126

Boswell, J. and Peters, J., 1997, *Capitalism in Contention*, Cambridge University Press, Cambridge

CBI (Confederation of British Industry), 2001, DTI review of structure, priorities and business support structure: CBI official response, available at www.cbi.org.uk, last accessed 12 August 2005

Cox, K., 1998, Spaces of dependence, spaces of engagement and the politics of scale, or: looking for local politics, *Political Geography*, 17, 1–23

Cox, K. and Mair, A., 1989, Urban growth machines and the politics of local economic development, *International Journal of Urban and Regional Research*, 13, 137–46

Cox, K. and Townsend, A., 2005, Institutions and mediating inward investment in England and the USA, *Regional Studies*, 39, 541–53

Garrahan, P. and Stewart, P., 1992, *The Nissan Enigma: Flexibility at Work in a Local Economy*, Mansell, London

Gordon, I., 2002, Industrial and regional policy: a London perspective, in J. Adams and P. Robinson (eds) *Devolution in Practice: Public Policy Differences within the UK*, Institute for Public Policy Research, London, 86–9

Grant, W., 1993, *Business and Politics in Britain*, Macmillan, Basingstoke

Hannah, L. and Kay, J., 1977, *Concentration in Modern Industry: Theory, Measurement and the UK Experience*, Macmillan, London

Harding, A. 1990, Public–private partnerships in urban regeneration, in M. Campbell (ed.) *Local Economic Policy*, Cassell, London, 107–27

Harvey, D., 2003, *The New Imperialism*, Oxford University Press, Oxford

Humphrey, L. and Shaw, K., 2004, Regional devolution and democratic renewal: developing a radical approach to stakeholder involvement in the English regions, *Environment and Planning A*, 36, 2183–202

Jessop, R., 1990, *State Theory*, Polity Press, Cambridge

—— 2001, Institutional re(turns) and the strategic-relational approach, *Environment and Planning A*, 33, 1213–235

John, P., Musson, S. and Tickell, A., 2002, England's problem region: regionalism in the South East, *Regional Studies*, 36, 733–41

Law, C., 1980, *British Regional Development since World War I*, Methuen, London

Lawless, P., 1994, Partnership in urban regeneration in the UK – the Sheffield Central Area Study, *Urban Studies*, 31, 1303–24

Logan, J. and Molotch, H., 1987, *Urban Fortunes: The Political Economy of Place*, University of California Press, Berkeley

Lynch, P., 1998, Reactive capital: the Scottish business community and devolution, *Regional and Federal Studies*, 8, 86–102

MacKinnon, D. and Phelps, N., 2001, Devolution and the territorial politics of foreign direct investment, *Political Geography*, 20, 353–79

Mawson, J., 1997, The English regional debate: towards regional governance or government? in J. Bradbury and J. Mawson (eds) *British Regionalism and Devolution*, Jessica Kingsley, London, 180–211

Molotch, H., 1976, The city as a growth machine: toward a political economy of place, *American Journal of Sociology*, 82, 309–32

Offe, C., 1985, *Disorganised Capitalism*, Polity Press, Cambridge

Paasi, A., 2001, Europe as a social process and discourse: considerations of place, boundaries and identity, *European Urban and Regional Studies*, 8, 7–28

Peck, J., 1995, Moving and shaking: business elites, state localism and urban privatism, *Progress in Human Geography*, 19, 16–46

Peck, J. and Tickell, A., 1995, Business goes local: dissecting the business agenda in Manchester, *International Journal of Urban and Regional Research*, 19, 55–78

Phelps, N., Valler, D. and Wood, A., 2005, Stealing the skills agenda? Devolution, business and post-16 education and training in Wales, *Policy and Politics*, 33, 559–79

Pilkington, C., 2002, *Devolution in Britain Today*, Manchester University Press, Manchester and New York

Raco, M., 2003, The social relations of business representation and devolved governance in the United Kingdom, *Environment and Planning A*, 35, 1853–76

Rallings, C. and Thrasher, M., 2005, Why the North East said 'No': the 2004 referendum on an elected Regional Assembly, ESRC Devolution Briefing No. 19, available from http://www.devolution.ac.uk/Briefing_papers.htm, last accessed 12 August 2005

Rogerson, R. and Boyle, M., 1998, Glasgow's reluctant mavericks and inward investment strategy: local dependence and its applications, *Scottish Geographical Magazine*, 114, 109–19

—— 2000, Property, politics and the neo-liberal revolution in urban Scotland, *Progress in Planning*, 54, 133–96

Salisbury, R., 1964, Urban-politics: the new convergence of power, *Journal of Politics*, 26, 775–97

Sandford, M., 2004, The governance of London: strategic government and policy divergence, in A. Trench (ed.) *Has Devolution Made a Difference? The State of the Nations 2004*, Imprint Academic, Exeter, 141–63

Saunders, P, 1979, *Urban Politics: A Sociological Interpretation*, Penguin, Harmondsworth

Savage, M., Stovel, K. and Bearman, P., 2001, Class formation and localism in an emerging bureaucracy: British bank workers, 1880–1960, *International Journal of Urban and Regional Research*, 25, 284–300

Shaw, K., 1993, The development of a new urban corporatism: the politics of urban regeneration in the North-East of England, *Regional Studies*, 27, 251–9

Strange, I., 1997, Directing the show? Business leaders, local partnership, and economic regeneration in Sheffield, *Environment and Planning C*, 15, 1–17

Tickell, A., Peck, J. and Dicken, P., 1995, The fragmented region: business, the state and economic development in North West England, in M. Rhodes (ed.) *The Regions and the New Europe*, Manchester University Press, Manchester, 247–72

Tickell, A., John, P. and Musson, S., 2005, The referendum campaign: issues and turning points in the North East, ESRC Devolution Briefing No. 20, available from http://www.devolution.ac.uk/Briefing_papers.htm, last accessed 12 August 2005

Tomaney, J., 2002, The evolution of regionalism in England, *Regional Studies*, 36, 721–31

Tomaney, J. and Hetherington, P., 2003, England arisen? in R. Hazell (ed.) *The State of the Nations 2003*, Imprint Academic, Exeter, 49–77

—— 2004, English regions: the quiet regional revolution, in A. Trench (ed.), *Has Devolution Made a Difference? The State of the Nations 2004*, Imprint Academic, Exeter, 121–39

Valler, D. and Wood, A., 2004, Devolution and the politics of business representation in Britain: a strategic-relational approach, *Environment and Planning A*, 36, 1835–54

Valler, D., Wood, A., Atkinson, I., Betteley, D., Phelps, N., Raco, M. and Shirlow, P., 2004, Business representation and the UK regions: mapping institutional change, *Progress in Planning*, 61, 75–135

Ward, K., 2000, From rentiers to 'rantiers': 'active entrepreneurs', 'structural speculators' and the politics of marketing the city, *Urban Studies*, 37, 1093–107

—— 2004, Challenging the machine from within: urban entrepreneurialism and representations of the city, in A. Wood and D. Valler (eds) *Governing Local and Regional Economies*, Ashgate, Aldershot, 277–300

Wood, A., 2004, Domesticating urban theory? US concepts, British cities and the limits of cross-national applications, *Urban Studies*, 41, 2103–18

Wood, A., Valler, D. and North, P., 1998, Local business representation and the private sector role in local economic policy in Britain, *Local Economy*, 13, 10–27

Wood, A., Valler, D., Phelps, N., Raco, M. and Shirlow, M., 2005, Devolution and the political representation of business interests in the UK, *Political Geography*, 24, 293–315

# 5  Harnessing all a region's capacities

## Inclusion issues

*Irene Hardill, Mia Gray and Paul Benneworth*

This chapter argues that the rise of the regions cannot be understood fully without unpacking how the variations in regional economic and political landscapes structure opportunities for inclusion to all citizens. One of the major issues to emerge when re-examining the region is that gendered relationships (as well as ethnicity and class) in the workplace and in the politics have an important – and unappreciated – effect shaping the form that particular places take. The English regions have historically had different kinds of social relations in the private and the public spheres, including the political sphere (McDowell and Massey, 1984; Massey, 1985). We argue that highlighting the distinctive ways in which gender relationships have unfolded in the English regions is critical to understanding the respective regions and provides a more insightful analysis of particular regional economic development coalitions.

One of the ways we have traditionally understood variation in the labour market is through labour market segmentation theory. This was first put forward as a framework to explain how firms with varying structural characteristics – such as conditions of competition and regulation – develop varying reward systems for discrete labour markets (Baron and Bielby, 1980; Edwards, 1979; Kaufman, 1983). But traditional explanations of stratification within the labour market and occupational system focus exclusively on variables related to social class, rather than gender. Feminist scholars challenged this by arguing that the gender typing of jobs is a basic feature of stratification (Hartmann, 1985; Remick, 1984; Reskin, 1988). The domination of one or another gender in different occupations is a widespread and persistent phenomenon, indicating that gender segregation is an important source of occupational differences (Baron and Bielby, 1980; England, 1992; Jacobs, 1989). The empirical evidence also indicates male dominance of stratification systems, the perpetuation of separate job structures for men and women, and the operation of different rules and procedures governing men's and women's occupations (Coverman, 1986).

In the last decade, geographers have made important contributions to the segmentation debate by highlighting the differentiation between labour markets and, in particular, stressing the importance of local labour markets (Peck, 1996; Wills, 1996). Thus, regional characteristics, such as the history of organised labour, local aspects of regulation, and types of industrial agglomeration, affect the ways in which segmentation occurs in regional and sub-regional labour markets. This suggests that variation in local characteristics, including gendered social relationships, creates labour markets particular to specific places. We use this chapter to explore this and argue that social network theory is an important companion to segmentation theory in that it allows us to examine the micro-practices which reinforce the local gendered segmentation.

Likewise we find much of the same segmentation and under-representation in regional and national electoral politics. Although women's political roles are growing, women remain significantly under-represented in political circles at almost all scales. A reassessment of the UK regions therefore seems to offer a useful opportunity to reconsider the progress that has been made in the mobilisation of women. We have chosen the case of gender to illustrate this wider point, and we identify a set of political drivers which account for the current landscape, and may yet exert further influence in shaping English regional development. We turn to examine the interplay between different types of regional economic and political structures and the opportunities and constraints presented to women, highlighting both the political and economic spaces of exclusion and inclusion and how the varied regional economic and political infrastructure result in uneven gendered rates of participation. We argue that exclusion in economic and political spheres is intertwined and can only be understood by assessing those two spheres together.

## Economic representation

In this section, we begin by exploring women's economic segmentation, and draw on social network theory to understand this process. Social networks, or bonds of affiliation, provide individuals with information, contacts and mentors, which extend individuals' range of knowledge and awareness of opportunities, which in turn result in job acquisition and promotion, knowledge diffusion, and increased effectiveness in economic and political life (Granovetter, 1973; Powell and Smith-Doerr, 1994; Gray and James, forthcoming). Networks are often conceptualised as a social resource, and, like many resources, are not distributed evenly in society, but instead vary with class, ethnicity and gender. The reasons for these divisions based on gender are complex.

First, men and women tend to socialise in gender-segregated networks – at work, at home and even in voluntary associations (McPherson and Smith-Lovin, 1986). Second, men's and women's networks have different compositions, with women's networks less diverse and more family- and friends-based than men's. That is, women's networks are often more homogeneous and have fewer powerful contacts in them than men's (Marsden, 1987). Third, women's networks are often more spatially constrained, with more local, neighbourhood ties than those of their male counterparts (Hanson and Pratt, 1991). Due to the homogeneous and spatially limited character of many networks, an individual's position in a social network both empowers, by generating benefits and opportunities, and constrains, by limiting some options while enhancing others (Burt, 1992).

As a result, social networks function differently in the labour market for women and men. For example, women who use social networks in the job search tend to find themselves in gender-segregated jobs (Drentea, 1998). Not only are these jobs female dominated, but they are typically lower paid, with less prestige and authority and fewer benefits, thus they reinforce gender segregation in the labour market. Likewise, in politics, having less well-placed mentors seriously affects women's motivation, resources and aspirational roles. So, the gendered micro-practices surrounding social networks at home and at work function to structure a particular pattern of opportunity open to women.

Elsewhere in this volume, the strong variations still found in the economic structure of the English regions (whereby regions such as the South East and the East have much more diverse – but also stronger – economies than regions such as the North East) are sketched out. For example, the regional economies of the South East and London have a much higher proportion of the working population with degrees, and higher rates of employment, while the North East and the South West have the greatest proportion of those without qualifications, reflecting population characteristics but also the types of jobs available in those places. These factors are heavily interdependent: a region's strength in a particular economic sector structures the opportunities and life chances that workers face in different regions. This structures and reinforces an individual's decisions about education, qualifications and labour market mobility as she or he responds to the local economic structure. Regions with a strong science base and high rates of corporate and institutional research and development will give workers a different range of opportunities as compared with regional economies dominated by tourism and personal services. In this way each regional economic structure presents an 'opportunity structure' to potential job seekers.

The gendered nature of this 'opportunity structure' becomes clear when we analyse the data on occupational employment (Figure 5.1). Although some occupations, such as associate professional and technical jobs, have an equal proportion of women and men, we see greater levels of divergence in the high and low ends of the labour market. Women are heavily over-represented in administrative and secretarial, personal services, and sales and customer services occupations, and under-represented in managerial and senior-official, skilled-trade and professional occupations. Furthermore, we see high levels of gendered occupational segregation whereby these female-dominated occupations tend to have poorer pay and prestige than male-dominated occupations (England, 1982; Jacobs, 1989). The homogeneity of gendered social networks reinforces this occupational segmentation by producing labour market information and job contacts within the 'feminised' occupation. Once an occupation effectively becomes 'feminised', men have little incentive to enter it and women have few opportunities to leave it, or to enter (or advance within) predominantly male occupations (Miller *et al.*, 2004).

This gendered occupational segregation can be seen in occupational structures, promotion patterns and wage differentials. For example, a study of engineers in the IT industry, an extremely male-dominated occupation, finds a wage gap

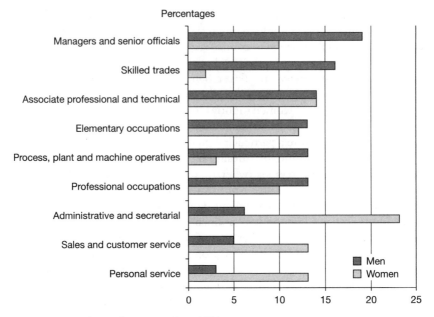

*Figure 5.1* Employees by occupation, 2003

*Source*: ONS (2003)

between women and men that is minimal (5 per cent) for younger workers but rises steadily with age so that women aged between forty and forty-four earn only 85 per cent as much as men of the same education, experience and age (Panteli *et al.*, 1999). Many scholars argue that the labour market positions and opportunities of men and women differ so radically that they actually represent separate stratification systems in the labour market (Acker, 1989). In addition, these figures themselves hide much of the variation found within these broad occupational categories. For example, within the professional and technical occupations, women are more likely to be found in the biological sciences than in electronics or engineering.

Even within a particular occupation, we see a lot of segmentation based on gender. For example, women engineers in the UK are most often found in supporting occupations, such as testing and customer service, rather than in core development engineering roles (Gray and Kurihara, 2005). Panteli *et al.* (1999) find a similar situation in the UK ICT industry, where women tend to hold only a small proportion of management posts and earn lower salaries. Similarly, US research on Silicon Valley found that women tend to be assigned menial tasks while men are given more demanding assignments (DiDio, 1997). Thus, gendered occupational segregation occurs on many different scales in the labour market – both between and within occupations.

What is not clear from Figure 5.1 is the extent to which we see regional variation in the occupational structure. For example, the South East Region has an occupational structure that is over-represented in skilled, elite occupations and under-represented in routine, manual work. Thus, 13.7 per cent of the working population in the South East is found in higher managerial and professional occupations, while only 7.2 per cent is found in routine occupations (compared to national averages of 10.7 per cent and 9.4 per cent, respectively). In contrast, in Yorkshire and Humberside the occupational structure is heavily weighted towards less skilled jobs, with 11.2 per cent of the working population in routine occupations and only 8.9 per cent in higher managerial and professional occupations (ONS, 2003). This regional variation in occupational structure, together with the gendered nature of the occupational segregation, suggests that each region has a particular gendered occupational structure.

Furthermore, there is a debate about the extent to which regional industrial structure may also affect gendered labour market segmentation. There exists a strong positive association between levels of formality or bureaucracy in the hiring and promotion processes and employment equity (Bridges and Villemez, 1994). Women and racial/ethnic minorities in a given sector experience less discrimination in hiring and other employment practices within firms which use more formal methods of hiring and promotion but more discrimination in small, informal firms which often rely more upon social networks and contacts in their hiring and promotion practices (Hodson and Kaufman, 1982; Kaufman, 1983). Therefore, within a given sector, regions which host established firms with formal labour market practices, whether government, educational institutions or private sector, should see less labour market inequality (although even formal hiring and promotion practices remain subject to the biases and preferences of the advantaged groups that are already dominant in desirable positions within the firm) than small firms with informal hiring and promotion practices. However, this idea is challenged by a study of top management in sixteen firms which finds that women are *more* likely to become CEOs in small, local corporations and in high-technology firms (Davies-Netzley, 1998). This study found that these small, and often high-tech, firms have a more fluid social system and are less characterised by an 'old boys' social network controlling job acquisition and promotion decisions, which, in turn, increases women's opportunities for advancement. Thus, some types of small firms may prove to have a more open promotion system, which may present greater opportunities for women and ethnic minorities in the region.

Therefore, although more research needs to be done to clarify the relationship between regional industrial structure and labour market segmentation, we can start to unpack the ways in which economic structures may intersect with labour market segmentation on a regional level. For example, we may find that regions in the UK with higher rates of high-tech small-firm start-ups, where social networks are new and unformed, may present a broader opportunity structure to women than regions dominated by more established firms. Additionally, regions with a large proportion of public sector jobs, characterised by formal hiring and promotion processes, where social networks are thus downplayed, may result in a higher proportion of women in management occupations.

Conversely, we may find that UK regions dominated by older industries with established old boys networks may show more severe levels of gendered labour market segmentation.

## Political representation

As we have already noted, a region's strength in a particular economic sector, the number and type of jobs available, structures the opportunities and life chances that workers face. In the remaining part of the chapter we focus on political representation. Women have long been under-represented politically on both the national and the regional levels. Although women make up 51 per cent of the population, they hold only 35.7 per cent of public appointments and ethnic minority women hold only 2 per cent of all national and regional public appointments (ODPM, 2003). Recognition of inequality (including, but not exclusively, gender-based inequality) has fuelled notions of inclusive and representative decision-making in debates surrounding governance (Humphrey and Pinkney, 2003: 2). Our argument goes one step further – that regions have had an emancipatory effect (we use such stark language with care) in terms of mobilising hitherto excluded regional assets. By creating political pathways for fairer representation of all regional residents, there are greater opportunities for political representation to shape the contemporary complex socio-political economic regional environments. These opportunities, and hence the gender emancipation, can be considered to have arisen in the English regions as a consequence of developments at three levels, including pressure from the European Union, policy from Westminster, as well as the example of the devolved administrations within Great Britain.

## National level

Westminster has played an important role in promoting gender mainstreaming in the regions. First, the Women's Unit at Whitehall was established in the Department of Social Security one month after Labour returned to office in May 1997, although it was criticised for its inability to promote its agenda, lack of policy orientation and high staff turnover, which prevented the development of core staff with specialist skills and networking ability essential to the success of a cross-cutting body. Significantly, since the inception of the Unit, the Minister for Women has had to combine her duties with another major departmental role, which brings into question New Labour's commitment to the Unit (Squires and Wickham-Jones, 2002: 66). While there was rhetorical commitment to inclusion, the practical mechanisms and strategies to bring this about were lacking. A significant change occurred after the 2001 election when there was a relaunch of the Unit as the Women and Equality Unit. The Unit's remit has been broadened and redefined, and it has been given an increased budget and more focused ministerial support (*ibid.*: 69). Part of its new policy focus has revolved around gender mainstreaming.

Women also influence policy at Westminster by applying pressure as activists, party members and think-tank researchers,[1] and by becoming MPs themselves to affect the policy agenda (*ibid.*: 63). In addition, there are gender budgeting initiatives which contribute to gender mainstreaming by focusing on the gender dimensions of government budgets,[2] both the revenue and expenditure sides, in order to produce a budget in which gender has been mainstreamed (Elson, 2003). However, while views are given, the message is not necessarily heeded or understood by government.

## Gender at a local level

It is often assumed that local/regional politics provides an easier and more direct route into power for women (for a critique, see Valiente, 1998). As is shown in Table 5.1, women's representation at the regional level across Europe is generally higher than it is at the national level (Greece and Italy, where national representation is slightly higher, are exceptions). Indeed, the UK and France are striking in that the number of women at the regional level is significantly higher than at the national level. Thus, while women make up under 18 per cent of Members in the House of Commons, and 29 per cent of Cabinet ministers (Humphrey and Pinkney, 2003: 2), they make up 37.2 per cent of Members of the Scottish Parliament, and since 2000 42 per cent of the National Assembly for Wales[3] – amongst the highest proportions of elected female politicians in the world – and 40 per cent of the London Assembly. As Humphrey and Pinkney (2003: 2) point out, the attainment of gender balance in Wales is the result of strategic intervention using the Government of Wales Act. Although women's representation at Westminster has been maintained at around 18 per cent since 1997[4] (it remained at roughly the same level in 2001[5]), research suggests that 30 per cent is the critical mass to bring about fundamental change (Lovenduski, 2001). Anne Phillips (2001: 64) comments, 'numbers alone are important, but the longer term significance lies in the opportunity for mobilising a wider range of voices, articulating concerns that would otherwise be discounted, and thereby developing more just social policies'.

*Table 5.1* Women in national and regional parliaments, 2002

| Country | Regional | National |
|---------|----------|----------|
| Sweden | 47.2 | 45 |
| Finland | – | 37 |
| Germany | 30.7 | 29.6 |
| Spain | 30.4 | 27.1 |
| UK | 27.3 | 17.1 |
| France | 25.8 | 8.7 |
| Denmark | 30.2 | 37.1 |
| Italy | 8.4 | 10.2 |
| Greece | 8.4 | 10.3 |

*Source:* http://www.db-decision.de

There has been remarkably little analysis of the engendering of the regional governance structures in England (for example, Tomaney and Mawson, 2002; Adams *et al.*, 2003), except the work undertaken by Lynn Humphrey (Humphrey and Pinkney, 2003) and by a team led by Fred Robinson (Robinson *et al.*, 2000). An analysis of governance structures in England in 2004 reveals that the proportion of board members who were women ranged from 21 per cent in the West Midlands to 43 per cent in the East Midlands (surveyed March 2004; Table 5.2). Moreover, women headed one Regional Assembly (Yorkshire and the Humber) and two RDAs (the South West and North East), while five of the nine Government Offices were headed by women. In Robinson *et al.*'s (2000) careful examination of the membership of all the directly and indirectly elected and appointed organisations charged with the governance of the North East Region, it is clear that governance remains a middle-aged, middle-class and male preserve, and it is this lack of diversity and exclusivity that Robinson *et al.* and Humphrey (Humphrey and Pinkney, 2003) question. The latter point out that although there are 22,000 public appointees in 834 public bodies,[6] women and members of minority groups are under-represented in the democratic process. An analysis of the visibility of women in other governance structures for the East Midlands reveals that they make up a smaller proportion of county councillors, MPs and MEPs than they do for RDA board membership (Tables 5.3, 5.4 and 5.5).

*Table 5.2* Regional Development Agency board members, 2004

| Region | Total | Male | Female | % Female |
|---|---|---|---|---|
| Yorkshire Forward | 15 | 9 | 6 | 40 |
| One North East | 15 | 10 | 5 | 33 |
| North West | 14 | 11 | 3 | 21 |
| East Midlands | 14 | 8 | 6 | 43 |
| Advantage West Midlands | 14 | 11 | 3 | 21 |
| South East England | 15 | 11 | 4 | 27 |
| East of England | 15 | 10 | 5 | 33 |
| South West of England | 15 | 11 | 4 | 27 |

*Source:* http://www.consumer.gov.uk/rda/innto/board.htm. Accessed 4 March 2004

*Table 5.3* Regional governance, 2004

| Organisation | Male leader | Female leader | % Female leaders |
|---|---|---|---|
| RGOs | 4 | 5 | 56 |
| Regional Assemblies | 7 | 1 | 12.5 |
| RDAs | 7 | 1 | 12.5 |

*Source:* Websites accessed May 2004

*Table 5.4* County council members in the East Midlands

| County | Total seats | Male seats | Female seats | % Female seats |
|---|---|---|---|---|
| Northamptonshire | 72 | 58 | 14 | 19 |
| Rutland | 26 | 24 | 2 | 8 |
| Leicestershire | 54 | 47 | 7 | 13 |
| Nottinghamshire | 63 | 48 | 15 | 24 |
| Derbyshire | 63 | 49 | 14 | 22 |
| Lincolnshire | 77 | 65 | 12 | 16 |
| East Midlands total | 355 | 291 | 64 | 18 |

*Source:* County council websites. Accessed March 2004

*Table 5.5* Members of Parliament in the East Midlands

| County | Total seats | Male seats | Female seats | % Female seats |
|---|---|---|---|---|
| Northamptonshire | 6 | 5 | 1 | 17 |
| Rutland | 1 | 1 | 0 | 0 |
| Leicestershire | 9 | 8 | 1 | 11 |
| Nottinghamshire | 11 | 11 | 0 | 0 |
| Derbyshire | 10 | 7 | 3 | 30 |
| Lincolnshire | 7 | 6 | 1 | 14 |
| Total | 44 | 38 | 6 | 14 |

*Source:* United Kingdom Parliament, 18 March 2004

## The devolved administrations

In Scotland, Wales and Northern Ireland women played a key role in campaigning for devolution and subsequently in the life of the devolved administrations. Alice Brown (1996: 28) comments that it was the distinctive dimension of the politics of Scotland and the challenges to the existing constitutional arrangements throughout the 1980s and 1990s that 'provided a political opportunity for women to articulate their own demands'. The Scottish campaign also influenced the devolution campaign in Wales, such that the Campaign for a Welsh Assembly 'aspired to an early state of equal representation of women and men' (Feld, 2000: 76). The strength of the Labour Party in Wales coupled with its decision to use a 'twinning'[7] system when selecting candidates resulted in a high proportion of women being elected to the Assembly. Unlike Westminster, the Welsh Assembly has a statutory duty with regard to equal opportunities which may have influenced those responsible for making appointments, as 50 per cent of the positions of responsibility within it are held by women (Beveridge *et al.*, 2000). In Northern Ireland, Policy Appraisal and Fair Treatment (PAFT) was established in 1994 to assess the impact of policy proposals on target groups, including women, in an attempt to overcome the divisive effects of religious and political discrimination, and so equality became a central issue in shaping devolution in the province (*ibid.*).

Crucially, some equality features form key building blocks of the new institutions in Scotland and Wales, including family-friendly working hours and observation of school holidays[8] (MacKay and Meehan, 2003). Some women who chose to be MSPs or AMs admit that the very location of the devolved administrations has made it feasible for them to enter politics and juggle that role with domestic commitments. They felt such a choice was not open to them in Westminster because of the geographical distance between 'work' (Westminster) and domestic commitments (Gill, 1999). In addition, the fact that women's networks tend to be more local and regional means that women are able to mobilise these networks on a regional level. Moreover, the devolved administrations place emphasis on committee structures, and politics is less adversarial, which has appealed to women (*ibid.*; see also Stephenson, 1998: 35). In addition to the adversarial male culture that characterises Westminster politics, childcare, cash and confidence are suggested as the other three of 'four Cs', or 'problems', facing women in the House of Commons (*ibid.*).

## Gender and the reshaping of regional governance structures

There is some commitment to mainstreaming in the English regions. For example, in the West Midlands the RDA, Advantage West Midlands (AWM), is the lead partner in two regional fora on gender equality.[9] Initially the focus was on raising awareness on gender, which was more acceptable to policymakers, but the shift towards mainstreaming led to the commissioning of a toolkit for general use in 2003. In the North East the Assembly has commissioned research on the participation of women in public life because of the possibility of an elected regional assembly in the North East by 2007 (Humphrey and Pinkney, 2003). These authors suggested a strategy for achieving greater female participation in public life, but to date the Assembly has not taken it up as was hoped (communication with authors).

The EU has had a large influence on gender mainstreaming in the English regions. Equality of treatment for men and women was enshrined in the Treaty of Rome, and UK equal opportunities legislation, enacted in 1975, was based on a fundamental article (119) in the Treaty, which affirmed equality of pay and treatment for men and women. More recently the EU has been proactive in developing gender mainstreaming. This involves incorporating gender equality concerns into all policies – instead of having separate policies for gender equality or adding on gender equality concerns to already formulated policies, programmes and procedures – and was adopted by the European Commission in 1996, when it committed to incorporate equal opportunities for women and men into all Community policies and activities. The EU's gender equality strategy has a dual-track approach of mainstreaming plus developing specific measures for women (see Table 5.6).

*Table 5.6* Gender balance of MEPs (June 2004)

| Region | Male | Female | % Female |
|---|---|---|---|
| East Midlands | 6 | 0 | 0 |
| Eastern | 7 | 0 | 0 |
| London | 5 | 4 | 44 |
| North East | 2 | 1 | 33 |
| North West | 8 | 1 | 11 |
| South East | 8 | 2 | 20 |
| South West | 6 | 1 | 14 |
| West Midlands | 5 | 2 | 29 |
| Yorks and Humber | 4 | 2 | 33 |
| Scotland | 5 | 2 | 29 |
| Wales | 1 | 3 | 75 |
| Northern Ireland | 3 | 0 | 0 |
| Total | 60 | 18 | 23 |

*Source:* http://www.europarl.org.uk/guide/Gelectionsmain.html

Additionally, the new governance structures for England envisaged an inclusive framework from the outset, as is illustrated by the rationale for appointments to these bodies, which promoted an appointments system inclusive of all sections of the community, with the emphasis being on skills and experience (DETR, 1997). The potential pool that candidates identified was from business, trade unions, local government and the voluntary sector (*ibid.*). In subsequent publications there was an acknowledgement that opportunities had been presented to women by regional government in Scotland and Wales. Moreover, the government has endorsed initiatives to increase women's participation in future regional assemblies in England, and in the 2002 White Paper announced its intention to apply the Sex Discrimination (Election Candidates) Act (2001) to the election of assembly members. However, the commitment to inclusivity cannot guarantee greater representation as it is dependent upon people putting themselves forward for public life. Barriers still exist that effectively prevent women aspiring to, and acquiring the necessary skills for, public life.

## Conclusion: the gender dimension to the rise of the English regions

In this chapter we have examined the levels and types of gendered segmentation and under-representation in political and economic spheres and explored the ways that this interacts with regional structure. First, we suggested that each region's economic structure presents a distinct series of local opportunity structures for women workers. For example, there exists a strong positive association between levels of bureaucracy in the promotion processes and equity in labour market outcomes. Thus, regions with a strong public sector may find more women able to transcend the 'glass ceiling'. However, the effect of having a local economy dominated by small, informal firms is less clear. On the one hand, small firms often rely more upon social contacts in their hiring and promotion practices, and this may increase segmentation due to the gendered nature of social networks. On the other hand, small firms may have a more fluid social system and be less characterised by an 'old boys' network controlling job acquisition and promotion. Thus, in the economic realm we have explored the extent to which the gendered social networks of different types of regional industrial structure may affect the extent of gendered segmentation found in the local labour market.

Likewise, women's visibility in political life cannot be fully understood without examining their positions in economic life, which in turn are shaped by domestic commitments. In the political realm, while it is true that a broader range of voices, including those of women, have been sought for new governance arrangements, we noted that the commitment to inclusivity does not itself guarantee greater representation. Numerous barriers, such as the difficulty of basing oneself far from home and juggling politics with domestic commitments, exist which function to minimise women's political participation. These barriers effectively prevent women aspiring to, and acquiring the necessary skills for, public life. This line of reasoning again highlights the continued importance of viewing the interconnections between the economic, the social and the political.

While women are more visible in the English regional governance structures than in Westminster, one key question is: has the reality of life in the English regions altered because of these changes? As they stand, the governance structures in place do not have the means or the will to bring about true equality between the genders. While there is much rhetoric to date on gender mainstreaming, strategies for more inclusive membership of public bodies have yet to be put in place. (Whether this will change when elected assemblies become a reality for some – but not all – English regions remains an unanswered question.) A greater visibility for half of the population of a region will inevitably reshape the issues that come to dominate regional policy and planning.

As pointed out earlier, women's lives are often lived more locally than men's, and their economic and political decisions are shaped by non-economic and social factors (caring commitments, equality in the home, distance between home and work, unpaid formal and informal voluntary activity). But, of course, gender does not determine life courses, and many groups are involved in the provision of these activities and services, but they are systematically absent from the political radar of key decision-makers. A greater visibility of these interests through a fairer representation of women in economic and public life therefore produces better decision-making for all regional residents. The valuing of the social fabric of communities (unpaid work, such as caring and voluntary activity) in regional economies, and the roles such activities play in bringing about socio-economic inclusion, would make regional policies and strategies strategically different, sustainability would have a social dimension, and we would argue for sustainable social regions, or sustainable socio-economic regions.

# Notes

1   Policies such as work–life balance, childcare (National Childcare Strategy) and family policy (Working Family Tax Credit) have been mainstreamed.
2   Gender budget analyses in practice are probably most developed in Australia and South Africa (Rake, 2002). See the work of the Gender Budget Group for the UK (www.gbg.org.uk) and the Women's Budget Group for Scotland (www.engender. org.uk).
3   An analysis of the career profiles of the women MSPs and AMs suggests that they have followed fairly traditional pathways into politics. In Wales an experience with quangos was important while in Scotland trade union links, work experience in local government or election as a councillor were all significant (Squires and Wickham-Jones, 2001: xiii).
4   As the *Daily Mirror* on 5 May 1997 suggested, 'they are young, intelligent, dedicated and strong, and for the first time they are bringing girl power to the mother of parliaments' (cited in Squires and Wickham-Jones, 2001: 89).
5   At the 2001 general election, the number of women in the House of Commons fell from 120 to 118. It was the first general election for over twenty years (since 1979) at which the number of women in Parliament had fallen. The result indicated a failure to sustain the progress achieved at the 1997 general election (Squires and Wickham-Jones, 2001: 48).
6   http://www.northeastassembly.gov.uk/gloabl/assets/documents/asset20030912092 807.pdf.
7   Constituencies are coupled, one selecting a female candidate and the other a male, in order to give equal opportunity at the selection stage.
8   An analysis of the 2001 election sponsored by the EOC (Elgood *et al.*, 2002: xv) included a survey of Parliamentary candidates, who were asked to consider the most important reasons why there are so few women in Westminster. Half of all the candidates cited family commitments or childcare issues; second was hours of work at Westminster.
9   Mainstreaming Equality for Disadvantaged Groups and the Equal Opportunity Forum.

# References

Acker, J. (1989) *Doing Comparable Worth: Gender, Class, and Pay Equity*, Philadelphia: Temple University Press
Adams, J., Robinson, P. and Vigor, A. (2003) *A New Regional Policy for the UK*, London: Institute for Public Policy Research
Baron, J.N. and Bielby, W.T. (1980) 'Bringing the Firms Back In: Stratification, Segmentation, and the Organization of Work', *American Sociological Review*, 45: 737–65
Beveridge, F., Nott, S. and Stephen, K. (2000) 'Mainstreaming and the Engendering of Policy-Making: A Means to an End?', *Journal of European Public Policy*, 7(3): 385–405
Bridges, W.P. and Villemez, W.J. (1994) *The Employment Relationship: Causes and Consequences of Modern Personnel Administration*, New York: Plenum Press (Studies on Work and Industry Series)
Brown, A. (1996) 'Women and Politics in Scotland', *Parliamentary Affairs*, 49(1): 26–40
Cabinet Office (2003) *Public Bodies 2003*. Available at http://www.thewnc.org.uk/ pubs/pb2003.pdf. Accessed 1 September 2004
Cabinet Office and DLTR (2002) *Your Region, Your Choice: Revitalising the English*

*Regions*. Available at http://www.odpm.gov.uk/stellent/groups/odpm_regions/documents/pdf/odpm_regions_pdf_607900.pdf. Accessed 1 September 2004

Burt, R.S. (1992) *Structural Holes: The Social Structure of Competition*, Cambridge, MA: Harvard University Press

Chaney, P. (2002) 'Women and Post-Devolution Equality Agenda in Wales', paper presented to Gender Research Forum, Women and Equality Unit, 11 February

—— (2003) 'Women and Constitutional Change in Wales', paper presented to workshop at the European Consortium for Political Research on Changing Constitutions, Building Institutions & (Re-)Defining Gender Relations, Department of Politics/School of Social Science & Political Studies, University of Edinburgh, 28 March–2 April

Coverman, S. (1986) 'Gender, Domestic Labor Time and Wage Inequality', *American Sociological Review*, 48: 623–37

Davies-Netzley, S.-A. (1998) 'Women above the Glass Ceiling: Perceptions on Corporate Mobility and Strategies for Success', *Gender and Society*, 12: 339–55

DETR (1997) *Building Partnerships for Prosperity*, Cmnd 3814, London: HMSO

DiDio, L. (1997) 'Boys' Club on Campus', *Computerworld*, 31: 68

Drentea, P. (1998) 'Consequences of Women's Formal and Informal Job Search Methods for Employment in Female-Dominated Jobs', *Gender and Society*, 12(3): 321–38

Edwards, R. (1979) *Contested Terrain: The Transformation of the Workplace in the 20th Century*, New York: Basic Books

Elgood, J., Vinter, L. and Williams, R. (2002) *Man Enough for the Job? A Study of Parliamentary Candidates*, Manchester: Equal Opportunities Commission

Elson, D. (2003) 'Gender Mainstreaming and Gender Budgeting', paper presented at European Commission, DG Education and Culture and Jean Monnet Project Conference on Gender Equality and Europe's Future, Brussels, 4 March

England, P. (1982) 'The Failure of Human Capital Theory to Explain Occupational Sex Segregation', *Journal of Human Resources*, 17(3), Summer: 358–70

—— (1992) *Comparable Worth: Theories and Evidence*, New York: Aldine de Gruyter

Feld, V. (2000) 'A New Start in Wales: How Devolution is Making a Difference', in A. Coote (ed.), *New Gender Agenda*, London: Institute for Public Policy Research

Gill, B. (1999) *Winning Women: Lessons from Scotland and Wales*, London: Fawcett Society

Granovetter, M. (1973) 'The Strength of Weak Ties', *American Journal of Sociology*, 78: 1360–80

Gray, M. and James, A. (forthcoming) 'Connecting Gender and Economic Competitiveness: Lessons from Cambridge's High Tech Regional Economy', *Environment and Planning A*

Gray, M. and Kurihara, T. (2005) 'Getting in, Staying in and Moving up: Career Pathways in ICT Engineering', Working paper: Regional Comparison of School to Work Networks

Hanson, S. and Pratt, G. (1991) 'Job Search and the Occupational Segregation of Women', *Annals of the Association of American Geographers*, 81: 229–53

Hartmann, H. (1985) *Comparable Worth: New Directions for Research*, Washington, DC: National Academy Press

—— (1986) 'The Impact of Industrial and Occupational Structure on Black–White Employment Allocation', *American Sociological Review*, 51: 310–23

Hodson, R. and Kaufman, R.L. (1982) 'Economic Dualism: A Critical Review', *American Sociological Review*, 47: 727–39

Humphrey, L. and Pinkney, E. (2003) *Women's Participation in Public Life – Towards a Regional Network in the North East*, Newcastle upon Tyne: Centre for Urban and Regional Development Studies, University of Newcastle upon Tyne

Jacobs, J.A. (1989) 'Long Term Trends in Occupational Segregation by Sex', *American Journal of Sociology*, 95(1): 160–73

Kaufman, R.L. (1983) 'A Structural Decomposition of Black–White Earnings Differentials', *American Journal of Sociology*, 89: 585–611

Lovenduski, J. (2001) 'Women and Politics: Minority Representation or Critical Mass?', *Parliamentary Affairs*, 54: 743–58

McDowell, L. and Massey, D. (1984) 'A Woman's Place?', in D. Massey and J. Allen (eds), *Geography Matters: A Reader*, Cambridge: Cambridge University Press/Open University

MacKay, F. and Meehan, E. (2003) 'Women and Devolution in Northern Ireland, Scotland and Wales', paper presented at Irish Association Seminar on New Relationships within and between These Islands, Dublin, 10 May

McPherson, J.M. and Smith-Lovin, L. (1986) 'Sex Segregation in Voluntary Associations', *American Sociological Review*, 51(1): 61–79

Marsden, P.V. (1987) 'Core Discussion Networks of Americans', *American Sociological Review*, 52: 122–31

Massey, D. (1985) *Spatial Divisions of Labour*, London: Macmillan

Miller, L., Neathey, F., Pollard, E. and Hill, D. (2004) *Occupational Segregation, Gender Gaps and Skill Gaps*, Manchester: Equal Opportunities Commission. Available at http://www.eoc.org.uk/pdf/occupational_segregation_ph1_report.pdf

Office for National Statistics (ONS) (2003) 'Labour Force Survey', in *Labour Market Trends*, London: ONS

Office of the Deputy Prime Minister (ODPM) (2003) 'Public Appointments Unit Annual Report'. Available at www.ofmdfmni.gov.uk/0203.pdf

Panteli, A. *et al.* (1999) 'Gender and Professional Ethics in the IT Industry', *Journal of Business Ethics*, 22(1): 51–6

Peck, J. (1996) *Workplace: The Social Regulation of Labour Markets*, New York: Guilford

Phillips, A. (2001) *Engendering Democracy*, Cambridge: Polity Press

Powell, W.W. and Smith-Doerr, L. (1994) 'Networks and Economic Life', in N.J. Smelser and R. Swedberg (eds), *The Handbook of Economic Sociology*, Princeton, NJ: Princeton University Press and Russell Sage Foundation

Rake, K. (2002) 'Gender Budgets: The Experience of the UK's Women's Budget Group', paper presented at conference on Gender Balance – Equal Finance, Basel, Switzerland, March

Remick, H. (ed.) (1984) *Comparable Worth and Wage Discrimination: Technical Possibilities and Political Realities*, Philadelphia: Temple University Press

Reskin, B.F. (1988) 'Bringing Men Back In: Sex Differentiation and the Devaluation of Women's Work', *Gender and Society*, 2: 58–81

Robinson, F., Shaw, K., Dutton, J., Grainger, P., Hopwood, B. and Williams, S. (2000) *Who Runs the North East . . . Now? A Review and Assessment of Governance in North East England*, University of Durham. Available at http://www.sustainable-cities.org.uk/database_files/WhoRunsNE.doc. Accessed 1 September 2004

Squires, J. and Wickham-Jones, M. (2001) *Women in Parliament: A Comparative Analysis*, Manchester: Equal Opportunities Commission

—— (2002) 'Mainstreaming in Westminster and Whitehall: From Labour's Ministry for Women to the Women and Equality Unit', *Parliamentary Affairs*, 55: 57–70

Stephenson, M.-A. (1998) *The Glass Trapdoor*, London: Fawcett Society

Tomaney, J. and Mawson, J. (eds) (2002) *England: The State of the Regions*, Bristol: Policy Press

Valiente, C. (1998) 'An Overview of the State of Research on Women and Politics in Spain', *European Journal of Political Research*, 33(4): 459–73

Walby, S. (1999) 'The New Regulatory State: The Social Power of the European Union', *British Journal of Sociology*, 50(1): 118–40

Wills, J. (1996) 'Uneven Reserves: Banking Trade Unionism', *Regional Studies*, 30: 359–72

Women's National Commission (2003) *Removing the Barriers*. Available at http://www.thewnc.org.uk/wnc_work/public_appointments.html. Accessed 1 September 2004

Yeandle, S., Booth, C. and Burns, D. (2003) *Thinking Gender First: Gender Mainstreaming in Thurrock*, Thurrock: South Essex Rape and Incest Crisis Centre

# Part II

Part II of this volume includes a set of regional chapters, explored through the theoretical lens already developed in Part I to provide some theoretical and background context for the re-emergence of regions as significant actors in economic development. These regional chapters are intended to gauge the significance of the regional evolutionary process, and whether what has taken place can be regarded as a rise. Our aspiration in this book is to take a fresh look at the English regions to understand the significance of these changes, in economic, social and political terms, and to try to find commonalities of process in the divergences of experiences across the English regions. Each regional essay thus presents a portrait of how each region has been shaped by, and has responded to, the unique interplay of global, national and local socio-economic and environmental challenges in their particular geographical area. Taken together, they offer some interesting insights into the extent to which a more general process of 'regional rising' is taking place in England as a whole, and examine the nature of that process.

Starting with the North East region, scene of the recent devolution referendum battle, nine regional chapters are presented, their boundaries corresponding with the current geographical boundaries of central government administration via Government Offices for the Regions (GORs). These boundaries are shown in Figure II.1. A glance at the accompanying statistical table (Table II.1) amply reveals the wide socio-economic diversity inherent between these regions, although, as most of the subsequent chapters demonstrate, often there are equally sharp divisions apparent at the intra-regional scale. Although there are many differences between the regions, some clear themes do emerge which begin to tell a story of why regional diversity is a 'real' issue. Parts of London, the South East and the East of England are locally articulated, rather than existing merely to support London as a world city. Conversely, a problem across the regions is the emergence of a network society in which pockets of affluence exist almost apart from their host regions, with far more connection with core cities and London as a world city. Although the fates of Grimsby, Barrow-in-Furness, Lowestoft and Norwich might appear somewhat divorced from each other, all are ultimately dependent on the way in which new forms of city-regional governance emerge which harness the dynamism of large cities to underwrite

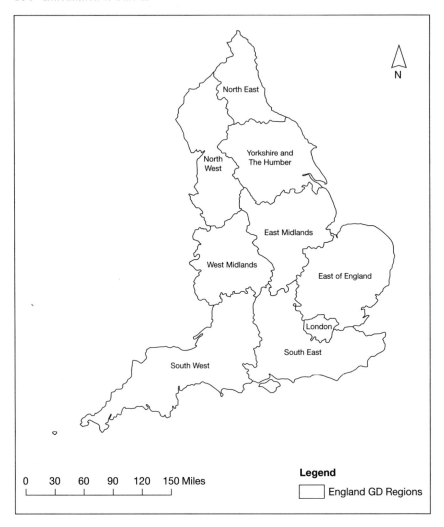

*Figure II.1* The English regions

declining peripheral communities. Although failure to address these problems might produce very different symptoms in different regions, the problems remain united and unified through the national governance system. These regional essays, written by a wide range of authors with extensive knowledge, expertise and experience of their particular regions, thus provide a rich seam of empirical findings that complement and extend the earlier theoretical discussions in setting the scene for the final concluding chapter, in which we turn to reconsider how England can be theorised as a coherent and vibrant nation, recognising the strengths and opportunities that lie within the diversity and dynamism of its constituent regions.

Table II.1 English regions: comparative regional statistics

| | United Kingdom | England | North East | North West | Yorkshire & Humber | East Midlands | West Midlands | East | London | South East | South West |
|---|---|---|---|---|---|---|---|---|---|---|---|
| Area (sq km) | 242,514 | 130,281 | 8,573 | 14,106 | 15,408 | 15,607 | 12,998 | 19,110 | 1,572 | 19,069 | 23,837 |
| Population (MYE 2004[1]) | 59.8m | 50.1m | 2.5m | 6.8m | 5.0m | 4.3m | 5.3m | 5.5m | 7.4m | 8.1m | 5.0m |
| % Population aged under 18[1] | 22.1 | 22.3 | 21.9 | 22.8 | 22.6 | 22.3 | 21.1 | 22.4 | 22.1 | 22.3 | 21.2 |
| % Population over 60[1] | 21.1 | 20.6 | 21.4 | 20.8 | 20.8 | 21.2 | 21.1 | 21.7 | 15.4 | 21.2 | 24.0 |
| % Population change (1994–2004)[2] | 3.4 | 3.9 | -1.7 | -0.2 | 1.6 | 5.1 | 1.6 | 6.1 | 8.1 | 5.2 | 5.9 |
| Standardised mortality rate (2002) (UK=100) | 100 | 98 | 111 | 109 | 101 | 99 | 101 | 92 | 98 | 91 | 90 |
| % Working population[3] with no qualifications (2003) | 15.0 | 14.6 | 18.8 | 17.5 | 16.2 | 17.1 | 17.6 | 14.0 | 13.4 | 10.6 | 10.7 |
| % Working population[3] with degree or equivalent (2003) | 16.3 | 16.6 | 11.3 | 13.3 | 13.4 | 13.0 | 12.7 | 16.2 | 24.7 | 19.9 | 16.2 |
| Average male weekly earnings[4] (April 2002) | £511.3 | £521.3 | £439.1 | £471.1 | £447.1 | £454.2 | £469.6 | £506.3 | £704.8 | £555.3 | £463.3 |
| Average female weekly earnings[4] (April 2002) | £382.1 | £388.0 | £332.1 | £354.3 | £345.0 | £334.8 | £353.0 | £375.1 | £503.6 | £398.6 | £350.0 |
| Unemployment rates[5] (Q3 2005) (%) | 4.7 | 4.7 | 6.6 | 4.4 | 4.6 | 4.4 | 4.7 | 4.0 | 6.7 | 4.0 | 3.6 |
| % Households receiving benefits[6] (2001–2) | 17 | 16 | 22 | 22 | 19 | 17 | 17 | 12 | 17 | 10 | 13 |

continued

Table II.1 continued

| | United Kingdom | England | North East | North West | Yorkshire & Humber | East Midlands | West Midlands | East | London | South East | South West |
|---|---|---|---|---|---|---|---|---|---|---|---|
| Average house prices (Q4 2005)[7] (UK=100) | 100.0 | 104.8 | 72.3 | 79.8 | 78.4 | 86.0 | 89.0 | 110.4 | 144.8 | 125.8 | 108.1 |
| GDP per head[8] (2001) (UK=100) | 100 | | 76.1 | 89.9 | 86.2 | 91.7 | 90.3 | 96.2 | 156.2 | 109.9 | 89.0 |
| GVA per head[9] (2004) | £16,800 | £17,200 | £13,400 | £14,900 | £14,900 | £15,400 | £15,300 | £18,300 | £22,200 | £19,500 | £15,600 |
| % GVA derived from manufacturing (2003)[10] | 15.2 | 15.0 | 19.6 | 19.1 | 20.0 | 21.6 | 19.5 | 13.4 | 8.5 | 11.6 | 15.2 |
| % GVA derived from services (2003)[10] | 83.4 | 83.9 | 79.3 | 79.9 | 78.5 | 76.4 | 79.2 | 85.0 | 91.3 | 87.6 | 82.6 |
| Recorded crime rate (2002–03)[11] | 11,327 | | 11,543 | 11,810 | 13,597 | 11,884 | 11,546 | 9,084 | 15,175 | 8,631 | 9,473 |

Notes:

1 2004 Mid-Year Estimate (ONS).
2 Based on corrected mid-year estimates for 1994 and 2004 (ONS).
3 Males aged 16–64; females 16–59.
4 Average weekly earnings for full-time employees on adult rates not affected by absences.
5 Percentage of total economically active, seasonally adjusted (ONS Labour Force Survey).
6 Households in which at least one member is in receipt of benefit; figures include Family Credit, Working Families Tax Credit and Income Support.
7 Based on House Price Index, November 2005 (ODPM).
8 GDP (Gross Domestic Product) calculated from figures published by Eurostat in *Eurostat News Release 21/2004*.
9 ONS First Release Gross Value Added (December 2005): 2004 provisional estimates at current basic prices, calculated on a residence basis (i.e. income allocated to where commuters live rather than their place of work).
10 ONS First Release Gross Value Added (December 2005): 2003 figures at current basic prices; 'services' includes all industry groups except manufacturing and primary industries.
11 Serious offences per 100,000 population.

*Source*: Unless otherwise stated, all statistics are from *Regional Trends No. 38* (2004), a publication of the Office for National Statistics (ONS), ISSN 0261-1783. This is also available on the ONS website www.statistics.gov.uk. Figures in the UK column in italics are for Great Britain.

# 6  Where and what is the North East of England?

*Dave Byrne and Paul Benneworth*

## Introduction

If the critics are to be believed, then the North East of England is both the birthplace and the graveyard of English regional devolution and regionalism (Figure 6.1). John Tomaney, speaking at his professorial inauguration in 2003, argued that the 'North' had a long history of autonomy from the English 'centre'. And yet, when on 4 November 2004 the people of the North East were invited to vote on an elected regional assembly, they spoke clearly, with 78 per cent of those voting (39 per cent of all those eligible to vote) rejecting the proposal and ending the current Labour government's devolution plans 'for a generation'. Part of the problem is that although regional identity is strong in the North East of England, the identity is complex, and simple narratives of 'Geordie pride' inevitably fail to catch that complexity.

Jenkins (1996: 75) remarks of identity that it is 'imagined but not imaginary'. However, imagination does not work in isolation from context and experience. They provide a repertoire on which an 'imagined community' (Anderson, 1992) can be constructed. In the case of regional identities, the repertoire is defined by historical experience in a specific space. Here, we identify an immediate problem for the North East. Until 1994, the region was the 'Northern Region' and included Cumbria, now transferred to the North West. Indeed, for many years the Northern Region also included the North Riding of Yorkshire.

These are administrative definitions and derive in origin from the regional organization in the inter-war years for the maintenance of supplies. The administrative regions were created in response to the perceived revolutionary threat of a general strike, a perception which persisted through the 1930s depression despite the ultimate failure of the 1926 strike. This administrative ad hoc mechanism acquired much more significance as the basis of devolved administration and coordination in the UK's wartime planned economy. Wartime arrangements then served as the basis of much post-war administration, particularly in health and in the regional organization of central government's own direct services in employment and national insurance. However, the 'North' has much more than just an administrative identity. The administrative mechanisms themselves reflected a particular historical geography. Of greatest significance was the

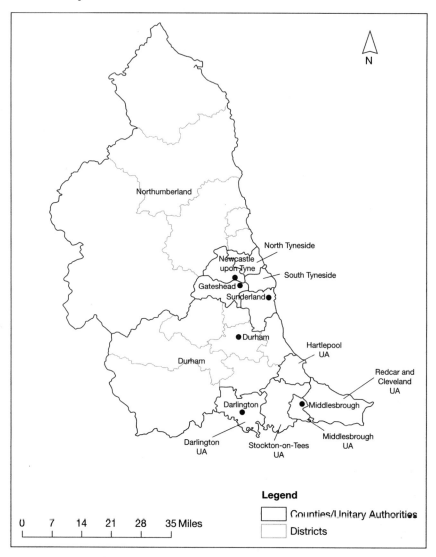

*Figure 6.1* The North East

historical geography of carboniferous capitalism during and after the industrial revolution. This experience is of an essentially unique combination of coal mining, iron and steel production, shipbuilding and heavy engineering, chemicals and seafaring, what the Germans call their *Montanenindustrien*. This was not an inward-looking frame. Perhaps the first use of 'North East' in a modern sense is to define the North East coast, the ports from Whitby (Yorkshire) to Blyth (Northumberland) which were involved in the eighteenth-century coal trade, which in the nineteenth century became global.

But that is by no means the whole story. The North is England's border region and all the original parts of it, including the old North Riding, were the 'English Marches' until the union of the Scots and English crowns in 1603. This medieval structure overlay the early modern religious continuities of the region of England which was originally Christianized by the Celtic rather than the Roman Church. The North has two broad interrelated dialects with much in common. In Northumberland and north Durham this is directly derived from Anglish whilst Norse content predominates elsewhere in the North: the internal boundaries can be read from a map by looking to see whether small streams are called burns (Anglish) or becks (Norse).

A key factor in this is the significance of immigration. The North East is rather homogeneously white but it is by no means simply English. Although there has been an excess of emigration from the region since the 1920s, for a hundred years before that, the region, and in particular industrial Tyneside, Wearside, Teesside and the Great Northern Coalfield, saw more immigration than any other industrial region of Britain. By 1911 about 40 per cent of the origins of the region's population were from outwith the Northern counties of England, with the largest single contribution being from Ireland, followed by Scotland. Differential Irish Catholic fertility over four generations has meant that about a fifth of the North East's gene pool is of Irish origin (see Byrne, 1996). However, the nature of the labour process in the dominant industries entailed a rapid assimilation of such immigrants into a heavily unionized industrial structure, the labour movement leaving little space for the emergence of Orange/Green[1] sectarianism in the region.

The industrial structure has been critical in building linkages through the period of industrial capitalism, with a modern version of regional identity emerging across today's regional boundaries. Cumbria is split, with the former Furness district of Lancashire and Cumberland and Westmorland south of Shap looking to the North West whereas the Eden Valley, the Northern Lakes, industrial west Cumbria and Carlisle identified with the North East. This is even more the case for the North Riding, because Teesside had long served as the industrial attractor and market for the North Yorkshire Dales and Moors and much of the Vale of York, and these functional relationships are evident to this day. In cultural terms industrialism is the medium which has nourished identity and to which all the aspects of identity relate. In Raymond Williams' terms (1973: 332), we have a 'structure of feeling' which is the source of identity and its expression, including, and indeed particularly, political identity.

In terms of 'the region' being an object of significant political identification, the first expression was in the North East Coast Exhibition of the 1920s in which local government and local industry came together to 'promote' the region in a time of structural adjustment. Likewise, the role of the Special Areas Commissioner, created in 1934 (and whose remit included west Cumbria), reinforced this conception of the region as a scale at which decline could be addressed. Likewise, North East Industrial Estates (which later became English Partnerships) also operated in Cumbria, despite its name, and through the 1950s was to become the leading regional institution, alongside another creation of the Special Areas Commissioner, the North East Housing Association (also active in Cumbria). This focus on addressing industrial decline inevitably encouraged two trends: the creation of a branch plant economy with little local control over production activities; and the reinforcement of the relative importance of manufacturing to the region. As the regional indicators presented in the introduction to Part II indicate, even today one-third of economic activity in the region is in the manufacturing sector, contrasting with the UK average of one-quarter.

## Economic and social change

It is clear that the experiences of carboniferous capitalism have exerted a profound influence on the emergence of regional identity in the North East, and have produced a regional identity with clear differences with the underlying national English and British identities. The defining basis of North Eastern identity has been first in class and second in industrial experience, which includes the experiences of women as social reproducers in industrial contexts through their centrality as domestic managers. Indeed, the domestic culture was strongly matriarchal, especially in the coalfield, as is generally the case in societies where there has been a substantial surplus of adult males.

Carboniferous capitalism was undoubtedly important to the North East of England; in the late nineteenth and early twentieth centuries, some 8 per cent of the population were employed in mining, a phenomenal dependence on the sector given the generally much lower participation rates than today. Ferrous metals, whilst never overtaking 'old king coal', grew to comparable size by the 1960s. In that decade, when the UK government published its White Paper on a regional policy for the North East (Board of Trade, 1963: 10), one-third of all male jobs were in four industries, 'compared with one eigth [*sic*] in the country as a whole'. An indication of the rise and fall of these industries over 150 years is given in Table 6.1, compiled from a variety of sources.

The other great factor to influence the industrial structure of the North East was the gradual and hidden emergence of a branch-plant and foreign-owned sector. In 1934, in response to the depression sweeping the UK, the government

*Table 6.1* Population and employment in carboniferous capitalism in the North East (thousands)

|  | 1841 | 1861 | 1881 | 1901 | 1931 | 1961 | 1971 | 1981 | 1991 |
|---|---|---|---|---|---|---|---|---|---|
| Population | 617 | 942 | 1,458 | 1,995 | 2,515 | 2,610 | 2,678 | 2,636 | 2,602 |
| Coal mining | 23 | 50 | 96 | 165 | 188 | 118 | 64 | 39 | 11 |
| Iron & steel | – | 13 | 31 | 34 | 23 | 57 | 56 | 22 | 10 |
| Shipbuilding | – | 7 | 15 | 42 | 51 | 64 | 39 | 26 | 8 |

*Source:* Benneworth (2002)

designated two 'trading estates', one in Treforest and the other in Team Valley in the North East, calling these places 'special areas' and giving them their own commissioner, Sir Sadler Forster. Advance units (i.e. vacant factories) were to be built to attract entrepreneurs and business activities to those locations (Loebl, 1987). This policy, which for the laissez-faire politicians of the time was a radical experiment, was followed up with a sequence of policy measures aiming to sustain employment in the region by attracting new companies. The net effect was the creation of what was later to be called the 'branch-plant economy', dominated by externally controlled firms which often failed to invest in modernization, and which were individually prone to closure during periods of economic downturn. Until the 1970s, the strength of the carboniferous industries obscured the significance of this emerging sector, but the changes were to influence the industrial culture of the region profoundly.

This was because the government policies of the 1940s to 1960s which created branch plants also created a very substantial female industrial proletariat employed in clothing, textiles and light engineering. This fact tends to be much neglected in general discussion of the North East's cultural character, but it is extremely important. This transformation was promoted by the governments of the day as a means of reinforcing the North East's position as the industrial heart of the nation, but it was also a side-effect reinforced massively by the general labourist character of identities and politics. This transformation policy was driven by two key reports, both dating from the 1960s, whose role in 're-placing' the North East within a national imagination cannot be over-emphasized. The Hailsham Report (Board of Trade, 1963) and *Challenge of the Changing North* (a planning report by the Northern Economic Planning Council – 1966) were both developed at a time when regional planning was coming for the first time into vogue and the decline of North Eastern industry had not played through to its climax.

The emergence of the branch-plant economy in the North East is well documented, and by the time of the UK's entry into the EEC in 1973, there was a foreign-owned sector (mainly of US origin) of some importance in the North East. Smith and Stone (1989) estimated that in 1971 there were 24,400 jobs in foreign firms, rising to 53,000 in 1978, at a time when total employment in the region was at a level of approximately one million (Office for National Statistics, 2001). These jobs were predominantly in manufacturing, and Hudson (1995) estimates that 75 per cent of the jobs created to that date by inward investment were in six sectors: chemicals, mechanical engineering, electrical engineering, rubber, automotives and printing.

## Regional politics and identity in the North East of England

The politics of the North East historically reflected the region's industrial character. However, the politics were not by any means exclusively Labour in the twentieth century. Rather, an original nineteenth-century politics became transformed through the inter-war years (see below). Its basis lay in a primarily radical liberalism – drawing particularly on coalfield support – confronted by a rural and manufacturing conservatism which drew on some skilled workers and white-collar industrial staff. External identification of the region is based on the distinctive general accent of those from Tyneside, Wearside, Durham and Teesside, and also encompasses the accents of North and West Cumbrians. This external labelling has been important, positive and amiable, and did feed back into the region itself, particularly of course through the massive general experience of young men and women in two world wars. Indeed, the region's distinctive military institutions – the county regiments (before 1968 the Royal Northumberland Fusiliers, the Royal Border Regiment and the Durham Light Infantry) and units of army corps drawn from the North East – have been important both as internal and as external symbols of identity.

The external identification reflects and reinforces internal identification, and here the significance of the inter-war period was – but perhaps is no longer – of very great importance. For the North East the inter-war slump represented a descent from the heights to the depths; a region characterized by industrial innovation, massive self-confidence, and the highest skilled and mining male manual wages in Europe became poor and 'depressed'. All the evidence suggests that this was a real psychic shock and it shaped views of collective selves through the Second World War and well into the 1960s. In part this was a matter of 'never again' but it also led to confusion in outward representations of the region. To some degree at this point traditional heavy industry was seen as having failed, and the symbols, particularly the working-class symbols, of the period of growth and confidence became confused with the symbols of depression and decline.

Industrialization had made the North East a globally significant region and North Eastern identities acquired a particular belated recognition in some of the key agencies of globalization. A popular regional BBC radio show of the 1950s, *Wot Cheor Geordie?* (this was when Newcastle was an important regional broadcasting centre), had as its theme tune the song 'Wherever ye gan ye're sure to find a Geordie'. In the maritime institutions of globalization this was and remains absolutely true, although, apart from mining engineers, North Easterners are much rarer away from tidewater. The expression 'Geordieland' has been in circulation ever since the 1960s to describe the whole of the North East, occurring repeatedly in military, maritime and engineering contexts.

The politics of regional workers defied simple explanation into the period between the 1950s and the 1970s, when manual workers and public service workers were Labour, and much of the industrial white-collar grades tended to support a Conservative Party led by people with manufacturing connections and a general 'one nation' (centre-right or patrician) orientation. Both the Labour Party and the Conservatives at this time had a strong regional orientation. The Hailsham Report, written by a Tory aristocrat in response to a request from a Conservative government led by a former North Eastern MP, Harold Macmillan, in the early 1960s, was indicative of this. The report was the first attempt by the central government to develop a regional economic development strategy for the North East, and it remains arguably the most realistic strategy to emerge for the region. It led to one of the most successful periods of regeneration in the North East.

The reconstruction processes of the 1960s reasserted the status of the region as the locus for coordinated interventions of an essentially corporatist form. A corrupt local politician, T. Dan Smith, was significant here in establishing a regional dominance by the Labour Party in the local government 'presence' on regional bodies. His assertion of regional identity was important in asserting Labour dominance over regional bodies. In parallel with this, Andy Cunningham, regional secretary of the General and Municipal Workers' Union (G&M), succeeded in making his the dominant general union in the new manufacturing plants and in nuclear west Cumbria. By careful manipulation, the G&M usurped the highly democratic National Union of Mineworkers' dominance of regional trade unionism and Labour politics, and it retains this position to this day, exercising power over Labour constituency parties. More generally, the politics of 'regeneration' has intimately shaped the regional level of politics in the North East. The North Eastern Development Corporation was created in the 1960s as a local response to industrial decline, and evolved during the 1970s and 1980s through an incarnation as the Northern Development Company (NDC) into the present Regional Development Agency, One NorthEast. From its time as the NDC onwards, the emphasis shifted towards the attraction of US and Far Eastern branch-plant and related incoming investment.

Most recently, the role of European Union regional funding has reinforced this tendency. Although the UK government attempted to dictate this process from Whitehall, in the North East as in other regions pressure from the European Commission led to genuine efforts for a wider local input. In parallel with this, the local authorities' regional association – now calling itself the North Eastern Assembly (of local authorities) – is a formally corporatist body with strong business representation. The rejection of an elected regional assembly in the North East means that it is this body which will receive the limited new statutory 'Chapter 2' powers over planning, transport and waste granted in the Devolution White Paper to all English regions (ODPM, 2002).

The old 'industrial' orientation remains very significant as a common bond among local government and business representatives. For example, the North East Chamber of Trade is strongly regionalist in orientation, reflecting its relationship with European institutions. The CBI component was against elected regional assemblies on the grounds that these existing corporatist regional institutions worked effectively and the proposed regional assembly had no such proven pedigree. It should be noted that the industrial connection extends into the North East's countryside, with agriculture figuring as another industry with structural adjustment problems. The presence of significant manufacturing and mining activities until quite recently, even in deep rural areas, and strong social relations between the rural and urban North East have reinforced this connection.

## North Eastern culture beyond economic development

Outside this corporatist sphere the regional agenda has re-emerged as a factor in civil society. In the Labour Party, this arose as a reaction to the national party's mid-1990s abolition of the Northern Region, when central party administrators folded the Northern region into a greater North East & Yorkshire organization run from Wakefield. North Eastern Labour figures as well as Liberal Democrats, Greens along with figures from the artistic, literary and 'regional intellectual' scenes, have all participated in the 'Campaign for a Northern Assembly' (CNA), which remains a significant presence in regional politics as a pressure group and popular movement. The CNA was instrumental in defusing Northern Labour opposition to the 1990s version of Scottish devolution, in contrast to the 1970s period when opposition from the Northern Group of Labour MPs resulted in the defeat of the government's devolution programme and ultimately the collapse of the Callaghan premiership.

The example of Scottish devolution has been important for the CNA in principle, if not always in practice, although recently the organization has developed closer ties with the Welsh Assembly, reflecting common interest between the North East and Wales in relation to regional funding allocations and a distaste for the style of Scottish Assembly politics. Alongside the CNA, UNISON, now the North's largest union although entirely a public sector organization, established a regional convention. This was supposed to imitate the Scottish convention, which had established the moral and political cases underpinning the creation of the Scottish Assembly since 1989. However, the prevailing corporatism in the North East led to a premature end for the convention, and the capture of the terms of the debate by a central government which was never anything other than sceptical of the value of regional government.

Of particular significance are regional cultural institutions. Historically the radical liberal press, the *Chronicle* in the north and the *Northern Echo* in the south of the region, have been of great significance, and remain important to regional politics, business and culture. Although Tyne Tees Television was important for a time, it has been absorbed into the ITV monolith, leaving very little regular regional production. Regional opt-outs from national news bulletins do currently remain important as assertors of regional identity and character. A distinctive broadcast media is now exclusively limited to the realm of local radio, a consequence of the BBC abandoning the North East as a regional radio centre in the 1960s.

There is a history of a distinctive North Eastern culture beginning with the music-hall tradition in the nineteenth century and continuing through the folk revival – an important connector of the urban and rural North East – and both drama and popular novels, with Catherine Cookson, even *post mortem*, remaining a major export industry for the region. Indeed, on a national and even global scale the work of Cookson and Clement and La Frenais (who wrote *The Likely Lads*) represents the North East to the world. Perhaps the very successful dramatic series *When the Boat Comes In*, written originally by Jimmy Mitchell, best conveyed the character of regional politics and industrial identity in the period of its consolidation.

The cultural sphere in the region is now very lively indeed, although it is rather disconnected, except in the visual arts and to a lesser extent music, from culture as a vehicle of urban regeneration. This is not a new phenomenon: there was a radical inter-war popular culture of North Eastern working-class novelists, and in particular Harold Heslop writing about mining. This never quite disappeared – Catherine Cookson often displayed rather radical sympathies – but it was only in the 1960s that it re-emerged across a number of fronts: traditional forms of drama, a radical poetry revival and a local rhythm and blues music scene rendered global through the Animals. Many of the significant contemporary assertors of regional identity – Live Theatre, Amber Films, the regional poetry scene – date back to this period. It is noticeable that the much-vaunted 'cultural regeneration' has engaged not so much with this locally embedded – although globally connected – cultural practice, as with regional versions of high culture in modern visual arts and classical music, leading to highbrow projects such as the Sage Music Centre and the Baltic Art Gallery. The North East has also been the base for a good deal of fiction writing at all levels, with David Almond's atmospheric children's books in particular acquiring an international reputation. This has been taken forward in its own 'highbrow' manner, with the recent opening of the Seven Stories centre for contemporary children's literature in the Ouseburn cultural quarter.

Sport also matters. An excellent guide to the regional significance and salience of football can be found in Harry Pearson's *The Far Corner* (1996) and it is worth noting that the North East's three big football clubs all draw on an essentially local and highly specific fan base. The three clubs, Newcastle, Sunderland and Middlesbrough, are all seen as North Eastern, in a sense which excludes Yorkshire, so it was long asserted that Leeds was Yorkshire's only Premiership club. (And from 2006 Sheffield United will adopt that mantle.) Middlesbrough, although within the cultural boundaries of historic Yorkshire, didn't seem to count. It clearly belongs to the North East, which is today a culturally distinct area from the Yorkshire Ridings. It is an assertion of some durability, given that Leeds' relegation from the top flight of English football has not led to a belated assertion of the 'Yorkshireness' of Middlesbrough Football Club by Yorkshire supporters seeking to follow the Premiership.

## The North East of England and the new economy

The North East is now essentially post-industrial; as the indicators show, two-thirds of the North Eastern economy is services, and we have to recognize explicitly that post-industrialism is a recent phenomenon and a sudden one. Indeed, in terms of lived daily point-of-production experience, the high point of North Eastern industrialism was only forty years ago, when traditional industries were still going strong and the enormous post-war development of a female industrial proletariat in clothing, light engineering and so on was at its height. This was in many ways a revival of the pre-1920 experience – in which very high household incomes were the norm in a predominantly industrial society. Things are now very different: fewer than 20 per cent of the North East's workers currently work in manufacturing; and on the most generous inter-pretation of 'industrial', fewer than 30 per cent of workers could be described as such.

Is the North East a knowledge economy? In one sense it is, but it is a rather specific sense. As with most post-industrial regions a very large proportion of jobs are now in locally produced and consumed public services which depend on labour forces with high levels of education and/or professional training. Much is made of the call centre industry, which currently employs some 30,000 people in the North East (although the Government Office of the North East's anticipated growth in this sector to 40,000 by 2008 seems highly optimistic in the light of job exports to India). Indeed, the indicators bear out all too clearly how far the North East lags even other peripheral regions in the UK in the move to the knowledge economy, with the highest proportion of unqualified labour market participants and the lowest proportion of the workforce with degrees.

It is important to recognize the continuing importance of the public sector to North Eastern employment. Since the interrelated decimation and privati-zation of the nationalized industries of carboniferous capitalism, the importance of coal, steel and shipbuilding has been supplanted by regional health service employment and employment in local government, schools, colleges and universities. Indeed, the five universities alone employ nearly 20,000 people. The region has served as a devolved centre of routine central government admin-istration for the UK since the head office of the then National Insurance was located here in the immediate post-war period. This routine data processing is in fact the characteristic form of knowledge economy employment in the North East, and the technical substitution of electronic record for paper file is the only difference over some fifty years for many of the workers. Byrne (1999) stylizes three types of workers in the knowledge economy, namely: rangers, artisans and drudges. The rangers were the entrepreneurs and higher service-class employees of IT who closely resembled the engineers and engineering capitalists of the early industrial revolution. The artisans were the programmers and system workers who corresponded to the millwrights and fitters and turners of that period – highly skilled labour with considerable labour market bargaining ability and a good deal of control over their own work process. Both of these groups of course existed in and were crucial for the industrial North East. However, most workers were drudges, tied to and working in relation to machino-facture. These days, call centre workers are unequivocally drudges, as are the majority of those involved in social security processing activities. There are some rangers and artisans in the private sector in the North East. The obvious example is in Sage UK, headquartered here with 1,400 employees. However, even in this innovative company, over 500 of the employees are call centre workers.

In 1999 the EU research database CORDIS identified engineering, biological and life sciences, and computing/IT as the main research and development (R&D) functions with a significant presence in the North East. The first is of course much decreased from its heyday, although a significant marine and mining consultancy and design resource has survived the massive erosion of production in these areas. The second is relatively limited and consists of Sage, some small and medium-sized enterprises and the outsourced activities from the Department of Work and Pensions. Pharmaceuticals are more important, although the loss of major chemical research by ICI on Teesside far outweighs some developments in life science and pharmaceutical R&D by AstraZeneca and other companies.

In general, it has to be said that the North East had a far more real knowledge economy in its industrial prime when it was a major centre for marine and power engineering, metallurgy, chemical production and mining engineering. Deindustrialization has massively reduced the knowledge base. This means that the region is essentially externally dependent, with a meagre degree of autonomous knowledge production in the private sector, reflected in low wage levels, low levels of gross value added, and a continuing dependence on state insurance benefits for supporting regional spending power.

The knowledge economy runs through the recently published *Northern Way* strategy for the three Northern English regions (the North East, the North West and Yorkshire and the Humber). As a consequence of the referendum result, this strategy is seen as being 'the only game in town'. *Northern Way* emphasizes the role of strong provincial cities as bulwarks against overcentralization around London. Knowledge activity, R&D and innovation are central to *Northern Way's* approach. But despite the apparent benefits of this approach, the North East once more faces being made the 'peripheral other', the strategy threatening greater concentration on Leeds and Manchester rather than a more general decentralization to all urban areas.

## Conclusions: placing the North East of England in the knowledge economy?

The cultural and spatial implications of this for the North East of England are as yet unresolved. The industrial culture remains the base motif on which cultural identity and cultural performance are constructed in the region as a whole. Many of the consumption habits which have led to the identification of Newcastle and other North Eastern city centres as party zones are to a considerable degree simply the consumption habits of a prosperous industrial working class in an exaggerated form – post-modernity, as Lash and Urry (1994) have it, as modernity on speed. Indeed, they echo the consumption habits of earlier industrial ages when high wages permitted ostentatious leisure consumption. There is an important difference in these new activities in that they are heavily outward facing, dominated by external companies, staffed in many cases by temporary residents and produced as a 'spectacle' as part of a tourism-driven reimagining of a post-industrial Tyneside.

However, what is certain is that the region is plagued by uncertainty, and regional identity reflects the stresses of dealing with long-term consequences of regional economic decline. The short lifespan of call centres illustrates the contingency of employment in a globalized world. There is no clear trajectory towards the future, and politicians are seen to have 'failed' the region. This has clearly left its imprint on regional politics, as the November 2004 referendum demonstrated. Early indications seemed to imply that the result reflected that the very limited powers of the proposed assembly were woefully inadequate to deal with the very real social and economic problems of the region.

The North East region today strongly reflects its roots in terms of its economic structure, its regional identity and regional politics. However, these all bear the imprint of the decades in which the North East has been a 'problem' region, and, as time has gone by, a problem which seems increasingly intractable. This has the effect of making regionalism seem irrelevant for the solution of these problems, and ultimately for delivering a better quality of life for the region's residents. The region is also held back by a national rhetoric which denigrates regional equalization policies as being bad for the British economy.

It is hard to see how the region moves forward from this position, harnessing its undoubted cultural strengths in an instrumental way to create a more unified and dynamic political environment capable of addressing these deep-seated problems. Looking north to Scotland, the new Parliament was able to articulate a vision of a society reborn through the emancipating opportunities of new technologies and science. Unfortunately for the North East of England, there is no clearly articulated conceptual map into the future, and by not providing such a clear vision, regional identity and culture continue to fail.

## Note

1   'Orange/Green sectarianism' is used to refer to the split between Protestant and Catholic Irish in the north of Ireland. Whilst Glasgow in particular exhibits strong Protestant and Catholic divisions in Irish diasporic groups, with each community adopting the symbols of the unionist and nationalist communities from the North of Ireland, this split has not been replicated in the North East.

## References

Anderson, B. (1992) *Imagined Communities: Reflections on the Origin and Spread of Nationalism*, London: Verso

Benneworth, P. (2002) 'Innovation and economic development in an old industrial region: the case of the North East of England', unpublished Ph.D. thesis, University of Newcastle upon Tyne

Board of Trade (1963) *The North East: A Programme for Regional Development and Growth* ['The Hailsham Report'], London: HMSO, Cmnd 2206

Byrne, D. (1996) 'Immigrants and the formation of the North Eastern industrial working class', *North East Labour History Bulletin*, 30: 29–36

—— (1999) *Social Exclusion*, Milton Keynes: Open University Press.

Hudson, R. (1995) 'The role of foreign inward investment', in L. Evans, P. Johnson and B. Thomas (eds), *The Northern Regional Economy: Progress and Prospects in the North of England*, London: Mansell

Jenkins, R. (1996) *Social Identity*, London: Routledge

Lash, S. and Urry, J. (1994) *Economies of Signs and Space*, London: Sage

Loebl, H. (1987) *Government Factories and the Origins of British Regional Policy, 1934–1948*, Aldershot: Gower

Northern Economic Planning Council (NEPC) (1966) *Challenge of the Changing North*, Newcastle upon Tyne: Northern Economic Planning Council

Office for National Statistics (NOMIS database) (2001) Census of Employment, London: HMSO

Office of the Deputy Prime Minister (ODPM) (2002) *Your Region, Your Choice: Revitalising the English Regions*, London: The Stationery Office

—— (2004) *Making it Happen: The Northern Way*, London: The Stationery Office

Pearson, H. (1996) *The Far Corner*, London: Abacus

*Report of the Royal Commission on the Constitution* (1973), London: HMSO, Cmnd 5460, paragraph 329

Smith, I. and Stone, I. (1989) 'Foreign investment in the North – distinguishing fact from hype', *Northern Economic Review*, 18: 50–61

Tomaney, J. (2003) 'Governing the region past, present and future', inaugural lecture, St Cuthbert's Day, University of Newcastle upon Tyne, 20 March, available at http://www.campus.ncl.ac.uk/unbs/hylife2/lib/files/5169tomaney.pdf, accessed 17 November 2004

Williams, R. (1973) *The Long Revolution*, London: Pelican

# 7 The North West

## Cultural coherence and institutional fragmentation

### Christopher Wilson and Mark Baker

### Introduction: Location, history and identity

The North West region extends over 14,140 square kilometres and has a population of 6.9 million and a labour force of 2.6 million, making it the second-largest region in Britain (Figure 7.1). Three-fifths of its population live in the major conurbations of Greater Manchester (2.6 million) and Merseyside (1.4 million) – both with population densities of over 2,000 person per square kilometre – with further concentrations in the largely Victorian industrial towns of Central and east Lancashire and north Cheshire. One of the world's first industrial regions, and still one of the country's leading manufacturing locations, it has been particularly badly hit by the process of deindustrialisation. It has a poor reinvestment record, the lowest rate of new firm formation in Britain, and poor regional performance in terms of inward investment (Tickell *et al.*, 1995). The region is peripheral to existing and emerging European markets, and has been hit hard by contemporary changes in defence-related industries.

However, it has a large market and good access to both domestic and other markets, and production costs are low. Manchester is England's most sophisticated financial centre outside London, and Manchester Airport is by far the largest provider of international services outside the South East. Its transport infrastructure is good, whilst its environmental settings are diverse. Intra-regionally, the impact of economic change has been uneven and fragmented, with Merseyside perceived in recent times as being in a state of continual crisis from which it is only now beginning to emerge. Greater Manchester has attempted to overcome structural decline through vigorous image building, whilst the less urban parts of Cheshire, Lancashire and Cumbria have demonstrated relative success (Williams and Baker, 2006).

At one level, compared to many of the English regions, the North West can be argued to have had, at least culturally and historically if not politically or administratively, a relatively strong identity and sense of 'self'. The historical development of England, particularly the geographically uneven industrial-isation of the country in the eighteenth and nineteenth centuries, and subsequent deindustrialisation, have ensured that most English citizens continue to identify 'the North' as being an area distinct from Southern and Midlands

*Figure 7.1* The North West

regions. At the same time, those living in the Northern region continue to differentiate between a North West region, based on a core of Lancashire, Greater Manchester and Merseyside, and a 'North Eastern' region of Yorkshire and Northumbria/Tyneside. Although this 'Northern' identity has been somewhat diminished by the globalisation of culture and the reduction of the North West's role as a key manufacturing centre, the sense of uniqueness remains, reinforced by regionally based media (*North West Tonight, Look North* and fictional programmes such as *Coronation Street*), sport and history as well as the practical distance between Manchester/Liverpool and England's other conurbations. Paradoxically, however, in terms of institutional collaboration and intra-regional rivalries, the North West is arguably one of the most fragmented of all the English regions. This issue, and its implications for regional governance and strategy development, is a matter returned to later in this chapter.

The region's separate historical and cultural identity has its origins in the Duchy of Lancaster, when this powerful medieval dukedom (composed of Lancashire and elements of modern Cheshire, Merseyside, Greater Manchester and Cumbria) dominated the Northern woollen trade and vied with its trans-Pennine rival, Yorkshire, for control of the monarchy (Defoe, 1974). The medieval 'War of the Roses' is even today reflected in sporting rivalries such as the annual 'Roses' cricket matches between Yorkshire and Lancashire and the intensity of the football confrontations, on the pitch and the terraces, between Manchester United and Leeds United. However, much of the region's current identity comes from the industrial era when the North West took an early lead in many industries, particularly textiles. Writing at the tail end of that era, Dury (1961) divides the region into two distinct zones, the first being the comparatively flat Lancashire–Cheshire Plain. Here the presence of an abundant coalfield and numerous small rivers led to the development of small villages, along key transport routes, into extensive industrial communities. By far the largest of the North West's industrial communities was the city of Manchester, which grew from a town of 36,250 in 1773 to a major city of 607,000 in 1901 (Smith, 1969: 23).

The elements of the textile process – coal mining (for power), spinning, weaving, bleaching and dying – were divided among the various towns and this necessitated the extensive communication of goods and labour by road, canal and later rail, creating a shared industrial identity and mutual dependence that has formed the core of the North West region (Smith, 1969). Also part of this network was the City of Liverpool. From this port city the raw cotton necessary for the textile process was imported from the Americas, and the finished products exported, linking the city into the North West region despite its geographical separation from the major urban areas of Lancashire and Greater Manchester. Like Manchester, the city grew extensively through its industrial success from 75,000 in 1800 to 700,000 in 1900, when the port was handling half the value of goods exported from the UK (against the quarter that went through London; Dury, 1961: 301).

A final element in this industrial identity comprises the coastal towns of Lancashire, of which Blackpool is the most prominent. With some exceptions these towns had little industry of their own but rather provided leisure and entertainment facilities for the industrial working class during the later industrial period. Through this service, the Lancashire coast became as closely linked to the North West's industrial identity as any of the manufacturing communities (Dury, 1961).

If the Lancashire–Cheshire Plain marks the core of the North West Region, then the periphery is marked by the upland areas of Cumbria and the Pennines. This area is dominated by smaller rural communities dominated by uplands agriculture and more recently by landscape tourism. Industry (outside the communities of Barrow and Carlisle) has been traditionally limited to mineral extraction, providing a more limited industrial link to the rest of the North West (Dury, 1961). Also outside of the industrial core of the North West, the flat lands of south and central Cheshire have little history of industrialisation, being historically dominated by farming, forestry and service-based economies (Smith, 1969).

The last forty years has seen the loss of much of the industry that spawned the North West's original identity. However, the region remains a major force in the UK's economy. The true power of the region's economy is best illustrated when it is compared with other European economies. In doing so we still find that the £60 billion pound economy is larger than that of five of the pre-2004 European member states – the Republic of Ireland, Finland, Luxembourg, Portugal and Greece (NWRA, 2004a) – giving the North West a formidable economic presence both nationally and internationally.

It is difficult to overestimate how much the industry of the past 200 years has shaped the physical and socio-economic landscape of the North West. Even with all that has been lost without trace over recent decades, it is hard to find an area of rural Cumbria, Lancashire or Greater Manchester that lacks evidence of quarrying or mill activity. The cities of Manchester and Liverpool may be trying hard to find their places in the new knowledge economy but many of the companies and workers who fuel that economy now reside in the redeveloped industrial buildings that still ring the city centres (Franklin, 1995). However, it is in the area of population demographics that industry has had its greatest impact. Throughout the industrial era the North West has drawn immigrants, attracted primarily by the hope of good manufacturing employment. The Chinese, the Irish and European Jews were perhaps the first groups to leave significant cultural marks on the cities, but they were subsequently eclipsed by extensive immigration from Southern Asia and Africa. As early as 1933, Priestley (1984: 239) could talk about the slum tenements of Liverpool in which the children 'were of all shades, and Asia and Africa came peeping out of their eyes'. The result of this influx has been a multiculturalism that today penetrates into almost every community.

In terms of sub-regional divisions, the formal county and metropolitan boundaries of Lancashire, Cumbria, Cheshire, Merseyside and Greater Manchester have little real bearing on the movement of goods and workers. The draft revision of the North West's Regional Planning Guidance (NWRA,

2004b: 17) describes the North West region as being a 'bi-polar, metropolitan region, in a coastal position and with extensive rural areas'. The region is therefore focused on its two primary urban areas – Liverpool and Manchester/ Salford – which, together with the belt of urbanised land between them, cut an east–west swath across the centre of the region. Both regional poles display the style and functions of regional capitals, providing the primary economic drivers of the region, although Manchester/Salford currently displays a more diverse range of functions and a greater economic strength. However, outside of this key belt area, the complex functional linkages between the dispersed towns and rural areas of Cumbria, Lancashire and Cheshire make further clear sub-divisions difficult (NWRA, 2004a).

## Economic and social change

As the last section discussed, it was the industrial revolution that defined much of the North West's cultural, economic and physical landscape. As early as the 1720s, Daniel Defoe in his *Tour through the Whole Island of Great Britain* (1974: 256) described Liverpool as having an 'opulent, flourishing and encreasing [*sic*] trade' becoming 'universal merchants', while Manchester had a rapidly growing manufacturing trade that made it, in Defoe's words, 'the greatest meer [*sic*] village in England' (p. 261). Bolton, Wigan, Kirby, Bury and Rochdale were also described as thriving cotton towns at this time. Writing at the tail end of the industrial revolution, Priestley (1984: 252) describes Manchester as a sprawling industrial city, 'an Amazonian jungle of blackened bricks', and is shocked by the ugliness of the cotton mills that dominated every view of Bolton, while Blackpool was turned into a 'huge mad place' by the millions of cotton mill workers who crowded in to enjoy its attractions each year. He labels the whole framework an 'industrial democracy' in which reliable and (relatively) well-paid industrial work, combined with growing opportunities for leisure and improvement, allowed the ordinary people of the North West to enjoy a standard of living that few could match at that time.

However, the cotton trade upon which this 'industrial democracy' was built ultimately proved fragile. Even at the time of Priestley's writing, the Great Depression was bankrupting whole towns and one former cotton baron was 'picking up cigarette ends in the street' (Priestley, 1984: 272). After the 1950s the decline of manufacturing became a continuous trend that would reshape the whole fabric of the region. The textile industry proved unable to compete with cheaper foreign imports primarily from the developing world, as did Lancashire's coal pits. In other cases technology drastically reduced the employment needs of key industries. Perhaps the most extreme example of this kind of employment loss is Liverpool Docks, where massive reductions in the workforce came not from a decline in trade – the docks still process largely the same amount of goods as they did forty years ago, albeit from a smaller number of ships – but rather from the containerisation of shipping, which reduced the number of workers required from over 90,000 in 1953 to fewer than 800 today (Aughton, 1990).

Between 1952 and 1971 total employment in the region fell by 3.5 per cent while the national trend was a growth of 7.5 per cent (Rodgers, 1980: 255). From 1971 to 1976 alone, the North West lost 19,620 jobs, the second-largest percentage loss after the West Midlands, with textiles, shipbuilding and mechanical engineering bearing the brunt of the loss (Reeve, 1978: 3). As employment opportunities were reduced, large numbers of people left the region, primarily for the more economically prosperous Southern regions. Between 1971 and 1975 alone, 17,000 individuals migrated out of the region, with loss rates that peaked in the late 1970s at 0.25 per cent per annum. Losses were particularly acute in the big cities, with Manchester losing 4 per cent of its population in the 1970s (Rodgers, 1980: 255).

This economic decline was not uniform, however. The heavily industrialised towns of Lancashire and the two core cities were severely hit, but the peripheral areas of Cumbria and Cheshire, which had always been far less dependent on manufacturing employment, had a softer fall (Rodger Tym & Partners, 1991). Cumbria in particular benefited from the growth of Lake District tourism, which went some way to replacing lost industries. For those communities that bore the brunt of decline the result was high unemployment, which in many cases produced excessive social problems in the forms of crime, loss of social cohesion and increases in limiting long-term illness. A particular legacy of economic and social change has been a decline in housing quality. Industrialisation, combined with subsequent social developments, has left a legacy of lower-value housing that subsequent residents have failed to maintain properly. In 1972, levels of unfitness in some Lancashire towns stood at 35 per cent (Rodgers, 1980: 293), while the current North West region still has 25,500 unfit homes, the second-highest regional rate in the country after the North East (ODPM, 2003b: 4). It is perhaps not surprising, therefore, that four of the nine Housing Market Renewal Pathfinders are located in the North West (ODPM, 2003a).

Despite the massive losses in secondary employment, the North West still remains strongly dependent on manufacturing. In 2001 the manufacturing sector accounted for 30 per cent of the region's GDP, compared to a national rate of 24 per cent (ONS, 2002). However, this should not disguise the massive growth in the service sector that has occurred over the last forty years. This service growth has fundamentally changed the North West's labour market, which is becoming increasingly feminised (although women still receive an average of £200 per week less than their male counterparts; Pion, 2003), with an increasing emphasis on educational qualifications which is boosting the importance of the tertiary and higher education sectors in the region.

The primary result of this economic change has been increasing diversity of employment within the North West. In line with broader trends, tertiary and service employment has increased to a position of dominance, albeit in a way that was more uneven and less rapid than in many other regions (Roger Tym & Partners, 1991). However, many of the North West's communities retain a base of manufacturing industry that continues to be essential to their economic health.

## The economic diversity of the North West

The region as a whole has an intermediate level of economic performance, with unemployment levels that put it in fifth position among the nine regions of England and levels of business start-up that are similarly median (Pion, 2003). However, in other areas, most notably life expectancy and housing quality, the North West continues to be the worst-performing region in the country (Roger Tym & Partners, 1991). These weaknesses may explain why the North West continues to be one of the few UK regions that is still actively losing population through out-migration. (The region lost 110,000 residents to out-migration in 2001, one of only three regions that lost more individuals than they gained; ONS, 2002.) However, these broad regional trends are less informative than what is occurring at the sub-regional level.

In terms of population, while the region as a whole saw a population loss of 3 per cent between 1981 and 2001, Cheshire, Cumbria, Lancashire and the Warrington area of Merseyside all saw some growth. This has primarily been the result of outflow from the two conurbations as people continue to search for suburbanised housing (Regional Intelligence Unit, 2003). With many of the smaller North West communities denuded of major employers, some North West towns are thus increasingly providing a dormitory function for the larger urban centres. Such movement is contributing to a steady rise in North West house prices, although house prices remain below Southern and Midlands averages (ODPM, 2003a). Generally, housing policy in the North West is linked to issues of urban regeneration rather than affordability, with Regional Planning Guidance (NWRA, 2004b) focusing development on the metropolitan belt area of Merseyside and Greater Manchester, where issues of low demand and market failure are most intense. Outside this area, individual Lancashire and north Cheshire market towns that are also felt to have declining markets are also prioritised.

In terms of transport, the region's position at a central point in Great Britain allows some communities to benefit from the movement of goods within the country. The North West is heavily dependent on two main transport routes – north–south via the M6 and West Coast main line and east–west via the M62 and trans-Pennine rail links. The Mersey Ports, although no longer a large-scale employer, does still represent one of the UK's key entry and exit points for goods. Manchester and Liverpool airports are also the key air transport hubs for Northern England (NWDA and NWRA, 2004). Together these make an effective transport network that gives the region the national and international access necessary for its economic success.

Also essential for the region's economic functioning are the road and rail links of the Mersey Belt which link Liverpool and Manchester. These are the region's busiest (and most congested) roads, but they provide essential lines of communication for goods and commuters, allowing the Mersey Belt to be increasingly considered as a single conurbation. They also allow Liverpool (the more geographically isolated of the two cities) better access to the wider transportation network. Outside the central belt area the transport picture is more mixed. Most of the larger towns are accessible only by regional railway lines and roads, while rural areas of Cumbria and east Lancashire suffer from poor public transport services (NWDA and NWRA, 2004). This puts many North West communities at a disadvantage when attempting to attract large employers. It is little surprise, then, that the region remains bipolar in its economic make-up, with Manchester and Liverpool remaining the primary drivers of the region.

The North West lacks the extensive knowledge clusters found in the South East, but Manchester has been able to build itself into one of the largest banking and finance centres outside London. Currently, 18 per cent of employee jobs in Greater Manchester are in the banking and finance sectors, bringing notable economic advantages, particularly to the central city. Manchester currently has the highest gross average earnings in the region, 14.9 per cent above average (Regional Intelligence Unit, 2003). Economic success has also fuelled a notable boom in commercial property within the central city, with prices far exceeding those of the rest of the conurbation.

The transformation of Manchester city centre over the last decade has been dramatic, with large-scale residential developments – both new builds and conversions of older industrial buildings – fuelled by the attractions of a twenty-four-hour city centre lifestyle, together with associated leisure and commercial developments. Distinct districts and quarters have emerged, from the industrial canalsides of Castlefields to the 'funky' northern quarter and the 'Gay Village' (indeed, the spending power of the 'pink pound' has itself contributed to rising economic prosperity). Furthermore, this transformation is still under way, with the growing number of new high-rise buildings for residential and commercial purposes beginning to change the skyline of the city. However, the industrial backdrop still remains strong, and 'the ghosts of old industrial Manchester wait round every gleaming new corner' (Somerville and Springings, 2005).

Liverpool has been slower to adapt to the new economy than Manchester. In the 1980s particularly, a reputation for high crime levels, combined with a local government system that was unresponsive to business needs, discouraged inward investment. That has changed, and both Liverpool and Manchester now aggressively promote themselves, with some success. In 2002 Manchester hosted the Commonwealth Games, which brought considerable regeneration benefits to the previously neglected eastern portion of the city (Commonwealth Games Legacy, 2003), while Liverpool has recently been named 'European Capital of Culture' for 2008, which it is hoped will have similar benefits – 14,000 extra jobs and £2 billion in extra investment are forecast for the city as a result of the successful bid (NWRA, 2004a). What is not yet in evidence, however, is any attempt by the two cities to cooperate in marketing or economic development, and an atmosphere of competition continues to dominate. Additionally, Liverpool remains excessively dependent on public sector employment, with 32.9 per cent of Merseyside jobs located in this sector. Tertiary employment still has some way to go before Liverpool can be seen as a fully equal economic partner to Manchester (Regional Intelligence Unit, 2003).

In terms of the region's skills base, the North West compares favourably with the national average. The number of people of working age with A levels or equivalent stands exactly equal to the national average (ONS, 2002), while the numbers with GCSE grades A★ to C is three percentage points above average. However, the number of North West working-age residents with a degree or equivalent stands at just 12.6 per cent, compared with a national average of 15.8 per cent (ONS, 2002), and there are significant pockets of poor educational attainment within deprived urban communities in Greater Manchester, Merseyside and east Lancashire.

A significant proportion of the landscape of the North West is agricultural, although agriculture itself makes only a small contribution to the regional economy, accounting for only 2.2 per cent of the region's exports in 2000–1 (Pion, 2002). The agricultural base of the North West is, however, diverse, encompassing most types of UK agriculture. Around the Fylde coast of Lancashire, for example, there is a significant belt of market gardens growing fruit, vegetables and garden plants for sale to commercial retailers or local garden centres. In central Lancashire and some areas of Cheshire, small-scale farming of animals and cereals is common, while the Pennines and Cumbrian hills are home to extensive upland farming of cattle and sheep. Cheshire and Cumbria also contain some areas of forestry. In most cases the areas of pastoral farming have been hard hit by recent downturns in the farming industry, and consider-able agricultural diversification is taking place. Most rural areas now boast innumerable barn conversions and small-scale property developments, while the Lake District National Park has seen a number of tourist accommodation developments and second homes. Even by the mid-1970s, the Lake District National Park Authority was processing more planning applications than all the other national parks combined (Acland, 1975). Such demands have contributed to a rural affordability crisis for local residents that increasingly equals that occurring in Southern regions.

In the North West's urban centres, immigration has left its mark on all the key urban centres. The traditional immigrant communities of Irish, European Jews and Chinese have receded into the background, but thriving Asian and West Indian communities have brought a cosmopolitan feel to these cold Northern towns. Early successes in places like the 'Curry Mile' of Rusholme in southern Manchester have allowed the development of an extensive ethnic business network throughout the region and beyond. Racial tensions remain an issue, however, and one that exploded violently in the Burnley and Oldham riots of 2001. In these communities and others in the North West, ethnic ghettoisation and deprivation continue to hold back the development of multiculturalism.

The tensions of Burnley and Oldham have served to emphasise the fact that many North West communities are still struggling to find a place in the new economy. However, change is coming. Over the last ten years most Lancashire towns have invested heavily in the infrastructure and appearance of their town centres. The result of this has been the development of a large number of high-quality retail cores in Preston, Stockport, Southport, Burnley, Warrington and many others. Outside of the cores many communities still struggle with legacies of poor-quality housing and social failure, but recent years have also seen the importing of large-scale regeneration schemes (previously witnessed only in Manchester and Liverpool), giving hope that the towns of the North West may be able to find their own places in the urban renaissance.

## Regional institutional and strategy development

Despite its cultural and historical identity, in terms of public administration the North West region has typically lacked coherence, with no regional administrative focus, possessing two regional offices of government throughout the 1980s and 1990s and 46 local authorities (3 counties, 25 shire districts and 3 unitary authorities, and 15 metropolitan districts). This has been compounded by institutional variety involving both the public and the private sectors, with such fragmentation within the region being considered to be high in comparison with other British regions. Thus, Bristow (1987) viewed the North West as one of Britain's most fragmented regions, with imprecise boundaries compounded by the diversity of its economy and the fragmentation of its polity, and with little experience of political responses at the regional level to the challenges posed by recession and decline. Strong traditions of political and economic rivalry have been particularly noticeable between Manchester and Liverpool: 'the culture of parochialism has tended to predominate, with local interests determining outcomes, and with areas often in conflict over resources' (Wong and Howe, 1995). Others have noted that the very looseness of possible regional coalitions unable to confront crucial issues likely to affect development has historically made the region unable to set any sort of strategic priorities.

Such concerns have been set within the wider context of increasing professional and academic interest in the organisation of the state as a territorial entity, and the multifaceted process of reterritorialisation that has gained in currency over the past decade, involving a commitment to break down historic preoccupations with a single national policy framework in order to deal with complex issues that involve systematic territorial differences (Roberts, 2000). Part of the received wisdom stemming from such 'new regionalist' perspectives centres on the widely held notion that regions such as the North West need to acquire a clear and coherent institutional identity if they are to induce improved economic performance. Deas (2005) notes that such arguments have been given added salience in the North West by three factors of particular relevance for the region – its history of institutional fragmentation, its historical experience of economic sluggishness, and reservations as to the region's ability to exploit emerging EU funding regime developments that focus on regional institutional coherence.

During the early 1990s, however, the North West saw the gradual emergence of a regional political consciousness, involving the modifying of local governance, pragmatic public–private cooperation, and the fledgling promotion of business leadership at the regional level (Williams and Baker, 2006). In the context of modifying local and regional governance, this involved both the restructuring of government administration within the region from a 'bottom-up' perspective involving the initial establishment of a North West Regional Association of local authorities and, following a 1992 manifesto commitment, a 'top-down' initiative of the then Conservative government establishing Government Offices for the Regions (GORs) in order to coordinate government activity. Alone amongst English regions, in the North West this new coordinated approach did not initially go so far as to centralise such coordination in one regional office, with the Government Office for Merseyside (GOM) and the Government Office for the North West (GONW) coexisting until 1998.

Meanwhile, the North West Regional Association was established as a consortium of all local authorities, with the aim of promoting the image and influencing the future prosperity of the region, as well as acting as a regional voice in lobbying the UK government and European institutions (NWRAss, 1993). This was clearly encouraged (by the European Commission and by the North West Business Leadership Team) to facilitate local cooperation for attracting additional investment and, in particular, to ensure that the North West remained competitive in gaining European structural funds. The driving force was clearly the gradual emergence of a regional elite within the region, consisting of leading politicians and senior officers from county councils and the large metropolitan districts, and regional business and employment interests (Peck, 1995; Peck and Tickell, 1995). This institutional development did not, however, simply come about in response to local perceptions of a need to adopt a unified and coherent approach; it was also connected with the undertaking of a number of specific tasks. Chief amongst these was the preparation of the first North West Regional Economic Strategy, some years before the creation of the North West Development Agency (Pieda, 1993). A parallel development also saw the emergence of the initial Regional Planning Guidance (RPG) for the region (NWRAss, 1993) as a framework for moving forward the focus of local development plans. These first-generation strategies put to the test the depth of political and institutional commitment to collaboration that existed within the region (Williams and Baker, 2006).

The return of a Labour government with a commitment to push forward the regional agenda in 1997 saw the launch of two separate but fundamentally interacting institutional structures, namely the North West Development Agency (NWDA) and the North West Regional Assembly (NWRA). However, it was clear from the outset that a tripartite regional framework would emerge between NWDA, NWRA and the existing regional office of government (GONW) (Baker, 2002). NWDA was formally established in April 1999, alongside RDAs in the other English regions (DETR, 1997), with staffing largely transferred from incorporated agencies, and an annual budget of £250 million (only around 1 per cent of public spending within the region). Its most pressing task was to produce a new regional economic strategy (RES) to be approved by government by the end of 1999. At the same time, a key component of emerging parallel central government policy and legislation was to be the establishment of a regional chamber organisation to represent local authorities and other major stakeholders within the region, this becoming known as the North West Regional Assembly (NWRA). The activities of the existing North West Regional Association were thus subsumed within its operation, but the regional association of local authorities was still expected to meet as a formally separate body when specific local government responsibilities were involved, in particular in relation to the preparation of revised RPG.

The main vision of NWDA's initial RES, published in December 1999, was to facilitate the creation of a region that would attract and retain the skilled and talented; bring everyone into the mainstream of community life; nurture its environment, heritage and culture; kindle creativity, innovation and competitiveness; transform its image; and strengthen its infrastructure (NWDA, 1999). Once this broad strategy had been adopted, the key intention was to develop a series of action plans to take forward the main areas of activity, with the NWDA attempting to work closely with the NWRA and GONW to integrate policy and programme delivery within the region.

It was always intended that the regional strategy be updated on a regular basis, and thus the initial RES was subsequently reviewed in an attempt both to take on board changes in national and regional policy and to take stock of the previous three years' experience. Whilst the main vision was not significantly amended, the challenges facing the region in the early twenty-first century were now seen to need concerted action on five key priorities centred on improving the region's transport and communications infrastructure; addressing the skills deficit and weakness in the education and learning infrastructure; improving the quality and delivery of business support services, and the provision of quality business sites and accommodation; securing significant increases in levels of public and private sector R&D; and enhancing the image of the region both nationally and internationally (NWDA, 2003).

As far as the strategy-making of the NWRA was concerned, a draft RPG was published in July 2000 and was intended as a spatial strategy which would establish 'a broad framework for the preparation of development plans by the North West's local authorities up to 2021' (NWRA, 2000: 1). The document was claimed by NWRA to take account of *Action for Sustainability*, the emerging sustainability framework for the region (GONW, 2000), and to support the vision set out in the NWDA's RES (NWDA, 1999). The overriding aim was to promote sustainable patterns of development and physical change, and the guidance was therefore built around six objectives, which, it was noted, cut across traditional planning objectives (NWRA, 2000: 5), embracing economic competitiveness and growth, an urban renaissance in the cities and towns, sustaining the region's smaller rural and coastal communities, creating an accessible region, ensuring the prudent management of the region's environmental and cultural assets, and securing environmental quality. An important aspect of the strategy to achieve these broad aims was a spatial development framework that emphasised the concentration of development and urban renaissance resources on the conurbations of Greater Manchester and Merseyside. This generally reflected continuity with earlier approaches to strategic and regional planning in the North West – dating back at least as far as the *Strategic Plan for the North West* (North West Joint Planning Team, 1974) – which had traditionally focused development on the Mersey Belt. This new strategy also took more of a 'polycentric' approach, whereby, outside the Mersey Belt, development was to be concentrated in the larger regional towns and cities within Lancashire and Cheshire and in the priority regeneration areas of east Lancashire, Lancashire's coastal towns and west Cumbria and Furness.

Other significant policy stances included a commitment to existing green-belt boundaries, except on Merseyside, and regional housing provision requirements (for 357,400 new dwellings), of which some 65 per cent overall were expected to be met on brownfield sites (rising to 85 per cent in the conurbations). The implication of this was that only local housing and employment needs would be met in the more affluent rural areas, such as Cheshire. This was despite the references in the NWDA's RES to an area running from south Manchester and northern Cheshire through to Chester and Ellesmere Port termed the 'Southern Crescent', identified as an area of economic opportunity and hence a potential engine for wider regional growth (NWDA, 1999). Unlike the NWDA, which saw potential in allowing further economic expansion in this area as a catalyst for enhanced regional development more generally, the NWRA clearly considered that letting development pressures rip here would seriously detract from the more pressing aim of renewal in the conurbations and metropolitan core, as well as having potentially serious adverse environmental impacts locally. This decision has subsequently had significant repercussions on new housing land allocations in virtually all areas of the region outside the conurbation cores and renewal areas. The resulting so-called 'moratorium' on new housing development has since been applied to an increasing number of local authorities within the region, causing much controversy in the construction industry and raising further questions in terms of the ability of such areas even to meet indigenous needs for affordable housing against a backdrop of rapidly rising house prices (HBF, 2005).

In contrast to the debate over RPG housing figures, and once again highlighting the extreme spatial diversity within the North West region, at around the same time the government launched the Sustainable Communities Plan (ODPM, 2003b, 2005), as part of which Housing Market Renewal Pathfinders were established to tackle problems resulting from housing market failure. Four of these nine Pathfinder areas were to be located in the North West and, as a result, amendments were also made to the final RPG13 to reflect this initiative. Equally significant, from a contemporary viewpoint of regional development prospects for the region, was the promotion of a growth strategy dimension for England's Northern cities, labelled the 'Northern Way' initiative (ODPM, 2003a, 2004). This has provided a core theme for current activities in connection with the preparation of the latest Regional Spatial Strategy (RSS) that are currently under way to replace RPG following the government's recent whole-sale reforms to the planning system (as part of the Planning and Compulsory Purchase Act 2004).

In summary, then, the final RPG13 reinforced the concentration of development in the Mersey Belt – or the North West Metropolitan Area (NWMA), as it was now called – with particular emphasis placed upon the two regional poles and their surrounding areas (the Liverpool and Greater Manchester conurbations). Subsequent strategy development for the region as a whole and its sub-regions has subsequently moved on to the process of developing the RSS, within the context of the broader Northern Way initiative, with current activities concerned with the consideration of strategic spatial options and the sub-regional dimension to regional planning within the region. As part of this exercise, briefs for the preparation of sub-regional strategies have been drafted by NWRA for a number of identified sub-regions: Liverpool/Merseyside City Region; Central Lancashire City Region; Greater Manchester City Region; Carlisle and North Cumbria; West Cumbria and Furness; and the Lake District. This has been complemented by work already undertaken on a West Cheshire/North East Wales sub-regional study (GVA Grimley, 2004). A draft RSS was published for consultation purposes at the beginning of 2006 (NWRA, 2006).

Whatever the detailed issues that emerge over the next few years, there thus remains a clear need to develop a robust long-term vision for the region, now linked to the government's broader Northern Way agenda, and where RSS becomes a significant delivery mechanism. In doing so, it is essential that greater integration occurs between the key players in terms of regional strategy-making, and particularly between the RSS and RES. It must do this, however, within an institutional context that is likely to remain as complex and fragmented as at any time over the years covered by this chapter. The resounding defeat in November 2004 of the proposals in the North East for a directly elected regional government effectively killed off any possibility of a similar institutional solution in the North West. Instead there is the prospect of a continuing tripartite arrangement of NWRA, NWDA and GONW, and the consequent emphasis on partnership, collaboration and shared ownership if any future strategic vision for the region is to stand any chance of implementation.

Nor is it certain that the failure of the devolution agenda will simply imply a continuation of the status quo. One potential consequence could well be a reduction in the support for, and importance of, the regional scale as a level of strategy-making generally, and the legitimacy of the NWRA in particular. Such a decline in the role of the region as a scale of strategy-making is already apparent in the Northern Way agenda, which emphasises an inter-regional vision on the one hand (embracing all three Northern regions) but based on a sub-regional 'city-region' agenda. This concept is not alien to the North West, as the focus on the Mersey Belt conurbations over the years has shown, but inherent in such an approach is the danger of increased rural–urban tensions in a region which, geographically, is predominantly rural in character. The Northern Way influence also suggests an increasing top-down, rather than bottom-up, influence on regional policy as the government realises it needs to be more proactive if its national sustainable communities plan is to be operationalised. Finally, the continued support of the private sector is not assured, as the increasing tensions between the public sector agencies involved in the HMR initiatives and the house-building industry, arising from calls for housing restraint, amply demonstrate.

## Conclusion

This chapter has charted the growth, decline and rebirth of the North West region since the industrial age. The North West has a historical and cultural sense of identity and uniqueness that is shared by few other contemporary English regions. This 'sense of place' can be traced back to the late medieval era, when the Duchy of Lancaster developed into an economic and political powerhouse, putting the North West into the heart of the English woollen trade. Later, industrialisation provided an even greater unifying force, bringing the region together in a web of trade and labour movement that gave birth to a working-class identity that was uniquely 'Northern'. What is perhaps more surprising is that this cultural identity has survived the loss of so much of this industry and has expanded to include thousands of new immigrants and new ways of working. Politically and institutionally, the region has certainly moved a long way from the fragmentation and rivalry between institutions and geographical areas that characterised early attempts at strategic planning and economic development at the regional scale, but the challenges ahead for the region and all those involved in strategic policy-making are still considerable.

The North West is no longer the economic powerhouse it once was – in 2000 the region had the second-lowest export value per capita, after Yorkshire and Humberside (Pion, 2002) – but it remains a centre for UK industry and, increasingly, service employment. Its nature means that economic power remains strongly focused on the core cities of Manchester, a key city for finance, IT and development, and Liverpool, previously a city of lesser economic power, but one that is now growing rapidly. All other population centres are necessarily subordinate to this core – a relationship that is not always healthy. Throughout the region small and medium-sized towns have suffered from decades of poor investment, poor infrastructure and an inability to compete with the Manchester/Liverpool core. The result has been pockets of intense social and economic deprivation equal to that occurring in the coalfield communities of the North East, despite good access to road and rail networks. Only recently have the North West's towns begun to take charge of their destinies, seeking to tackle their own social and economic problems and carve new niches for themselves as individual retail or economic centres. Whether this will lead to a newly resurgent North West as an economic and social entity remains to be seen.

# References

Acland, C.H.D. (1975) 'Lake District'. In M. Bell (ed.), *Britain's National Parks*, David & Charles, Newton Abbot

Aughton, P. (1990) *Liverpool: A People's History*, Carnegie Press, Preston

Baker, M. (2002) 'Government offices for the regions and regional planning'. In T. Marshall, J. Glasson and E. Wilson (eds), *Contemporary Issues in Regional Planning*, Ashgate, Basingstoke

Bristow, R. (1987) 'The North West'. In P.J. Damesick and P. Woods (eds), *Regional Problems, Problem Regions and Public Policy in the UK*, Clarendon Press, Oxford

Commonwealth Games Legacy (2003) *Regeneration/Legacy*. Available at http://www.gameslegacy.com/cgi-bin/index.cgi, accessed 24 March 2004

Deas, I. (2005) 'The contested creation of new state spaces: contrasting conceptions of regional strategy building and land use planning in North West England'. In M. Tewdwr Jones and P. Allimendinger (eds), *Territory, Identity and Space: Spatial Governance in a Fragmented Nation*, Routledge, London

Defoe, D. (1974) *A Tour through the Whole Island of Great Britain*, J.M. Dent & Sons, London

Department for the Environment, Transport and the Regions (DETR) (1997) *Building Partnerships for Prosperity*, The Stationery Office, London

Dury, G. (1961) *The British Isles: A Systematic and Regional Geography*, Heinemann, London

Franklin, K. (1995) *Manchester: 50 Years of Change*, HMSO, London

Government Office for the North West (GONW) (2000) *Action for Sustainability for the North West*, GONW, Manchester

—— (2002) *Regional Planning Guidance for North West England (RPG13): Draft for Consultation*, GONW, Manchester

GVA Grimley (2004) *Sub-regional Study of West Cheshire and North East Wales*, GVA Grimley, Manchester

Housebuilders' Federation (HBF) (2005) *The Economic Importance of House Building in the North West*. Report for HBF by Nathaniel Lichfield & Partners

North West Development Agency (NWDA) (1999) *Regional Economic Strategy for North West England*, NWDA, Warrington

—— (2003) *Regional Economic Strategy*, NWDA, Warrington

North West Development Agency (NWDA) and North West Regional Assembly (NWRA) (2004) *The North West's Strategic Transport Priorities*, North West Regional Assembly, Wigan

North West Joint Planning Team (1974) *Strategic Plan for the North West*, HMSO, London

North West Regional Assembly (NWRA) (2000) *People, Places and Prosperity: Draft Regional Planning Guidance for the North West*, NWRA, Wigan

—— (2003) *2001 Census Results, Population Counts, Summary of Results: North West*, North West Regional Assembly, Wigan

—— (2004a) *North West Region*. Available at http://www.nwra.gov.uk/region/index.php, accessed 10 March 2004

—— (2004b) *Partial Review of Regional Planning Guidance for the North West (RPG13)*, North West Regional Assembly, Wigan

—— (2006) *The North West Plan: Submitted Regional Spatial Strategy for the North West of England*, NWRA, Wigan

North West Regional Association and North West Business Leadership Team (NWRAss) (1993) *Regional Economic Strategy for North West England: Main Report*, NWRAss, Wigan

Office of the Deputy Prime Minister (ODPM) (2003a) *Making It Happen – The Northern Way*, ODPM, London

—— (2003b) *Sustainable Communities: Building for the Future*, ODPM, London

—— (2004) *Northern Way: Moving Forward*, ODPM, London

—— (2005) *PPS1: Delivering Sustainable Communities*, ODPM, London

ONS (2002) *Region in Figures: North West*, ONS, London

Peck, J. (1995) 'Moving and shaking: business elites, state localism and urban privatism', *Progress in Human Geography*, 19: 16–46

Peck, J. and Tickell, J. (1995) 'Business goes local: dissecting the business agenda in Manchester', *International Journal of Urban and Regional Research*, 19: 55–78

Pieda (1993) *Regional Economic Strategy for North West England*, NWRA/NWBLT, Manchester

Pion Economics (2002) *North West Strategy Review Economic Report*, Pion Economics, Salford

—— (2003) *State of the North West Region: Vital Signs*, Pion Economics, Salford

Priestley, J.B. (1984) *English Journey*, Heinemann, London (first published 1934)

Reeve, D.E. (1978) *Working Paper No. 7: Trends in the Distribution of Employment in the North West: An Analysis of Change from 1971 to 1976*, North West Industry Research Unit, School of Geography, University of Manchester, Manchester

Regional Intelligence Unit (2003) *State of the Northwest Economy: Sub-regional Report*, Regional Intelligence Unit, Lancaster

Roberts, P. (2000) *The New Territorial Governance*, Town and Country Planning Association, London

Rodgers, B. (1980) 'The North West and North Wales'. In G. Manners, D. Keeble, B. Rodgers and K. Warren (eds), *Regional Development in Britain*, John Wiley & Sons, Chichester

Roger Tym & Partners (1991) *The North West: Inward Investment and Regional Development*, Roger Tym & Partners, London

Smith, D.M. (1969) *Industrial Britain: North West*, David & Charles, Newton Abbot

Somerville, P. and Springings, N. (2005) 'Housing and local policy futures'. In P. Somerville and N. Springings (eds), *Social Policy: Contemporary Themes and Critical Perspectives*, Routledge, Abingdon

Tickell, A., Peck, J. and Dicken, P. (1995) 'The fragmented region: business, the state and economic development in North West England'. In M. Rhodes (ed.), *The Regions and the New Europe*, Manchester University Press, Manchester

Williams, G. and Baker, M. (2006) 'Strategic planning and regional development in North West England'. In H. Dimitriou and R. Thompson (eds), *Strategic and Regional Planning in the UK*, Spon, London

Wong, C. and Howe, J. (1995) 'Destined for rivalry? The case of two city regions in North West England'. Paper presented at Regional Studies Association (RSA) International Conference, Gothenburg, April

# 8  Yorkshire and the Humber

*Tony Gore and Catherine Jones*

## Regional identity: one Yorkshire or many?

Apart from some marginal gains and losses on its southern and northern fringes, the current Government Office Region of Yorkshire and the Humber (Figure 8.1) is in essence the latest incarnation of an ancient administrative division, the history and heritage of which remain a potent motivating and marketing force. Dating from Anglo-Saxon times in the sixth and seventh centuries, Yorkshire was formally adopted as a separate unit following the Danish and Norse settlement of the eighth century. Long renowned as the largest county in England until its dissolution under local government reorganisation in 1974, it was also distinct in being divided into three segments, or 'ridings' (derived from the Danish word *treding*, meaning a third part): East, North and West (Bentley, 1973). Its association with the House of York, the losing side in the fifteenth-century Wars of the Roses, later led to the adoption of the White Rose as the county emblem. This warring imagery has persisted through to modern times, with any sports match between football, cricket or Rugby League teams from Yorkshire and Lancashire referred to as a 'Roses clash'.

The area and its inhabitants are traditionally characterised in equally distinctive ways, sometimes justifiably, sometimes stereotypically. Thus, native Yorkshire folk are colloquially known as 'Tykes', speaking with a strong, broad accent that features many dialect words that hark back to their Nordic forebears. They have a reputation for speaking their mind, for not suffering fools gladly but at the same time calling complete strangers 'love', for showing resourcefulness and determination in the face of adversity ('Yorkshire grit'), and for not squandering their hard-earned money on trifles or baubles. It should also be noted that the region's primary contribution to British cooking, the Yorkshire pudding, is in its home patch traditionally eaten as a first course, with gravy, rather than as an accompaniment to the Sunday roast.

All this might suggest that there is a strongly delineated and entrenched regional identity in Yorkshire and the Humber. However, while this has some validity at one level, in many senses it is only skin-deep. For a start, as with the UK generally, the region has undergone considerable change over the last thirty years, especially in terms of population composition, occupational and industrial

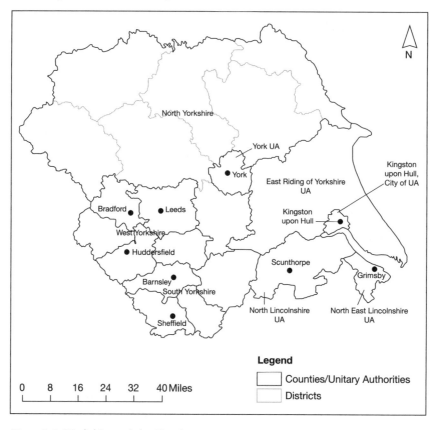

*Figure 8.1* Yorkshire and the Humber

structure and lifestyles. More importantly, though, one of the region's abiding features has always been its geological and geographical variety, offering a home to as wide a range of landscapes and activities as anywhere in Britain. To capture this range in a simple image: while Yorkshire pride usually dictates that the area be known as 'God's own country', it also plays host to the 'Devil's Arrows', a grouping of Neolithic standing stones near Boroughbridge in the north of the region (Wragg Elgee and Wragg Elgee, 1971). In terms of physical geography, the region splits into eight broad zones: the South Pennines; the Yorkshire Dales; the Magnesian Hills; the Vale of York; the North Yorkshire Moors; the Yorkshire Wolds; Holderness and the Humber Estuary; and the East Coast (Allison, 1976; Bentley, 1973; Jones, 2000; Raistrick, 1970).

### The South Pennines

This line of hills forms the south-western part of the region, and is made up of gritstone moors covered in heather, crags and scars where the rocks outcrop, and deeply incised valleys containing fast-flowing rivers and streams. The latter were instrumental in the early development of industry, giving rise to the iron and steel foundries of Sheffield and environs in the south, and the woollen textile mills of the Bradford–Huddersfield–Leeds area further north. These industries, which were the cornerstones of the industrial revolution in the region, attracted migrants from elsewhere in the country, as well as from Ireland (Singleton, 1970). Both industries were able to expand and intensify because of the existence of abundant coal measures close to the surface of the eastern flanks of these hills, and their successful exploitation, particularly in the Barnsley area (Jones, 2000).

### The Yorkshire Dales

Around the middle part of Airedale near Skipton and the north end of Ilkley Moor, these gritstone hills gradually merge into a different type of landscape, characterised by extensive expanses of massive carboniferous limestone. This gives rise to a series of rocky, sparsely vegetated hills interspersed with several long, steep-sided valleys or 'dales'. The latter are green and pastoral, the main farming activity being sheep and cattle rearing. Fields are delineated by drystone walls, which march up and across the hillsides as well as criss-crossing the valley bottoms. Most of the population lives in villages or small market towns like Hawes, Richmond and Settle, with a small scattering still battling on in isolated hill farms. The whole area is designated as a national park, and is probably the best-known part of Yorkshire, being especially popular with outdoor pursuit aficionados like walkers, climbers and cyclists.

### The Magnesian Hills

These comprise a ten-mile strip of rolling limestone hills, acting as a buffer between the South Pennines and the southern reaches of the Vale of York. The hills themselves peter out north of Wetherby, and the zone is incorporated into the plain, although the limestone sub-stratum continues. For most of its extent it has something of a dual character. On the one hand, its good soil and decent building stone have enabled the development of productive mixed farming, fine woodland and a scattering of archetypal English villages. On the other, it was also the first location affected by the eastwards migration of the coal-mining industry during the first half of the twentieth century, on the back of the technological advances in pumping and excavation that allowed mining to proceed at greater depths underground. As a result, some existing villages were transformed into mining settlements, whereas in other places, like Maltby, brand-new pit villages were built (Jones, 2000).

### The Vale of York

The central swath of the region is taken up by a wide, low-lying plain that separates the western and eastern hill ranges. All the major Yorkshire rivers drain through here, including the deflected Derwent, which flows counter-intuitively westwards from its source near the East Coast through the Vale of Pickering to join the Ouse at York. All the others also eventually join the Ouse at various points, to divulge as one through the Humber Estuary (see below). The vale is a flat, fertile area, essentially being a northward extension of the Midland Plain, and like most of the latter has in the past been subject to extensive drainage and agricultural improvement works. This is particularly noticeable in places like Thorne, to the north-east of Doncaster, and the Isle of Axholme in north Lincolnshire. The natural wealth of this largely arable area is reflected in its main settlements, which include old ecclesiastical centres like York and Selby, and prosperous market towns such as Thirsk and Northallerton. These have also benefited from their location on the major north–south transport links through the region, the Great North Road (A1) and the East Coast main line railway.

## The North Yorkshire Moors

This is a roughly square-shaped area lying in the north-east of the region, comprising a central dissected plateau of heather and peat-clad moorland, fringed with steep-sided limestone hills to the south-west, west and north. The latter rear abruptly from the Vale of York, and are famous for the Kilburn White Horse, which can be seen from many miles away. While most valleys have a north–south orientation, the main river of the area (the Esk) runs from west to east to reach the sea at Whitby. The steep sides and narrowness of these valleys and the harshness of the moorland terrain still make communications difficult, and many places retain a feeling of remoteness. Although there are vestiges of past ironworking at places like Rosedale, today there is little in the way of industry and no major urban centres, and the whole area is protected by its designation as a national park.

## The Yorkshire Wolds

This area describes a gentle curve from the north bank of the Humber Estuary to reach the East Coast at Flamborough Head, to the south of Scarborough. Mainly comprising undulating chalk hills, it shares much in common with the Downs of Southern England. However, the west-facing escarpment is heavily dissected by several steeply incised valleys, some dry, some containing misfit streams. The highest parts in the west are still covered in grass and given over to sheep grazing, while the more rolling hills further east are covered in large amalgamated fields devoted to cereal growing. The area is predominantly rural, with several small, straggling villages and only two minor urban centres, Beverley in the south and Driffield in the north-east.

## Holderness and the Humber Estuary

Formed where the Ouse and the Trent join, the Humber punches its way eastwards out to the North Sea between the narrow bands of chalk forming the Yorkshire and Lincolnshire Wolds. These hills apart, the adjacent estuarine lands are low-lying and flat, curving southwards to the low sand spit of Spurn Point. To the north-east, there is a triangular extension of this flat terrain known as Holderness, stretching as far as Bridlington and characterised by large, open arable fields interspersed with knots of woodland on old morainic mounds. The main urban centres of Humber, Hull and Grimsby, lie respectively on the north and south banks. These have both traditionally looked outwards to the sea, rather than towards the rest of the region, partly via trading links with Northern Europe, latterly centred on the extensive facilities at Immingham. More especially, their maritime heritage stems from the fishing industry, extensive in its heyday, but now a mere shadow of its former self. Nevertheless, both trading and fishing connections have resulted in a continued concentration of port-related industries in the area, especially involving food processing and packaging, oil refining and chemicals.

## The East Coast

The North Sea coast of Yorkshire and the Humber stretches approximately 120 miles, mostly in a north-west to south-east direction. It can be divided into four main segments. First, in the north there are the dramatic cliffs where the North Yorkshire Moors reach the sea, dotted with old fishing villages clinging to narrow inlets, like Staithes and Robin Hood's Bay. Second, the stretch around Scarborough has a mixture of rocky outcrops and long sandy beaches, the latter being the prime reason for the town's erstwhile status as the region's holiday destination of choice. South from here are the chalk cliffs between Filey and Bridlington (two of the region's other main holiday resorts), home to thousands of sea birds in the nesting season. Finally, there is the Holderness and north Lincolnshire coast, split by the Humber Estuary but having in common a line of low boulder clay cliffs that in places have visibly receded through erosion in living memory, but also fronted by fair beaches that support smaller-scale tourist developments at places like Hornsea and Cleethorpes.

From this it is clear how, even until fairly recently, the economies of different parts of the region have been strongly shaped by their natural resources. This in turn has tended to give a differentiated slant to people's outlooks and attitudes in the constituent parts of the region, frequently to the point of parochialism. At present this geographical variability is reflected in an administrative structure that is likewise far from uniform. This has not always been the case, however. Indeed, the aim of the first round of modern local government reorganisation in 1974 was to create a standard two-tier arrangement across the whole of Great Britain. Through this the ancient county of Yorkshire and its ridings disappeared, to be replaced by a fourfold division into the counties of Humberside, North Yorkshire, South Yorkshire and West Yorkshire. Combined, these made up the Standard Statistical Region of Yorkshire and Humberside, although this amalgam had no administrative status at this stage. The main difference between the four new parts was that the first two were shire counties, whereas the latter two, covering the region's most urbanised areas, were designated as metropolitan counties. This mainly entailed differences in the division of duties and responsibilities between the county and the lower district, or borough, tier, and reflected the greater capability of (and perhaps power wielded by) some of the larger metropolitan boroughs.

Throughout their brief existence, both metropolitan counties in Yorkshire (West and South) were continually under Labour control, and they adopted a strongly interventionist stance, particularly in terms of their support for traditional industries and in generous subsidies to public transport. Indeed, for such reasons the epithet 'the Socialist Republic of South Yorkshire' was widely used at the time. Inevitably, this was not to the liking of the Conservative government led by Margaret Thatcher, and the confrontation between them culminated in the abolition of all six metropolitan counties in 1986. The metropolitan boroughs thus became the first of England's unitary authorities, taking on most functions, with only a few powers – such as transport, fire and police – remaining under a cross-borough remit. These arrangements remain in place today, but have now been joined by further changes resulting from the third stage of modern local government reorganisation in the mid-1990s.

A precursor of these latest readjustments was the establishment of the Government Office for Yorkshire and Humberside in 1994, essentially as a means of bringing the administration of key central government functions in the region together under a single integrated banner. This was closely followed by a patchwork reorganisation of local government arrangements in Humberside and North Yorkshire. The former always had an uneasy existence, with no history as a 'shire' and seen as being imposed from above. It also originated from the late 1960s economic development idea of the moment, estuarine growth zones, and more specifically from the feasibility study published by the government on the Humber itself (DEA, 1969). The fixed-link Humber Bridge between the northern and southern banks, opened in 1981, was also intended to bind the two sides together and give greater coherence to the sub-region. However, there remained strong antipathy to the loss of the East Riding, and also to the perceived ruling of northern parts of Lincolnshire by their Yorkshire neighbours.

The upshot was that in 1996 the county of Humberside disappeared, to be replaced by a set of unitary authorities, along with the restoration not only of the East Riding, at least in name, but also of the historic boundary between Yorkshire and Lincolnshire south of Goole. To mollify the sensibilities of the traditionalists further, the territory covered by these new councils was henceforth referred to as 'the Humber' sub-region. Hence was born the regional label 'Yorkshire and the Humber'. In contrast, the changes in North Yorkshire were relatively minor. The main modification here was the provision of expanded boundaries for the city of York, which also became a unitary authority and hence freed itself from the dictates of the county council. The remainder of the area retained its two-tier set-up of county and districts, however.

In many ways these recent local government reshuffles have been generally cosmetic when compared to the growth of agencies and institutions operating at the wider regional level over the last eight years. Principal amongst these is the establishment of Yorkshire Forward, the regional development agency, in 1999. As with most English RDAs, this has been charged with the task of promoting accelerated economic growth as a means of addressing the regional disparities in wealth that characterise the country, particularly between those in the North and those in the prosperous South East. As such, it has taken on responsibility for a wide range of policies and funding programmes, being involved in business development, inward investment, place marketing and promotion, site servicing and provision, training and skills development, urban and rural regeneration, transport and environmental sustainability.

In addition, the Government Office has been boosted by the addition of further functions operating at regional level, such as culture, media and sport, health and the Home Office. More significantly, key agencies and actors in Yorkshire and the Humber have strongly supported the development and operation of a broad-based regional assembly (the YHRA), formed by a merger of the original local-authority-focused assembly and the regional chamber. Of course, with the referendum indefinitely postponed, this still only involves indirect representation, but at least it brings together nominated delegates from local authorities and other key public sector agencies with counterparts from the private and voluntary sectors. It has also taken on a small permanent staff to shoulder its responsibility for such matters as preparation of the Regional Spatial Strategy (currently in progress), the Regional Transport Strategy and the revision of the Regional Planning Guidance. This has enabled a more collaborative approach compared to what had existed before (Stephenson and Poxon, 2001), and has ensured that, in its consultative role on all matters regional, the YHRA acts as an important counterbalance to the official might of the Government Office and the financial clout of Yorkshire Forward (Bache, 2000).

Perhaps in response to these regionalising trends, a number of other collaborative organisations have arisen to give voice to other interests. The most developed of these is the Yorkshire and Humber Regional Forum, a vehicle for the voluntary and community sector not only to coordinate its activities across the region, but also to formulate and then articulate its stance on different issues concerning its future shape and development. There are also a number of other regional structures that have emerged, mostly connected to specific subjects or matters of concern, such as the sub-national offices of the Lottery distribution boards, Yorkshire Universities, the Regional Environmental Network and the recently formed Yorkshire and Humber Faiths Forum.

## Economic and social change: the last thirty years

Today Yorkshire and the Humber accommodates approximately 10 per cent of the population of England on 12 per cent of its land area. The composition of its population has changed radically in the post-war period due to migration flows, especially to the urban and industrial heartlands of the region (the South Pennines zone). This was nothing new: the area had already experienced strong in-migration during the nineteenth century. The growth in job opportunities in the nascent factories attracted migrants from elsewhere in the UK; as with the North East of England, significant numbers of immigrants were attracted from Ireland without recreating the sectarian tensions that were to plague the West Coast of Scotland. In addition, in the later nineteenth century German Jews settled in Leeds and Bradford, playing a pivotal role in the development of the textile and clothing trade. In the post-war period job opportunities attracted migrants from the Commonwealth, such as West Indians, Indians and Pakistanis, and more recently migrants from further afield have also enriched urban settlements in the region. The patterns of in-migration have thus been strongly shaped by labour demand, and flows have been predominantly to whichever urban areas were then rapidly growing. While the more industrial western parts of the region are culturally more diverse today, this is not the case for the communities in the more rural north and east of the region.

During the last three decades the economy of the region has diverged from the national (England) average, while more southerly regions like the South East have surged ahead. The scale of divergence can be illustrated with reference to a wide variety of indicators. Table 8.1, for example, shows the growing and now persistent productivity gap between the region, the South East and England. The same pattern exists for a range of other indicators, most notably economic activity rates and household income. Setting aside the undoubted economic dynamism of the South East, for Yorkshire and the Humber the major factors behind this productivity gap have been the massive extent of deindustrialisation during the 1980s and early 1990s, the associated restructuring of surviving industries, and the relatively sluggish pace of service sector expansion (Newby, 2004).

The first two were especially linked to the 1980s monetarist policies of the Conservative government under Margaret Thatcher. Its hugely deflationary

*Table 8.1* GDP per head (£)

|  | 1975 | 1980 | 1985 | 1990 | 1995 | 2000 |
|---|---|---|---|---|---|---|
| Y&H | 1,566.00 | 3,165.00 | 4,714.00 | 7,533.00 | 9,301.00 | 12,057.00 |
| South East | 1,878.00 | 3,710.00 | 5,694.00 | 9,572.00 | 11,889.00 | 16,555.00 |
| England | 1,689.00 | 3,485.00 | 5,204.00 | 8,692.00 | 10,759.00 | 14,260.00 |

*Note:* Figures for 2000 relate to GVA; all others to GDP

*Source:* Central Statistical Office

policies had a deleterious impact on those traditional industries that formed such a substantial part of the region's original economic base. The prime example is of course the demise of coal mining, particularly after the 1984–5 miners' strike. (In 1981 70,200 men were employed in the Yorkshire coalfield. By 2004 this had fallen to 3,200 (Beatty *et al.*, 2005).) The Yorkshire coalfield played host to many of the notable landmarks and set-pieces of this confrontation: Cortonwood colliery, whose proposed closure triggered the dispute; the Orgreave coking plant, where secondary picketing was met head-on by the police; and the headquarters of the National Union of Mineworkers (NUM) in Sheffield. Today the economic landscape of South Yorkshire is virtually devoid of coal mines, and the associated landscape is gradually being transformed as a result of land reclamation and redevelopment.

Alongside tourism, fishing was the key employer on the East Coast of the region from the mid-nineteenth century until the mid-1970s. Following the 'Cod War' against Iceland around that time, it entered into a steep decline, accelerated as a result of the catch quotas introduced by the EC during the 1980s. Although the scale of job loss was smaller when compared to steel and coal, and the consequent effect on the region less dramatic, there were major localised impacts, particularly on Hull and Grimsby, that are still being felt today.

In contrast, the textile industry in West Yorkshire has been experiencing a more gradual decline for over fifty years (Hardill, 1987), and surviving firms have had to adjust their activities in the face of growing overseas competition (Hardill and Wynarczyk, 1996). As a result, there is little or no primary production undertaken these days, with the focus being mostly on garment making or finishing using imported cloth. The main area affected has been the Bradford–Dewsbury–Huddersfield belt. Apart from Huddersfield, which benefits from its location on the main trans-Pennine transport corridor, these places have struggled to revive their economies, in spite of diversification into activities such as mail-order and internet-based selling.

The situation in Yorkshire and the Humber mirrors the pattern of change and restructuring in Nord-Pas-de-Calais in France, and in the early 1990s Sheffield and Lille closely resembled each other. However, concerted French government intervention in coal mining and strong local investment in textiles saw the emergence of several new high-technology businesses concentrating on e-commerce and environmental engineering (Schulz *et al.*, 2004). By contrast, the laissez-faire approach of the UK government has squandered any chance that large 'new economy' or high-technology industries might emerge in Yorkshire and the Humber. Instead, regional manufacturing has been left with a large rump of low-technology, low-value-added production firms. Difficult trading conditions and the mere struggle to survive have meant that many of these have lacked the foresight but more critically the wherewithal to invest in new plant and processes. While they can still find a market, they see no pressing need to innovate or change. Arguably, if they had done so en masse the job losses of the 1980s and early 1990s would have been even more substantial.

This is borne out by the experiences of the steel industry in South Yorkshire. This was subject to severe rationalisation in the early 1980s in the face of world overcapacity. This process weeded out the unproductive plants and at the same time prompted survivors (mostly working in special steels) to invest heavily in state-of-the-art technology and processes, leading to huge productivity gains over a short period of time. Such investments were also driven by company mergers and takeovers by foreign steelmakers. The result was that the actual volume of steel production did not fall in parallel with the shrinking workforce, but through escalating productivity gains stayed much the same. However, as recent experiences (like the closure of the Stocksbridge works) illustrate, the sector remains extremely vulnerable to further sudden shocks as a result of global competition, especially from China.

One interesting aspect to note here about the Sheffield steel industry has been the advances made in materials science and technology on the back of research and development in the city's two universities, and the adoption of many of these innovations by the region's steel forgers and toolmakers. Exploiting such collaboration is a key facet of contemporary regional development theory, and it has found further expression in the region in the shape of the developing advanced manufacturing park at Waverley, on the Sheffield–Rotherham border close to the M1 motorway. This development incorporates the site of the old Orgreave coke works (see above), and its first occupier is to be the R&D wing of the US aerospace firm Boeing.

Another sector where new and innovative processes have been introduced has been food processing, particularly involving improved freezing and other storage techniques that give products a longer shelf-life, such as cook–chill preparation. While these may be commonplace across the industry, and not just in the region, their adoption has enabled considerable growth of such factories on the south bank of the Humber. This has also been accompanied by jobs growth, although such posts tend to be relatively low skilled and poorly paid. However, in replacing low-skilled jobs lost in other local industries, their creation is highly welcome for the area (Jonas *et al.*, 2002). There has also been some growth (or re-emergence) of local craft-based food products, made more prominent by their widespread region-based marketing, both internally and to the nation as a whole. Many of these have used the internet as their means of reaching a wider market. Examples include Wensleydale cheese (which came to global prominence as a result of the animated film *A Close Shave*), beer from the Black Sheep brewery and a number of organic meat producers.

All of these have strong roots in the Yorkshire countryside and in some respects their efforts form part of the fightback being mounted after the depredations of the foot and mouth disease outbreak in 2001. This particularly affected the sheep farmers of the Dales, Moors and Wolds, with far-reaching knock-on effects on the rest of the rural economy due to the severe restrictions on access to the hills. This crisis served to underline the extent to which the tourism sector in the region had changed, with the long-standing holiday resorts on the coast managing to survive, in a slimmed-down form, on the back of day-trippers and those

*Table 8.2* Tourist visitors and expenditure: Yorkshire's share, 2002 (%)

|  | Visitor trips | | Expenditure | |
|  | UK | Overseas | UK | Overseas |
| --- | --- | --- | --- | --- |
| Yorkshire | 9.0 | 4.4 | 7.7 | 2.9 |
| South East | 8.1 | 9.8 | 6.5 | 6.4 |
| England | 100.0 | 100.0 | 100.0 | 100.0 |

*Source:* Regional Trends 38, Table 13.15, available online at:
http://www.statistics.gov.uk/STATBASE/ssdataset.asp?vlnk=7854

taking short breaks. The growth areas for visitors to the region have been the national parks and historic places like the World Heritage sites of Fountains Abbey and Saltaire, and the city of York (Andrews, 2003). Even so, the region does not punch its weight as far as visitor numbers or expenditure is concerned, falling short especially in terms of those from overseas (see Table 8.2).

All these changes have entailed a decrease in the numbers working in these traditional sectors. However, unlike Southern regions, Yorkshire and Humber has seen a much slower rise of the service economy and consequently has struggled to generate new jobs on a scale sufficient to replace those lost. The major exception to this has been the revitalisation and growth of Leeds. This city traditionally acted as the mercantile and financial centre for the West Riding woollen textile industry, and as such was well placed to redirect its focus towards the growing financial, legal and business services sectors. These have all expanded enormously, and the city has also benefited from the electrification of its rail link to London, and from a growing concentration of public agencies (Unsworth and Stillwell, 2004). These include most of the regional institutions mentioned above, such as the Government Office and Yorkshire Forward, as well as the decentralised portions of government departments such as the Department of Health. Even so, some of its communities were badly affected by loss of blue-collar jobs in engineering, and are still struggling to readjust, prompting concerns about Leeds becoming a 'two-speed' city (Bruff, 2002).

As elsewhere, the region has also witnessed a growth of out-of-town retailing and related specialist outlets. The opening of the Meadowhall Centre near Sheffield in 1990, on the site of a former steelworks, perhaps remains the most iconic expression of the transformation it then denoted (and still denotes). At the time it had a markedly adverse impact on surrounding retail centres, especially Sheffield and Rotherham. Of the two, Sheffield is now bouncing back with a range of new offices, galleries, hotels, refurbished buildings, housing developments and high-quality public spaces. Its progress may be gauged by the fact that, after years of wrangling, agreement has finally been reached between the NUM and the city council over redevelopment of the former's old headquarters next to the City Hall for high-quality offices.

Other aspects of service industry growth include a proliferation of call centres, not only in the major cities but in the former South Yorkshire coalfield along the Dearne Valley. Redevelopment here has been helped by its designation as an enterprise zone in 1995. This has proved to be an attractive location due to its new road links, tax concessions, access to a pool of young workers and availability of serviced sites and modern buildings. Call centre operators attracted to this location have been of all types, the area now having a mixture of private firms and public sector agencies operating their own services, as well as firms such as Ventura that provide them on behalf of a range of contracted clients.

In parallel there has also been a growth of logistics and distribution depots close to motorway interchanges along the M1, the A1(M) and the M18, alongside smaller rail freight depots at Doncaster and Wakefield. The main locations for these are in the south of the region, particularly around Doncaster, but also at the western end of the Dearne Valley link road close to the M1, just south of Barnsley. As elsewhere there has also been the emergence of several smaller retail parks dotted across the region. Perhaps the most significant of these is the one occupying the site of the Cortonwood pit, which now provides a home to B&Q.

With all these new developments occurring, there is a sense in which Yorkshire and the Humber is beginning once more to make progress in economic terms (see Yorkshire Futures, 2004). The jobs growth associated with the attraction of these new activities has recently been mirrored by new house-building in previously unmarketable areas such as inner-city Leeds and Sheffield and the coalfield. The processes of regional policy-making and sub-regional partnership working have prompted many places in the older industrial areas to begin looking forward rather than back, and to redefine a new role for themselves in an attempt to take advantage of current opportunities and strategic locations. Generally this involves a rebranding exercise, not only as an external marketing tool, but to differentiate themselves from their neighbours.

Thus, Barnsley now calls itself a twenty-first-century market town, and has tentatively reimagined itself as a northern Tuscan village; Doncaster claims to be the transport gateway to Yorkshire and the North (a role being cemented by the development of the Robin Hood Airport at the former RAF Finningley air base); Huddersfield is presented as the regional creative industries capital; and Sheffield is trying to reinvent itself as a green knowledge economy city. For the latter, it will be interesting to see if winning the gold medal in the recent European Entente Florale (*Guardian*, 22 September 2005) helps to change its image in the wider world. At the same time, other places have found it more difficult to carve out a similar niche; examples here include Rotherham, Bradford and Wakefield. One potential difficulty is that there may not be sufficient additional economic activity for everywhere to share in any regional prosperity that ensues. The likely situation is that in the future, as now, the benefits will remain very patchily distributed in terms of both places and people.

Thus, contemporary intra-regional disparities remain wide. Turning first to the Index of Deprivation (2004), the sub-regions of South and North Yorkshire present virtually mirror images of each other. Thus, 37 per cent of neighbourhoods in South Yorkshire are classed as being in the most deprived quintile,

*Table 8.3* Average house prices (£)

|  | *April–June 2000* | *April–June 2005* |
|---|---|---|
| Harrogate | 116,062.00 | 226,543.00 |
| York | 85,732.00 | 181,830.00 |
| Leeds | 74,908.00 | 145,614.00 |
| Barnsley | 54,780.00 | 107,556.00 |
| Hull | 79,231.00 | 84,350.00 |
| England & Wales | 101,303.00 | 183,241.00 |

*Source:* UK Land Registry, available online at:
http://www.landreg.gov.uk/propertyprice/interactive/

compared to 5 per cent for North Yorkshire. At the other end of the scale, 7 per cent of neighbourhoods in South Yorkshire are within the least deprived quintile, compared to 31 per cent in North Yorkshire (ODPM, 2004). This growing socio-economic divide within the region is also expressed through developments in the housing market (see Table 8.3). Gains in the 'Golden Triangle' of Leeds, Harrogate and York are matched by market failure in poorer parts of the region, with low levels of demand, low and static house prices and even abandonment in parts of Hull and Doncaster. On the other hand, as Leeds and its immediate hinterland begin to overheat, some areas like Barnsley and Calderdale have begun to benefit as people look to other areas in search of affordable homes and more efficient, less congested transport links.

An important consequence of economic restructuring and the transition to a post-industrial social order is the divided city, with a bifurcation in both the quality of life and the economic resources of urban dwellers (for a fuller account, see Bruff, 2002; Byrne, 1999). The wealth gap in cities is often dramatic, as is illustrated by the case of Sheffield. Within the city there is a pronounced east/west contrast of poverty and wealth, such that, according to a recent survey by Barclays, Sheffield Hallam is the most affluent parliamentary constituency outside London and the South East (seventeenth overall). In contrast, school-children in Sheffield Brightside are eight times less likely to go to university than their Hallam counterparts. These very different situations for people in east and west Sheffield mean that they essentially live parallel lives – disconnected spatially, socially and economically – in a 'two-speed' city.

This polarisation in the life chances and lived experiences of residents is seen in east Yorkshire as well. Data on earnings (Table 8.4) are matched by compa-rable data on economic activity, and paint a picture of an increasingly affluent East Riding beginning to 'pull away' from the much more becalmed Hull econ-omy. These increasing social and economic divisions are matched by increasing environmental differentiations. One-third of the region's land is designated as either national park or area of outstanding natural beauty (with the amount of the former being greatest of any English region), whereas in 2004 its urban and industrial zones contained the second-largest expanse of vacant and derelict land after the North West (ODPM, 2005). Similarly, there is a huge disparity in terms

*Table 8.4* Earnings by residence (£)

| | Gross weekly pay (£) | | | |
| --- | --- | --- | --- | --- |
| | Kingston upon Hull | East Riding of Yorkshire | Yorkshire and the Humber | Great Britain |
| All full-time workers | 344.8 | 450.1 | 394.8 | 422.9 |
| Male full-time workers | 394.5 | 477.6 | 435.1 | 464.5 |
| Female full-time workers | 253.6 | 361.9 | 330.5 | 359.0 |

of quality of life and living conditions, with a recent Channel 4 television programme ranking Harrogate third best in the UK as a whole, while Hull trailed in at the bottom of this particular league table. Perhaps the most interesting facet of this rather dubious exercise is that, London aside, Yorkshire and the Humber was the only region to be represented in both the top and the bottom ten.

## Fragmentation or unity: current directions in the region

Uneven development within the region is being addressed through four main policy vehicles at present, including the Regional Economic Strategy (RES), *Advancing Together* (Yorkshire Forward, 2005). A first revision of the original document of 2000, this consultative draft document focuses on business start-ups and survival; the promotion of seven knowledge-based clusters (digital industries; food and drink; advanced engineering and metals; chemicals; bioscience; environmental technologies; and healthcare technologies); improved educational attainment and targeted training in skills required to assist cluster development; connecting people to jobs via employability initiatives, childcare take-up and transport initiatives; improvements to transport and other infrastructure; and urban and rural development. Critically, the RES identifies the need for national government spending in the region, but outwith regional control, to be increasingly shaped to invest in the kinds of productive activities that have genuinely regional benefits.

A second important document is the Regional Spatial Strategy (RSS); again this is currently a consultative draft document, proposing a spatial framework which is based on six sub-areas (Leeds city region; South Yorkshire; the Humber Estuary; the East Coast; Vales and Tees Links; and Remoter Rural), plus the York area of influence, which cuts across three of the above sub-areas. All the sub-areas are linked by main and secondary 'movement corridors'. In each sub-area the aim is to identify the key issues around economic development, housing, transport, environmental protection and social development (Yorkshire and the Humber Regional Assembly, 2004).

South Yorkshire is an Objective 1 area, and the aim is to secure fundamental economic restructuring in the area based on the main urban centres and three strategic economic zones (two along the motorway corridors of the M1 and

M18; one in the coalfields enterprise zone in the Dearne Valley). The strategy to achieve economic development is envisaged through business support for innovation, wider marketing and inward investment, and site and infrastructure provision. To support this, a range of individual skills development initiatives, community development programmes and social inclusion mechanisms is also being put in place across the sub-region in an effort to improve the socio-economic infrastructure and assets of the area. The programme began in 2000, and will run until 2006, with individual projects being delivered through to 2008.

The first three policies focused on developments within the region, but there are also cross-region developments in the form of the Northern Way (see Chapters 6 and 7; and there is a Midlands Way – see Chapters 9 and 10). The Northern Way seeks to foster a coordination of efforts at economic development, infrastructure and physical development, transport links, education and training, and social inclusion initiatives across the three Northern regions of England. Its fundamental aim is to secure productivity improvements that start to reduce the gap between the North and the South, in other words to plug the North/South divide. The key themes of the Northern Way include strengthening the North's knowledge base; building a more entrepreneurial North; capturing a larger share of global trade; improving external transport linkages, especially via airports and sea ports; creating improved transit systems between constituent city regions; meeting employers' skills needs; marketing the North to the world; and securing improved housing, security and community cohesion for all (Northern Way Steering Group, 2004). In Yorkshire the strategy is being rolled out through three 'city-region' development plans, based on Leeds, Sheffield and Hull.

There appear to be some important mismatches between these different policy approaches, particularly in terms of spatial development. The RES uses a sub-regional approach, based on the four 'county' areas, as well as in tying development very much to a polycentric model of the central places in each of these areas. On the other hand, the RSS focuses on six different zones, and while there is some commonality with the RES, the spatial focus is different. The biggest criticism of the RSS is that it lacks any clear policy or governance mechanisms to achieve integration between its sub-areas. In contrast to the other two, the Northern Way places particular emphasis on city-regions, similarly in a way that cuts across existing administrative and governance arrangements. Although there are embryonic structures developing, at present these are extremely fragile, and will probably remain so until the outcome of the next government spending review is known in 2007. The other issue about the Northern Way is that it lacks region-wide inclusivity, with all activity revolving around the three main cities, and the role of any territories outside their sphere remaining unclear.

However, in this welter of strategies and documents it is possible to detect some common components that comprise current regional development policy for Yorkshire and the Humber. First, sustained economic growth is being led by Leeds and the M62 corridor. Elsewhere employment is focused on the main urban centres and the Objective 1 strategic zones. Development is also planned for the Humber Trade Zone. The promotion and development of the industrial clusters is to occur in all of the above-mentioned areas. Rural economic development is designated for North Yorkshire and the East Riding, based on closer links between agriculture and food-processing industries, on the one hand, and diversification into areas like tourism, on the other.

At the regional scale, there is less attention to the integration of constituent sub-regions into Yorkshire and the Humber as a whole, with a greater focus on the main city-regions (Leeds, Sheffield, Hull/Humber ports). This perhaps implies an acceptance of the unbridled openness of regional economies, certainly based on a view of cities as 'economic drivers' of their hinterlands. But it also embodies a recognition of political realities, such as the slim and distant prospects of regional government, and city authorities exercising power in trying to ensure they all get the most out of the newly emerging approach. This would imply that other places will need to find ways of linking themselves into these growth zones. Whether the one to which they are allocated is best for them may be debatable. Thus, at present Barnsley is positioning itself to play a role in both the Leeds and the Sheffield city-regions. Similarly, Grimsby arguably might have a brighter future if it could link itself to the booming Leeds economy, rather than attempting to share the crumbs from the relatively meagre table of the Humber area alone. A crucial aspect here is how the Northern Way is able to improve the connections between places for the region's residents, particularly via enhanced skills development and improved transport linkages.

At the inter-regional and international scale, Yorkshire and the Humber can be conceived as acting as the 'crossroads' of the Northern Way. This image is partly based on fluid commuting and trading flows and links along its north–south and east–west corridors of development. In a wider sense the region can also be imagined as forming a 'land bridge' to Europe. However, on a cautionary note the benefits of being a trade route are unclear, except in terms of an increase in port traffic, but there are potential environmental costs and risks. The key aspect will surely be to generate economic activity in the region that can feed into these trading patterns. One way of achieving this would be to ride on the outward 'ripple effects' from the UK/EU economic core. What is unclear with this approach is whether it will still be possible when the next downturn in the economic cycle arrives. Questions must also be asked regarding the sustainability of this model of economic development. Yorkshire and the Humber has chosen to plug itself into globalised manufacturing and trade, and is busily attuning itself to trading, service provision and commuting patterns which are irrevocably contingent on petrol-based transport. Given the limited nature of oil supplies, and recent price rises in energy, there is the question of whether the region will be able to sustain this position.

## Conclusions

While there may be a 'Yorkshire' identity, its currency and role within the region is a relatively minor one, as a factor either influencing political decision-making or driving economic development. However, it remains fairly powerful in terms of external image, both in terms of how many residents portray themselves and how the region is perceived by outsiders. However, as with all stereotypes, the image is in many respects backward-looking. It is instructive that the region is home to perhaps more territories or 'countries' defined in fictional ways by TV series or literature than any other – *Heartbeat*, *Emmerdale*, *Summer Wine*, Herriot, Brontë. These tend to portray a rather romanticised picture, but their strong traditional elements make them ideal for marketing campaigns for products like Allinson's bread and Yorkshire tea. Films, on the other hand, have often portrayed the grim but determined side of the region, as seen most recently in *Brassed Off* and to global acclaim in *The Full Monty*.

In the last few years, though, things have definitely changed, and a more complex version of a modern multicultural Yorkshire is emerging. There is certainly a limited appetite in the region for a directly elected regional assembly, and regional opinion was always divided over the government's proposals in 2004. This reflects the wider reality of the Yorkshire and the Humber situation: that there are huge disparities within the region, and almost any economic policy choice will create winning and losing communities. Certainly the aim of making Yorkshire and the Humber a mercantile crossroads for Britain and the western EU is full of imponderable issues and difficulties. The challenge for the region lies more in moving beyond the temptations of lowest common denominator decision-making, and in tying together the undoubted strengths that exist within the region to the wider regional benefit. However, progress towards this is not being helped by the divergent paths taken by the main regional policy vehicles, and the current framework may exacerbate existing competition between sub-regions, cities and towns.

This brings us neatly to the starting point of this chapter, which was the fact that despite a superficial strong regionalism and regional identity, a better way of thinking of Yorkshire is as a 'diverse patchwork' of complementary places which come together to make 'God's own country'. In this situation, one-size-fits-all policy-making has no means to articulate policies which can offer a vision for places as diverse as Leeds, Settle, Sheffield and Thirsk. The brightest future for the region may lie in a strong polycentric urban corridor broadly linking Leeds and Sheffield generating the wealth and dynamism to revitalise and reinvigorate the region. However, it goes without saying that equally important to delivering this future success is finding a way to incorporate the lower-key strengths of the 'Yorkshire' brand – the attractive landscapes, the unique Yorkshire products, good accessibility to most of the UK, and the pride and determination of its people – into this bigger picture of regional success.

## References

Allison, K. (1976) *The East Riding of Yorkshire Landscape*, London: Hodder & Stoughton

Andrews, D. (2003) The future of tourism in the Yorkshire and Humber region, *Yorkshire and Humber Regional Review*, Vol. 13, No. 1, pp. 19–20

Bache, I. (2000) Government within governance: network steering in Yorkshire and the Humber, *Public Administration*, Vol. 78, No. 3, pp. 575–92

Beatty, C., Fothergill, S. and Powell, R. (2005) *Twenty Years On: Has the Economy of the UK Coalfields Recovered?* Sheffield: Centre for Regional Economic and Social Research, Sheffield Hallam University

Bentley, P. (1973) Yorkshire, in J. Hadfield, ed., *The Shell Guide to England*, London: Book Club Associates/Michael Joseph, pp. 718–25

Bruff, G. (2002) Two-speed city: narrowing the gap in Leeds, *Yorkshire and Humber Regional Review*, Vol. 12, No. 2, pp. 4–6

Byrne, D. (1999) *Social Exclusion*, Milton Keynes: Open University Press

Department for Economic Affairs (1969) *The Humber Estuary: A Feasibility Study*, London: HMSO

Hardill, I. (1987) *The Regional Implications of Restructuring in the Wool Textile Industry*, Aldershot: Gower

Hardill, I. and Wynarczyk, P. (1996) Technology, entrepreneurship and company performance: British textile and clothing SMEs, *New Technology, Work and Employment*, Vol. 11, No. 2, pp. 110–17

Jonas, A., Gibbs, D. and While, A. (2002) *The Estuary Strikes Back? The Environment and Economic Development in North East Lincolnshire*, Hull: Case Study Working Paper No. 2, Governance and Regulation in Local Environmental Policy-making, Department of Geography, University of Hull

Jones, M. (2000) *The Making of the South Yorkshire Landscape*, Sheffield: Wharncliffe Books

Newby, L. (2004) Rediscovering true north: trends and prospects for regional economic performance, *Yorkshire and Humber Regional Review*, Vol. 14, No. 2, pp. 2–4

Northern Way Steering Group (2004) *Moving Forward: The Northern Way*, available at http://www.thenorthernway.co.uk/

Office of the Deputy Prime Minister (2004) *The English Indices of Deprivation 2004 (Revised)*, London: ODPM

—— (2005) *Previously Developed Land that May be Available for Development. England 2004*, London: ODPM

Raistrick, A. (1970) *The West Riding of Yorkshire*, London: Hodder & Stoughton

Schulz, C., Dorrenbacher, H.P. and Liefooghe, C. (2004) *Far Away, So Close? Regional Clustering of Mail Order Firms and Related Business Services in the Lille Metropolitan Area/France*, Birmingham: Earth & Environmental Sciences Working Papers No. 14, University of Birmingham School of Geography

Singleton, F. (1970) *Industrial Revolution in Yorkshire*, Clapham, Yorks.: Dalesman Publishing

Stephenson, R. and Poxon, J. (2001) Regional strategy making and new structures and processes for regional governance, *Local Government Studies*, Vol. 27, No. 1, pp. 109–24

Unsworth, R. and Stillwell, J., eds. (2004) *Twenty-first Century Leeds: Geographies of a Regional City*, Leeds: Leeds University Press

Wragg Elgee, F. and Wragg Elgee, H. (1971) *The Archaeology of Yorkshire*, London: Methuen

Yorkshire and the Humber Regional Assembly (2004) *Developing the Regional Spatial Strategy: Draft Spatial Vision and Strategic Approach*, Wakefield: PLANet Yorkshire and Humber, YHRA (consultation document)

Yorkshire Forward (2005) *Regional Economic Strategy for Yorkshire and Humber 2006–2015*, Leeds: Yorkshire Forward (consultation draft)

Yorkshire Futures (2004) *Advancing Together: Progress in the Region 2004 – Key Findings and Policy Implications*, Leeds: Yorkshire Futures: the Regional Intelligence Network

# 9  The West Midlands

## The 'hinge' in the middle

*Anne Green and Nigel Berkeley*

## Where and what is the West Midlands?

The West Midlands lies in the heartland of the country (Figure 9.1). It has curiously been described as 'a rump left over . . . when the more recognisable surrounding regions of England and Wales have been identified' (Wood, 1976: 15). It is unique in being the only landlocked English region (Chapman *et al.*, 2000). Outside of the South East, it is also unique in being dominated in its urban core by one city: Birmingham. It is this contrast, alongside racial and cultural diversity, that gives the region strength and character, but it also means that regional identity is weak and a regional image poor (AWM, 2004). Moreover, it has been argued that parts of the counties which comprise the rural region have more in common with neighbouring regions than with each other (Wood, 1976). Also, medieval Coventry was linked, through its woollen and leather trades, to Nottingham, Northampton and Leicester in the East Midlands (Dury, 1978; and see Chapter 10).

Geographically, the region extends from the Malvern Hills and Cotswolds in the south to the Peak District in the north. It is bounded by the Welsh border to the west, and the East Midlands to the east. In the centre of the region is the UK's second-largest conurbation, connecting Birmingham, the Black Country and Coventry. A second conurbation, the Potteries, lies in the north of the region. Administratively, the region comprises five counties, the ancient shires of Warwickshire, Worcestershire, Staffordshire, Shropshire and Herefordshire.

These counties surround the former West Midlands County, created by boundary changes in 1974 to bring together independent 'urban' boroughs – Coventry, Birmingham, Dudley, Sandwell, Solihull and Walsall – previously part of Warwickshire, Worcestershire and Staffordshire (European Commission, 1999). The creation of the West Midlands County recognized the linkages between the boroughs in economic and functional terms, and commuting, and the need to take a more regional view of service delivery (Upton, 1999). Its formation provides an interesting insight into regional identity. For Upton, the county 'was always a contentious creation' in that it incorporated Coventry through its industrial links, but excluded Cannock, a town which shares a tradition of mining. Upton maintains that 'an arbitrary imposition of boundaries' failed to engender any sense of loyalty and identity.

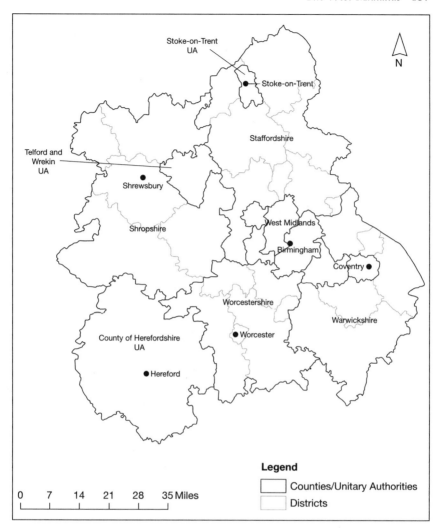

*Figure 9.1* The West Midlands

The issue of regional identity has re-emerged in recent years. Evidence shows calls for an elected regional assembly in the region to be weak (Walker, 2002). The West Midlands Regional Assembly, in its response to the Devolution White Paper, commented that public interest and engagement in the regionalism debate were at a low level (West Midlands Regional Assembly, 2002). Part of this lack of enthusiasm may lie in the fear that an elected regional assembly would be located in Birmingham and would serve only to exacerbate the city's dominance (captured in the phrase 'Big Brother Birmingham') over the rest of the region. Both the Regional Development Agency and the Government Office are headquartered in Birmingham, and the Regional Assembly and regional media are based there. Moreover, the urban–rural divide which characterizes the region has generated conflict between separate interests: on the one hand urban–industrial; on the other rural–residential (Wood, 1976).

Interestingly, though, this lack of regional loyalty in terms of the population contrasts sharply with a strong history of regional working and collaboration which serves to bind the region, both urban and rural, artificially together. Ayres *et al.* (2002) suggest that regional collaboration dates back to post-war planning when the shires and the conurbation were encouraged to work together to find regional solutions to the population, housing and economic growth of Birmingham. Since the 1960s the region can boast an unbroken tradition of regional strategic planning associations matched only by the South East.

Physically, the heart of the region lies in the watershed of two major river systems – the Trent and the Severn–Avon – and it was here that the 'spectacular and epoch making growth' associated with the industrial revolution occurred (Wood, 1976: 17; see also Rowlands, 1987). The industrial revolution led to a power shift from the county towns to Birmingham, the Black Country and the Potteries. Although metal and textile trades have been features of the region from medieval times, it is to Abraham Darby's Ironbridge Works that the roots of the modern industrial region can be traced. The smelting of iron with coal in 1709 was the change-making event. The region was rich with mineral resources in the form of coal, iron and limestone, and continued innovations in the use of these resources, alongside developments in transport and technology, helped the region take full advantage. The Black Country, which had the mineral deposits, and Coventry and Birmingham, which already had skilled labour to produce finished goods, became the centre of the metal industry. The region's watershed location ensured it was well placed to exploit the emergence of canals as a mode of transport. Its centrality gave it advantages as the railways, and later the roads, developed to get goods to and from markets and suppliers. Developments in steam power helped to expand productive capacity and open up new markets (Wood, 1976; WMRO, 2004).

The industrial identity of the region is found in the growth, character and distinctive products that put the industrial centres on the map. Birmingham became famous for guns, buttons, 'toys', trinkets, jewellery and the motor industry; the Black Country for coal mining, heavy industry, bicycles, cars, armaments, machine tools and aero engines. Coventry, developing from its 'medieval greatness', produced watches, sewing machines, bicycles, motorcycles, aero engines, tractors, machine tools and cars; while the Potteries made china (e.g. Wedgwood), earthenware, bricks, tiles and pipes (WMRO, 2004; Upton, 1999; Rowlands, 1987; Dury, 1978; Wood, 1976). The availability of work served to increase greatly the urban population, drawing people in from the countryside. Birmingham doubled in size between 1785 and the early 1800s to reach one million inhabitants and become England's second city in 1881. Coventry's population increased by 140 per cent between 1901 and 1931 from 70,000 to 167,000 (Rowlands, 1987; Dury, 1978). Despite the forces of deindustrialization over the last three decades, the region remains closely associated with manufacturing.

Although the region is dominated by its urban and industrial core, some 80 per cent of the land is rural. The Countryside Agency has identified thirteen local authority districts within the region as rural, four of which are described as 'remote rural' (WMRO, 2004). Centuries of agriculture have left a legacy of traditional spa and market towns and supportive industries. Economic diversification has led to a broad industrial structure in rural West Midlands incorporating traditional service and business activities and manufacturing, alongside rural sectors of land-based industries, food and drink manufacture and tourism. In south Warwickshire towns, engineering and automotive component manufacturing firms play important roles, but tourism-related industries account for the largest share of employment. Many of the region's rural towns offer unique branded products: Hereford cider, Worcester porcelain, Worcester Sauce and Rugby cement. Elsewhere, new towns such as Telford have developed and been hugely successful in attracting overseas inward investment.

The region's diversity and rich cultural heritage are celebrated in many ways. The industrial heritage is reflected in attractions such as the Ironbridge Gorge World Heritage site and the Potteries. The region's medieval past is highlighted through attractions such as Warwick Castle and towns like Stratford-upon-Avon – the heart of 'Shakespeare Country'. Landscape tourism is popular in the Cotswolds, the Malvern Hills, the Marches and parts of the Peak District.

## Economic, social and demographic trends and implications

During the long post-war boom from 1945 to the early/mid-1970s the West Midlands emerged as one of the more prosperous regions in England, seeing rapid population and employment growth. It was second in prosperity only to London and the South East. There was in-migration from the rest of England and from overseas. Indeed, during this period there was diversion of growth from the West Midlands (along with the South East) to the assisted regions of Northern England, South Wales and Central Scotland. However, the reliance on manufacturing industry, and particularly car production (the sector most closely associated with the region), metal goods, metal manufacturing and mechanical and electrical engineering in this Fordist heartland left the region exposed to foreign competition and the shift to service employment. The last year when regional GDP exceeded the UK average was 1975. Job losses in the latter part of the 1970s and in the 1980s were on such a scale that on the basis of economic statistics and in the geographical imagination the region moved from the 'affluent South' to the 'declining North' (Henry *et al.*, 2002): the West Midlands had fallen from being near the top of the England rankings in the 1960s to near the bottom by the mid-1980s (WMRO, 2004). The region's economic performance improved in the 1990s, but GDP per capita has remained below the national average.

As noted in the *State of the Region Report* (WMRO, 2004), the economy is the main driving force behind the state of the region, so it is worthy of more detailed examination. In 1965 nearly two-thirds of the labour force in the West Midlands was employed in manufacturing. By 1982 less than a third of regional employment was in manufacturing, and by 1992 less than a quarter. In 2002 manufacturing accounted for around 470,000 jobs (just over 18 per cent of the regional total). Despite the loss of over 250,000 manufacturing jobs in a twenty-year period, manufacturing remains more important regionally than it does nationally (Green *et al.*, 2004). The demise of MG Rover and rationalization at Jaguar have heralded further major job losses in manufacturing: in April 2005, 5,000 workers at MG Rover's Longbridge plant were made redundant, plus as many again in the supply chain and dealerships (in the West Midlands and beyond).

However, despite a decline in jobs in manufacturing, regional employment has expanded over the period from 1982 to 2002, with business and other services showing the fastest growth: by 2002 over 585,000 of the region's jobs were accounted for by this broad sector, compared with 335,000 in 1982. Nevertheless, distribution, transport and communications and non-marketed services still account for more jobs than business and other services. Over the medium term, job losses in manufacturing and the primary sector are projected to continue, albeit at a slower rate than formerly and alongside rises in output and productivity (at least in the case of manufacturing), while the expansion of employment in services is expected to continue apace. As in other regions, women have been the main beneficiaries from employment restructuring. They have played an important role in some traditional industries (for example, in the ceramics industry in the Potteries heavy work was undertaken by men while those jobs requiring manual dexterity tended to be done by women), but across the region men have borne the brunt of job losses in manufacturing and manual occupations.

The revitalization of Birmingham city centre and regeneration in the 'Bullring' and the city's east side exemplifies (in a fairly extreme form) the changing sectoral composition of employment. Birmingham now prides itself on offering 'world class shopping', while Brindleyplace – with its bars, restaurants and shops – represents the jewel of canal regeneration, and the Mailbox (a former sorting office) houses cafés, bars and designer shops. In the Jewellery Quarter, a quintessential industrial district a mile to the north-west of the city centre, the city council's vision is of 'new economy', and an 'Urban Village' is being constructed in the physical and symbolic space of the 'old' manufacturing-dominated economy (Pollard, 2004).

The change in the sectoral basis of the region's economy has been accompanied by marked changes in the occupational structure of employment. Between 1982 and 2002 around 100,000 jobs in each of skilled trades and elementary occupations were lost. There was a decline of around 50,000 jobs for machine and transport operatives over the same period. In 1982 these three occupational groups accounted for over 50 per cent of the region's employment. By 2012 they are expected to account for less than 20 per cent. Professional occupations, associate professional and technical occupations and managers and senior officials have witnessed increases in employment (although the regional share of employment in such occupations remains below the national average), as have personal services occupations (often associated with part-time employment) and sales and customer service occupations.

As in other regions, economic restructuring has impacted most on those individuals and areas associated with manual and unskilled work in traditional industries. However, compared with other regions, the West Midlands has low levels of skills in the workforce and poor literacy and numeracy amongst school leavers. Data from the 2002 Labour Force Survey indicate that nearly 20 per cent of the working-age population in the West Midlands have no qualifications (and in areas such as the Black Country this proportion rises considerably higher), compared with 16 per cent across England. Problems of poor basic skills and intermediate skills comprise one of the foremost challenges recognized in the West Midlands Framework for Regional Employment and Skills Action, given a trend towards the skills intensification of employment.

In demographic terms the West Midlands is characterized by slow growth: the population increased by about 3 per cent over a twenty-year period, from 5.19 million in 1981 to 5.3 million in 2002. The region is second only to London in the proportion of its residents from minority ethnic groups. According to the 2001 Census, 89 per cent of the regional population is White (and 86 per cent is White British), 7 per cent is Asian or Asian British (3 per cent Pakistani and 3 per cent Indian), 2 per cent is Black or Black British (with those identifying themselves as Black Caribbean dominant in this category), 1 per cent is from Chinese or other groups and 1 per cent is from a Mixed background. The urban areas display the greatest ethnic and cultural diversity: 30 per cent of Birmingham's population is from non-White ethnic groups, with those of Pakistani origin accounting for 11 per cent of the total (at over 100,000, the Pakistani community is the largest in any local authority outside London), those of Indian origin for 6 per cent, and the Black Caribbean group making up 5 per cent of the total.

There is a significant correlation between areas of highest ethnic minority population and the highest levels of deprivation and unemployment in the region. On the English Indices of Deprivation, 2004 (ODPM, 2004), Birmingham has very high levels of severe multiple deprivation and the districts of Wolverhampton, Walsall and Sandwell all have severely deprived neighbourhoods, with further localized concentrations evident in Coventry and Stoke-on-Trent. Birmingham, Stoke-on-Trent, Sandwell and Wolverhampton are amongst the thirty most deprived districts in England; 26.5 per cent of Super Output Areas (SOAs) in the West Midlands fall within the most deprived 20 per cent of SOAs in England (a similar proportion to London and Yorkshire and the Humber, but less than the North East and North West); while 12.6 per cent of the SOAs in the West Midlands fall within the least deprived 20 per cent of SOAs in England. This indicates that the region suffers somewhat greater levels of deprivation than the English average.

However, as well as being associated with some of the highest levels of deprivation in the region, the areas of Sparkhill and Sparkbrook in Birmingham are synonymous with the 'Balti Belt' – an area of restaurants specializing in a type of cuisine originating in the mountains of north Pakistan. The 'Balti Belt phenomenon' has been attributed with putting '"Birmingham on the culinary map" and its restaurants are estimated to bring an annual turnover of £7 million into the city' (BBC, 2002). Moreover, it is illustrative of the role of 'ethnic entrepreneurs' and of ethnic community-based economic networks in some West Midlands cities (most notably Birmingham), which is indicative of a process of what Henry *et al.* (2002) term 'globalization from below', drawing on the distinctive histories and transnational links of residents.

## Changing governance: driving the region forward

As noted above, the West Midlands has an established tradition of regional working, particularly in respect of regional planning, dating back to the mid-1940s (Ayres *et al.*, 2002). Examples include the establishment of the West Midlands Planning Authorities Conference in 1968 and the West Midlands Regional Forum of Local Authorities. The latter provided a framework for coordination between urban and rural, the conurbation and shire authorities, most notably in the preparation of Regional Planning Guidance and the region's first European Strategy. Ayres *et al.* contend that this history and legacy of regional working helped in the transition to more formalized structures of regional policy.

Regional governance began to take shape in the mid-1990s with the emergence of Government Offices for the Regions. This agenda has continued apace with regional development agencies (RDAs) and the more recent drive to elected regional assemblies. In the West Midlands Region four key institutions have emerged and developed which are at the heart of regional governance: the Government Office for the West Midlands (GOWM), Advantage West Midlands (AWM) (the RDA), West Midlands Local Government Association and the West Midlands Regional Assembly. These four have since come together under the Regional Concordat, which facilitates the collaboration and coordination of policies and programmes by providing a framework for regional working and the integration of regional strategies. Given that the regional institutions are working alongside each other on a range of regional policy issues, the potential for overlap is considerable. The framework seeks to 'clarify the multitude of territorial boundaries and organisational remits' that have emerged and provide the 'quality of partnership working required to tackle the challenges facing the region' (Ayres *et al.*, 2002: 71).

The problems, challenges and opportunities facing the region are being tackled strategically through the RDA and its partners. AWM was established in 1999 with a responsibility for 'establishing regional development priorities with local partners, and bringing to bear AWM's own economic development programmes and budgets' (Ayres *et al.*, 2002: 67). AWM's first key task was to formulate a Regional Economic Strategy (RES). *Creating Advantage* was published in 1999. In conjunction with a supporting 'Agenda for Action' in 2001, this provides a framework within which AWM and regional partners can target resources worth some £30 billion and drive the region forward and upward in the twenty-first century. Revised in 2004, the RES is founded on four main policy 'pillars': developing a diverse and dynamic business base; promoting a learning and skilful region; creating conditions for growth; and regenerating communities (AWM, 1999). To deliver on these policy priorities three foci for action, in which resources are targeted and concentrated, were identified: business clusters, regeneration zones and high-technology corridors. These foci are reflections of the region's industrial legacy described earlier, and the need to modernize and diversify if competitiveness is to be sustained. Moreover, AWM recognized that challenges will be met only if delivery targets 'companies and communities where the challenges and opportunities are the greatest' (AWM, 2004: 40).

In a similar fashion to clusters policies elsewhere in England, the region has identified ten business clusters at various stages of development (AWM, 2004). Five are 'established', reflecting the industrial history and development of the region previously described: transport technologies, building technologies, food and drink, tourism and leisure, and high-value-added consumer products (including ceramics, jewellery, glassware and clothing). In these clusters the agenda is to modernize and diversify, embracing new technologies, upskilling and moving 'upmarket'. A further three clusters are supported due to their growth potential: business and professional services, ICT and environmental technologies. The remaining two clusters, media and medical technologies, are described as 'embryonic', and support is provided to nurture development. The clusters policy is supported by an action plan and £250 million of resources over the next five years.

Focusing resources in regeneration zones reflects the uneven nature of economic development within the region following decades of deindustrialization and the fragmented nature of subsequent policy intervention. The six zones focus effort on areas of long-standing deprivation in both urban and rural parts of the region. They include the majority of the 20 per cent most deprived wards, incorporating much of the Black Country, parts of Birmingham and Coventry, and the Potteries, as well as the most remote rural areas. The approach to support in the zones is large scale and long term, looking towards creating sustainable job opportunities and ultimately narrowing the gap between these areas and the regional average. Projects and initiatives are set out in Zone Improvement Plans and funded to the tune of £400 million (AWM, 2004).

The need for diversification and modernization is reflected in the establishment of high-technology corridors as the third focus of action. Three have been set up in the region to attract and develop high-tech and value-added companies exploiting the knowledge base of research and higher education institutions. They are located in areas with a high dependency on the motor vehicle industry and funded to the value of £55 million (AWM, 2004).

The emphasis on regional governance has led to an increased demand from regional stakeholders for greater intelligence in terms of shared, high-quality information on the region. This demand led to the establishment of the West Midlands Regional Observatory (WMRO) in 2002, initially under the parentage of AWM, but with a remit to become independent as soon as is practical. WMRO's key objectives are: to review the state of the region against its development objectives (a *State of the Region Report* was published in 2004); to provide effective access to information and intelligence; and to engage partners in establishing priorities in terms of information and research. WMRO has a useful role to play in supporting partners in regional working.

The growth of partnership working in economic development in the region is reflected in the increased proliferation of sub-regional partnerships. These have emerged often as a reaction to the demands of funding regimes for public–private partnership. Coventry, Solihull and Warwickshire Partnership Ltd (CSWP) provides a good example. It was created as a company, limited by guarantee, in 1994 to enable private, public, educational and voluntary agencies to work together for the growth and prosperity of the sub-region and its inhabitants. CSWP partners include constituent local authorities, Warwick and Coventry universities, FE colleges, private businesses, community and voluntary organizations, AWM, the health sector and Coventry and Warwickshire Chamber and Business Link. It originally came about to coordinate sub-regional bids under City Challenge and then the Single Regeneration Budget (SRB) programme. The partnership has also formulated sub-regional economic regeneration strategies, the latest of which was launched in October 2002, to provide a vehicle for delivering the RES at the sub-regional level (CSWP, 2002). The partnership also has a long-standing researchers' forum. This group ensures that strategies and policies are both evidence-led and effectively monitored, and has responsibility for producing a biannual economic assessment of the sub-region which underpins strategy review and formulation (CSWP, 2003). The ten-year existence of the partnership is testament to the commitment of partners and provides a model of working that is more effective than short-term alliances, which previously characterized activities in economic development.

A similar sub-regional partnership has existed in the Black Country since 1999. The Black Country Consortium was created as a public, private and voluntary sector partnership to explore sub-regional ways of working where added value to existing district-level working could be achieved. It has developed a strategic framework for partners to work within clear priorities and objectives, and is working on a number of initiatives to achieve its vision. One such initiative has been the establishment of the Black Country Observatory in 2002 to coordinate sub-regional intelligence and information effectively.

Sub-regional working recognizes that problems, challenges and opportunities facing the region are not uniform in character. This is apparent from the industrial development and character of the region outlined previously, and, interestingly, since 2002 GOWM has coordinated its tasks on a sub-regional basis, creating a northern division (Staffordshire and the Black Country), western division (Shropshire, Herefordshire and Worcestershire) and a south-eastern division (Birmingham, Solihull, Coventry and Warwickshire).

## Conclusions: in the middle – looking outwards from the centre

The West Midlands can claim to be England's heartland. The picture that emerges from the description above is one of a region dominated by a large conurbation and retaining a strong manufacturing heritage in the face of deindustrialization and growth in service employment. Despite intra-regional tensions and lack of a strong regional identity on the part of many residents, the region can point to successes in regional and sub-regional working over a prolonged period.

On many socio-economic indicators, as in geographical terms, the West Midlands emerges as a 'middle-ranking' or 'intermediate' region. It does not fit easily with notions of a 'North–South divide' in England (Baker and Billinge, 2004). Rather, it is 'disputed territory' (Martin, 2004), as it was at the time of the industrial revolution: 'too far south to be northern' and 'too far north to be southern: . . . truly betwixt and between' (Billinge, 2004: 99). The southern parts of the region fit in with Steed's (1986) conceptualization of an 'outer core', while the rest of the region is part of the 'inner periphery', as Warwickshire, Coventry, Solihull and Birmingham benefit to a greater extent from changing sub-regional employment patterns than areas such as north Staffordshire and the Black Country, as employment gravitates towards the south and east of the region and away from the north and west.

On the basis of long-term growth in service jobs over the period from 1975 to 2000 and decline in manufacturing jobs over the same period, Martin (2004) notes that the West Midlands emerges as a 'hinge region' – dividing the service-based South from the deindustrialized North. This befits a region that in geographical terms is at the centre of England, lying at the heart of the motorway network, just as in an earlier era (as noted above) its position gave it a primacy in the transport network of rivers and canals (WMRO, 2004). At the start of the twenty-first century, the West Midlands is again capitalizing on its central position to 'look outwards', with Birmingham promoting itself as the 'Meeting Place' (not only of Britain, but of Europe) with the National Exhibition Centre, the National Indoor Arena and the International Convention Centre (Pollard, 2004).

However, despite its central position, might there be a danger that the West Midlands is 'overlooked' by regional policy and by national policies with spatial implications? A study of the media portrayal of the West Midlands has shown that there is a low awareness of the region as an entity, and confusion over its boundaries (indeed, the fact that the West Midlands is the only English region that is landlocked perhaps means that there is greater potential for such confusion). National government remains centred in London, while the Northern regions of England have been at the forefront of debates concerning regional devolution. There has been mounting concern from the Midlands that it is being squeezed between the growth area agenda of the South East (with concerns in the West Midlands that the Milton Keynes and South Midlands Growth Area could drain investment from Birmingham and Coventry) and the three Northern regions working together effectively in the Northern Way for the development of a growth strategy for Northern England (Blackman, 2004). *The Midlands Way* – focusing on the West and East Midlands – was published several months later. Under the banner 'SMART Growth', the vision is to '[d]rive forward the engines of economic growth across the English Midlands, nurturing and re-igniting the indigenous sparks of innovation, enterprise and connectivity, to accelerate the evolution and delivery of sustainable communities fit for the 21st century' (AWM and East Midlands Development Agency, 2004; and see Chapter 10).

## References

Advantage West Midlands (AWM) (1999) *Creating Advantage: The West Midlands Economic Strategy*, Birmingham: Advantage West Midlands
—— (2004) *Delivering Advantage: The West Midlands Economic Strategy and Action Plan 2004–2010*, Birmingham: Advantage West Midlands
Advantage West Midlands (AWM) and East Midlands Development Agency (2004) *SMART Growth: The Midlands Way – A Report for Consultation*, Birmingham and Nottingham: Advantage West Midlands and East Midlands Development Agency. Available at http://www.advantagewm.co.uk/downloads/smart-growth---the-midlands-way.pdf
Ayres, S., Mawson, J. and Pearce, G. (2002) 'Institutional collaboration in the West Midlands region', in J. Tomaney and J. Mawson (eds), *England: The State of the Regions*, Bristol: Policy Press, pp. 63–80
Baker, A.R.H. and Billinge, M. (2004) *Geographies of England: The North–South Divide, Imagined and Real*, Cambridge: Cambridge University Press
BBC World News (2002) 'Balti Belt "neglected", restaurants claim', 23 December. Available at http://news.bbc.co.uk/2/hi/uk_news/england/2601227.stm
Billinge, M. (2004) 'Divided by a common language: North and South, 1750–1830', in A.R.H. Baker and M. Billinge (eds), *Geographies of England: The North–South Divide, Imagined and Real*, Cambridge: Cambridge University Press, pp. 88–111
Blackman, D. (2004) 'The way ahead', *Inside Housing*, 28 May 2004: 30–2
Chapman, C., Harridge, C., Harrison, J., Harrison, G. and Stokes, B. (2000) *Region and Renaissance: Reflections on Planning and Development in the West Midlands 1950–2000*, Studley: Brewin Books
Coventry, Solihull and Warwickshire Partnership Ltd (CSWP) (2002) *An Engine of Growth: The Economic Regeneration Strategy for the Coventry, Solihull and Warwickshire Sub-region*, Coventry: CSWP Ltd
—— (2003) *Driving the Sub-region Forward: The Coventry, Solihull and Warwickshire Economy*, Coventry: CSWP Ltd

Dury, G.H. (1978) *The British Isles*, London: Heinemann

European Commission (1999) *The West Midlands: An English Region in the European Union*, Brussels: GO Business Publishing

Green, A., Homenidou, K. and Wilson, R. (2004) *Working Futures: Regional Report 2003–04*, Coventry: IER, University of Warwick. Available at http://www.ssda. org.uk/pdfs/wf-rcgional.pdf

Henry, N., McEwan, C. and Pollard, J.S. (2002) 'Globalization from below: Birmingham – postcolonial workshop of the world?', *Area*, 34, 2: 118–27

Martin, R.L. (2004) 'The contemporary debate over the North–South divide: images and realities of regional inequality in late-twentieth-century Britain', in A.R.H. Baker and M. Billinge (eds), *Geographies of England: The North–South Divide, Imagined and Real*, Cambridge: Cambridge University Press, pp. 15–43

Office of the Deputy Prime Minister (ODPM) (2004) *The English Indices of Deprivation 2004*, Wetherby: ODPM Publications

Pollard, J.S. (2004) 'From industrial district to urban village? Manufacturing. money and consumption in Birmingham's Jewellery Quarter', *Urban Studies*, 41, 1: 173–94

Rowlands, M.B. (1987) *Regional History of England: The West Midlands from AD 1000*, London: Longman

Steed, M. (1986) 'The core–periphery dimension of British politics', *Political Geography Quarterly*, 5: 90–102

Upton, C. (1999) *Regional Identity and the West Midlands*, Comenius Project seminar presentation, University of Caen

Walker, D. (2002) 'Power to the people', *Public Eye*, newsletter of the Association of Chartered Certified Accountants, 39, February

West Midlands Regional Assembly (2002) *Your Region, Your Choice: The Assembly's Response to the White Paper for the English Regions*, Birmingham: West Midlands Regional Assembly

West Midlands Regional Observatory (WMRO) (2004) *Real Lives, Real Issues: A State of the Region Report 2004*, Birmingham: West Midlands Regional Observatory

Wood, P. (1976) *Industrial Britain: The West Midlands*, London: David & Charles

### Key website references

Advantage West Midlands – www.advantagewm.co.uk

Black Country Consortium – www.blackcountryconsortium.co.uk

Coventry, Solihull and Warwickshire Partnership – www.cswp.org.uk

West Midlands Regional Observatory – www.wmro.org

# 10 The East Midlands

## The missing middle?

*Irene Hardill, Chris Bentley and Mike Cuthbert*

### Introduction: where and what is the East Midlands?

Is the East Midlands a region? Many people within the region obviously do not think so or there would be no need for campaigns such as the Great East Midlands Campaign (http://www.gemcampaign.org.uk/), which is dedicated to raising the profile of the region, or for East Midlands Airport to change its name to Nottingham East Midlands Airport so that people, both within the region and abroad, know where it is (*Nottingham Evening Post*, 4 July 2003 and 20 January 2004).

The East Midlands was part of the old Anglo-Saxon kingdom of Mercia, and forms part of 'Middle England' and part of the English Plain (Demangeon, 1927; see Chapter 9). For W.G. Hoskins (1949: v) the region was 'the most unknown and neglected part of England', and what constitutes the 'East Midlands Region' has been much debated by geographers (for example, Demangeon, 1927; Fawcett, 1960; Dury, 1963). For Dury, the East Midlands[1] 'does not constitute a geographical region . . . the "portion" of Britain left over when other, more recognisable, regions – Yorkshire, Wales, South-East England and so on – were filled in. Any coherence, physical, social or economic, the East Midlands might be attributed collapsed as soon as you started serious study of any topic' (cited in Daniels, 1994: 3; see also Gough, 1985). Moreover, the internal diversity of the region was emphasised by Edwards (1954: 6, 12) in the first issue of the *East Midland Geographer*.[2] He acknowledged that while the East Midlands does not constitute a 'geographical region', with very little regional consciousness, it is an administrative region, and has been so since 1939; 'through organisation, which is an expression of policy rather than by any inherent qualities of the region, the East Midlands, to repeat Carl Sauer's phrase, may be regarded as a "functionally coherent" unit'.

Daniels (1994) has drawn attention to the fact that it is the very lack of consistent physiography, livelihood, culture or popular consciousness that has allowed various constructions of the East Midlands around the particular visions of individuals (see also Stobart, 2001: 1309). Midland England – between the Chilterns and the Trent – signified for Hoskins (1949: v) the centre of national identity, 'so solidly in the middle of England . . . in some way the most

English'. For Hoskins, this Englishness was the result of people descended from Scandinavian yeomen stock, their vernacular culture the epitome of English character (Daniels, 1993). For K.C. Edwards (1954: 2), the East Midlands was significant nationally because of the region's coalfields, an engine of growth for 'the economic development of the country'. Moreover, Edwards argued that the region's variety of landscapes and human activity provided 'an epitome of the English scene' (see also Kilbrandon, 1973: 70–1).

It has been argued that the absence of functional and spatial integration on a region-wide basis during the industrial era served to limit the development of a strong and wide East Midlands identity (Stobart, 2001: 1321), and regionalism in the East Midlands retained a pre-industrial structure (Everitt, 1979). The nebulous character of the East Midlands in the pre-industrial era has been emphasised by others. For example, in an analysis of the East Midlands of the pre-industrial era Laughton *et al.* (2001: 336) placed London as the apex of the region's urban hierarchy because of the strength of trade links with the capital – from large towns like Leicester, but also from smaller towns such as Melton Mowbray and Wellingborough. They also identified Coventry as *the* commercial centre for the East Midlands (pp. 337–8; see also Chapter 9).

The industrial East Midlands lacked the internal coherence of other industrial regions that emerged in the nineteenth century and were founded on a single industry, or a clustering of operationally linked industries as seen in the metal-working and engineering trades of the West Midlands, for example (Stobart, 2001: 1309). Uniquely in British industrialisation, the established political, cultural and economic centres within the county towns of the East Midlands became the pre-eminent industrial centres of the industrial era. Thus, industrialisation reinforced local and county identities. The Kilbrandon Report of 1973 pointed to the differences between the East and West Midlands. It noted that the East Midlands was not dominated by a large conurbation but was an area of many free-standing towns of varying size, and highlighted a growing diversification of industry, which was reducing the distinction that once existed between the West and East Midlands. It also mentioned that links between the two regions were increasing (Kilbrandon, 1973: 69).

Constructions of the East Midlands as a broad unitary spatial entity are the result of the activity of planners, geographers and historians in the twentieth century (Daniels, 1994; Stobart, 2001). While the 'East Midlands' has been around for administrative purposes since the nineteenth century (Figure 10.1), it was first formally defined (as the North Midlands) in 1939 for Civil Defence organisation, and retained for post-war planning and reconstruction. The work of Edwards (1949, 1954) helped to reorientate the official name of the region to East Midlands in the 1960s (Daniels, 1994: 7).

An examination of *Regional Trends 38*[3] reveals that the East Midlands Region is a 'middling' region when it comes to its relative performance in a range of socio-economic indicators (see Table II.1, p. 105), but the 2003 figures for GVA per household reveal that the East Midlands ranked sixth out of the nine English regions, lagging considerably behind London and the South East. But

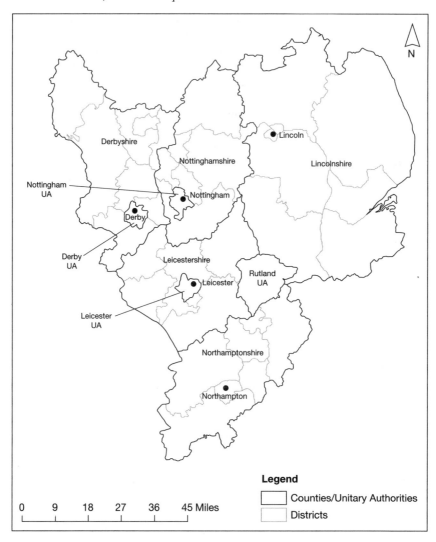

*Figure 10.1* The East Midlands

to generalise about the East Midlands is 'difficult and misleading, since it is a region with little uniformity' (Crewe, 1995: 166), and indicators of economic prosperity for the region as a whole mask important internal spatial differences in economic structure and development (see below).

The region's natural environment has been affected by mineral extraction over the centuries, such as in the northern coalfield area. While very little deep coal mining survives, coal continues to be extracted by opencast, and mineral extraction is found in the Peak District National Park, and in rural locations such as Leicestershire. Intensification in agriculture, especially drainage schemes, has also had an impact on the environment in the Fenland parts of the region, where drainage has reduced the elevation of the land, and the topsoil is prone to removal. One important recent development has been the establishment of the National Forest (Wade *et al.*, 1999), and extensive gravel workings continue to change the landscape in the Trent, Welland and Nene valleys. The East Midlands is composed of a mosaic of physical and socio-economic landscapes (Edwards, 1954). These range from the intensively farmed Fens in the east – a 'curiously Dutch landscape' (Priestley, 1984: 280) – to the hills of High Peak in the west – 'high country . . . good Pennine stuff' (p. 118). There is also a range of scarplands in the central part of the region, along with a cluster of free-standing urban centres, the so-called 'core cities', such as Nottingham, in the Midland Plain. Interestingly, for Hoskins the most characteristic urban place in the region was not one of these core cities[4] but Stamford in Lincolnshire (Daniels, 1994: 6).

Currently the East Midlands comprises the counties of Derbyshire, Leicestershire, Nottinghamshire, Northamptonshire and Lincolnshire, and the unitary authorities of Derby, Leicester, Nottingham and Rutland. The current East Midlands Regional Spatial Strategy (ODPM, 2005) identifies five sub-areas which have some internal coherence:

- *Southern sub-area* – Northamptonshire and the most southerly parts of Leicestershire; has close functional relationships with adjacent regions (South East, West Midlands and Eastern England); has experienced rapid growth in recent decades;
- *Three cities sub-area* – Derby, Nottingham and Leicester and surrounding districts, which act as major administrative and cultural centres, and while they are strong engines of existing and potential growth, they also have major pockets of economic, social and physical deprivation;
- *Peak sub-area* – National Park and surrounding areas; largely rural in character;
- *Northern sub-area* – has been adversely affected by economic restructuring, especially colliery closures; also considerable downsizing of textiles and clothing companies; currently a priority area for regeneration. A range of settlements have been adversely affected, from larger towns, such as Mansfield and Chesterfield, to smaller rural settlements, such as Clay Cross and Shirebrook;
- *Eastern sub-area* – Lincolnshire, Rutland and eastern parts of Leicestershire; predominantly rural in character, with a traditional settlement structure of dispersed towns and rural hinterlands. Parts of the area suffer from peripherality (East Midlands Local Government Association, 1998, 2003; Green, 1999a: 83).

## Economic and social change

Three key drivers have structured and restructured the East Midlands: the industrial and agricultural revolutions, deindustrialisation and finally tertiarisation and globalisation and the emergence of a post-industrial landscape. The industrial revolution was centred on the county towns and a small number of established industrial centres (Stobart, 2001: 1309). This emerging economy was captured by Daniel Defoe in his eighteenth-century *Tour through the Whole Island of Great Britain* (1978: 408). But vast areas of the region were untouched by industrialisation; indeed, the principal activity through much of Northamptonshire and southern Leicestershire remained agricultural.[5] The novels of H.E. Bates and the poetry of John Clare focused on the landscapes and the lifestyles of this countryside, their native Northamptonshire, though they were not so fixed on their own space (for a fuller discussion, see Stobart, 2001). Lincolnshire remained rural, and parts of the county were drained and improved in the nineteenth century (Priestley, 1984). During the nineteenth century a growing divide emerged between the industrialising north and west and the craft industry and rural/agricultural south and east, and so the region 'became a microcosm of the national space economy' (Stobart, 2001: 1311).

Indeed, even within the industrial north and west, the core of this industrial area was the northern coalfield. Coal-based industry served to 'divide rather than unite local economic activity' in the region (Stobart, 2001: 1313). Coal mining occurred in isolated communities set in a largely rural landscape in Nottinghamshire and Derbyshire. D.H. Lawrence was born and grew up here (in Eastwood) and the area formed the backcloth for his novels, such as *Lady Chatterley's Lover* and *Women in Love*. Lawrence himself once worked in Nottingham, which is the setting for *Sons and Lovers*. The novels of James Prior were also set in this area. In addition to mineral extraction, a diverse industrial economy developed in an area extending from the industrial west and north to Northamptonshire in the south, and included pharmaceuticals, tobacco, textiles, clothing and footwear, engineering and railways (Kilbrandon, 1973: 69; see Box 10.1). In common with the North West and Yorkshire and the Humber, women – single and married – formed a key part of the industrial workforce of the East Midlands. Their (relative) economic 'power' and independence were commented upon in Alan Sillitoe's novel *Saturday Night and Sunday Morning*.

Industrialisation was accompanied by urbanisation and rapid population growth. Migrants from rural England were attracted to these industrial centres as well as from further afield (in the nineteenth century from Ireland and in the twentieth from mainland Europe and the former colonies and dominions). These migrants altered the social composition of the region's population as they became members of a socially and culturally diverse urban proletariat (Box 10.2). Industrialisation also created an urban bourgeoisie, who were responsible for usurping the economic and political power from the old elite.

The second key driver has been deindustrialisation. Since 1945 the economy has been restructured due to the continued erosion of primary industry and the

*Box 10.1* The evolution of the East Midlands

The term 'East Midlands' has been around for some time, though the area we now call the East Midlands Region has for much of the last century been included in an area termed the North Midlands. Starting with the 1881 Census of Population, the five counties of Derbyshire, Nottinghamshire, Lincolnshire, Leicestershire and Rutland constituted the North Midlands, with Northamptonshire included in the South Midlands. In 1923 a larger region, termed the Midlands, was formed for statistical purposes, comprising most of the present East and West Midlands, though most of Lincolnshire was placed in the North Eastern Region and High Peak in the North Western. Following some more boundary tweaks in 1937, in 1939, just a few days before the outbreak of war, the North Midlands was reinstated, including Derbyshire (without High Peak), Leicestershire, all of Lincolnshire, Northamptonshire, the Soke of Peterborough, Nottinghamshire and Rutland. High Peak joined briefly between 1941 and 1946 and then in 1962 the North Midlands and the (West) Midlands recombined as the Midlands region. In 1965 Lincolnshire was transferred to a short-lived Yorkshire and Lincolnshire Region.

In 1966, when the East Midlands was formed, the standard region was as the pre-war North Midlands but without the Lindsey part of Lincolnshire, which went to a new Yorkshire and Humberside Region (except for Lincoln City, which remained in the East Midlands), and without the Soke of Peterborough, which finally broke its ties with Northamptonshire and transferred to East Anglia. Finally we arrived at the current area in 1974 when West and East Lindsey Districts came back to the region and High Peak was reunited with Derbyshire. This was not to say that all government departments immediately changed their administrative arrangements to coincide with these boundaries; indeed, for some purposes High Peak still has links with the North West and it was only on 1 April 2002 that the Department of Health reorganised to the current GOR boundaries.

However, despite the lack of a coordinated regional policy at the government level, East Midlands local authorities began to develop regional awareness through the East Midlands Regional Planning Forum, set up originally in 1990 to advise on the first Regional Planning Guidance that was issued in March 1994. By 1997, when the East Midlands Local Government Association was formed, the Regional Planning Forum had already diversified into other areas, particularly relationships with Europe through the EU's Committee of the Regions, and had become a leading player in the English Regions Association.

*Box 10.2* Industrial activity in the East Midlands

England's first factory – a silk mill built for John and Thomas Lombe between 1717 and 1721 – was located in Derby. The city has been associated with Royal Crown Derby since 1750, and since the nineteenth century with the railways, when workshops were established to repair vehicles. Other engineering concerns also set up in the city, culminating in the arrival of the infant firm of Rolls-Royce in 1908. The company was formed in Manchester in 1904, but moved to Derby to begin the era of aero-engine manufacture in the city. Nottingham became synonymous with lace, but three nineteenth-century industrialists were Jesse Boot (pharmaceutical products), John Player (tobacco) and Frank Bowden (cycles), all of whom achieved international fame and repute (Hardill, 2002). Cycle manufacture was immortalised by Allan Sillitoe in *Saturday Night and Sunday Morning*.

Industrial Leicester, according to Priestley (1984: 92), had its 'name stamped on thousands of bales of stockings and underclothes', including Wolsey socks, and the Imperial Typewriter Company was headquartered there. East Midlander Thomas Cook, the founder of the modern tourism industry, started his travel business empire with a round trip from Leicester to Loughborough in 1841. Northampton has been associated with the manufacture of footwear since Cromwellian times, and includes Church shoes, which has manufactured high-quality men's shoes since 1873. Until recently the cult Doc Martens boots were also made in the county by Griggs. The family business was formed in 1901 and specialised in solid workwear. In the 1950s it acquired the exclusive licence to produce the air-cushioned sole, developed by Maertens and Funck, and Doc Martens were manufactured in Northamptonshire from 1960. Production, however, was moved to China in 2002, a typical example of the recent trend of 'outsourcing'.

manufacturing base. But the region remains relatively reliant on manufacturing, particularly lower-value activities (see Table II.1, above), including textiles and clothing, which will continue to shed labour. While some jobs have been lost due to their transfer to countries with lower labour costs,[6] the majority have been lost due to technological change and automation and the drive for profits. Economic restructuring has perhaps for the first time in more than a century resulted in young working people facing poorer economic prospects than their parents did at the same age.

The decline of coal mining has had devastating social and economic effects on the coalfield communities, which are characterised by high levels of long-term unemployment, particularly among men. As late as the 1980s the East Midlands produced more coal than any other region, more than one-third of

*Box 10.3* The urban proletariat: case study of St Ann's, Nottingham

A large deteriorated district, geographically distinct, with a certain sense of identity; perhaps, it might be expected, even a sense of community . . . extraordinary variety of residents, the Poles and Ukrainians from war time days, the Italians shortly after, more recently the Asians and West Indians . . . the Scots and Irish, the Geordies and Liverpudlians, all drawn to the Midlands in the pursuit of work. Some stay [in St Ann's] for a few days or weeks . . . but they all live with, in and among the people born and bred in St Ann's, a key part of Nottingham's working class.

*Source:* Coates and Silburn (1970: 95–6)

the national total (Crewe, 1995: 168). Economic decline has adversely affected these once tightly knit communities and they tend to have high levels of ill health, particularly long-term illness (CRESR, 2002). Considerable effort and funding – including the Single Regeneration Budget – have gone into the former mining communities to ameliorate the worst effects of pit closure and economic decline (Smith, 1999). A consequence of the erosion of the region's manufacturing base has been the depletion of those industries and services that were once the cornerstone of urban living, especially in the smaller old industrial centres where particularly low male economic activity rates are also recorded (CRESR, 2002).

The third driver has been tertiarisation and globalisation, which together have created a 'new landscape' of employment over the last few decades (Green, 1999a). The East Midlands workforce of the new economy has become increasingly feminised but also casualised, and for all social classes there is increased insecurity in the employment relationship (*ibid.*; Beck, 1992; Sennett, 1998). The skills and expertise demanded, including 'generic skills' (e.g. IT skills, teamworking, customer care skills, verbal and written communication, problem-solving and an ability to work independently), are very different to those demanded in an industrial economy (Green, 1999a). While education and training policy in the region is regarded as occupying a position of paramount importance, and despite an increase in skill intensity in many jobs, there are a substantial number of jobs – often in the service sector and with low rates of pay – that do not require high levels of skill. The service sector now dominates the region's economy, and investment is concentrated away from the nineteenth-century coalfield core to Northamptonshire, the core cities and adjacent to the main axes of communication.

During the third period of change the East Midlands has moved into the scientific core of the UK space economy. In 1970 Buswell and Lewis argued that the West Midlands was better poised than the East Midlands to benefit from proximity to the scientific core of the economy, but in the following discussion we will highlight that it has been the East Midlands which has really seen the science overspill and related growth, rather than the West Midlands.

## The East Midlands and the new economy

The region as a whole has recorded a net population growth (4.3 per cent from 1991 to 2001, compared to 3.2 per cent nationally),[7] mainly due to in-migration,[8] and this growth is projected to continue (ONS, 2004: 32–3). This reflects the increasing popularity of parts of the region as places to live and work, and places to retire to or 'opt out' in (Hardill, 1998, 2006; Lewis, 1998; ONS, 2001). The southern counties, especially Northamptonshire and parts of Leicestershire, have witnessed population growth because of their proximity to the prosperous markets of the Greater South East, while some communities in Lincolnshire are expanding because of retirement and pre-retirement migration (Hardill, 1998, 2006). And growth in the southern part of the region is set to continue, as under the Sustainable Communities Plan (ODPM, 2003) Northamptonshire has been earmarked for major new growth clustered around Northampton, Corby, Kettering and Wellingborough.

Parts of the region derive economic benefit from their nodal location in the new economy, as indeed Daniel Defoe noted in the eighteenth century (1978: 430).[9] The M1 links Northampton, Leicester, Nottingham, Derby and Sheffield, and the A42/M42 links the core of the region to Birmingham and the West Midlands conurbation. To the eastern side of the region, the A1 also acts as a north–south connector, linking Peterborough, Stamford, Grantham and Newark, and since the completion of the A46 dual carriageway also Lincoln. In the 1990s, prior to the construction of the A14 trunk road, which links the A1, M1 and M11, there was a lack of major east–west connectors, and this is still the case in the northern part of the region. Three other key trunk roads in the region are the A52, the A47 and A46, which are intensively used. But other parts of the region remain relatively inaccessible, especially parts of Lincolnshire, particularly along the coastal strip, the Peak District in Derbyshire and north Nottinghamshire. Here, residents reliant upon public transport find it difficult to access the economic, social and cultural opportunities – jobs and amenities – found in more thriving parts of the region, especially in the core cities. Some residents in these less accessible areas experience spatial entrapment as their job searches are confined to local labour markets where employment opportunities remain limited and some lives are characterised by social exclusion.

Warehousing, logistics and distribution have developed as companies have opted for sites at nodal locations on the region's transport arteries, such as the Daventry International Rail Freight Terminal (DIRFT)[10] and the adjacent logistics complex at Junction 18 of the M1 in Northamptonshire. In recent decades the economy of Northampton has diversified from footwear to logistics (such as Argos, and Tibbett & Britten) and financial services. Nottingham East Midlands Airport is also at a key motorway intersection (M1 and M42) and (with Gatwick) is one of the two largest air freight centres in the UK.[11]

The service sector in the region, however, lacks high-value growth sectors, including knowledge-intensive sectors, when compared to London and the South East. The region does, however, possess a number of advantages, such as lower land prices, house prices and commercial rents than those in London and the South East. That said, there have been fewer inward investment projects when compared with the West Midlands, though Derbyshire was successful in attracting the Japanese car manufacturer Toyota in 1989. The Inland Revenue chose to relocate to Nottingham in 1995, rather than being wooed by the city, and more recently the American bank Capital One also opened its European headquarters in the city (Hardill, 2002). In addition, in the Nottingham/Derby area there are a number of call centres, such as those servicing Egg, Powergen, Experian and Capital One. But with the much-publicised relocation offshore, especially to the Indian subcontinent, of some call centres, the future of this sphere of economic activity in the region may not be long term.

In common with Leeds, Birmingham and Newcastle, Nottingham has become a major post-industrial centre, with new industries and services – including the creative industries, banking, insurance and finance. Nottingham-born, internationally famous fashion designer Sir Paul Smith epitomises these changes, and he retains strong links with his home city.[12] Nottingham city centre has a long tradition of being a place in which to socialise (see, for example, Sillitoe's *Saturday Night and Sunday Morning*). This local function is now serving a wider geographical area, and the city is emerging as an important cultural/entertainment centre for a national market of young adults, with the evening economy making a significant contribution to the city (Crewe and Beaverstock, 1998). It is estimated that over 50,000 young people socialise in the city centre at weekends (BBC, 2004), and, like Prague and Dublin, Nottingham is favoured by youngsters from outside the region, especially for weekend stag nights and hen parties. This partying has had some bad press, though, focusing on binge drinking and violence.

There are concerns about the skills base of the region, and the region's workforce is on the whole relatively poorly qualified, in terms of the proportion of the workforce with NVQ-level qualifications. A significant number of districts have a higher than average proportion of adults with poor literacy and numeracy skills. Moreover, ICT usage per employee is relatively low compared to that in other regions; and managers, administrators and professional occupations are under-represented in the region. Finally, while the region is a net importer of undergraduates, it is a net exporter of graduates.

By far the greater part of the landscape of the East Midlands remains primarily agricultural, but farming is no longer the foundation of the rural economy, nor is it the linchpin of rural society (MacFarlane, 1998). Despite very high levels of support and protection under the Common Agricultural Policy, farmers' incomes have generally been under pressure, including those practising hill farming in the Peak District and those involved in more extensive farming in Lincolnshire, where wages remain low compared with the rest of the region

(Green, 1999b). In some parts an almost feudal atmosphere is retained, with the survival of some large estates, including the Duke of Devonshire's estate centred on Chatsworth House in Derbyshire; the estate of the Duke of Rutland centred on Belvoir Castle in Leicestershire; and Earl Spencer's Althorp Estate in Northamptonshire. But the region still produces some outstanding agricultural produce, such as Stilton cheese[13] from the Vale of Belvoir, and it is associated with Lincolnshire Poacher, Red Leicester and Sage Derby cheeses, as well as with nationally known foods such as Bakewell tart, Derby scones, Lincolnshire sausage and Melton Mowbray pork pies.

As noted above, increasing numbers of people are choosing to live in the accessible rural parts of the East Midlands, especially in Northamptonshire, south Lincolnshire, Leicestershire and Rutland, irrespective of whether they also work there (Lewis, 1998). This process has accelerated in the last two decades within a context of increasing affluence and a rising rate of private car ownership. Rural in-migration has radically altered the rural landscape, economically and socially, and has adversely impacted on locals in a number of ways. There is now a shortage of affordable housing, caused by the sale of rural council housing (which had in any case always been in short supply) and by rising house prices due to demand from in-migrants. Socio-economic polarisation is acute in rural areas, and as more wealthy people leave the towns for the rural areas this is set to increase. Hidden unemployment is higher in rural parts of the region and a higher proportion of rural people are dependent on part-time work and seasonal jobs in both agriculture and tourism (CRESR, 2002). In addition, poverty in rural areas is a significant and persistent problem, though less prevalent than in urban areas.

In the post-war period some urban centres have been enriched by migration flows from Europe (such as Poles and Ukrainians), the former colonies and dominions (South Asia and the West Indies) and more recently from other locations, such as Vietnam, Somalia, Kosovo and the Middle East. Some urban centres in the East Midlands have a rich cosmopolitan feel, and the transnational social networks and business connections of some of the region's diasporic communities have been used to foster business and employment opportunities. Ethnic minority enterprise is, for example, playing a significant role in the economic restructuring of Leicester through the development of the vibrant multicultural Belgrave business district[14] (Hardill and Raghuram, 1998; Leicester Business School, 2001). But on the whole, a number of the region's ethnic minority communities are clustered in some of the most materially and socially deprived areas in England, as measured by the Indices of Deprivation[15] (Hardill *et al.*, 2001).

In some respects those parts of the East Midlands that have been reshaped by the new economy are examples of what Auge (1995: 44) has described as a 'landscape of mobility' (motorway service stations, airport terminals), 'non-places', the 'fleeting', the 'temporary' and 'ephemeral'. As Cresswell (2001: 19) comments, 'not only does the world appear to be more mobile but our ways of knowing the world have become more fluid', and this applies to the East

Midlands: in a number of respects it can be a region one passes through socially and spatially. This is illustrated by the population growth figures for parts of the region – while some in-migrants work in the region, they are just as likely to commute to work in the West Midlands or the South East, and towns and villages in Lincolnshire are attracting people as they approach state pension age. In addition, every day people and goods pass through, as they use the road and rail networks that link areas outside the region with London and the South East. But there is another image of the East Midlands: as a region of solidity. Some parts of it, especially the smaller towns and rural areas, are felt to be almost in a time warp – and this solidity is valued by residents and attracts in-migrants.

## Conclusion

In this chapter we have charted the evolution of the region since the industrial era. What is remarkable about regional formation in the East Midlands, then, is the resilience of local allegiances during industrialisation and deindustrialisation. East Midlanders continue to have a low level of identity with the region. It does not necessarily have an identity expression, but the fact that it is an 'activity place' makes it quite distinct from surrounding regions. It could be argued that the East Midlands' 'style' or atmosphere is that locals or in-migrants come together and get by and achieve things. The East Midlands is a wealthy region compared to most European regions and its population is growing, thanks largely to in-migration by working-age adults from other parts of the country and abroad, and by older adults as part of a pre-retirement or retirement strategy. Some of those have chosen to reside in the region but not work there, and may commute to the South East. Furthermore, the levels of vehicular traffic on the M1, M69 and M42 provide vivid evidence of the strong commuter flows between the East and West Midlands (see Chapter 9).

But it can also be argued that the life worlds of the residents of the post-industrial East Midlands are far more complex today than ever before. Within each of the five sub-areas of the post-industrial East Midlands there are a number of overlapping economic, social and cultural landscapes, each occupied by communities with very different lifestyles and levels of economic and social wellbeing. Within each sub-area residents live parallel and unconnected lives: for example, affluent and deprived households live side by side as socio-economic polarisation is being accentuated, and members of different cultural and ethnic communities and groups inhabit splintered urban areas. The new landscapes of the East Midlands include vibrant multicultural cities with a '24/7' rhythm to life, but with some people 'excluded' – socially, economically and culturally – from fully participating in this life. Indeed, the members of some diasporic communities have hyphenated identities: they exist in one place, the urban centres of the East Midlands, but in their own minds they live elsewhere, and have social networks that extend beyond the boundaries of England. Those residents in less accessible locations, such as those in isolated former mining communities or in inaccessible rural areas, encounter economic and social exclusion; and while there are dynamic market towns and quiet rural villages, these are often favoured by in-migrants, who have lifestyles and life chances that many of the local population cannot share or aspire to.

The post-industrial East Midlands is characterised by dynamic flows and is perceived to offer a good quality of life, and while property prices are lower than in the South East, and may appear attractive to those from outside the region, current prices penalise local people attempting to get on the property ladder. The southern part of the region is being asked to respond to the agenda of the South East in addition to that of the East Midlands, as it has been earmarked for major housing development to solve a housing shortage that has its origin outside the region. But it remains to be seen if the necessary resources for infrastructure provision to accommodate these households will also flow from the South East to the East Midlands. A final question centres on whether the accessible parts of the region can retain their relative attractiveness centred on nodality as people become less mobile with the reinvention of cities and more sustainable and restrictive transport policies, and huge increases in the costs of fossil fuels, all of which will adversely affect haulage, whether it be road or air transport.

While the administrative boundaries of the region have changed, it is significant that in all this boundary adjustment the vast majority of the region's inhabitants have had no idea what region they live in, nor did the boundary adjustments affect them personally in any substantial manner. However, although a strong regional identity does not have to lead to more regional democratic control, it would be foolish to think that the East Midlands can attain its desired goals without the population in that region giving it some support. Despite this, there are a number of examples of 'joined-up' thinking and action which began with local authorities cooperating as part of the European Regional Project, in an effort to secure EU funding. This spirit of cooperation has been built upon since 1999 with the English Regional Project. Plans to develop a regional concept since 1999 have been limited because it has not been an essential prerequisite to ensure service delivery as part of the regional project. However, it should be noted that the region's Integrated Regional Strategy (East Midlands Regional Assembly, 2000), an example of joined-up thinking, has been commended externally; indeed, the role of the third sector has been recognised as a key component in achieving economic and social inclusion. The spirit of joined-up thinking is also witnessed in intra-regional cooperation, as illustrated by the 'Midland Way' (see Chapter 9). It has been argued that the amorphous character of the region offers opportunities for those who wish to shape a new vision of this region (Beckett, 1988: 10). Moreover, Stobart (2001: 1322) argues that the East Midlands 'may become the archetypal post-industrial region'.

## Notes

1  In his book *The East Midlands and the Peak*.
2  This publication was established in an era when regional geography was a core part

of undergraduate geography degrees, and was founded and has been subsequently edited by geographers at the University of Nottingham.

3 *Regional Trends* is a series of compendiums of statistics about the regions published by ONS. *Regional Trends 38* was published in 2004.

4 The core cities are Nottingham, Derby and Leicester.

5 Particularly the fattening of animals for the London market.

6 Including the movement offshore of production of Raleigh cycles, Avon cosmetics and Doc Martens boots.

7 Only three LADs – West Lindsey, Corby and Mansfield – experienced a population decline over the period 1981–2000 (ONS, 2001).

8 For example, 69 per cent of the region's population growth between 1991 and 2000 was due to net migration rather than natural change (ONS, 2001).

9 He commented upon the quality of the region's transport infrastructure and the importance to the economy of its trade links with London: 'The badness of the roads, through all the midland counties . . . these are counties which drive a very great trade with the city of London, and with one another, perhaps the greatest of any counties in England.'

10 For example, the nationwide Eddie Stobart haulage company has its main depot at DIRFT.

11 Since 2000 Nottingham East Midlands Airport has been DHL's European hub. There are almost 100 companies located at the airport and adjacent business park, employing over 6,000 people (East Midlands Regional Assembly, 2002: 18).

12 He is a graduate of Nottingham Trent University as well as currently a visiting professor there. His company has five warehouses in Nottingham and employs 250 people in the city.

13 Defoe (1978: 424) refers to Stilton as 'our English Parmesan'.

14 It is recognised that, for many, self-employment has been adopted as a survival strategy because of disadvantage and discrimination in the labour market. The Belgrave area of the city was an important locus for economic activity during the industrial revolution and has undergone a remarkable economic revival over the last few decades. It is now a dynamic space for manufacture, wholesale and retail activity due to Asian business development, and is one of the key Asian commercial sites in the country. This could provide a model for other ethnic minority business clusters elsewhere in the region.

15 In 2000 new Indices of Deprivation were produced as measures of deprivation for every ward and local authority area in England. These combine a number of indicators which cover six domain scores (income, employment, health deprivation and disability, education skills and training, housing and geographical access to services) based on thirty-three indicators into a single deprivation score for each area (DETR, 2000). The 2000 indicators enable a focus on deprivation at a small geographical level, which was not possible with the 1998 index (DETR, 2000: 5).

# References

Auge, M. (1995) *Non-places: Introduction to Anthropology of Supermobility*, London: Verso

BBC (2004) 'Last Orders', *Panorama*, broadcast 6 June. See http://news.bbc.co.uk/l/hi/programmes/panorama/3766637.stm

Beck, U. (1992) *Risk Society: Towards a New Modernity*, London: Sage

Beckett, J. (1988) *The East Midlands from AD 1000*, London and New York: Longman

Buswell, R.J. and Lewis, E.W. (1970) 'The geographical distribution of industrial research activity in the United Kingdom', *Regional Studies*, 4, 3: 297–306

Coates, K. and Silburn, R. (1970) *Poverty: The Forgotten Englishman*, Harmondsworth: Penguin

CRESR (2002) *Hidden Unemployment in the East Midlands*, Centre for Regional Economic and Social Research, Sheffield Hallam University, September. Available at http://www.eastmidlandsobservatory.org.uk/loosefiles/hu%5FHiddenUnemp EastMidlandsreport250702finalversion%2Epdf, accessed 25 February 2003

Cresswell, T. (2001) 'The production of mobilities', *New Formations*, 43: 11–25

Crewe, L. (1995) 'The East Midlands', *Geography*, 80, 2: 166–71

Crewe, L. and Beaverstock, J.V. (1998) 'Fashioning the city: cultures of consumption in contemporary urban spaces', *Geoforum*, 29, 3: 287–308

Daniels, S. (1993) *Fields of Vision: Landscape Imagery and National Identity in England and the United States*, Princeton, NJ: Princeton University Press

—— (1994) 'Inventing the East Midlands', *East Midland Geographer*, 17, 1: 1–2

Defoe, D. (1978) *A Tour through the Whole Island of Great Britain*, Harmondsworth: Penguin (first published 1724–6)

Demangeon, A. (1927) *Les Isles Britanniques*, Paris: Librairie Armand Colin

Department of Environment, Transport and the Regions (DETR) (2000) *Our Towns and Cities: The Future Delivering an Urban Renaissance*, London: The Stationery Office

Dury, G. (1963) *Regions of the British Isles: The East Midlands and the Peak*, London: Nelson

East Midlands Local Government Association (1998) *Regional Guidance for the Spatial Development of the East Midlands*, Leicester: Leicestershire County Council

—— (2003) *Regional Guidance for the Spatial Development of the East Midlands*, Leicester: Leicestershire County Council

East Midlands Regional Assembly (2000) *England's East Midlands Integrated Regional Strategy*, Melton Mowbray: East Midlands Regional Assembly

—— (2002) *England's East Midlands*, Ilkeston: Bragdate Publishing

Edwards, K.C. (1949) 'The East Midlands', in G.H.J. Daysh (ed.), *Studies in Regional Planning*, London: George Philip, pp. 135–68

—— (1954) 'The East Midlands: some general considerations', *East Midland Geographer*, 1: 3–19

Everitt, A. (1979) 'Country, county and town: patterns of regional evolution in England', *Transactions of the Royal Historical Society*, 29: 79–108

Fawcett, C.B. (1960) *Provinces of England: A Study of Some Geographical Aspects of Devolution*, London: Hutchinson (first published 1919)

Gough, J. (1985) *British Rail at Work: East Midlands*, Hersham: Ian Allan

Green, A.E. (1999a) 'The Midlands', in M. Breheny (ed.), *The People: Where Will They Work?* London: Town and Country Planning Association, pp. 65–88

Green, A.E. (1999b) 'Employment opportunities and constraints facing in-migrants to rural areas in England', *Geography*, 84, 1: 34–44

Hardill, I. (1998) 'Trading places: case studies of the labour market experience of women in rural in-migrant households', *Local Economy*, 13, 2: 102–13

—— (2002) *Discovering Cities Nottingham*, Sheffield: Geographical Association

—— (2006) 'A place in the countryside: migration and the construction of rural living', in P. Lowe and L. Speakman (eds), *The Ageing Countryside: The Growing Older Population in Rural England*, London: Age Concern Publishing

Hardill, I. and Raghuram, P. (1998) 'Diasporic connections: case studies of Asian women in business', *Area*, 30, 3: 255–61

Hardill, I., Graham, D.T. and Kofman, E. (2001) *Human Geography of the UK*, London: Routledge

Hoskins, W.G. (1949) *Midland England: A Survey of the Country between the Chilterns and the Trent*, London: Basford

Integrated Regional Strategy (2000) *England's East Midlands Integrated Regional Strategy*, Nottingham: East Midlands Regional Assembly

Kilbrandon, Lord (1973) *Royal Commission on the Constitution 1969–1973*, London: HMSO

Laughton, J., Jones, E. and Dyer, C. (2001) 'The urban hierarchy in the later Middle Ages: a study of the East Midlands', *Urban History*, 28, 3: 331–57

Leicester Business School (2001) *Barriers and Drivers for Ethnic Minority Business in the East Midlands*, Leicester: Leicester Business School, De Montfort University

Lewis, G. (1998) 'Rural migration and demographic change', in B. Ilbery (ed.), *The Geography of Rural Change*, Harlow: Longman, pp. 131–60

MacFarlane, E.R. (1998) 'What – or who – is rural Britain?', *Town and Country Planning*, 67, 5: 184–8

Middleton, S. (1989) *Vacant Places*, London: Arena

ODPM (2003) *Sustainable Communities: Building for the Future*. Available at http://www.odpm.gov.uk/stellent/groups/odpm_communities/documents/page/odpm_comm_022184.hcsp, accessed 11 August 2004

—— (2005) *Regional Spatial Strategy for the East Midlands*, London: The Stationery Office

ONS (2001) *Region in Figures – East Midlands*, Summer 2001 edition, London: ONS

—— (2004) *Regional Trends 38*. Available at http://www.statistics.gov.uk/downloads/theme_compendia/Regional_Trends_38/rt38.pdf, accessed 11 August 2004

Priestley, J.B. (1984) *English Journey*, London: Heinemann (first published 1934)

Prior, J. (1901) *Forest Folk*, London: Heinemann

Sennett, R. (1998) *The Corrosion of Character*, New York: Norton

Sillitoe, A. (1993) *Saturday Night and Sunday Morning*, London: Flamingo

Smith, C. (1999) 'Coalfield's joy at £24m cash boost', *Nottingham Evening Post*, 15 July

Stobart, J. (2001) 'Regions, localities, and industrialisation: evidence from the East Midlands circa 1780–1840', *Environment and Planning A*, 33: 1305–25

Wade, M., Sheail, J. and Child, L. (1999) 'The National Forest: from vision to reality – creating a new Midlands forest', *East Midland Geographer*, 21, special issue

# 11 The East of England

## A nebulous region in transition

*Mia Gray, Ron Martin and Peter Tyler*

### Introduction: locating and defining the region

Something rather curious has been happening in the discussion of 'regions'. On the one hand, it is widely argued – by geographers and increasingly by economists – that, contrary to what might be expected in an era of accelerating globalization, regions have assumed heightened importance as the loci of economic growth, innovation and governance: we are witnessing a 'resurgence of regions' (see, for example, Kitson *et al.*, 2005; Fujita *et al.*, 1999; Porter, 1996, 2001, 2003; *Regional Studies*, 2003, 2004; Scott, 1998, 2001; Storper, 1997). Yet, at the same time, it is also argued that defining 'regions' – always a contentious issue – has become more difficult. Geographers have long grappled with the question of how to conceptualize and define 'regions'. The very idea of a region conjures up an image of a distinct geographical area of the national territory that is at once both internally coherent in some way and different from other geographical areas (regions). Thus, Ann Markusen (1987: 16), a leading American economic geographer and regional planner, suggests that

> [a] region is an historically evolved, contiguous territorial society that possesses . . . a socio-economic, political and cultural milieu, and a spatial structure distinct from other regions and from the other major territorial units, city and nation. This relational definition delineates regions through both (1) their mutual contrasts and distinctions and (2) their location on the scale of units.

Similarly, according to the geographer David Harvey (1985: 146), what differentiates one 'regional economic space' from another is the specific 'structured coherence' that characterizes each:

> There are processes at work . . . that define regional spaces within which production and consumption, supply and demand (for commodities and labour power), class struggle and accumulation, culture and life style, hang together as some kind of structured coherence within a totality of productive forces and social relations.

But unlike Markusen's definition, there is nothing in Harvey's conceptualization to restrict the regional notion to any particular spatial scale.

More recently, however, this view of a region as a fixed, bounded, internally coherent space has given way to a more 'relational' concept, as an internally discontinuous, non-fixed entity, shaped by ever-shifting flows and networks rather than by fixed places and spatial structures (Allen *et al.*, 1998; Amin *et al.*, 2003). Under this perspective, economic regions do not exist 'out there' as pre-given entities with hard and fixed, easily identified geographical boundaries waiting to be mapped and measured:

> regions (more generally, 'places') only take shape in particular contexts and from specific perspectives. There will always be multiple, co-existing, characteristics of particular spaces/places . . . There is . . . no 'essential place' that exists in its real authenticity waiting to be discovered by the researcher.
>
> (Allen *et al.*, 1998: 34)

Rather, there are different regional representations of economic space, depending on the specific processes being studied and the purpose of enquiry.

Yet, in practice, political imperatives typically dictate a need for fixed geographical spaces for administrative and related purposes, and such 'regions' sometimes have their own corresponding institutions (such as regional development agencies or even governments). The problem arises when these 'regions of convenience' become seen as somehow representing meaningful economic units, when they are in fact cartographic constructions imposed from above:

> A 'region' was once a realm, a distinct society. In its modern sense, by contrast, it is from the beginning a subordinate part of a larger unity . . . What has then happened is that the real and powerful feelings of native place and a native formation have been pressed and incorporated into an essentially political and administrative organisation, which has grown from quite different roots . . . It is here that the element of artifice is most obvious, when the terms of identity flow downwards from a political centre.
>
> (Williams, 1983: 126)

Irrespective of whether 'regions' were indeed once 'distinct societies', Williams is right to argue that today they are invariably artificially delineated spaces defined from above rather than coherent socio-economic entities that emerge through indigenous processes from below.

Such official delineation and institutionalization may, of course, impart a degree of internal regional coherence and identity, of the sort discussed by Markusen and Harvey. But, in general, it is rare that an administrative or policy region is also a meaningful and coherent functional economic space, a fact that can pose constraints and limits on the efficacy and impact of regionally based polices and development strategies. At the very least, officially defined regions are almost certain to be highly discontinuous internally, and highly porous at the boundaries.

The East of England Government Office Region (Figure 11.1) exemplifies all of these issues. Since 1998 the region has comprised the old post-war East Anglia Standard Region, made up of the counties of Norfolk, Suffolk and Cambridgeshire, together with the counties of Essex, Bedfordshire and Hertfordshire, all previously part of the South East Standard Region. Although historically dominated by agricultural communities, it would be hard to argue that the old East Anglia Region was in any real sense a coherent and integrated socio-economic space, with a common cultural identity – other than having

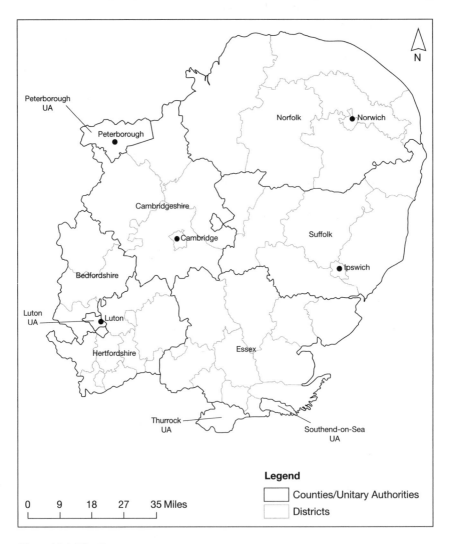

*Figure 11.1* The East

the generally conservative politics characteristic of many rural areas. Nor did the enlargement of the old East Anglia Region in 1998 to the new East of England entity have any real basis in economic or functional logic. However, it has extended and intensified what was already a marked distinction, even discontinuity, between the southern and northern parts of the region. In the south, the region now abuts directly on to Greater London. In fact, the southern half of the region – in effect that part within about an hour's train journey of London (reaching to Ipswich in the east, and Cambridge and Peterborough in the west) – is firmly within London's commuter belt, and significantly orientated to the capital. It is also, as we will see, the most economically prosperous and dynamic part of the region. The northern and eastern parts of the region – much of northern Cambridgeshire, Suffolk and Norfolk – are, by contrast, much less accessible to London, and less prosperous and dynamic.

Despite the official boundaries, it is difficult to know where Outer London stops and the southern margins of the East of England Region begin: the southern suburban zone stretching from Brentwood to St Albans and Watford feels more like suburban Outer London than part of the East of England. Likewise, along its north-western boundary the region adjoins the East Midlands, but where one begins and the other ends is again debatable: is Peterborough, where the long vowel sounds of the South turn abruptly into the short ones of the North, in the East of England or the East Midlands?

The division between the southern and northern halves of the region is also, to a large degree, one of economic history. Historically, the bulk of the region was largely bypassed by industrialization (though the region had seen a number of significant innovations in agricultural production techniques). Indeed, Norfolk, Suffolk and Cambridgeshire have long been rural and agricultural (arable and livestock in the first two of these counties, primarily horticulture in the last-named). What industry they had was typically closely related to agriculture (machinery, fertilizers, food processing). It is in the west and south that there is more of an industrial history (for example, car production in Dagenham and Luton, aircraft parts in Hatfield), although even here the bulk of the industrial base has been light and clean in nature. Partly because of this difference in industrialization, and partly because of its close proximity to – and closer economic links with – Greater London, the southern area of the region is far more built up and urbanized than the basically rural northern half, an asymmetry accentuated by the lack of any major city to attenuate the pull or influence of London. In fact, the Eastern Region contains no provincial capital (or 'core city', to use the current political parlance), but rather a number of modest-sized centres – notably Norwich, Ipswich, Colchester, Chelmsford, Cambridge and Peterborough – together with several so-called 'new towns' (Basildon, Harlow, Stevenage, Welwyn) created after the Second World War as part of the (regional) policy of dispersing population and jobs away from London.

## A key region in the new economy . . .

Until the late 1960s, the region (and particularly that part of it that was East Anglia) was not particularly noted for its economic performance, although it was already clear that it was beginning to attract overspill and new town activity from the Greater London conurbation and benefiting from the pronounced urban–rural shift that has been such a prominent feature of the geography of post-war Britain. Since then, the region has emerged as one of the better-performing areas in the UK. In terms of per capita GDP, the region is second only to London and the South East (Figure 11.2), and for this reason is usually regarded as falling in the prosperous Southern part of the much-debated 'north–south divide' (Martin, 2004), or in what some, adopting an alternative core–periphery view of the UK's economic geography, refer to as the 'outer core' (Steed, 1986).

Other statistics also point to the East of England having a favourable position in the broad hierarchy of UK regions. Thus, the region has a high rate of population growth, in large part attributable to high rates of in-migration: over the period 1982–2002 the population grew by 11.2 per cent, compared with a national (UK) average of only 5.2 per cent. The region has one of the lowest unemployment rates in the UK, 3.6 per cent in January–March 2005, compared to the UK average of 4.7 per cent, and bettered only by the South East (3.5 per cent). It also has one of the lowest economic inactivity rates (18 per cent in January–March 2005, compared to the UK average of 21.4 per cent). The region ranks fourth in terms of average house prices (£172,075 in May 2005, compared to £289,655 in Greater London, £221,055 in the South East, and £196,819 in the South West), and indicators of social deprivation also point to a lower incidence in the region, with an example being the percentage of households receiving household benefit at 12 per cent, compared with a national average of 17 per cent. Over the period 1975–2000 the East Region taken as a whole has been able to expand its employment base by just over a quarter, compared with a national United Kingdom average of about 9 per cent. This impressive rate of employment growth has reflected a number of factors, not least that the region has not suffered to the same extent as other more urban and industrial regions in the shake-out of manufacturing jobs.

Moreover, not only is the region now viewed as one of the more prosperous, it is frequently invoked as a leading region of the so-called new 'knowledge-driven' economy, and the nation's centre of high-tech R&D activity (Table 11.1 and Figure 11.3). Its relative lack of industrialization in the past, and the success and reputation of Cambridge University, its premier higher education institution, has given the region a definite advantage in the new phase of high-tech post-industrialization. As we shall now see, however, this is only part of the story, and moreover a part that only applies to certain areas in the region; other areas have yet to participate in this high-tech-based economic boom, and remain relatively poor. The challenge posed by this inequality is the dual one

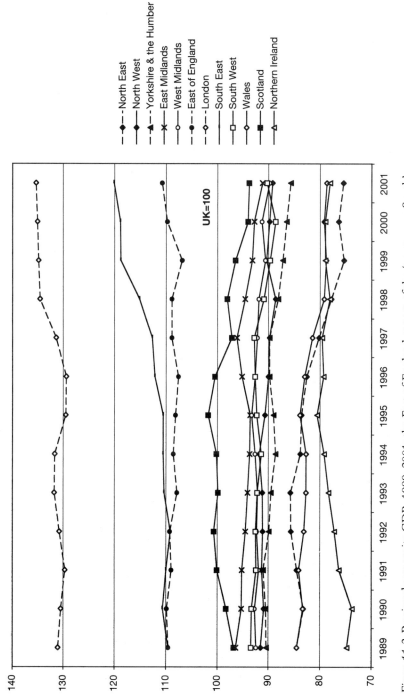

*Figure 11.2* Regional per capita GDP, 1989–2001: the East of England as part of the 'prosperous South'

Table 11.1 The East of England Region and the knowledge economy

| Region | Private sector R&D expenditure as % of GDP, 2002 (Rank) | Business start-up rates, 2003 (Rank) | Proportion of knowledge-based businesses (Rank) | Venture capital activity – % of companies, 2000–3 (Rank) | Education and skills – % of working population with NVQ4+, 2002–3 (Rank) | Gross value added per head (current prices), 2002 (Rank) |
|---|---|---|---|---|---|---|
| London | 0.46 (9) | 5.0 (1) | 28.6 (1) | 20 (1) | 126.2 (1) | £20,990 (1) |
| South East | 2.12 (2) | 3.8 (2) | 26.9 (2) | 24 (2) | 114.5 (3) | £18,411 (2) |
| **East** | **3.07 (1)** | **3.4 (3)** | **21.6 (3)** | **10 (3)** | **91.7 (5)** | **£17,452 (3)** |
| South West | 1.58 (5) | 3.2 (4) | 18.7 (5) | 5 (7) | 103.5 (4) | £15,038 (5) |
| East Midlands | 1.63 (3) | 3.0 (5) | 16.6 (8) | 4 (8) | 82.4 (10) | £14,505 (7) |
| West Midlands | 0.84 (6) | 2.9 (6) | 17.6 (6) | 7 (6) | 85.6 (9) | £14,538 (6) |
| North West | 1.59 (4) | 2.8 (7) | 20.2 (4) | 8 (5) | 88.4 (7) | £14,346 (8) |
| Yorks–Humber | 0.46 (10) | 2.4 (8) | 15.6 (9) | 5 (7) | 86.3 (8) | £14,222 (9) |
| Scotland | 0.75 (7) | 2.4 (9) | 17.0 (7) | 9 (4) | 115.9 (2) | £15,409 (4) |
| N. Ireland | 0.63 (8) | 2.4 (10) | 15.2 (11) | 2 (9) | – | £12,971 (10) |
| Wales | 0.46 (11) | 2.2 (11) | 14.1 (12) | 3 (8) | 90.9 (6) | £12,629 (11) |
| North East | 0.37 (12) | 1.8 (12) | 15.4 (10) | 3 (8) | 80.0 (11) | £12,629 (11) |
| UK | 1.19 | 3.2 | 21.2 | 100 | (GB) 100 | £16,383 |

Sources: ONS (2005), British Venture Capital Association (2004), Local Futures (personal communication), Robert Huggins Associates (2005)

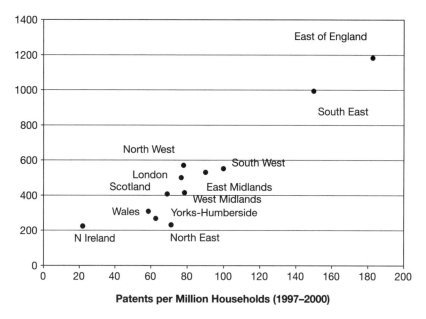

*Figure 11.3* The East of England's lead in the high-tech economy

of promoting growth across the region as a whole whilst managing and ensuring the continued success of those locations whose very growth is threatening to undermine itself.

## . . . But with unequal growth

Indeed, it has been the western areas – Cambridgeshire (including Peterborough) and Hertfordshire–Bedfordshire – that have led the growth process, with the rest of the region lagging somewhat. As a result, these two parts of the region have diverged in recent years (Figure 11.4). Thus, in 1995, GVA per head ranged from £8,200 in Southend to £11,998 in Hertfordshire, but by 2002 the gap had widened from £11,856 in Norfolk to £19,443 in Hertfordshire. In other words, growth has tended to concentrate in those areas close to and straddling the major north–south transport routes (into London and to Northern Britain), namely the M11 and A1 trunk roads, and the fast rail links into the capital. As Figure 11.4 shows clearly, over the past decade a major gap in growth and prosperity has opened between this highly buoyant and thriving part of the region on the one hand and much of the north and east of the region on the other.

In part this gap also reflects the very uneven development of the high-tech economy across the region (Figure 11.5). Much of the growth of the science-based knowledge-driven high-tech sector of the East of England's economy over the past thirty years has concentrated in a zone centred on Cambridge, and

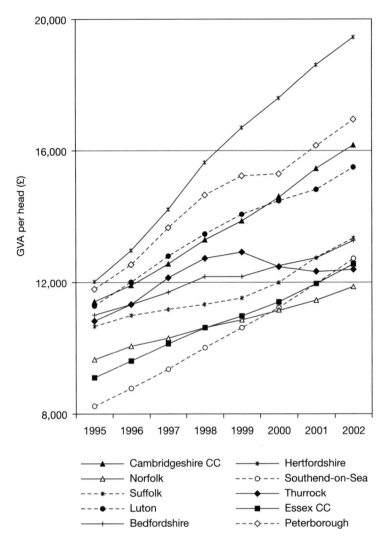

*Figure 11.4* Sub-regional growth trends in GVA per head (NUTS3 areas),
1995–2002

extending southwards into Hertfordshire, and northwards to Ely, Huntingdon
and Peterborough. The Greater Cambridgeshire area – that area within a 20–
25-mile radius of the city – contains what has become a much-celebrated
'cluster' of knowledge-based companies, often referred to as the 'Cambridge
Phenomenon'.

The story of the growth of the Cambridge high-tech sector has been discussed
at length, and we do not seek to repeat it here (see, for example, Segal *et al.*,
1985, 2000; Gonzales-Benito *et al.*, 1997; Library House, 2004). However, it is

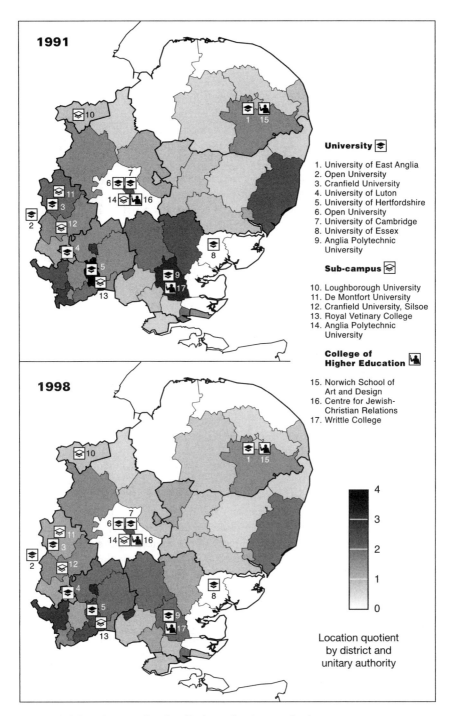

*Figure 11.5* Location quotient by district and unitary authority

*Source:* map based on Ordnance Survey material with the permission of Ordnance Survey on behalf of the Controller of Her Majesty's Stationery Office © Crown Copyright.

difficult to overestimate the importance of the Mott Report in 1969, which recommended that the exploitation of the area's knowledge base be more actively encouraged through some relaxation of the hitherto extremely restrictive stance on land use, and led to the establishment by Trinity College of the Cambridge Science Park just to the north of the city in 1970, followed by the St John's Innovation Centre in 1987. Since then, several other science, innovation and incubator parks have appeared in and around Cambridge. As a consequence, it is estimated that, over the period 1971–2001, some 60,000 jobs have been created in the science-based knowledge economy of the Greater Cambridgeshire area, accounting for more than a third of the total job growth of 150,000 in the sub-region (Greater Cambridge Partnership, 2003).[1] Many of the high-tech jobs have been filled by in-migrating workers.

The theme of mixed prosperity can be seen most clearly through an analysis of the labour market in the East of England. This region is clearly not a single, homogeneous labour market, but many distinct, overlapping local labour markets that display as many differences as similarities. The local nature of these labour markets reflects demand-side factors – such as the differences in the sub-regional economic base, employers' need for skilled labour, and employers' boundaries in the labour search – as well as supply-side factors – such as variation in the skill and education of the workforce, employees' boundaries of job-search areas, and viable commuting patterns.

The region contains many local areas where the population displays high economic activity rates, low levels of unemployment and high incomes; however, other parts of the region are lagging behind and the population in these areas show multiple signs of economic deprivation. This situation in the East mirrors many of the problems of the South East region, where areas of economic growth are juxtaposed with large pockets of decline, leading to what Allen *et al.* (1998) term the 'holes in the doily' of regional growth. This section explores this regional variation in the East of England, which is based on extremely different economic structures and proximity to London.

Reflecting the sub-regional variation in economic structure, the local labour markets in the northern and eastern parts of the region tend to display higher rates of unemployment, lower rates of education, and more signs of economic deprivation. Although there are pockets of poverty spread throughout the region, the greatest concentrations of low-income wards are found in rural areas, the coastal areas, the north of the region, and in many urban areas, such as Luton, Basildon and Peterborough (EEDA, 2004).

In contrast, although there are pockets of poverty in these parts of the region as well, overall the labour markets in the south and western sectors tend to show higher rates of employment and educational attainment, and have lower rates of poverty. The labour markets in the south and west are affected by their proximity to London and function to supply labour to firms in London and the South East as much as supplying labour to firms in the Eastern Region. In fact, in 2001 over 14.2 per cent of the entire population commuted to work outside the region (ONS, 2003). The great majority of these commuters are travelling

*Table 11.2* Working population commuting to London, by county (%)

| | |
|---|---|
| Essex | 18.64 |
| Norfolk | 0.82 |
| Bedfordshire | 6.39 |
| Suffolk | 1.76 |
| Cambridgeshire | 2.68 |
| Hertfordshire | 20.43 |

*Source:* Census, 2001, Origin–Destination Table, W107

from Essex and Hertfordshire (Table 11.2). More detailed analysis shows great variation within these counties, with over a third of the working population in places such as Epping Forest and Brentwood in Essex, or Broxbourne in Hertfordshire, commuting daily into London.

In addition, the housing market in the south-west of the region has been affected by the area acting as a bedroom community for London commuters, which has increased housing demand and prices for those who seek to live and work in the south and western parts of the region. In 2002, housing prices in the region were second only to London and the South East regions (ODPM, 2003: Table 5.5).

As a result of the strength of the economy and the high-tech growth particularly concentrated in the south and west of the region, much of the population in the East of England has experienced low unemployment rates and relatively high average incomes which compare favourably to those in most other regions in the UK. For years, the region has had unemployment rates that are lower, and average income figures that are higher, than those found in most other regions in the UK. For example, in 2001 the male population of the Eastern Region received a higher average weekly income, £529, than any other region in the UK except for London and the South East. Similarly, the East's male unemployment rate, standing at 3.4 per cent in the autumn of 2004, was tied with the South West Region as the lowest regional male unemployment rate in the UK, compared to a national average of 5 per cent (Labour Force Survey, ONS, 2005).

However, mirroring the sub-regional variation in economic structures discussed above, the Eastern Region comprises distinct local labour markets that exhibit different histories and growth trajectories. The regional figures on unemployment and average income presented above conceal this variation and it is only by analysing the sub-regional labour markets that we can under-stand the East of England's economy. We find great divergence in the health of the labour market when analysing the data at this level. For example, while Hertfordshire and Cambridgeshire enjoyed extremely low unemployment rates of 3.1 per cent and 3.2 per cent, respectively, in 2002–3, Luton experienced over double that rate, at 7.2 per cent (Table 11.3).

In the same manner, we can analyse county and unitary authority data on weekly earnings to see the sub-regional variation. Although average male weekly

*Table 11.3* Unemployment rate, by sub-region, 2002–3

| | |
|---|---|
| Great Britain | 5.2 |
| East of England | 4.0 |
|     Luton UA | 7.2 |
|     Peterborough UA | 4.9 |
|     Essex | 4.6 |
|     Thurrock UA | 4.3 |
|     Southend-on-Sea | 4.2 |
|     Norfolk | 4.1 |
|     Bedfordshire | 3.9 |
|     Suffolk | 3.4 |
|     Cambridgeshire | 3.2 |
|     Hertfordshire | 3.1 |

*Source:* Annual Local Area LFS, ONS

*Table 11.4* Average gross weekly earnings, by sex and sub-region, April 2003

| | Males Average (£) | Females Average (£) |
|---|---|---|
| United Kingdom | 523 | 395 |
| East of England | 529 | 383 |
|     Norfolk | 447 | 349 |
|     Suffolk | 455 | 358 |
|     Peterborough UA | 490 | 359 |
|     Southend-on-Sea | – | 367 |
|     Essex | 540 | 377 |
|     Luton UA | 513 | 383 |
|     Bedfordshire | 546 | 383 |
|     Cambridgeshire | 561 | 403 |
|     Hertfordshire | – | 426 |

*Note:* no data available on Thurrock UA

*Source:* New Earnings Survey, ONS

earnings in the East are slightly above the UK average and second only to London and the South East, there is great differentiation in income in the region. The population in the coastal rural counties of Suffolk and Norfolk have wages that are the lowest in the region and are significantly less than the regional average, or the average for the UK, while the population of counties such as Cambridgeshire have some of the highest earnings outside of London and the South East (Table 11.4).

Significantly, although women's average earnings also show great differentiation, the gap between the lowest and highest average earnings is smaller than with men. This highlights the strong gendered occupational segregation that exists and suggests that women are occupying less well-paid jobs wherever they are employed within the region. Thus, gendered labour market segmentation is as prevalent in areas with a high-tech economic base as it is in areas with more agricultural or service-based economies.

The Eastern Region's uneven growth pattern extends to the skilled labour market for graduate labour. The region has a number of excellent universities, including the Open University, the University of East Anglia and Cambridge University, one of the world's top-ranked universities. Many regional growth theories incorporate the assumption that a strong local university is one of the keys to creating regional economic growth, as it is particularly necessary to support clustered, specialized, high-tech sectors. For example, theories on regional clusters, regional innovation systems and the triple helix all assume that local universities, especially first-class, well-funded universities with an international reputation, such as Cambridge, help explain the dynamism of the regional high-tech economies (Florida, 1995; Saxenian, 1994; Porter, 2000; Etzkowitz *et al.*, 2000; Etzkowitz and Leydesdorff, 2000). However, whatever other role they may play in promoting new firm formation or technology transfer, the universities in the East of England actually play a smaller part in providing a highly skilled, graduate labour force than do universities in many other regions. In fact, in 1993 the Eastern Region accounted for only 7 per cent of the UK's stock of graduates, lower than any other region except for Northern Ireland. (But exceptional growth in the 1990s meant that by 2000 the region almost doubled its rate and accounted for 13.4 per cent of the UK's stock of graduates (EEDA, 2003).) In addition, the region had the lowest rate of graduation retention of any English region.

The low rate of graduate retention is in large measure due to the relatively low demand for highly educated workers in the region. Despite the strength of the knowledge-based economy in some parts of the Eastern Region, the importance of agriculture and personal services in much of the region leads to relatively low levels of private sector demand for graduate labour. Moreover, there are significant regional variations in the demand for graduates. For example, in the southern and western sectors the demand for graduates is far higher than in predominant rural areas of the region. In fact, despite the high rates of innovative activity in some areas, the local RDA argues that the low level of local demand makes the Eastern Region 'a classic low-skill equilibrium labour market' (EEDA, 2003).

To the extent that regional firms do generate demand for local graduates, they must often compete with firms external to the Eastern Region for graduate labour. The region's high-tech firms have long suffered from particular skills shortages in areas such as electronic engineering and software programming and find themselves in intense competition with similar firms around the country for high-quality graduates in these fields. Additionally, the international reputations of regional universities, such as Cambridge, reinforce the outward flow of graduates, since the institution does not just serve regional demand but provides graduates for a national and even international labour market. In fact, the majority of Cambridge University graduates take positions in London and the South East, where demand for graduate labour is high.

The uneven nature of economic growth within the Eastern Region makes labour market adjustment difficult. The needs of the rural and coastal communities are very different from those of the southern and western areas. Thus, the England Rural Development Programme produced in 2000 (MAFF, 2000) highlighted that the agriculture, forestry and fishing sector accounted at that time for just over 8 per cent of total employment in the district of north Norfolk and workers on average tended to be older than in other sectors, with a tradition of unattractive working hours that was unappealing to the younger working population. Ensuring an adequate supply of training and take-up thereof is becoming ever more important in the sector as it becomes more market driven rather than production orientated. During the last ten years the region has benefited from having four Rural Development Areas (parts of rural Norfolk, rural east Suffolk, the Fens and Tendring District in Essex). Financial assistance has been given to help the agricultural sector to assist with business development and training.

Labour market policies intended to ease unemployment and stimulate growth in the less prosperous parts of the region can exacerbate skills shortages in the other parts and vice versa. This tension is often expressed institutionally, through regional bodies such as the East of England Development Agency (EEDA). Their remit is region-wide and there is a constant tension between devoting resources to promoting high-tech growth in the west and south or spreading growth into less prosperous parts of the region.

## Maintaining the momentum: tackling the key constraints

This chapter has painted a picture of the East of England Region as one of the United Kingdom's relative economic success stories over the last thirty years. Across its often quite different economic space it has been a region in transition. In some parts, this has seen the emergence of new, dynamic sectors. Where growth has occurred it has been associated with, and has in itself encouraged, quite rapid growth in population with attendant pressures on infrastructure and consequential impacts on the demand for housing. In part, pressures on housing and infrastructure have been affected by proximity to London and the increased commuting flows this has produced over the study period, as well as the growth of second homes in the region, particularly on the Suffolk and Norfolk coasts. In its fast-growing parts, the region reflects the range of problems associated with the United Kingdom's relatively successful areas.

As in many other growing areas, economic growth has created problems with house-price inflation, housing availability, land scarcity, traffic congestion and demands on the local tax base. For example, average house prices are now almost eight times the average income in the East of England (NHF, 2005) and this affordability gap is increasing. Average housing prices in the East almost doubled from 1999 to 2004 (showing a 99 per cent increase), while average income increased by only 15 per cent in the same period (*ibid.*). Again, this problem has been particularly pronounced in high-growth parts of the region such as Hertfordshire, Cambridge and Essex. In response, growth coalitions have emerged in some high-tech 'hot-spots', such as Cambridge, to pressure the local and national state for a relaxation of planning rules and increased provision of the housing and infrastructure needed to sustain economic growth in the region (While *et al.* 2004).

Elements of how it is proposed that the region will respond to the challenges it faces are to be found in a number of documents, including the Regional Planning Guidance for East Anglia (RPG6), Regional Planning Guidance for the South East (RPG9) and the Milton Keynes/South Midlands Sub-Regional Strategy (MKSM). The unifying document, the Regional Spatial Strategy (RSS) for the East of England, is presently under review. The draft revised document is referred to as the East of England Plan with a remit encompassing the whole of the East of England. After an examination in public it is anticipated that the final RSS for the region will be available in late 2006.

The draft RSS has proposed that some 478,000 new homes should be built, alongside substantial provision for further industrial and commercial floorspace and associated infrastructure. Figure 11.6 indicates how the region features in the government's Growth Zone plans. To say that some of the recommendations of the draft RSS have met with opposition would perhaps be an understatement!

The East Region looks set to maintain its relatively favourable position in the United Kingdom league of regions, but the extent to which it can maximize its relative growth depends on how well it is able to tackle the problems associated with its unequal growth in terms of spatial inequalities and congestion. There is, in particular, an urgent need to overcome the infrastructure shortages that constrain the ability of the region to reach its true economic potential over the longer term.

Space here does not permit an adequate exposition of all of the relevant issues, but recent research (Baxter *et al.*, 2005) points to the need to ensure that the pace of institutional change matches that of the economic. Enterprising regions meet the needs of their businesses and residents by adjusting their resource base through coordinated actions by the relevant parties from across the public and private sectors. The key to overcoming key infrastructure constraints is to ensure a joined-up institutional response. Successful areas in this respect are those that:

- enhance the *core competencies or attributes* of their area so that it is a relatively attractive place for businesses to want to invest in and for people to live in;
- bring together the relevant *agents of change* from across all sectors, be it government, business or the voluntary sector; and
- adopt a *strategic* approach.

In line with the other English regions, the East has established its own Regional Development Agency (EEDA). Its Regional Economic Strategy (RES) (EEDA, 2004) has brought together the views of a number of key stakeholders from across the region and sets out a clear vision statement that embraces the need

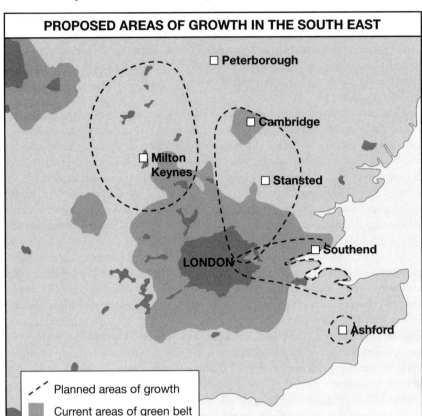

*Figure 11.6* Proposed areas of growth in the South East

to build on the region's economic strengths, capitalize on its distinctive opportunities and challenges as well as spread the benefits of economic growth to those areas in the region that have hitherto been somewhat left behind. Throughout, the strategy recognizes the need to build on the underlying principles of sustainable development, encouraging urban and rural vitality, fostering equality and diversity, while ensuring that there is regional leadership, coherence and cohesion. The overall vision is for 'a leading economy, founded on our world-class knowledge base and the creativity and enterprise of our people, in order to improve the quality of life of all who live and work here' (EEDA, 2004).

The RES makes a number of proposals as to how its objectives might be achieved and how it can be delivered on the ground. It is suggested that the best way forward might be to have two overarching regional partnerships. One might be the Regional Skills and Competitiveness Partnership (RSCP), which would bring together activities from a Regional Skills Partnership, a Strategic Advisory Board for Business and the Science and Industry Council in the region.

The other, a Sustainable Communities and Infrastructure Board (SCIB), would focus on ensuring that the region was a high-quality place to live, work and visit, securing social inclusion and ensuring the development of international gateways and national and regional transport corridors. It is envisaged that the SCIB might bring inputs from the Community Development Board, a Transport and Infrastructure Board supported by the Regional Centre of Excellence for Sustainable Communities, and a Growth Areas Board.

At the present time, these proposals are being developed, as are the mechanisms by which actions at the regional level might be coordinated with the work of the region's sub-regional economic partnerships. However, besides coordinating issues around the regional economy, there is an urgent need in the RSS to ensure that the traditional boundaries of local governance at the district and county level in the region mesh with the geographies of the region's economic clusters as they have been developing on the ground, particularly in relation to knowledge-based activity. Existing planning structures may not fit particularly well with the central government's Sustainable Communities Agenda, which identifies three Growth Areas that either lie within or overlap with the region (Thames Gateway–South Essex, London–Stansted–Cambridge– Peterborough, and Milton Keynes–South Midlands). It is a time of considerable institutional flux, but the identity of the Eastern Region will continue to be affected by the seemingly relentless economic growth of Southern England. At the same time the relatively uneven economic pace of economic growth across the different parts of the region will exacerbate the tensions described earlier in this chapter.

The extent to which the region will be able to overcome its key infrastructure constraints on growth, as well as share its economic prosperity more evenly across its residents, will depend crucially on its ability to resolve a number of key strategic planning issues, not least that relating to Cambridge and its relationship to its hinterland. There is also an urgent need to identify how the infrastructure needs of the region can be financed in the years ahead so that many bottlenecks and inequalities can be overcome.

## Note

1   In the Greater Cambridgeshire Partnership Report, the Greater Cambridgeshire area is defined as all the wards in Cambridge, South Cambridgeshire, East Cambridgeshire and Huntingdonshire; in Uttlesford, the wards of Ashdon, Littlebury, Saffron Walden (Audley), Saffron Walden (Castle), Saffron Walden (Plantation), Saffron Walden (Shire), the Chesterfords, Wendon Lofts; in Fenland, the wards of Benwick and Doddington, Chatteris East/North/South/West, Manea; in Forest Heath, all wards except Brandon East, Brandon West, Lake Heath; in St Edmundsbury, all wards except Barningham, Cavendish, Clare, Honington, Hundon, Ixworth, Kedington, Pakenham, Rouggham, Santon, Whelnetham.

## References

Allen, J., Massey, D. and Cochrane, A. (1998) *Rethinking the Region*, London: Routledge

Amin, A., Massey, D. and Thrift, N.J. (2003) *Decentering the Nation: A Radical Approach to Regional Inequality*, London: Catalyst Publications

Baxter, C., Tyler, P., Moore, B., Morrison, N., McGaffin, R. and Otero Garcia, M. (2005) *Enterprising Places: Sustaining Competitive Locations for Knowledge Based Business*, CMI-MIT

British Venture Capital Association (BVCA) (2004) *Report on Investment Activity*, London: BVCA

East of England Development Agency (EEDA) (2003) *The Graduate Labour Market in the Eastern Region*, Cambridge: East of England Development Agency

—— (2004) *Regional Observatory*

Etzkowitz, H. and Leydesdorff, L. (2000) 'The Dynamics of Innovation: From National Systems and "Mode 2" to a Triple Helix of University–Industry–Government Relations', *Research Policy*, 29, 2, pp. 109–23

Etzkowitz, H., Webster, A., Gebhardt, C. and Terra, B.R.C. (2000) 'The Future of the University and the University of the Future: Evolution of Ivory Tower to Entrepreneurial Paradigm', *Research Policy*, 29, 2, pp. 313–30

Florida, R. (1995) 'Towards the Learning Region', *Futures*, 27, pp. 527–36

Fujita, M., Krugman, P. and Venables, A. (1999) *The Spatial Economy: Cities, Regions and International Trade*, Cambridge, MA: MIT Press

Gonzales-Benito, J., Reid, S. and Garnsey, E. (1997) *The Cambridge Phenomenon Comes of Age*, Research Papers in Management Studies WP22/97, Cambridge: Judge Institute of Management Studies, University of Cambridge

Greater Cambridgeshire Partnership (GCP) (2003) *Greater Cambridge Sub-Regional Economic Strategy*, Cambridge: GCP

Harvey, D. (1985) 'The Geopolitics of Capitalism', in D.J. Gregory and J. Urry (eds), *Social Relations and Spatial Structures*, London: Macmillan.

Kitson, M., Martin, R.L. and Tyler, P. (eds) (2005) *Regional Competitiveness*, London: Routledge

Library House (2004) *Flight to Quality: The Cambridge Cluster Report*, Cambridge: Library House

Ministry of Agriculture, Fisheries and Food (MAFF) (2000) *The East of England Development Programme.*

Markusen, A. (1987) *Regions: The Economics and Politics of Territory*, Totowa, NJ: Rowman & Littlefield

Martin, R.L. (2004) 'The Contemporary Debate over the North–South Divide: Images and Realities of Regional Inequality in Late Twentieth Century Britain', in A.R.H. Baker and M.D. Billinge (eds), *Geographies of England: The North–South Divide, Imagined and Material*, Cambridge: Cambridge University Press

National Housing Federation (NHF) (2005) *England's Housing Crisis: In the East, 2005*, London: National Housing Federation

Office of the Deputy Prime Minister (ODPM) (2003) *Sustainable Communities*

Office for National Statistics (ONS) (2003) *Go East*

—— (2005) *Regional GDP*, available at www.statistics.gov.uk

Osmond, J. (1988) *The Divided Kingdom*, London: Constable

Porter, M.E. (1996) 'Competitive Advantage, Agglomeration Economies and Regional Policy', *International Regional Science Review*, 19, pp. 85–94

—— (2000) 'Location, Clusters and Company Strategy', in G.L. Clark, M.P. Feldman and M.S. Gertler (eds), *The Oxford Handbook of Economic Geography*, Oxford: Oxford University Press

—— (2001) 'Regions and the New Economics of Competition', in A.J. Scott (ed.), *Global City-Regions: Trends, Theory, Policy*, Oxford: Oxford University Press

—— (2003) 'The Economic Performance of Regions', *Regional Studies*, Special Issue, 36, 6/7, pp. 549–78

*Regional Studies* (2003) 'Rethinking Regional Development', *Regional Studies*, Special Issue, 36, 6/7, pp. 545–751.

—— (2004) 'Regional Competitiveness', *Regional Studies* Special Issue, 38, 9, pp. 991–1120

Robert Huggins Associates (2005) *The Changing State of the Nation, 1997–2005*

Saxenian, A.L. (1994) *Regional Advantage: Culture and Competition in Silicon Valley and Route 128*, Cambridge, MA: Harvard University Press

Scott, A.J. (1998) *Regions and the World Economy*, Oxford: Oxford University Press

—— (ed.) (2001) *Global City-Regions: Trends, Theory, Policy*, Oxford: Oxford University Press

Segal, N., Quince, R. and Wicksteed, B. (1985) *The Cambridge Phenomenon: The Growth of High-Tech Industry in a University Town*, Cambridge: Segal, Quince, Wicksteed

—— (2000) *The Cambridge Phenomenon Revisited*, Cambridge: Segal, Quince, Wicksteed

Steed, M. (1986) 'The Core–Periphery Dimension of British Politics', *Political Geography Quarterly*, 5, 4, pp. 90–102

Steers, J.A. (ed.) (1965) *The Cambridge Region*, London: British Association for the Advancement of Science

Storper, M. (1997) *Regional World: Territorial Development in a Global Economy*, Cambridge, MA: Harvard University Press

While, A., Jonas, A.E.G. and Gibbs, G. (2004) 'Unblocking the City? Growth Pressures, Collective Provision, and the Search for New Spaces of Governance in Greater Cambridge, England', *Environment and Planning A*, 36, pp. 279–304

Williams, R. (1983) *Towards 2000*, London: Chatto & Windus

# 12 The South West economy

## Potential for faster economic development

*Amer Hirmis*

## Introduction

The South West Region of the United Kingdom is a paradoxical one. It is made up of a number of geographically contiguous administrative areas that stretch from one of the most western tips of Great Britain to the fringes of the economic hinterland of London. As a coherent regional entity, however, it appears to lack a unity of purpose and appears to fall into John Lovering's (2001) category of 'unfortunate regionalism'. That is, there is a tendency for many influential academics, policy-makers and practitioners to reify the region, and to insist upon its centrality as the contemporary basis of analysing economy and society, with reference to the complexities of geographical scale and the material distribution within it. In examining its potential for economic development, the region's paradoxical nature therefore becomes more apparent.

The South West Region covers the traditional West Country and most of the historical area of Wessex. Its political administration consists of the six counties of Cornwall (including the Isles of Scilly), Devon, Dorset, Gloucestershire, Somerset and Wiltshire. These are illustrated in Figure 12.1.

Towns and cities of note include Bath, Bournemouth, Bristol, Dorchester, Exeter and Weymouth. The total population in 2001 was 4.9 million, the seventh largest in England although spread over the largest English region, with an area of 23,829 square kilometres. This large spread is both a benefit and a cost to the region, particularly in respect of the distribution of the major economic activities of tourism and agriculture.

The region has a powerful literary history, from *Lorna Doone* and 'The Hound of the Baskervilles' to the works of Thomas Hardy, which powerfully recreated the idea of a Wessex culture being slowly eroded by creeping industrialisation. It is also home to strong sporting traditions, most notably in the fields of Rugby Union and cricket, but also football. These two aspects of culture are also testament to the paradoxical and often fragmented nature of the South West as a region whose identity is not a particularly shared one, and which consequently has had to be manufactured, despite claims from the Regional Development Agency (RDA) of the existence of an 'amazing regional identity'.

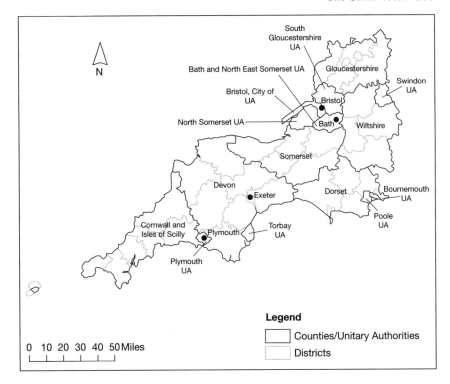

*Figure 12.1* The South West

It is recognised, however, that the region is made up of a number of sub-regional identities (Deacon, 2004). Although the Kilbrandon Report of 1973 argued that the South West had the strongest regional identity, this was a period when much of the eastern part of the current South West Region was located in the old South Region, centred on Southampton (HMSO, 1973).

The identity that appears to be the strongest is that of Cornwall, a historic nation whose claims to statehood have never really disappeared. Cornwall was the first place in England really to undergo any kind of industrialisation, with the emergence, and then disappearance, of the tin-mining industry producing a shared regional economic experience which fostered a collective regional identity. The preservation of this distinctiveness rests on the continued existence of its language (now recognised as a European minority language) as well as claims to some form of democratic self-determination through the establishment of the Cornish Constitutional Convention. Despite the later launch of the South West Regional Convention in April 2001, the strong attachment to local identities makes the construction of a coherent region difficult. Marketing campaigns aimed at business and potential inward investors have been promoted by the key regional institutions (such as the RDA, Chamber of Commerce, etc.). However, as Deacon (2004: 219) notes:

In the regional discourse of the peak institutions of the new regionalization the image of the South-West as rural, maritime and diverse, cohering around a politically and economically driven project of regional construction, is seen as separate from cultural identity, the self-identification of the inhabitants. When identity is recognized, it is found at a different scale.

Although this could be said to be a challenge for all the English regions, it appears to be especially marked in the South West. That separation of economic coherence and cultural dissimilarity is important in order to understand the economic geography of the region and the degree of diversity of its economy and intra-regional scale of economic peripherality: the South West Region is home to wealthy Dorset and Bristol but also to Cornwall, which in per capita terms is the poorest English county. This raises the problem of trying to draw a sketch of the South West, because although it is easy to write a compelling economic portrait, a cultural and social picture of the region is either so general as to be meaningless or loses its rigour underneath a sea of conflicting and incoherent local anecdotes and stories. In this chapter I therefore confine myself to the economic sphere, where the South West can truly be said to have a meaningful existence. It is clear that the South West has risen as a region, in purely economic terms, and this provides my main focus. This chapter differs from others in this book because of its emphasis on economic development and performance. It does so because of the paradoxical nature of the region: a region situated in the wealthy South of England is likely to be the last in England to continue to receive Objective 1 support from the European Union, under the changes announced under the Agenda 2000 reforms of the Structural Funds Programme.

The aim of this chapter is therefore to provide a strategic view of some of the economic characteristics and issues in the South West Region. It does not provide a sub-regional or local (microeconomic) view, although it is fully recognised that many of the sub-regional and local characteristics and issues are critical in shaping the macro picture. The analysis is couched predominantly in terms of positive, not normative, economics, looking at medium- and long-term change.

The chapter begins by setting out the economic geography of the region, followed by an examination of the key economic characteristics of the South West. It then moves on to examine these in more detail, looking at demand, output, supply, costs and prices. The final sections cover some of the critical spatial characteristics shaping the region's economic prospects, followed by some reflections on the key regional policy issues in the South West, on which some tentative conclusions are offered.

A key conclusion of this chapter is that the South West has been performing below its potential. The region suffers from a negative output gap; that is, total economic demand is below the productive potential of the region. Improving the current policy framework and making the business environment more conducive to additional investment will go some way towards accelerating income and productivity growth rates to take them above the historical trend. The key question for national, regional and local institutions and policy-makers is whether the combination of cultural diversity and identity, as well as the region's spatial fragmentation, can be managed in such a way as to overcome economic peripherality and development at consistently less than the region's capacity.

The current set of administrative institutions and structures assumes regional commonality. However, as this chapter shows, the scale of economic disparity tends to reinforce regional divergence. The imposition of a region (in terms of boundaries and institutions) by the fiat of administrative actors makes no sense unless the regional scale is used as the basis of a thoroughgoing analysis of the economy of the South West and the appropriate lessons drawn. An important lesson for current UK regional policy is whether the South West will meet the Public Service Agreement (PSA) agreed between central government and the region's economic development agency, the South West Regional Development Agency (SWRDA). This is most questionable in the particular target that has been set for the South West to increase its economic growth rate to that of the UK average by 2012. These considerations are at the heart of the discourse of this chapter.

## Economic geography within the South West Region

The paradoxical nature of the South West has been described above, and its economic geography tends to reinforce this sense of paradox. The combination of the six counties into a single regional entity makes for a very challenging economic geography. It contains not only the business growth poles of Bristol, Bournemouth and Poole, and Swindon but a notable number of sub-poles where private housing costs are among the highest in the UK (for example, Exeter). Yet on a national income per head basis (GVA per capita) the South West is one of the poorest regions in Western Europe. Furthermore, although the relatively wealthy conurbations of Bournemouth and Poole are formally part of the South West Region, their real economic hinterland is the corridor of the South East Region that stretches up to London along the M3 motorway, and these towns are much more dependent on the economic success of the capital than they have the scope to act as motors for the wider regional economy.

The main business activities of the region are concentrated in a numerical sense on the agriculture and tourism sectors. However, the main drivers of income and productivity growth (1995–2001) were very different sectors, particularly in business services, manufacturing and wholesale and retail. The sub-regional, spatial economic picture in the South West points to notable concentration of economic activity in, and around, Bristol, as can be seen from Table 12.1.

The table clearly shows concentration of economic activity in Bristol, in terms of employment as well as GVA levels. A distinct feature of the region is that, although Bristol tends to be the powerful sub-region, there is no one dominant

*Table 12.1* Key economic variables for county councils (CC) and unitary authorities
(UA) in the South West, 2001

| Area | Full-time employment | Gross domestic product (GDP), £m | Productivity[1] (£000 per worker) |
|---|---|---|---|
| Bath and NE Somerset UA | 72,863 | 2,494 | 34.229 |
| Bournemouth UA | 66,481 | 2,024 | 30.445 |
| Bristol UA | 222,626 | 7,824 | 35.144 |
| Cornwall and Isles of Scilly | 166,991 | 4,545 | 27.217 |
| Devon CC | 270,982 | 8,222 | 30.341 |
| Dorset CC | 142,644 | 4,819 | 33.783 |
| Gloucestershire | 229,960 | 7,739 | 33.654 |
| North Somerset UA | 68,405 | 2,370 | 34.647 |
| Plymouth | 106,812 | 3,128 | 29.285 |
| Poole | 61,416 | 1,949 | 31.734 |
| Somerset | 189,368 | 5,783 | 30.538 |
| South Gloucestershire UA | 116,358 | 3,962 | 34.050 |
| Swindon UA | 103,782 | 4,921 | 47.417 |
| Torbay UA | 46,903 | 1,051 | 22.408 |
| Wiltshire CC | 181,916 | 6,268 | 34.455 |
| **South-West** | **2,047,507** | **67,099** | **32.736** |

Note:
1 Labour productivity = GDP/worker

Source: Plymouth University, SW Regional Accounts for 2001 (the latest available)

centre for the region around which the economic geography is articulated.
Higher productivity is critical for economic development since in the long run
per capita income, and the general level of prosperity, depends on the productivity performance of the region. I have already noted that there are significant
wealth disparities, and these are closely correlated with significant intra-regional
disparities in productivity levels: high-technology Swindon records the highest
(£47,417 per worker), mainly due to the existence of a strong automobile
industry, followed by Bristol (£35,144 per worker). At the other end of the
scale, Cornwall recorded £27,217 per worker, consistently lower than elsewhere
in the region, a perhaps unwelcome position which it has occupied throughout
the recent past.

The combination of low population density and the geographical extent of
the region presents a significant challenge in developing the coherence of the
economic geography. For example, central government policy programmes to
address the needs of small and medium-sized enterprises and encourage greater
entrepreneurship run into the problem that it is difficult to provide business
support at a common level across the region. Despite the promise of programmes
like the Regional Venture Capital Fund (RVCF), the region's economic
geography constrains the opportunity sets that would lead to a greater fulfilment
of entrepreneurial activity.

## Key economic characteristics of the region

A key characteristic of the South West regional economy is its size. In 2002, the South West had a GVA of £69.2 billion at current basic prices, making it the fifth largest of the nine English regions. Whilst the annual rate of growth of the economy since 1992 was around 3 per cent (higher than the UK average of 2.5 per cent), its relative size to GVA in England remained unchanged at 8.9 per cent. In contrast, the South East had increased its share in national GVA by around 2 per cent (to 19.1 per cent) in 2002 and the North East had decreased its contribution by nearly 1 per cent (to 3.8) in 2002.

These figures suggest that the South West has not played a significant part in affecting the dynamics of the overall regional change in England. Indeed, ONS figures show that the average annual growth in GVA (at current prices) in the South West is slightly higher than in England as a whole, with both growing at an average of around 5 per cent per annum over the period 1992–2002. The highest growth rate was in the South East Region (6 per cent in 2001) and although the growth rate in the South West was higher than that of London in the same year (4.4 per cent), the differential is insufficient to say that there has really been a meaningful convergence with the national figure. Government intervention to alter the structure of the regional economy played some part in its growth performance but if the South West is to 'catch up', then clearly growth will need to be significantly above the national trend.

A second key characteristic of the South West is that labour productivity, already very uneven within the region, has been consistently lower than in England by around 10 per cent over the past ten years. This has been on average nearly 30 per cent below that in London and 13 per cent below the South East. Labour productivity is closely related to the level of average earnings, and so it is unsurprising that average earnings in the region have been consistently around 9 per cent lower than the average gross weekly earnings in England.

A third characteristic is the standard of living (or 'level of prosperity'), which ultimately derives from wealth production, productivity levels and wage rates. In 2002, GVA per head in the South West was £13,900, or 11.1 per cent below the average for England, 39.5 per cent below London and 29.1 per cent below the neighbouring South East, although 14.4 per cent above the North East.

Finally, the employment rate in the South West has been consistently above the average in England since 1994. ONS data show the region enjoyed a significantly higher employment rate over the ten-year period to 2004 of between 76.5 per cent and 78.7 per cent compared to between 72.5 per cent and 74.7 per cent for England as a whole. However, this means it is still slightly below the East of England (79 per cent) and the South East (79.1 per cent). The total number in employment in the South West was 2.44 million between August and October 2004, representing an increase of 10,000 on the previous year. Whilst in most English regions employment growth was driven by the public sector compensating for loss of employment in the private sector, in the South West employment grew in both sectors.

These characteristics suggest that despite the paradox of above-average employment growth, the regional demand (generated by disposable income and expenditure) is insufficient for the South West to close the gap with neighbouring regions that perform above the national average. This raises several questions. For example, why is the South West undershooting the national average in terms of key economic performance indicators (except employment rate)? Does the region suffer from negative output gap? What are the key policy challenges in the region? What are the opportunities which, if seized, could accelerate GVA growth above the historical trend and contribute to higher prosperity in the South West?

The remainder of this chapter attempts to address these questions and paradoxes from a more formal economic perspective.

## Demand in the region

As elsewhere in the country, recent economic growth in the South West has been supported by strong consumer spending and retail sales. Increased consumption in turn has been supported by low inflation (of around 2 per cent) and wage increases during 1995–2003: wages rose at a higher rate than GDP growth, at around 4.5 per cent per annum. In addition, the phenomenal increases in house (asset) prices in the South West, which ran in recent years at an average annual level of around 16 per cent, compared to the national average of 11 per cent, created a 'wealth effect', leading to increasing demand for goods and services. The greater apparent value of their assets encouraged individuals to borrow money against rising house prices, and this money was used to fund increased consumption. The issue of rising house prices, partly generated by second-home ownership, is a major concern for managing economic inequality in the region.

The quarterly survey of the South West Chamber of Commerce and Industry (Winter 2004) revealed some recent deterioration in sales growth, employment and investment. The picture was patchy and varied according to sector and size of firm. There was one distinct improvement compared with the previous quarterly survey, in that it showed a marked recovery back to the high levels typical of 2003 and early 2004. However, more worrying is the fact that there is extreme volatility in confidence. This has the potential to destabilise the regional economy by giving an uncertain context for investment decisions. Changes, including those taking place since Q1 in 2001, are shown in Figure 12.2. The upper line shows the proportion of firms enjoying increased sales while the lower line shows the proportion suffering a reduction. The gap between the lines gives an indication of domestic sales growth.

Another element of demand is exports and imports of goods and services. As the figures on exports and imports of goods are more reliable, we look at the balance of trade in the region. HM Customs and Excise figures show that the South West has a trade deficit with the outside world, but this is not as severe as that of the UK as a whole. In 1999, the trade deficit (imports of goods minus

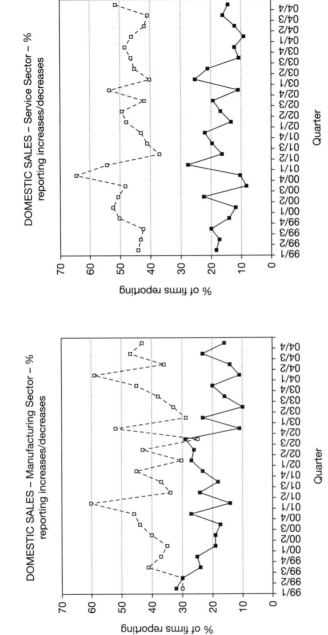

*Figure 12.2* Domestic sales: manufacturing and service sectors (%)

exports of goods) was 1.6 per cent of the region's GVA, compared to a UK figure of 2.1 per cent. However, in 2002 the region's trade deficit rose to 3.9 per cent, compared to 2.0 per cent nationally. This means that the region's contribution to the national trade deficit has increased relative to other regions over the course of three years. This would seem to suggest that the wealth effect mentioned above has fuelled increased consumption of consumer goods which have been imported, and has had little driving effect on the regional economy outside the retail, distribution and warehousing sector. However, further work is needed to examine whether this sudden increase in the trade deficit is due to increased investment in productive capacity or in housing and services.

Encouragingly for the region, Customs data also show continued rapid growth in the number of South West firms exporting to non-EU markets, although the number of exporters to the EU has declined marginally. This is perhaps a reflection of improving comparative advantage of the region.

Investment is a vital ingredient of economic development. Measured as gross fixed capital formation (GFCF), ONS data show that GFCF in the region was £12.5 billion in 2000, an investment rate of 20.4 per cent. This is slightly higher than England's 18.9 per cent and slightly lower than London's 20.6 per cent. The GFCF share of the region in England also increased from 8.7 per cent in 1998 to 9.5 per cent in 2000.

Figure 12.3 shows GFCF data for 2000 broken down by key sectors. It should be noted that much of the investment was in sectors which have a tendency to be less productive in the long run, such as real estate and housing. In manufacturing, for example, although the proportion of investment looks greater than in the South East, in absolute terms it was much less than in the North West, Yorkshire and Humberside, West Midlands, the East and the South East.

A similar picture emerged particularly in transport and communications, a vital determinant of economic growth and development in the new knowledge economy. At £1.4 billion investment in 2000, the region's investment in this sector was only 20 per cent of the amount of investment in London, and only 25 per cent of what was invested in the South East. It is not entirely clear from the statistics to what extent this moderate size of investment explains the poor accessibility of most parts of the region (except for Bristol and its immediate hinterlands). It may well be a strong explanatory variable, and if this is the case, then more investment in transport and communications – closing this infrastructure investment gap – in the region should be seen a critical policy objective for the future.

A tentative conclusion at this point, to be tested as we progress in the chapter, is that the demand side of the South West economy is not being driven by increased productive capacity of the economy, but by consumer spending and increased imports. Given the uncertainties over the housing market in the UK at present, the South West may be excessively vulnerable to an economic downturn, given its negative output gap and rapid house-price growth in recent years. Consequently, the degree to which economic peripherality and inequality can be overcome is also constrained.

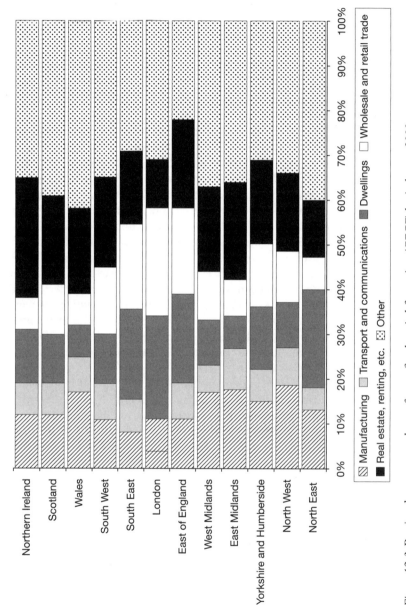

*Figure 12.3* Regional percentage share of gross fixed capital formation (GFCF) by industry, 2000

*Source:* Cope and Flanagan (2003: 39)

## Output in the region

The competitiveness of a region depends on its productivity levels, and these are a function of the way that physical capital, labour and the state of technology are organised to ensure the production of goods and delivery of services. Regional output levels are determined, *inter alia*, by the nature of the sectoral mix in the region's economy (because productivity levels show strong sectoral correlations), as well as business size and ownership, on which we focus here. Data for 2001 from ONS show that slightly over 50 per cent of GVA in the South West is generated by three sectors – business services (22 per cent), manufacturing (17.7 per cent) and wholesale and retail trade (12.5 per cent). Data for 2002 reveal the same picture.

The economic dynamics of the region during the period 1995–2001 (Table 12.2) show that the main business sectors driving economic growth in the South West have been hotels and restaurants (with 8.2 per cent growth), business services (8.1 per cent), wholesale and retail (6.0 per cent) and manufacturing (3.8 per cent). The public sector has also contributed to growth in creating most of the new jobs in the region (see the next section) and also by creating new demand for goods and services. The region as a whole grew at the same rate as nationally, averaging 5.5 per cent, and with the main sectors growing at a rate close to the national average. In terms of sectoral contribution to regional GVA growth, the sectors scoring highest contributions from 1995 to 2001 at 28.3 per cent, 13.4 per cent and 13.3 per cent were business services, manufacturing and wholesale and retail, respectively. Corresponding national growth rates were 33.1 per cent, 9.8 per cent and 14.1 per cent, respectively. In other words, the manufacturing sector in the South West has seen faster growth than nationally and therefore has become more important to the regional economy in generating GVA.

Table 12.3 compares sector structure in the region with that of England as a whole, using specialisation indices (GVA location quotient). It can be seen that the South West has been relatively more specialised in mining and quarrying, hotels and restaurants (important elements of the tourism industry). It has been as specialised as the national average in manufacturing and business services, but less specialised in transportation.

The overall size structure of businesses in the region is highly similar to that for England as a whole: the majority of South West business sites are small, with around 69 per cent employing fewer than five people, and around 84 per cent employing ten people or fewer. Business sites with more than 100 employees contributed around 42 per cent of total employee jobs in England, but only 38 per cent of those in the South West. Larger businesses, in employment terms, tend to be concentrated in a few industry sectors, particularly in energy and water, manufacturing, public administration, education and health, with larger concentrations of small firms in agriculture and fishing, distribution, hotels and restaurants, and business services.

The ownership structure of the region's firms appears to be an important determinant of the South West's productivity and thus has the potential to turn

Table 12.2 Industry contributions to GVA[1] growth: 1995–2001[2] (%)

| | South West Region | | England | |
| | Annualised growth rate (1995–2001) | Contribution to total growth (%) | Annualised growth rate (1995–2001) | Contribution to total growth (%) |
| --- | --- | --- | --- | --- |
| Agriculture, hunting, forestry and fishing | -4.0 | -2.4 | -4.1 | -1.1 |
| Mining and quarrying of energy-producing materials | -1.3 | 0 | -2.3 | -0.1 |
| Other mining and quarrying | 5.1 | 0.6 | 3 | 0.1 |
| Manufacturing | 2.5 | 10.4 | 1.2 | 5.1 |
| Electricity, gas and water supply | -1.4 | -0.9 | 0.4 | 0.2 |
| Construction | 6.4 | 7.9 | 6.4 | 7.2 |
| Wholesale and retail (including motor) | 5.7 | 15.0 | 5.7 | 15.0 |
| Hotels and restaurants | 8.1 | 6.5 | 7.4 | 9.3 |
| Transport, storage and communication | 5.3 | 7.4 | 5.2 | 9.3 |
| Financial intermediation | 0.2 | 0.2 | 2.7 | 3.6 |
| Real estate, renting and business activities | 7.8 | 33.5 | 8.6 | 39.8 |
| Public administration and defence | 1.4 | 2.5 | 2.0 | 2.2 |
| Education | 7.3 | 9.2 | 6.4 | 7.4 |
| Health and social work | 4.4 | 6.5 | 4.8 | 6.5 |
| Other services | 7.5 | 7.2 | 7.6 | 7.5 |
| Total[3] | 4.6 | 100 | 4.8 | 100 |

Notes:
1 Based on ONS 'headline' regional GVA series in current prices, calculated using a five-year moving average
2 Provisional estimates
3 Includes adjustments for financial services indirectly measured (FISIM)

Source: www.swo.org.uk

*Table 12.3* Sectoral production specialisation in the South West (output location
quotient)

|  | 1995 | 2001 | 2002 |
|---|---|---|---|
| Other mining and quarrying | 2.31 | 2.55 | 2.50 |
| Manufacturing | 0.88 | 1.01 | 1.00 |
| Wholesale and retail trade (including motor) | 1.01 | 0.98 | 1.00 |
| Hotels and restaurants | 1.15 | 1.22 | 1.21 |
| Transport and communications | 0.76 | 0.78 | 0.75 |
| Real estate, renting and business activities | 1.00 | 0.91 | 0.91 |

*Source:* author's calculations based on ONS data

around the negative output gap. Almost 50,000 people (18 per cent of the total)
worked in foreign-owned manufacturing firms. These firms are estimated to
have contributed around 26 per cent of output for that sector during 2000. This
would suggest that average labour productivity (GVA per worker) in foreign-
owned firms, at £60,400 per worker per annum, is nearly 60 per cent higher
than average labour productivity in the domestic firms (£38,400 per worker).
But it would be wrong to generalise this conclusion. Many UK-owned firms
in the manufacturing sector are highly competitive in global markets, for
example in the aerospace, ICT, biotechnology and nano- and micro-systems
sectors, which are not strongly represented in aggregate in the region.

The size structure of the region's firms also poses severe limitations on realising
economies of scale, externalities and productivity gains from innovation and
commercialisation of new ideas. It also implies that firms will be severely
constrained to allocate budgets for, let alone plan, training their workforce to
introduce and use new technologies. Eventually this will pose severe constraints
to improved productivity in the region as a whole to meet regional or national
policy objectives in these respects. The paradoxes of the region's economy
therefore constrain its potential in overcoming historical problems of geography,
culture and identity.

## The labour market

The paradoxical nature of the region is borne out when we look at the labour
market. The South West has had the fastest-growing civilian labour force in
England, increasing by 5.3 per cent in the period 1996–2001, almost twice as
fast as in England as a whole. Unlike every other region in England, the South
West saw a growth in the number of jobs of 32,000 between 2000 and 2001,
concentrated in the services sectors. As noted above, recent figures for the South
West highlight a (seasonally adjusted) employment rate of 78.4 per cent in late
2004. This relatively strong position is significantly above the national average
of 74.7 per cent.

In the 1995–2002 period, total employment rose by 9.4 per cent in the region
to 2,450,000. Employment in manufacturing increased by 0.3 per cent to

329,000 in 2002, and in services it increased by 14.3 per cent to 1,883,000, showing that the shift to a service-based economy is as important to the South West as it is to the rest of England. Between August and October 2004, total employment in the South West had risen to 2,680,000. The seasonally adjusted International Labour Organisation (ILO) unemployment rate for the same period was 3.2 per cent in the South West, the lowest of all the English regions. So the South West clearly has a very strongly performing labour market, but despite this it is failing to transform the regional economy. There are relatively few high-technology jobs: just over 5 per cent of all employees are involved in the high-technology sector, lower than in several other English regions, as is shown in Figure 12.4. This relative position is essentially due to loss of manufacturing jobs generally and also to increased competition globally and the resulting relocation of manufacturing activities to lower-cost locations outside the UK.

The region's potential is also limited by the relatively low proportion of research and development (R&D) jobs, which feeds through into not only potential employment in this sector but greater total employment through a higher overall level of demand. ONS data show that R&D as a proportion of GVA is significantly lower in the South West (just above 1.5 per cent in 2001), compared with the East (3.4 per cent). Also, across regions, expenditure on R&D is higher in the manufacturing sector than in the services sector. R&D expenditure in manufacturing in the East was 15.8 per cent of GVA in 2001, while the next highest spend was in the South East, at 12.8 per cent of GVA. The South West expenditure on R&D was around 2.0 per cent. Does this mean that a much lower proportion of the workforce in the South West is engaged in relatively lower value-added activities, compared with, say, the South East and East? If so, this may be part of the explanation for the relatively low share of foreign direct investment (FDI) in the region. The problem is that although foreign-owned firms are more productive, they are not performing the high-technology R&D activities that might attract other high-technology activities. Thus, although the region might have a strong foreign-owned sector, this is likely to decline under pressure of cost competition, particularly from emerging economies such as China and India. The loss of the foreign-owned sector could potentially be a big blow to the regional economy.

Another characteristic of the South West's relative weakness is that labour productivity (GVA per workforce job) has been consistently around 10 per cent lower than the national average, and more so in the manufacturing sector, as is shown in Figure 12.5. A paper by Eric McVittie (2004: 22, 25) suggests:

> The answer lies in the number of highly-skilled residents employed outside the region, not employed at all, or only working part-time. Some of this effect is a result of the older population, and peripheral location, of much of the South West . . .
>
> The effect of this was that, whilst the average skill level of South West residents is relatively high, the average skill level of those individuals who

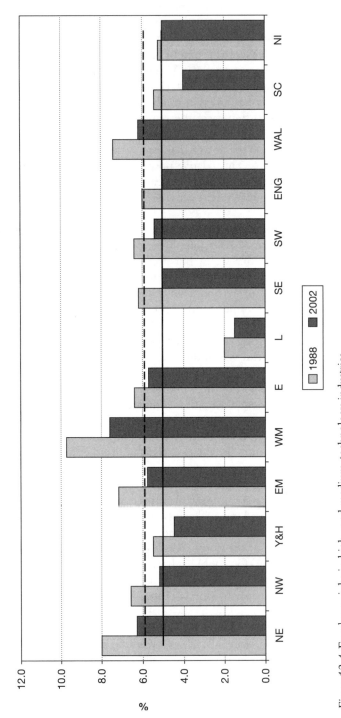

*Figure 12.4* Employee jobs in high- and medium-technology industries

*Source*: DTI and ONS (2004: 27)

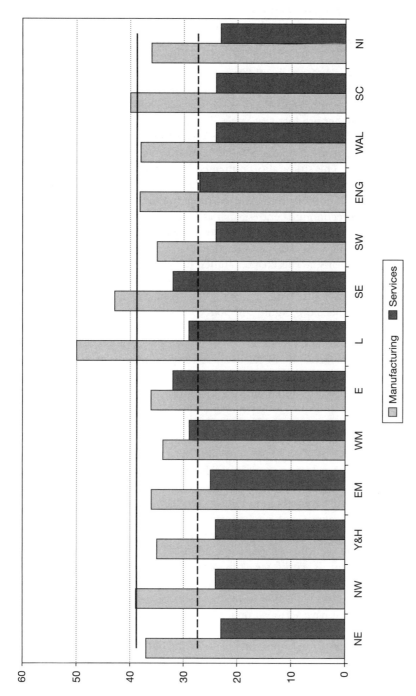

*Figure 12.5* Gross value added (GVA) per workforce job, 2001 (£000)

*Source:* DTI and ONS (2004: 9)

are actually employed within the South West is lower, and lower than that of the UK as a whole. This pattern appears to be related to the demographic structure of the South West's workforce. Much of the region's skills base, or 'human capital', is in the brains and hands of older residents, who are more likely to be economically inactive or to work shorter hours.

Overall, this analysis suggests that differences in skills levels explain some of the measured productivity differences between the UK regions, and between the sub-regions of the South West. Regions with a more highly skilled workforce seem to exhibit higher productivity levels. This conclusion has been confirmed by a recent study that the University of the West of England and University of Bath published in April 2005 for SWRDA, *Meeting the Productivity Challenge* (SWRDA, 2005). The study also confirmed the widely held view that the peripherality of some parts of the region could disadvantage the South West's regional economy if not fully mitigated by strong (physical and electronic) connectivity to major economic centres, such as London. The study also provides a number of other reasons for the relatively lower productivity in the South West compared with the UK average. Of particular significance is insufficient investment, particularly, as this chapter argues, in productive capacity. This and other reasons for lower productivity should be taken as serious issues for policy consideration in the South West so that the region may realise its potential for faster growth. Furthermore, significant policy interventions will be needed for the region to overcome the historical problems of its geography, particularly connectivity and accessibility.

An associated characteristic of relatively lower productivity in the region is lower average earnings. At almost £359 per week at the time of writing, average earnings in the South West (on a workplace basis) are around 11 per cent lower than the England average of £400 per week. Part of the explanation for this is that 'the South West has the oldest population structure of all the English regions. The percentage of retirement age is expected to increase from 21% of the total in 2002 to 27% in 2021' (South West Observatory, 2004: 143). A changing population profile not only will have important implications for the allocation of public funds to different services (e.g. health and welfare) but will mean lower demand for goods and producer services in the region, and slower growth in GVA. A number of labour market policy measures will need to be brought forward, including retaining people of retirement age in the workforce, promoting flexible working patterns, upgrading skills and encouraging 'economic' in-migration. If workforce skills across the region (not just in Bristol and its hinterlands) are not significantly upgraded in the medium term (five to seven years), the region will suffer from severe shortage of labour supply in the long term. This will have serious implications for the economic development prospects of the region.

Finally, perhaps the most important characteristic of the labour market in the South West in recent years has been the composition of employment growth, as is shown in Figure 12.6. It is clear that employment growth has been mainly

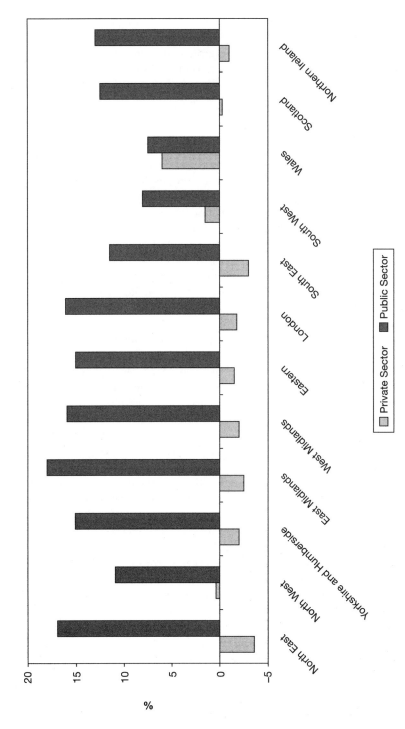

*Figure 12.6* Regional employment change in the public and private sectors, 1997–2004

Private Sector   Public Sector

in the public sector; that is to say, in the service sectors, or, as some might argue, in the non-productive parts of the economy. So, although the South West economy has been growing, driven by growth in domestic income and demand engendered by public sector employment growth, investment in the productive capacity of the region has been less forthcoming. This could constrain the capacity of the region to grow in future at faster growth rates than it has in recent years.

## Capacity utilisation in the region

At the start of this chapter it was pointed out that a negative output gap constrained the development of the regional economy. If the South West region is to 'rise', then capacity utilisation is an important indicator of future potential. Accurate measurement of output gap is essential to gauge instability in the economy and assess how growth might be improved. Capacity increases are dependent on increased demand, the accumulation of capital by investment (in equipment and buildings) and the accumulation of labour skills through the introduction of new technology and training. One way of measuring output gap is by assessing the level of capacity utilisation in manufacturing and services. Some qualitative data on capacity utilisation in the manufacturing sector in the region are shown in Figure 12.7.

In the manufacturing sector, the average capacity utilisation over thirteen quarters (Q4 2001 to Q4 2004) was 38 per cent. This leaves quite a significant amount of 'spare' capacity not utilised, which would translate into higher prices to absorb costs and, equally seriously, would be less price-competitive. However, throughout 2004, capacity utilisation declined and the short-term prospects were far from rosy. A similar picture emerges from the CBI survey (CBI, 2005) for manufacturing. This suggests that a balance of +62 of companies were working below capacity, and the balance of firms reporting increased output was −19. The fact that the region's manufacturing sector has the potential to grow faster is particularly apparent when compared with the private service sector. The experience of firms in the service sector differed significantly from that of manufacturers. Both the British Chambers of Commerce (BCC, 2005) and the CBI (CBI, 2005) surveys show that there was a marked increase in the proportion of businesses of all sizes working at full capacity in this sector. Although these are short-term changes in important sectors of the economy, they provide strong indications of the under-utilised potential of the South West economy. The question is, how much faster would the economy of the South West grow if both manufacturing and services businesses were operating at full capacity? Another issue relates to costs and prices in the region. With the exception of house prices in some areas, the South West does not suffer a cost and price disadvantage vis-à-vis the other English regions or nationally.

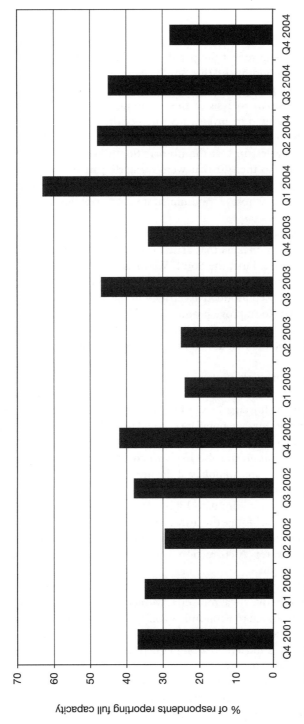

*Figure 12.7* Capacity utilisation in the manufacturing sector in the South West

*Source:* Boddy *et al.* (2005)

## Conclusions

Is the South West likely to rise or fall as the potential of its economy is either fulfilled or continues to reflect the paradoxes of the region itself? This chapter has explored the economy of the South West in order to investigate the challenges that this region presents to its inhabitants and policy-makers at various governmental levels. An analysis of the economy, the degree and scale of its peripherality, can be used to investigate whether the constraints of geography and history might be overcome in order to create greater regional coherence. The challenge is greatest in that the historic South West has been combined with two large areas to the east that were formerly part of another region to form a larger administrative but not economic territory. These two areas, moreover, are places whose economic hinterland stretches into two other regions.

These challenges, combined with various opportunities, suggest grounds for intervention by policy-makers that arise from the analysis of the South West economy set out above. First, the South West has a clear potential to grow at a faster rate. This conclusion is based mainly on two premises: the region has considerable non-utilised productive capacity in the manufacturing sector; and there is the potential to improve productivity. The challenge here is to expand domestic and export markets to increase utilisation rates in manufacturing and address the sets of factors that are constraining faster productivity growth rates in the region.

Second, the labour market in the South West provides both challenges and opportunities to have a greater impact on the regional economy over the longer term. The potential shortage of workforce in the region due to ageing and slower growth of working-age population could be addressed through improving higher skills and increasing labour productivity. Relatively higher house prices and lagging housing supply are also likely to constrain labour mobility within, and into, the region (an area of policy at the heart of current government policy on sustainable communities).

Next, the region must stimulate higher levels of investment in additional productive capacity, including the attraction of new FDI. Most of the recent investment and new jobs have come from the public sector, rather than the more productive private sector. A correction is required to ensure higher long-term prosperity of the region.

Fourth, national economic policy must support regional growth in the South West through more active fiscal measures. Monetary policy in the UK since the late 1990s has contributed to economic stability and lower inflation and interest rates. However, the effective rise in taxation has meant lower real disposable income in recent years and a reduction in the potential to increase consumption (and demand) in the economy.

Finally, an agreed realistic and practical vision and policies for the South West Region must address the economic constraints to the region's growth and development in the context of increasing global competition and possible changes in political, environmental, technological and societal spheres over the next twenty to thirty years. Government and various institutions – including SWRDA, the Regional Assembly and the CBI – must assume this responsibility, and provide sufficient funding for development in the long-term interest of the region.

The South West is an economically paradoxical region. Perhaps this is a more appropriate description than a 'peculiar' region, given its diverse economic geography, culture and identity. In concentrating on analysing its economic development, performance and potential, this chapter can make a contribution to understanding whether this paradoxical region will rise or if inclusion of such diverse elements within a single Government Office region will ultimately limit its potential. Addressing this issue lies at the heart of making sense of what is one of the most attractive regions in the UK, but also one that is not currently meeting the needs of all its citizens.

## Acknowledgements

The author is grateful for the generous assistance received from Anthony Plumridge, Senior Lecturer, University of the West of England, Bristol, and Eric McVittie and Rachel Fryett of the University of Plymouth Business School.

## References

BCC (2005) *Quarterly Economic Forecast*, London: British Chambers of Commerce

Boddy, M., Hudson, J.R., Plumridge, A. and Webber, J. (2005) *Regional Productivity Differentials: Explaining the Gap*, mimeo, Bristol: University of the West of England

CBI (2005) *Quarterly Business Survey*, London: Confederation of British Industry

Cope, I. and Flanagan, S. (2003) Regional and Sub-regional Gross Fixed Capital Formation, *Economic Trends*, 601: 36–68

Deacon, B. (2004) Under Construction: Cultural and Regional Formation in the South-West of England, *European Urban and Regional Studies*, 11(3): 213–25

Department of Trade and Industry (DTI) and Office for National Statistics (ONS) (2004) *Regional Competitiveness Indicators and State of the Regions*, London: The Stationery Office

Gough, J. (2004) The North/South Divide and 'Real' Regional GDP, *Business Economist*, 35(2): 8–15

HMSO (1973) *Devolution and Other Aspects of Government: An Attitudes Survey Commission on the Constitution*, Research Paper 7, London: HMSO

Lovering, J. (2001) The Coming Regional Crisis (and How to Avoid It)', *Regional Studies* 35(4): 349–54

McVittie, E. (2004) Productivity in the South West, in *The State of Regional Research*, Taunton: Association of Regional Observatories

Massey, G. (2002) The Attraction of Inward Investment to the South West Region, in Per Gripaios (ed.), *The South West Economy – Trends and prospects: 2002*, 14th edition, Plymouth: University of Plymouth

South West Observatory (2004) *State of the South West*, Taunton: South West Observatory

South West Regional Development Agency (SWRDA) (2005) *Meeting the Productivity Challenge*, Exeter: SWRDA

University of Plymouth (2004) *South West Regional Accounts for the South West Region* Plymouth: University of Plymouth

### Data sources

GDP/GVA growth: www.statistics.gov.uk
Tourism – overseas visitors: www.statistics.gov.uk
Business activity: www.rbs.co.uk/pmireports
Employment: www.rbs.co.uk/pmireports
House prices: www.nationwide.co.uk/hpi/
Unemployment rates: www.statistics.gov.uk
Transport: DTZ Pieda Consulting
South West economy: www.swo.org.uk

# 13  Looking for the South East

*Allan Cochrane*

## Introduction

Of all the British regions, the South East is the one whose conceptualisation is most awkward. It almost (but not quite) surrounds London, stretching from Southampton and Portsmouth in the south to Milton Keynes and Banbury in the north; and from Dover in the east to Reading, Newbury and Oxford in the west. The Government Office and the headquarters of the regional development agency are in resolutely suburban Guildford, perhaps reflecting the absence of any defining urban centre (apart from London) around which a regional identity might cohere.

The 'official' government region is somehow far too big and too fragmented to have a popular identity, and yet at the same time too small to capture the flows and networks that might define it as an economic activity space. It incorporates some 13.5 per cent of the population of the UK (with the highest population – at 8 million – of any UK region), and it accounts for over 15 per cent of UK GDP. It has an area of over 19,000 square kilometres and a coastline of 1,682 kilometres. At least according to the South East Economic Development Agency (SEEDA), its economy 'is the 22nd largest in the world'. In the 1990s, the region's economy grew faster than that of any other UK region and it also exports more goods than any other UK region (SEEDA, 2002a: 2). The average gross income of local residents is the highest in the UK. Over a quarter of regional GDP (2001 figures) is generated by financial and business services (significantly higher than the UK average). It is the location for one major international airport (Gatwick) and closely borders another (Heathrow). More surprisingly, perhaps, the share of engineering (at 7.2 per cent) is also higher than the UK average, and, although manufacturing as whole is less important than the UK average, in absolute terms manufacturing output (at £18.8 billion) in the region is still very high, behind only the North West (£20.4 billion) and the West Midlands (£18.9 billion) (SEEDA, 2002a).

The South East incorporates five urban areas with populations over 200,000 – Southampton, Portsmouth, Brighton, Milton Keynes and the Medway towns – as well as other major centres, such as Reading and Oxford. Internally, its sub-regions are diverse and sharply differentiated (see, for example, SEEDA,

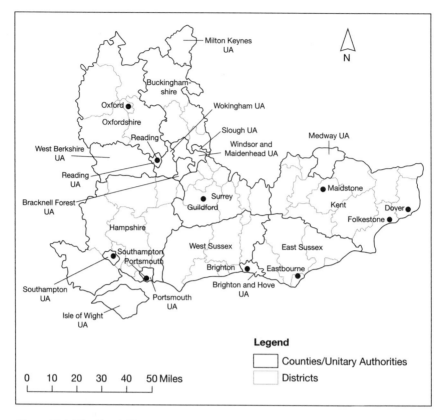

*Figure 13.1* The South East

2002a: 11–13), and planning documents point to the 'polycentric and rural nature' of the region (SEERA, 2003: 60). These divisions also find an expression in the institutional relations within the region. As John *et al.* (2002: 738) note, 'The region is fragmented into counties and sub-regions, which jealously guard their autonomy and fear centralization'. They point to the existence of a 'maze of competing partnerships'.

According to a survey conducted by MORI for the South East of England Regional Assembly (SEERA, 2004b), residents are more likely to identify two areas that are not in the 'South East' (Essex – by 29 per cent of those responding; and London – 25 per cent) as part of the region than three that are (Buckinghamshire – 22 per cent; Isle of Wight – 19 per cent; and Oxfordshire – 16 per cent). Although a relatively high proportion of the population (67 per cent) confirm that they are 'proud' to live in the region, a significant proportion (41 per cent) also agree that the South East is too diverse to be thought of as a single region. There is, however, at least one respect in which it is not particularly diverse. Whereas in the 2001 Census 29 per cent of people living in London did not describe themselves as 'white', that is true of only 5 per cent of those living in the South East, a figure well below the average for England and Wales. Of course, however, that also masks significant differences within the region, with significantly higher representation in some urban areas (such as Slough – 36 per cent; Reading – 13 per cent; Oxford – 13 per cent; Wycombe – 12 per cent; and Crawley – 11 per cent) and much lower ones in the commuter belts of Kent, Surrey and Buckinghamshire.

Regional 'stakeholders' interviewed for the MORI survey are explicit about the problems of regional identity. 'It just doesn't really work as a region,' says one. 'There is absolutely no [common] interest at all between Dover and Milton Keynes.' And another comments, 'We are not really a proper region. There are such enormous differences between the deprivation of Hastings and the huge prosperity of the Thames Valley, Berkshire and Oxfordshire . . . There is no community of interests. The only thing that links us is affordable housing.' As John *et al.* (2002: 734) confirm, 'Elite networks rarely identify with the South East region, nor do they mobilize behind regional institutions.'

Through another lens, however, it could be argued that the problem is a rather different one. Perhaps the region does not quite work because the administrative boundaries which define it are simply too restrictive. So, for example, from a popular perspective, the identity of the South East of England continues to be defined in large part by the presence of London as its (formally absent) core. Closeness to London is explicitly identified by residents in the MORI survey as one of the fundamental reasons for their satisfaction with life in the region. And, of course, it remains the place of employment for many of those who live in the South East – over half a million commuters travel in by rail every day. And much of the industry (whether production, financial services, knowledge based or logistics) in the South East is located there precisely because of its closeness to London. Some 6 per cent of London's GDP is generated by commuters from the South East, while 11 per cent of the residents of the South East who are in employment travel to London to work (Robinson, 2004: 14).

At the same time, the growth of the South East seems to bring ever more of England into its ambit, reflected, for example, in the plans for 'sustainable communities' which have led to the identification of 'sub-regions' that cut across the official regional boundaries as strategies have been developed for Milton Keynes and the South Midlands and for the Thames Gateway (ODPM, 2003). The former sits astride the South East, the East Midlands and the East of England; the latter incorporates parts of the South East, London and the East of England.

The remainder of this chapter focuses on three different ways in which the region is being and has been defined. The next section considers the construction of an 'official' government region, increasingly defined by the actions and plans of a range of regional agencies. That is followed by a section which explores arguments for the emergence of a 'Greater' South East (bringing together the government regions of the South East, London and the East of England). The third of these sections reflects on approaches that seek to define the region in 'relational' terms; that is, through the social and economic flows and networks that cut across it. Finally, a concluding section briefly considers the implications of each of these approaches for public policy.

## Official representations: making up a region

Development agencies were set up throughout England in 1999, and fostering the competitiveness of regions was presented as a means of providing them with a secure (competitive) economic base, capable of underpinning the financial well-being of their residents (moving beyond welfarism – see, for example, Morgan, 1997). Collectively, the competitiveness of individual regions was seen as a way of enhancing the overall competitiveness of the country, but the regional agenda was also presented as a route to political and economic redistribution. It was intended to 'promote sustainable economic development' (DETR, 1997), with a 'greater focus on wealth creation and jobs' (John Prescott, quoted in Jones and MacLeod, 1999: 301). In the coded language of New Labour politics, a focus on the 'regions' offered a means of acknowledging the existence of economic inequality, as well as promising a programme of renewal through a form of economic self-help, rather than redistribution.

The arrival of the new regionalism, however, had a particular significance for the South East of England. Unlike the era of the Keynesian welfare state in the middle of the twentieth century, when 'regional policy' was explicitly oriented towards shifting 'growth' from the more prosperous to the less prosperous regions of the country, this time the South East, too, is a region, apparently driven by similar needs to the others. Regional policy is no longer a policy for a set of 'regions', defined as those places with economic and social problems which lie outside the golden heartlands of London and the Home Counties. *Every* region is being enjoined to improve its economic competitiveness. SEEDA makes no bones about its purpose, with a strap-line that promises that it is 'Working for England's World Class Region' and the explicit claims that it is the 'driving force of the UK's economy' and the 'powerhouse of the UK economy' (see SEEDA, 1999, 2002a, 2002b).

While joint planning arrangements (given the Soviet-style acronym of SERPLAN) pre-dated the creation of the regional development agency and its associated regional assembly, they had little authority in shaping any emergent South East regional identity or, indeed, its economic direction, even if they did cover a wider area and included London in their remit (see, for example, Lock, 1989). Alongside the significantly expanded Government Office of the South East (GOSE), the development agency has taken on the role of giving the region more of a shared identity and, perhaps more important, attempting to shape its economic direction. Not surprisingly, the new agencies start from the borders they have been given and seek through planning and promotional practice to give them a meaning that goes beyond the bureaucratic. Following the logic of the new regionalism, the region is effectively to be defined by its competitive position; formally its competitive position with respect to regions elsewhere in Europe, but at least implicitly within the UK, too.

SEEDA explicitly defines the South East of England in terms of its economic success – as the UK's growth region, the region whose prosperity drives that of the rest of the country. The drive to regional competitiveness is therefore identified as a national as well as a regional imperative, since although the South East is understood to have grown faster than other regions of the UK – and, indeed, faster than London – over the last decade, it is also stressed that the South East's competitors are outside the UK, and particularly in Europe (see, for example, SEEDA, 2002a). So, while in one context the scale of the South East's economy is stressed (as larger than some national economies), in this context it is emphasised that the South East's GDP is twenty-third among the regions of Europe (SEEDA, 2002a: 9). If the South East does not succeed in claiming its rightful place among Europe's elite regions, it is implied, then the UK (and the UK's other regions) will also suffer.

SEEDA's Regional Economic Strategy (RES) forefronts an image of the region as 'a dynamic, diverse and knowledge-based economy that excels in innovation and turning ideas into wealth creating enterprise'. The aim of the strategy is to ensure that by 2012 the region is acknowledged to be one of the fifteen 'top performing regional economies' in the world (SEEDA, 2002b: 8; see also Huggins, 2001, 2003). The South East is said to be the UK's 'global gateway' and 'an international region', providing a way into both the UK and Europe for multinational companies, attracting almost as much foreign direct investment as London (SEEDA, 2002b: 13). Stress is placed on the knowledge industries, and from this perspective it is simply taken for granted that it is a more or less coherent 'region' capable of being understood as a unified whole.

But the current policy game has another vitally important aspect, which encourages a focus on the differences within the region and particularly the differences in income levels and prosperity within it. Just as others point to the differences in wealth between regions, so in the South East emphasis is placed on differences within it. Since the current politics of regionalism require regional actors to emphasise the problems they face in order to attract resources, there has recently been a remarkable turnaround in official representations. Where it was once left to agencies such as the South East Economic Development Strategy (SEEDS, a local-authority-sponsored initiative of the 1980s) (SEEDS, 1987; see also Breugel, 1992) to point to divisions within the South East, now the new regional agencies sponsor research to identify them so that they have bargaining chips to use in the search for state funding.

The broad divisions identified in the various texts of the regional agencies are clear enough. A growth belt – or 'area of economic success' – is identified in the west of the region, stretching from Winchester to Milton Keynes and Newbury to Gatwick, while a coastal belt to the east, incorporating areas bordering the Channel and the Thames Estuary, is identified as facing problems of decline (in both tourism and other traditional industries). Finally, an area is identified that has a concentration of declining industries, particularly those associated with defence or port activities (see, for example, SEEDA, 2002b: 12–14).

There is an explicit focus on 'tackling disadvantage' within the region. So, for example, although unemployment is low, the point is made that the numbers unemployed in the South East are high in absolute terms; while educational achievement is high in Buckinghamshire, it is low in Portsmouth; while the employment rate for the region as a whole is higher than the national average, it is lower in the Isle of Wight, Brighton and Hove, and Southampton (SEEDA, 2002b: 10). The South East Region Social Inclusion Statement (SIS), published in 2002, lists areas suffering deprivation; in particular it highlights the extent to which there are pockets of deprivation in the region's coastal towns, such as Hastings and Thanet. Of the 119 wards identified as being among the 20 per cent most deprived in the country, 94 are in coastal towns (GOSE, 2002: 40); 46 of the 50 most deprived wards in the region are in Hampshire, Sussex and Kent, 'mainly along the "coastal strip"' (SEERA, 2003: 27).

The impact of the closure of the east Kent coalfields is also noted as an issue in the SIS, since this is said to have left 'social scars', as well as dereliction, while individual wards in some of the region's urban areas contain significantly deprived populations – particular attention is drawn by GOSE (2002: 40) to a ward in Portsmouth in which child poverty is a particular problem and to a ward in Brighton where a poor skills level is identified as an issue of major concern, while a ward in Slough is identified as having the worst problems of poor housing and overcrowding in the region. Even in a region that seeks so strongly to present itself as a centre for knowledge-based industry, the variation in educational and skills levels between different parts can be stark. Nearly 60 per cent of working-age adults who live in Wokingham have qualifications at NVQ level 3 or above, but in Medway the figure is below 35 per cent (SEERA, 2003: 27).

Rural decline is also an issue that concerns the various agencies, both because of the fall in available agricultural employment and because of the reduction in housing available for local residents and their children. Not surprisingly, perhaps, attention is drawn to the fact that the experience of social exclusion may be worse for people trapped in more prosperous areas (like those in the South East), because access to appropriate services may be restricted by lack of overall demand (GOSE, 2002: 40–1). And, although in proportional terms deprivation in the South East is clearly far lower than in other regions of the UK, SEEDA (2002b: 42) also stresses that the 'sheer size of the South East means that the actual number of excluded people in the region is comparable to and can exceed those in regions that are better known for their high levels of deprivation', while the Draft Regional Plan also notes that the disparities between the incomes of individuals within the region are the widest of any English region (SEERA, 2004c: 2).

The search for a spatial pattern to issues of deprivation and social exclusion is ultimately unconvincing, however, since the most deprived wards are scattered like a rather disconnected necklace along the coast from the Thames Gateway, through Thanet and Hastings, to Brighton and Hove and on to the Isle of Wight and Southampton, with a few others dotted around in a series of urban areas – in Reading, Slough, High Wycombe, Milton Keynes and Oxford.

The explanations for the problems facing people who live in these wards owe little to any shared set of 'regional' issues. On the contrary, listing the areas concerned helps once more to indicate the relative incoherence of the region being so actively constructed in the planning documents and economic strategies. They are discussed together not because they have much in common, but because they happen to have been clustered together in a newly invented region.

If one vision for the South East focuses on competitiveness and growth, stressing what is seen to be the region's key role in underpinning the UK's economic prosperity, a second is defensive, recognising the inevitability of growth, but seeking to protect residents from its environmental and other impacts. In a sense this captures key tensions within the region – it incorporates the old 'Home Counties' (see, for example, Hamnett, 1984), reinforced by the rise of an extended suburbia at the same time as being the location for expanding service industries, particularly in financial and business services. One characteristic of development in the 1990s was the attempt to construct forms of suburb that drew on images of rurality in the South East, apparently to escape from urban sprawl into the protected space of the countryside (Murdoch and Marsden, 1994; Marsden *et al.*, 1996; see also Allen *et al.*, 1998: chs 3 and 4). The growth of employment in the new industries both underpins the prosperity of local residents and threatens their 'quality of life'. It is in this context that the language of 'sustainability' is so effectively mobilised to protect the new middle classes from growth's more unpleasant consequences.

'Sustainability' is, of course, a term that can take on many meanings. Sometimes the emphasis is on finding ways of ensuring that economic growth will be sustained (e.g. through the provision of necessary infrastructure, or housing for key workers), while on other occasions the emphasis may be placed on ways of protecting areas from environmental depredation, ensuring that transport networks remain effective, flooding is avoided or the quality of life for residents is maintained (see, for example, Robinson, 2004; Foley, 2004). The tension between these approaches is particularly apparent in the different ways the language is mobilised by the new regional agencies. SEEDA is more concerned with the former, while SEERA is more likely to emphasise the latter, particularly as a means of defending the relatively privileged position of existing residents of the South East. An Integrated Regional Framework has been developed with a range of regional partners, and an explicit emphasis is placed on finding ways 'to reduce the negative effects of economic growth' (SEERA, 2004a).

In the draft South East plan approved for consultation by SEERA in 2004, the tension is explicitly acknowledged:

> On the one hand economic growth and concomitant development has been a necessary condition for prosperity and social and environmental action. On the other, some consider that the price of that growth in terms of resource consumption and other impacts is too high and unsustainable in the long-term.
>
> (SEERA, 2004c: 4)

Despite the care of its authors to present the tension explicitly, when the draft plan was presented to the Assembly in November 2004, the range of proposals for housing growth in the region was rejected and a lower range was agreed for wider consultation. In other words, for however brief a moment, the protective instincts of the interests represented in the Assembly overcame the sponsors of growth. Their core concern is to find ways of coping with the 'problems of success' (Foley, 2004). This has been expressed more positively in the conclusions of the report of the Commission on Sustainable Development in the South East (2005), which was supported by the South East's county councils and undertaken through the Institute for Public Policy Research. The report suggests that it is possible to reconcile continuing prosperity for the region with environmental sustainability and greater social equality through a strategy focused on 'smarter growth', in contrast to what is perceived to be the narrower growth agenda of SEEDA and the government.

'Affordable housing' is a mantra shared by all the agencies involved in the region, and a clear concern of residents in the MORI survey referred to above. However, the understanding of what is meant by 'affordable housing' is not necessarily shared in quite so straightforward a fashion. For residents, of course, it is a complaint about the costs they incur by living in the South East, although (in some areas, at least) tempered by a desire to ensure that development does not threaten their lifestyles. For SEEDA, GOSE and the Office of the Deputy Prime Minister (ODPM), 'affordable housing' is a coded expression of the need to provide the necessary infrastructure to underpin continued growth. These issues are particularly clearly identified in the Barker Report, commissioned by the Treasury and the ODPM, within which it is strongly argued that substantial additional growth in housing supply will be required (particularly in the South East) if house prices are not to continue to rise dramatically (Barker, 2004). If growth in the 1980s and 1990s was held back by labour market constraints and overheating (see, for example, Peck and Tickell, 1995), then the task must be to find ways to reduce the likelihood of a similar occurrence. Providing housing for those who are needed to sustain the boom, even when (like teachers and other public sector workers, but also the growing army of service workers in retail, distribution, hotels and catering) they are not highly paid 'knowledge workers', is identified as a priority (see, for example, ODPM, 2003).

It is in this context that the language of social exclusion and deprivation, of internal divisions within the region, and the search for ways of tackling these problems also has the paradoxical policy benefit of offering an apparently painless way of resolving the tensions – growth may be delivered through the regeneration of deprived areas (such as the Thames Gateway, the other areas on the 'coastal strip' and parts of Kent) as well as development on the edge of the region (in Milton Keynes – to which there is a long tradition of shifting development to defend the leafy suburbs of south Buckinghamshire) (see, for example, Charlesworth and Cochrane, 1994). The quality of life of the prosperous 'core' can be protected, while growth is diverted to those parts of the region that are identified as needing it.

Although the focus of the regional agencies is on the narrowly defined South East as a more or less coherent entity, there is also a recognition that its connections to and linkages with neighbouring regions are significant. The existence of boundaries is taken for granted, but the potential importance of 'cross-boundary links' is acknowledged (SEEDA, 2002b: 13). There is even an acknowledgement that there may be a shared interest between Kent (particularly its coastal towns) and regional authorities in northern France. The South East is identified as an 'integrated region' – that is, a region 'integrated' into a wider national context – and, in this context at least, the interrelationship with London is recognised as paramount. Other explicitly identified linkages include the central South Coast (which stretches from Portsmouth and Southampton into the South West region) and the Oxford to Cambridge arc (which rather optimistically promises the creation of a major cluster of knowledge-based industries that stretches across the north of the region from Oxford to Cambridge in the East of England) (see O2C Arc, 2003). The most significant linkages, however, are probably those associated with the Thames Gateway and Milton Keynes and the South Midlands, since they (along with Ashford, on a smaller scale) have been identified as areas for significant growth in the government's plans for the development of 'sustainable communities' (ODPM, 2003, 2004; GOSE *et al.*, 2004). The extent of these proposals and their likely impact (as populations double in size and major investment takes place in infrastructure and housing) make it difficult to sustain a narrow focus on the official South East, since many of the most important development decisions affecting that region will be taking place either outside it or on its extreme edges, even if one of the reasons for focusing development there may be to protect the heartlands from the impact of growth – maintaining a relatively 'green and pleasant land' for those in the suburbs and 'rural' exurbs of the region.

## Bigger is better: the 'Greater' South East

If the curiously truncated and incoherent official region is unconvincing as a representation that reflects either popular understanding or economic linkages, is there any other basis on which the 'South East' may be understood and identified?

Until 2001, when the most recent Regional Planning Guidance (RPG) was issued (GOSE *et al.*, 2001), for planning purposes the South East continued to be defined as including London and the counties of Essex, Bedfordshire and Hertfordshire, so that the South East was made up of London and the rest of the South East. The latter was effectively the doughnut around London, which meant (in principle at least) that a rather different regional vision was in play. Some of the same features remain identifiable (Milton Keynes and Ashford are identified for growth and the Thames Gateway is identified as a priority for regeneration), but the region is seen as a whole and at least some of today's border regions – those with London and the East of England – are in the centre rather than on the edge of the region (and the fourth of the ODPM's sustainable communities of growth, stretching from London north into Cambridgeshire, is also included).

In this context, perhaps those who espouse the notion of a 'Greater' South East have a stronger claim to be identifying a more coherent approach to understanding the region. In their discussion of the South East as a 'core region', Breheny and Congdon (1989) start from this understanding of the region (and sometimes go further to include other parts of the 'Western crescent' identified by Hall *et al.*, 1987). They suggest that this South East is 'an example of a "core" region, occupying a dominant position, economically, politically and culturally, within a capitalist economy which exhibits distinct and enduring uneven development' (Breheny and Congdon, 1989: 1).

Gordon (2003, 2004), too, argues strongly that the focus should be on the 'Greater' South East, in his case incorporating the East of England as well as the government regions of London and the South East. His starting point is an understanding of this super-region as a city-region, one whose central focus is London. It is the spread of activities building on the strengths of the London economy, coupled with a transport network that focuses on London, that helps to define the region. However, Gordon emphasises that developments since the 1970s have begun to redefine the region, as the spread of business services functions and high-tech industry has helped to build a wider range of centres with their own linkages into national and international networks. As he puts it: 'In this regionalized version of London, outer areas now substantially contribute to its agglomeration economies, as well as continuing to benefit from those rooted in central London' (Gordon, 2004: 41).

In their commentary on the results of the 2001 Census, Dorling and Thomas (2004: 183) highlight the extent to which this area can be seen as the making of a new metropolis, 'with a dense urban core, suburbs, parks and a rural fringe'. Garreau (1991: 108) similarly suggests that the South East of England (which he calls 'London') is a particularly powerful example of the spread of edge cities, which he identifies as fundamental to contemporary urban development in the USA. Building on the work of Dorling and Thomas (2004), Gordon *et al.* (2004: 30) argue that 'the effective London economy extends well beyond the borders of Greater London, encompassing most of South Eastern England and perhaps some areas beyond, in what is for many purposes a single labour market'.

Gordon *et al.* are identifying the emergence of a region whose coherence is not simply a function of its core. They draw on the work of Simmie *et al.* (2002) to highlight the interdependence of the different parts of the region – both noting the dispersal of innovative firms across the region (i.e. not simply clustered in London) and emphasising that regional connections (including air services and labour markets) sustain the region's growth. Simmie (2003: 614) confirms that the Greater South East 'contains the highest concentration of innovative firms in the UK'. Pain (2004) looks at advanced producer services, exploring the extent to which the South East is becoming polycentric, with functional connections emerging between sub-centres and not just through London. Evidence strongly suggests that links through London are still the most important but also highlights linkages that cross-cut the region between Cambridge and Reading, Reading and Southampton, and Milton Keynes and Southampton (see also SEERA, 2004c: 43–4, which presents evidence from the same research project to support the argument for the emergence of a series of functional urban – commuting – regions across the Greater South East, as well as highlighting the growth of cross-commuting between towns in the wider region, and not just to London).

Gordon (2004: 42) argues that such are the interconnections within this region that it is only through regional success that internal divisions and inequalities can be minimised: 'For spatial equity within the GSE, as well as for its overall employment rate, it is the competitive performance of the region as a whole which matters.' From this perspective, the current structures of regional governance and planning not only are inappropriate but may actually have negative consequences for the development of the region and, because of its centrality to the UK economy and its wider role as a centre for innovation, for the well-being of the country as a whole.

Gordon shares the emphasis of SEEDA (albeit for the wider region) on the need for the South East to be supported in achieving economic success, and for this reason he maintains that 'it deserves serious attention to its needs and management on a continuing basis and structures which maximize the chance of this occurring' (Gordon, 2004: 64). 'The Greater South East', it is argued, 'is now effectively one economic and labour market region to which policies need to be developed in an integrated way' (Gordon *et al.*, 2003: 9). Gordon acknowledges a potential split between the 'region' with which people may identify as residents and the Greater South East for which he argues there needs to be coherent planning and political leadership. His own suggestion is for a political leader connected into national government, heading up 'a single, strengthened super-regional Government Office' which would work with a more fine-grained and disaggregated set of regional assemblies and agencies, although not necessarily at the same scale. (Barker (2004) draws a similar con-clusion, suggesting that an independent regional planning executive be given the responsibility for advising on housing growth.) In other words, Gordon's way of dealing with the tensions between the expectations of residents and the needs of the national economy is explicitly to separate the role of representation (the various regional and sub-regional agencies) from that of planning and fostering economic development (a super-government office).

## Beyond the boundaries

Another way of moving beyond the existing boundaries is to consider regions as what Allen *et al.* (1998) refer to as 'spatialised social relations'; that is, as places which are actively constructed by the economic and social networks and linkages within them and which connect them to other places. Unlike the fixed entities generated by the texts and the rhetoric of the official regionalism, this approach suggests rather more fluid possibilities and implies the possibility of overlapping regions of different sizes. These are regions that may vary across time and are made and remade by human interaction (within which – of course – the cartographers, government officials and regional politicians play their own parts). These regions do not have clear and permanent boundaries, and are defined by their positions within networks, which stretch out much wider nationally and internationally through a series of interconnections.

Allen *et al.* (1998) argue that in the 1980s and 1990s the 'South East' was defined and understood itself as a 'growth' region, and specifically a region of neo-liberal growth. Its national dominance was expressed through this definition, which reflected a particular confluence of political, cultural and economic dynamics. Although it was presented as a model of deregulated growth, in practice it relied on a high degree of state intervention to achieve the particular forms of 'deregulation' that were driven through and tended to advantage the South East, as well as significant investment in large-scale public infrastructure (e.g. road construction, from bypasses to the M25). The growth of the South East was predicated on decline elsewhere in the UK, in the wake of large-scale (state-sponsored) industrial restructuring. In other words, it was not possible to view the region as self-contained and simply building its own competitiveness.

Viewing the South East as a 'growth' region confirms the limitations of more static definitions, and it also highlights some of the difficulties of utilising generally available data in pursuing dynamic processes of change. There is no single correct definition of the 'growth' region. It stretches far beyond the 'standard' region for some forms of economic and cultural relationships (e.g. to Cambridge, through the threads connecting high-technology industry, and pulled to Wiltshire by the tentacles of the luxury – 'country' – housing market, as well as the M4 corridor) (see Gordon *et al.*, 2003). Meanwhile, within the 'standard' region there are substantial spatio-social discontinuities – holes and hot spots (the holes represented by the high-water mark of Fordism in places like the Medway towns, Eastleigh and Southampton, and the hot spots represented by Gatwick Airport, developments around Heathrow, the western 'wedge' and the new town of Milton Keynes). From this perspective, it could be argued that the region is spatially discontinuous, in the sense that some places currently defined as being in the South East are not (e.g. much of Kent and the coastal South), while other places located far away from the current borders of the region should be seen as part of it, precisely because they are so tightly connected through economic and cultural networks, in what Dorling and Thomas (2004: 183) identify as the 'provincial archipelago of city islands'.

Some have gone further to argue that the formal and informal networks that define the 'power' of London and the South East are national (and potentially international), rather than regional. Peck and Tickell (1992) see this as a weakness as well as a strength. They argue that in the boom years of the 1980s the 'region enjoyed strong economic growth as a result of its privileged place in *national* regulation strategies and *international* accumulation strategies, but subsequently was shown to lack appropriate *regional* regulatory mechanisms for the sustenance of growth' (Peck and Tickell, 1992: 359). For Amin *et al.* (2003:

9–12), this is a fundamental issue which sets the 'South East' in a longer cultural history. They relate its national role back to a 'courtly' structure (focused on the crown and state) through which the apparently necessary centrality of London and the South East is reproduced in terms of the institutional relations of class and politics with their associated powers of exclusion and inclusion. 'London is the presumptive location of the national,' they argue. 'It is in this sphere that the political meets the economic meets the national imaginary' (Amin *et al.*, 2003: 13). Amin and Thrift (1994: 17) acknowledge that the South East does not exhibit the rich set of finely grained and regionally focused cultural and economic networks that might be characterised as 'institutional thickness' (often seen as a prerequisite for economic growth), but it is where the national elites learn to be elites.

Amin *et al.* (2003: 17) question the extent to which the North/South divide should be seen simply as a consequence of the working out of market forces. On the contrary, they suggest that the centralisation of power in London and the South East means that a significant element of 'national policy making effectively functions as an unacknowledged regional policy for the South Eastern part of England'. So, for example, they suggest that national economic policy is overly influenced by the state of the regional economy in London and the South East, with steps being taken to restrain the economy when the region is 'overheating', even when the rest of the country still has significant capacity for growth (see also Morgan, 2002: 800). In sharp contrast to the arguments of Gordon *et al.* (2003: 65–80), who suggest that the South East is a net contributor to the rest of the country through its taxes and the public expenditure for which they pay, Amin *et al.* (2003) suggest that even in these terms the super-region is treated favourably. They argue, for example, that tax policy which reduces income tax for high earners in practice shifts resource to London and the South East because of the concentration of high earners in the region.

Effectively, Amin *et al.* (2003) turn the claims often made for the South East as a 'growth' region that drives the British economy on their head. Instead they suggest that it tends to work as a drain on the rest of the country. If the South East is a 'core' region, then, according to this analysis, it is one whose relationship with the rest of the British economy has been rather peculiar, since in the 1980s 'in effect the political economy of the south east as "growth region" operated in ways which restricted the possibility of growth in other regions of the UK' (Allen *et al.*, 1998: 119). Amin *et al.* (2003) highlight the drain of graduates to the region from elsewhere in the UK, which reinforces the centralisation of the knowledge economy in London and the South East at the expense of other parts of the country.

Hepworth and Spencer (2003) similarly highlight the extent to which London and the South East dominate the British knowledge economy and refer to the existence of an 'uneven or centralised geography of the knowledge economy', pointing to the impact of '"brain drains" that undermine capacity building, graduate underemployment and local bottlenecks for people with intermediate qualifications'. There is, they argue, 'a relatively distributed pattern of growth

in qualifications and the graduate labour pool contrasting with a highly concentrated pattern of knowledge-intensive job creation that favours London and its
hinterland, and the South East more widely' (Hepworth and Spencer, 2003:
Executive Summary). Among graduates who move to work in a region which
they did not study in or originate from, the Greater South East is the most
favoured first destination (Uzzell, 2004: 20). This argument is reinforced by the
extent to which the South East (and London, in particular) draws in migrants
(both technically skilled and unskilled) from other countries to replace those
who move out to other regions, or relocate within the wider South East (see,
for example, Uzzell, 2004). In the early 1990s, Fielding (1992) noted the role
of the South East as an 'escalator' region. His research indicated that the South
East effectively attracted the upwardly mobile young into high-end occupations
and also into the South East housing market. At a later stage of the life cycle he
suggested this allowed them to trade in their assets and move out to other
regions, albeit still predominantly in the South of the country (helping to create
a wider 'South East').

## What sort of South East?

The three versions of the South East that have been discussed in this chapter all
have a strong claim to represent the 'real' South East and each has significant
implications for public policy.

The first is in a sense the embodiment of current public policy, in the context
of a newly regionalised England. The regional agencies play an active part in
defining the region, identifying relations (including divisions) within it and
giving some meaning to the borders around it, not least as they identify cross-
border linkages and internal inequalities and divisions within the region. But
they also embody some of the tensions within the policy, in particular those
between the drive for 'growth' and the desire of residents to defend their quality
of life (particularly those residents in relatively privileged enclaves) – given
institutional expression to some extent in the different roles of SEEDA and
SEERA, and ultimately policed by GOSE. And they reflect the difficulties of
managing a 'region' whose borders are so porous and which does not include
many of the areas whose development effectively shapes what is possible within
it. The drivers of change are not 'regional' drivers, at least if the existing borders
of the government region are held to incorporate them.

The second finds a route through by identifying a Greater South East that
seeks to capture the broader economic linkages and to create an entity within
which plans can be given some meaning. The institutional tensions reflected in
the first model are overcome by suggesting that economic and regional planning
(i.e. planning for growth in the interests not only of the region but of the
country as whole) would be conducted under the aegis of a super-government
office, which would work with and negotiate with a wide variety of regional
and local agencies capable of reflecting the wishes of those they represented.
The extent to which such a powerful agency could ever be created is of course

an open question, and it is perhaps worth pointing out that the population of this super-region would be almost half that of England. Its construction in this way would have fundamental (and potentially threatening) consequences for the rest of England (as well as the devolved countries of the UK).

The third (certainly as articulated by Amin *et al.*, 2003) takes an approach that implicitly questions the value of regional structures of the sort that currently exist, but also questions the extent to which (whatever its borders) the South East can be seen as a positive driver of the UK economy. On the contrary, it is argued, the central role that is currently accorded to the South East in the UK economy and society masks the extent to which it effectively undermines growth elsewhere in the country, by sucking in talent as well as public and private investment. Instead of a programme of redistribution from the South East to the rest of the country, however, they argue for a different starting point, in which public policy is 'decentred' and the activities which it is currently simply assumed will be undertaken in London and the South East are instead located elsewhere.

Like the first, the third also emphasises the significance of inequalities within the region, but its proponents suggest that issues of distribution are not best handled through the promotion of further growth. Like the second, the third also highlights the emergence of an expanded economic and social activity space, even if it has little interest in seeing it expand further – at least at the expense of the rest of the country. The vision of the South East captured on both the second and the third approaches suggests that it dominates the 'rest of the country'. One challenge this presents for policy-makers is how this such domination is to be interpreted: whether it should be (or can be) managed positively to benefit the country as a whole, or whether it needs to be challenged rather more fundamentally. Given the balance of population as well as economic activity between the Greater South East and the 'rest of the country', this issue needs to be resolved quickly – otherwise the 'core' region will be dominant not only because of the linkages and networks that flow through it, but because in absolute terms it contains the majority of the country's population as well as the bulk of its economic activity.

## References

Allen, J., Massey, D. and Cochrane, A. (1998) *Rethinking the Region*. London: Routledge.

Amin, A. and Thrift, N. (eds.) (1994) *Globalisation, Institutions and Regional Development in Europe*. Oxford: Oxford University Press.

Amin, A., Massey, D. and Thrift, N. (2003) *Decentering the Nation: A Radical Approach to Regional Inequality*. London: Catalyst.

Barker, K. (2004) *Review of Housing Policy: Delivering Stability: Securing Our Future Housing Needs*. Final Report, London: The Stationery Office.

Breheny, M. and Congdon, P. (1989) Introduction, in M. Breheny and P. Congdon (eds.), *Growth and Change in a Core Region: The Case of the South East*. London Papers in Regional Science 20, London: Pion.

Breugel, I. (ed.) (1992) *The Rest of the South-East: A Region in the Making?* Basildon: SEEDS.

Charlesworth, J. and Cochrane, A. (1994) Tales of the suburbs: the local politics of growth in the South-East of England, *Urban Studies*, 31, 10: 1723–38.

Commission on Sustainable Development in the South East (2005) *Final Report*. London: Institute for Public Policy Research.

Department of the Environment, Transport and the Regions (DETR) (1997) *Building Partnerships for Prosperity*. London: HMSO.

Dorling, D. and Thomas, B. (2004) *People and Places: A 2001 Census Atlas of the UK*. Bristol: Policy Press.

Fielding, A. (1992) *Migration and the Metropolis: Patterns and Processes of Inter-Regional Migration to and from South East England*. Final Report, Department of the Environment Research Contract PECD 7/1/378.

Foley, J. (2004) *The Problems of Success: Reconciling Economic Growth and Quality of Life in the South East*. Commission on Sustainable Development in the South East, Working Paper 2, London: Institute for Public Policy Research.

Garreau, J. (1991) *Edge City: Life on the New Frontier*. New York: Doubleday.

Gordon, I. (2003) Three into one: joining up the Greater South East, *Town and Country Planning*, 72, 11: 342–3.

—— (2004) A disjointed dynamo: the Greater South East and inter-regional relationships, *New Economy*, 11, 1: 40–4.

Gordon, I., Travers, T. and Whitehead, C. (2003) *London's Place in the UK Economy 2003*. London: London School of Economics for the Corporation of London.

—— (2004) *London's Place in the UK Economy 2004*. London: London School of Economics for the Corporation of London.

Government Office for the South East (GOSE) (2002) *South East Region Social Inclusion Statement*. Guildford: Government Office for the South East.

GOSE, GOEE and GOL (2001) *Regional Planning Guidance for the South East (RPG 9)*. Department of the Environment, Transport and the Regions, London: The Stationery Office.

GOSE, GOEM and GOEE (2004) *Secretary of State's Proposed Changes: Milton Keynes and South Midlands Sub-Regional Strategy: Alterations to Regional Spatial Strategy for the East of England, East Midlands and South East of England*. Nottingham: Government Office for the East Midlands.

Hall, P., Breheny, M., McQuaid, R. and Hart, D. (1987) *Western Sunrise: The Genesis of Britain's Major High Tech Corridor*. Hemel Hempstead: Allen & Unwin.

Hamnett, C. (1984) Life in the cocktail belt, *Geographical Magazine*, 56, 10: 534–8.

Hepworth, M. and Spencer, G. (2003) *A Regional Perspective on the Knowledge Economy in Great Britain*. Report for the Department of Trade and Industry, London: Local Futures Group.

Huggins, R. (2001) *Global Index of Regional Knowledge Economies: Benchmarking South East England*. Report prepared by Robert Huggins Associates, Guildford: SEEDA.

—— (2003) *Global Index of Regional Knowledge Economies: Benchmarking South East England 2003 Update*. Report prepared by Robert Huggins Associates, Guildford: SEEDA.

John, P., Musson, S. and Tickell, A. (2002) England's problem region: regionalism in the South East, *Regional Studies*, 36, 7: 733–41.

Jones, M. and MacLeod, G. (1999) Towards a regional renaissance? Reconfiguring and rescaling England's economic governance, *Transactions of the Institute of British Geographers*, NS 24: 295–313.

Lock, D. (1989) *Riding the Tiger: Planning the South of England: A Discussion Paper.* London: Town and Country Planning Association.

Marsden, T., Flynn, A., Murdoch, J., Lowe, P. and Munton, R. (1996) *Constructing the Countryside: An Approach to Rural Development.* London: UCL Press.

Morgan, K. (1997) The learning region: institutions, innovation and regional renewal, *Regional Studies*, 3: 491–503.

—— (2002) The English question: regional perspectives on a fractured nation, *Regional Studies*, 36, 7: 797–810.

Murdoch, J. and Marsden, T. (1994) *Reconstituting Rurality: The Changing Countryside in an Urban Context.* London: UCL Press.

O2C Arc (2003) *The Spirit of Innovation.* Oxford2Cambridge Arc.

Office of the Deputy Prime Minister (ODPM) (2003) *Sustainable Communities: Building for the Future.* London: Office of the Deputy Prime Minister. Available at http://www.odpm.gov.uk/stellent/groups/odpm_communities/documents/page/odpm_comm_022184.hcsp

—— (2004) *Thames Gateway.* London: Office of the Deputy Prime Minister.

Pain, K. (2004) The city-region: an overview of the city-region, visions, practices, spatial ideas. Paper presented at Regional Studies Association Conference on City Regions: Creating New Urban Futures? London, 18 October.

Peck, J. and Tickell, A. (1992) Local modes of social regulation? Regulation theory, Thatcherism and uneven development, *Geoforum*, 23, 3: 347–63.

—— (1995) The social regulation of uneven development: 'regulatory deficit', England's South East and the collapse of Thatcherism, *Environment and Planning A*, 27: 15–40.

Robinson, P. (2004) *Going for Growth: Comparing the South East's Economic Performance.* Commission on Sustainable Development in the South East, Working Paper 1, London: Institute for Public Policy Research.

South East Economic Development Agency (SEEDA) (1999) *Building a World Class Region: An Economic Strategy for the South East of England.* Guildford: South East Economic Development Agency.

—— (2002a) *An Economic Profile of the South East of England.* Guildford: South East Economic Development Agency.

—— (2002b) *Regional Economic Strategy for South East England 2002–2012.* Guildford: South East Economic Development Agency.

South East Economic Development Strategy (SEEDS) (1987) *South–South Divide.* Stevenage: South East Economic Development Strategy.

South East England Regional Assembly (SEERA) (2003) *Regional Monitoring Report.* Guildford: South East England Regional Assembly.

—— (2004a) *Integrated Regional Framework 2004: A Better Quality of Life in the South East.* Guildford: South East England Regional Assembly.

—— (2004b) *Perceptions of the South East and Its Regional Assembly.* Report prepared by MORI for the South East England Regional Assembly. Available at http://www.southeast-ra.gov.uk/publications/surveys/2004/mori_report_july_2004. pdf

—— (2004c) *South East Plan Consultation Draft, November 2004.* Guildford: South East England Regional Assembly.

Simmie, J. (2003) Innovation and urban regions as national and international nodes for the transfer and sharing of knowledge, *Regional Studies*, 37, 6/7: 607–20.

Simmie, J., Sennett, J., Wood, D. and Hart, D. (2002) Innovation in Europe: a tale of networks, knowledge and trade in five cities, *Regional Studies*, 36, 1: 47–64.

Uzzell, S. (2004) *Skills Mismatches and Skills Forecasts*. Supplementary Paper 3, *A Skills Review 2004*. Guildford: Skills Insight.

# 14 London

## From city–state to city–region?

*Leslie Budd*

### Introduction: the context of regionalism

The famous lexicographer and narrator of London Samuel Johnson stated, 'a man that is tired of London is tired of life'. As a capital city – and, as some claim, a global city – London excites praise and opprobrium in equal measure. The challenge for any analysis of 'London as a region' is the complex interaction between London as a metropolitan area and its impact on the surrounding region. What is the direction of causality? Is the metropolis creating the region or is the region sustaining its focal metropolitan point? This immediately provokes the question of what is a 'region'. Does London correspond to any meaningful definition of this term? In a book about the rise of the English regions, should a chapter even be devoted to London?

In much of the literature that discusses the case for regionalism in the UK, scant attention is paid to what is a region and how a region should be conceptualised. In a recent intervention, John Lovering (2001) warns of the danger of falling into the snare of regionalism, just as many have fallen into the trap set by globalisation. He argues that the advocates of 'new regionalism' are creating an orthodoxy of regional development without 'an empirically informed theoretical understanding of the region as a socio–economic system' (p. 349). Whilst not defining the region *sui generis*, exploring the region as a socio–economic entity creates greater analytical purchase, particularly in exploring the peculiar regional position of London.

For some, the relationship between nations and regions is complex and symbiotic: nations are amalgams of regions that comprise them, and national cultures are regional cultures imposed on other regions (Marquand, 1991). For others, the relation between space and place is the basis of conceptualising the region (Allen *et al.*, 1998). The Kilbrandon Commission on the Constitution reported in 1973 that the concept of the 'region' was both understood and established among the majority of the population (HMSO, 1973). In response to the question of whether regionalism and, by implication, regional identity can be manufactured, Kilbrandon concurred.

A way of conceiving of regions is to treat them as different territories:

- geographical territories;

- administrative/financial territories;
- historical/cultural territories.

In the UK, the region is a geographical territory and the current regional divisions are partly a combination of the Standard Regions and the administrative distribution as represented by the Government Offices for the Regions and Regional Development Agencies (RDAs). In the late nineteenth century, local government evolved from parish-based and privileged corporations to more interventionist modes as agents of central government programmes. The logic of more powerful and larger local authorities was resisted by the implementation by the Conservatives in 1888 of countervailing county councils. The semi-regionalisation or federalisation of the country passed with the failure of the 'Radical Programme' in 1885. 'Unfortunate regionalism', as it became popularly phrased in respect of continental Europe, dominated political and cultural discourse until early in the next century, which saw the rise of more pluralist politics (Harvie, 1991).

In France, the region was a historical and cultural territory that reinforced the administrative and financial territory rendered by the Socialist decentralisation of the early 1980s, which devolved formal government to the regions and departments. Regions represented a historic bulwark for royalists against the centralising and modernising tendency of republicanism. In the 1970s, decentralisation represented a radical democratic project for the union of the left against the central government of the right.

The foundation of modern Germany was laid in 1866 when the customs union comprising many of the states (*Länder*) established in 1834 became a nation-state following Prussia's military victory over Austria and the subsequent victorious war against France five years later. The contemporary federal Germany was imposed by the United States after the Second World War to combat centralising tendencies, which were seen as crucial to the rise of the Third Reich. By imposing US-style federal administrative and financial structures in the context of Germanic historical and cultural territories, a deeper, legitimate and accountable sense of region ensued.

Within this dance of identity and politics, government and governance, a more comprehensive concept of the region is lost. In locating the conception of the region in the relations between space and place, there is a danger of a degree of abstraction that renders any consistent theorisation redundant.

Given the incomplete nature of the regionalism in the UK and the complex interaction of centre–periphery relations in respect of what constitutes government and governance, a way out of the current conundrum is to conceive of the region as an informal organisation: that is, locating this conception in the spaces between firm and market as adumbrated in the literature of institutional economics and transaction costs literature. This conceptual challenge is beyond our current purpose, however.

Where does London fit into this taxonomy? Is the 'London region' a geographical territory; an administrative/financial territory; or an informal organisation? Or is it a capital city whose hinterland is interwoven with the centre in myriad complex connections that warrants the title 'city-region'? This chapter explores the taxonomy of sites and regions in respect of London and some of the issues it throws up.

## What is London?

As a geographical entity, London can be conceived of at a number of spatial levels: traditional City of London; Inner London or the County of London; and Greater London. The latter conforms to the present administration and fiscal boundaries, which have not altered since the abolition of the Greater London Council (GLC) in 1986 and its partial reinvention as the Greater London Authority in 2000. The analysis of this chapter concentrates on the Greater London area, but the symbiotic nature of its relationship with the neighbouring South East and Eastern regions cannot be overlooked. This chapter, therefore, should be read in conjunction with the contributions on these regions in this book to gain a fuller understanding of the complex territory that is London.

## Government and governance

The City of London and its administration, the Corporation of London, was the original site of London. Offices that date back to the Middle Ages are characterised by both ceremonial and administrative powers. These offices include that of the Sheriff and the Alderman and reflect their long-standing importance in the government of the City of London. The office of Sheriff is of greater antiquity than any other in the City of London. Until the institution of the Mayoralty in 1189, Sheriffs or 'Shire Reeves' governed the City as the King's representatives, collected royal revenues and enforced royal justice. Today two Sheriffs are elected on Midsummer's Day every year in Guildhall by the City livery companies. Since 1385, when the Court of Common Council stipulated that every future Lord Mayor should 'have previously been Sheriff so that he may be tried as to his governance and bounty before he attains to the Estate of Mayor', the shrieval year of an Aldermanic Sheriff is a sort of testing-ground for a person who aspires one day to be elected Lord Mayor of London. Edward III established Westminster, the current site the UK's governmental functions, as the political bulwark against the trade and commercial power of the City of London (Porter, 1994). As the city expanded to an international metropolis, this duality and consequent tensions grew, with the latter being subordinated to the former, at least from a governmental perspective. Today, the implicit power of the City of London remains, through the internationalisation of its markets and its position as the wealthiest borough in the world.

The London County Council (LCC) was the principal local government body for the County of London from 1889 until 1965, when it was replaced by the Greater London Council. It covered the area today known as Inner

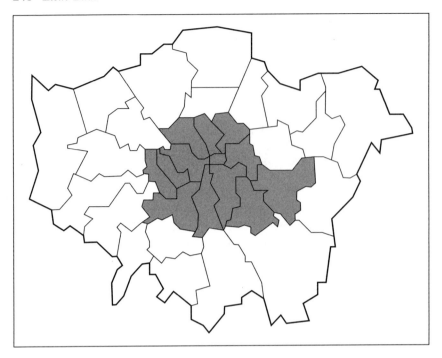

*Figure 14.1* County of London (Inner London) and Greater London

London. Figure 14.1 shows the current boundaries of Greater London and the boundaries of the County of London.

The successor Greater London Council was the top tier of local government administration for Greater London from 1965 until its abolition in 1986. After over a decade without a central governing body for London, a slimmed-down version of the GLC, the Greater London Authority, was set up in 2000, with an elected Mayor as the strategic head. The boundaries of the GLA are the same as the old thirty-two boroughs of the GLC and the Corporation of London, covering the City of London. The Mayor and the GLA represent the strategic direction of London, compared to the much more public administration and management role of the GLC on a metropolitan scale. Figure 14.2 shows the distributions of functions at different governmental levels.

Devolved government and governance are heavily conditioned by central government, through the Government Office for London (GOL). The role of GOL is to deliver programmes in the London Region on behalf of nine central government departments. GOL manages over forty programmes for the central government departments. It had a programme budget of £3 billion for 2004–5, of which the greater part, over £2.5 billion, is grant given to the Greater London Authority and its functional bodies: Transport for London and the London Development Agency. There are also five ministers in central government that have special responsibility for London: Minister for London; Minister

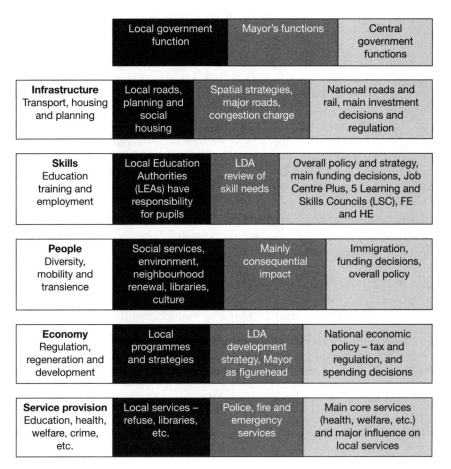

| | Local government function | Mayor's functions | Central government functions |
|---|---|---|---|
| **Infrastructure** Transport, housing and planning | Local roads, planning and social housing | Spatial strategies, major roads, congestion charge | National roads and rail, main investment decisions and regulation |
| **Skills** Education training and employment | Local Education Authorities (LEAs) have responsibility for pupils | LDA review of skill needs | Overall policy and strategy, main funding decisions, Job Centre Plus, 5 Learning and Skills Councils (LSC), FE and HE |
| **People** Diversity, mobility and transience | Social services, environment, neighbourhood renewal, libraries, culture | Mainly consequential impact | Immigration, funding decisions, overall policy |
| **Economy** Regulation, regeneration and development | Local programmes and strategies | LDA development strategy, Mayor as figurehead | National economic policy – tax and regulation, and spending decisions |
| **Service provision** Education, health, welfare, crime, etc. | Local services – refuse, libraries, etc. | Police, fire and emergency services | Main core services (health, welfare, etc.) and major influence on local services |

*Figure 14.2* Distribution of functions

*Source:* Hirmis (2005)

for Transport in London; Minister for London Schools; Minister for London Resilience; Minister for Health in London. These ministers do not hold posts in the Cabinet but report to their respective secretary of state and to the Deputy Prime Minister in the case of the first and fourth functions.

Economic governance rests with the London Development Agency (LDA), the Regional Development Agency (RDA) for London, created in 2000. The role of the RDAs in England is somewhat constrained by the Government Offices for the Regions (GORs), which are central government bodies located in the regions and representing the major central government departments, thus cross-cutting regional development. The other RDAs are non-departmental public bodies (NDPB) but the LDA is formed as a local authority reporting to the Mayor and the GLA, who approve the LDA economic strategy and expenditure to implement it (Syrett and Baldock, 2004).

Devolved economic governance in London is further constrained by the system of local governance in the UK, which is allowed little local or regional discretion by central government, unlike in many of the UK's continental European neighbours. Funding for London comes from GOL, and whilst the Mayor negotiates a London-wide precept on the community charge of the thirty-two London boroughs, the latter is effectively settled by central government. Moreover, the funding for the London Underground is undertaken through a complex financing vehicle, the Public–Private Partnership (PPP), underwritten by the Treasury. The other difficult issue comprises the benefits of economic governance flow across London's regional boundaries, as in any large metropolis, but London's system of government and governance has limited remits in managing the costs and benefits of these flows. The chronology of the evolution of London's current economic governance is given in Table 14.1.

London's economic governance is also cross-cut by a number of institutional relationships and programmes – for example, the Single Regeneration Budget, Selective Area Assistance, Thames Gateway, Park Royal Partnership, etc. – as well as a range of official and quasi-official agencies covering enterprise support and training and skills. The range and jurisdictions of these bodies make an articulate and comprehensive account of London's economic governance very difficult, to the point of being impossible. These governmental and governance boundaries, however, cannot contain the tragedy and farce that is London's

*Table 14.1* Chronology of London's economic governance, post-GLC

| | |
|---|---|
| 1986 | Abolition of the Greater London Council (GLC), replacement by London Planning Advisory Committee (LPAC) |
| 1990 | Creation of Training and Enterprise Councils (TECs) (seven across London in 2000) |
| 1994 | Business Links set up to support small and medium-sized enterprises with 10–200 employees |
| 1994 | Government Office for London formed as one of ten Regional Government Offices |
| 1998 | Formation of the London Development Partnership (LDP), forerunner to the LDA |
| 2000 | Publication of LDP's economic strategy, *Building London's Economy* |
| 2000 | Ken Livingstone elected Mayor for London and twenty-five representatives elected to the London Assembly |
| 2000 | Formal establishment of the London Development Agency as the executive arm for London's economic regeneration activity |
| 2001 | Business Link for London (franchise of national Small Business Service) and Local Learning and Skills Councils (LSCs) (five across London) officially come into operation |
| 2001 | Publication of London's economic development strategy by the LDA, *Success through Diversity* |
| 2002 | Publication by the Mayor of London of *The Draft London Plan* |

history and complex present, nor guide the inquisitive to how it should be conceived of as a region or a city-region or a metropolis or a city-state. The key question is whether government and governance actually match what London is. We return to history to consider this question.

## Metropolis or city-state?

The fourteenth-century poet St Erkenwald likened London to the ancient city of Troy, which he saw as both an ideal type of city and a city-state. The latter would surprise contemporary commentators, given London's topographical patchwork and fuzzy borders. London as a metropolis goes further back, to the Venerable Bede and William the Conqueror, who both used the term (Keene, 2004). The essence of the meaning of 'metropolis' is that of mother-city, seat of government and dominant centre of a nation's wealth and commerce. A straightforward definition suggests: 'a major concentration of population and economic activity' (Mogridge and Parr, 1997: 98).

The meaning of London as a metropolis expanded in the nineteenth century to become 'a conceptual identity for a collection of places and administrative units' (Keene, 2004: 461). The shifting meaning of London as a metropolis reinforces the notion of a capital city with expanding and fuzzy borders that continuously penetrates its surrounding region, thereby giving rise to the question of 'city or region', or perhaps both. Given London's international economic activities, it could be deemed a city-state. After all, the financial districts of London have been called an 'international offshore financial entrepôt' (Budd, 2000).

Compared to the classic Italian city-state or *City-Länder* of Germany, London has limited claim to city-state status. However, through informal and indirect processes, London has had a 'high degree of wider influence that might be characterized as city-state by negotiation with the kingdoms of which it has formed part' (Keene, 2004: 466). In the present context, this view can be construed as 'London versus the regions'. It can be objected that London is a capital city whose influence over the rest of the United Kingdom is what one would expect. However, the expansion of London, as first a European city and then a world city, has had three historical phases, each of which resulted in proportionately greater influence:

- *Up to 1500:* The population peaked around AD 1300 but London's share of national wealth and international trade grew at a faster rate than its population expansion.
- *Up to 1700:* London became the dominant city in Europe in respect of urban and commercial growth.
- *1700 to present:* The rapid expansion of provincial port and industrial centres accelerated London's growth, especially during the nineteenth century, despite the relative decline in the share of world trade and some catching up by other cities.

According to Keene (2004), the current territory of London, under the control of the Mayor and the GLA, represents the fullest and most consistent administrative manifestation for 400 years. However, Greater London creates a dual problem between its economy and the identity of those who work within it. In 1991 a fifth of the population who worked in London lived outside it, and the trend has grown since. The lives of this commuting population are heavily determined by London, but their sense of place exists outside, in the regions of the South East and the East. In economic performance London has always significantly punched above its national weight. It contributes 20 per cent of the tax revenue of the UK but contains only about 12 per cent of the population. (In 1666 it contributed half, with a tenth of the national population; in 1812 it contributed 40 per cent; Schwartz, 2000; London School of Economics, 2003.) On a per head basis, London's productivity (measured by gross value added) is one and a half times the UK average (ONS, 2003).

Financial London can be said to be both virtual and real: that is, the claim to world or global city status rests on London (effectively the City of London and the financial and business services district of Canary Wharf in Docklands) as an offshore financial entrepôt. Here financial services are traded through digital media around the world or between financial and business firms densely packed into the 'Square Mile'[1] and its environs. But it was ever thus. As Roy Porter (2000: 40) notes, London become the epicentre of England as a trading nation in the seventeenth and eighteenth centuries: 'London, proclaimed Addison, had become "a kind of Emporium for the whole Earth", a view extended to the nation at large by Daniel Defoe's *Tour Thro' the Whole Island of Great Britain* (1724–7), that national anthem to progress, agricultural, commercial and financial.' The international trading role was to be reinforced as London's axial position in the production and reproduction of culture was established between the Restoration of Charles II (1660) and the coronation of George III nearly a century later. This dominant London as an 'imaginary addictive space' (Porter, 2000: 35) was praised and pilloried in equal measure, as it is today:

> The shift from Court to Town helped make London the metropolis *à la mode*. Visitors marvelled at the ceaseless throb of activity, the flutter of news, personalities, fashion, talk, and diversion to be found from Cheapside to Chelsea . . . The capital became a non-stop parade, bursting with sites for culture-watchers, a festival of senses . . . London became a lead character in its own right in Georgian art and thought, if often cast in the villain's role.

Once one starts to examine beyond London as a city-state, however, the prospect of London as a polycentric urban region (PUR) or multi-centred urban region (MUR) starts to suggest itself. In doing so, however, the 'London region' starts to become disassociated with London as a capital city and more associated with a large functional region that incorporates most of the neighbouring regional territory.

## London's regional structure: polycentric, mega or multi-centred?

Defining London as a city, city-state, city-region, region or some other entity will depend on the criterion chosen. Mogridge and Parr (1997: 98) suggest:

> As a starting point it may be argued that London comprises its continuously built-up area, an area which today can be specified fairly precisely, due largely to the effects of green belt policy and other land use regulation throughout the post-war period. On the surface, at least, such a definition seems reasonable. It not only conforms to the popular view of London as a wholly urbanized area, but also captures the important feature of London as a metropolis . . . which may be compared and contrasted with similar concentrations in the UK or elsewhere.

As the authors note, this would be a reasonable definition if London is conceived of as a homogeneous mass whose boundaries set significant interaction in terms of social organisation and markets, but this has not been the case for a significant period. One has to distinguish between conceiving of London as an 'imaginary addictive space', a 'global galaxy' or 'the global city' advanced by the chattering commentators and London as an economic or functional entity. The combination of the ebb and flow of immigration and changing demographics, the structure of inter-regional and intra-regional markets and their flows, suggests that London's patchwork topography is more powerful than land-use containment policies and regulations in shaping its development. The social structure of Kensington is different from that of Finsbury Park, which is different from that of Hayes in Middlesex, which is different from that of Bromley in Kent, but they are all of the piece that is London.

Other commentators suggest that London has extended beyond the boundaries of the South East Region because of population expansion and its outward location, negative externalities like land costs and congestion, and a dense radial transport network enabling long-distance commuting (Hall, 2004). Hall has developed a view of London as a mega-city region, which he says (2004: 2)

> arises through a long process of very extended decentralisation from big central cities to new adjacent smaller ones. It is a new form: a series of anything between twenty and fifty cities and towns, physically separate but functionally networked, clustered around one or more larger central cities, and drawing enormous economic strength from a new functional division of labour. These places exist both as separate entities, in which most residents work locally and most workers are local residents, and as parts of a wider functional urban region connected by dense flows of people and information along motorways, highspeed rail lines and telecommunications cables carrying the 'space of flows' (Castells 1989).

Hall builds this concept on an extended functional urban region (FUR): an urban region defined by a core of employment and density and a connecting ring conditioned by daily commuting patterns. The mega-city region (MCR) then represents the aggregation of a number of FURs. The key characteristic is the contiguity of the FURs to form an MCR. On this basis, Hall asks whether the Greater South East of the UK is an MCR with London as its core. The concept rests on the meaning of 'contiguity'. In its straightforward sense it is defined merely as displaying common borders or physical proximity. Hall's claim concerning the aggregation of FURs into an MCR based on physical proximity rests on the degree of polycentricity that is measured by distribution of population among FURs and in his case the number of relatively independent FURs in the region, on which the Greater South East scores quite highly.

However, straying into the territory of polycentricity poses several problems, not least because there appears to be a conflation of a number of concepts to create the MCR. According to Kloosterman and Musterd (2001), PURs:

- consist of a number of historically distinct cities;
- have no clearly dominant city in respect of socio-economic and cultural activities and political structures;
- consist of a small number of larger cities complemented by a larger number of small cities with the former not differing much by function and importance;
- are concentrated in one part of national territory and located in close proximity, the limit being defined by maximum commuting distance;
- have constituent cities that are independent political units that are spatially separate.

Parr (2004) adds more detailed conditions to elicit a definition of a PUR:

- *Clustering of centres:* a set of urban centres separated by open land, but with a sufficiently clustered distribution within the national spatial system.
- *Upper limit on centre separation:* a maximum level of separation exists as a condition, otherwise the concept of the PUR becomes progressively denuded of meaning. Although arbitrary, a maximum of one hour's commuting time from the centre.
- *Lower limit on centre separation:* a minimum level of separation exists between centres in order to distinguish a PUR from a conventional conurbation or a multi-centred metropolitan region (MMR).
- *Size and spacing of centres:* a closer spacing between centres than within a benchmark region. That is, for a given region, centres will be more closely spaced in a PUR.
- *Interaction among centres:* the level of economic interactions and linkages within a PUR will be greater than in a comparable benchmark region.
- *Size distributions of centres:* there is no pronounced difference in size among the larger centres, so no centre has a population dominance.

- *Centre specialisation:* there exists a specialised economic structure in the centres that comprise the PUR compared to the centres that make up the benchmark region.

On the basis of Kloosterman and Musterd's classification and Parr's conditions, Hall's claims for the mega-city region of the Greater South East fall down on a number of issues, principally the population dominance of London and the variegation of the economic structure. Hall appears to conflate the concept of the PUR with that of a 'megalopolis'[2] or mega-city.[3] The absence of marked population centres suggests that the 'megalopolis' of the US eastern seaboard should not be considered a PUR because of the dominance of New York City (Parr, 2004).

The London Region could be considered to be an MMR, which differs from a PUR in respect of better transport and communications affording a continuous form of urban development. MMRs are driven by the twin forces of decentralisation and recentralisation, based on the redistribution of specialised economic activities (Gottdiener and Budd, 2005). Many MMRs started life as PURs, but the London Region is an incomplete MMR because of the lack of continuous urban sprawl redolent of US examples, like Los Angeles.

London's trajectory from city-state to city-region coincides with the early stages of development. In 1901, the increased provisions of public services to the citizens of the UK's cities provoked the remark: 'the modern city is reverting in its importance to the position of city-state in classical antiquity' (Daunton, 2000: 13). Ironically, this reference was to Glasgow, whose later development could be referred to as a PUR (Bailey and Turok, 2001). London's internal fragmentation and imperial city role made the metropolis of the time unlike a city-state (Keene, 2004). However, in the late modern period the notion of London versus the regions, and the bad economics and bad politics leading to London receiving a greater proportion of public expenditure than the English regions, begin to acculturate its inhabitants to the idea of London as a city-state.

This section has avoided explicit discussion of London as a world or global city and the associated literature. The next section, however, explores the role of the London economy in advancing its global status. The reasoning behind this lack of detailed discussion is that the plethora of concepts used to explore 'what is London?' are often part of an intellectual play zone and they take us no further in exploring London's regional context. A similar logic can be applied to policy-makers and practitioners who promote PURs. They often argue, without providing evidence, that the concept should be the strategic focus of a region as it represents a more efficient economic structure than existing ones. Parr (2004: 238) uses the following quotation to demonstrate the difficulty facing these promoters:

'In many cases the map and pencil seem to decide the shape of PURs. It is the invocation – the appeal to future functional cohort developments, to cultural identities – that counts most. As a result image making is a crucial part of a PUR. The present popularity of the term is apparently the hidden expression of a more basic need, that is, the need for the image of urban structure, in order to have a conceptual basis for organizing network-based strategies for urban development in a world dominated by issues of competitiveness (Van Houtum and Lagendijk, 2001).'

A similar observation can be made of MCRs, global city-regions and so on. The latter also suffers from definitional clarity, as the following quotation amply demonstrates:

> From a geographic point of view, global city-regions constitute dense polarized masses of capital, labour, and social life that are bound up in intricate ways in intensifying and far-flung extra-national relationships. As such, they represent an outgrowth of large metropolitan areas – or contiguous sets of metropolitan areas – together with surrounding hinterlands to a variable extent which may themselves be sites of scattered urban settlements. In parallel with these developments, embryonic consolidation of global city-regions into definite political entities is also occurring in many cases, as contiguous local government areas (counties, metropolitan areas, municipalities, etc.) club together to form spatial coalitions in search of effective bases from which to deal with both the threats and the opportunities of globalization. So far from being dissolved away as geographic entities by processes of globalization, city-regions are by and large actually thriving at the present time, and they are, if anything, becoming increasingly central to the conduct and coordination of modern life (cf. Taylor, 2000).
>
> (Scott, 2001: 814)

The burgeoning literature on city-regions may afford a path out of this definitional confusion. A city-region is a geographical area that comprises a large urban core, functionally connected to a set of smaller urban centres and rural hinterlands. Economic and social interdependence, reinforced by a range of political institutions and governance arrangements, is the key factor in identifying and narrating a city-region (CURDS, 1999). These interdependencies and interconnections are historically determined and reflect dominant socio-economic forms. More simply, 'city-region' is the current term for the interaction of central places with their regional hinterlands.

London's patchwork complexity and uniqueness, however, defy the imperative of the pencil and the map. Simply classifying London as a world city, a global city, a mega-city region or a global city-region denies its historical trajectory. At one time or another London has been a number of these things. It is the basis of its economy, however, that leads to many of the misspecifications. We explore the London economy in the next section.

# The London economy

If the question of 'what is London?' is difficult to answer, defining and drawing the boundaries of the London economy is equally challenging. It is apparent that there are not significant differences between the formal London Region and its neighbours. The difficulty is untangling the spillover effects from activities of the core and its surrounding regional neighbours. It is when we investigate the London economy that we find its boundaries cannot easily be contained, and when we look at the role of its financial services, the idea of London as an 'addictive imaginary space' becomes reinforced. Some claim that the London economy is covered by a 100-kilometre radius from the centre; others that it is contained within the boundaries of the M25 orbital motorway (Gordon, 2004a). The other challenging issue is the measurement of inter-regional trade in the UK – a significant contributor to the uneven development of the UK economy.

The London economy accounts for 15.8 per cent of gross domestic product and 15.3 per cent of employment, has 12.5 per cent of the UK population and contributes a net fiscal surplus of around 4 per cent (Hirmis, 2005; Gordon, 2004a).

In the past few years, there has been a plethora of reports on the London economy for and by a variety of organisations (Corporation of London, 1995, 2004; Llewelyn-Davies et al., 1996; Association of London Government, 1997). Whatever their individual merits, they all share the same policy conclusion: the 'golden goose' of financial and business services should be promoted in order to sustain the ability of this sector to maintain its global comparative advantage. In American parlance, this sector is known as FIRE (finance, insurance and real estate). This policy bias stems from a view of London as a global city, a view that conditions both *The London Plan: Mayor's Spatial Development Strategy* (Mayor of London, 2004) and *Sustaining Success: Developing London's Economy*, the economic development strategy (LDA, 2004). Despite the nods in the direction of balanced economic development, the variegated nature of the London economy and its complex interactions at different scales tend to get overlooked.

The literature on world cities (Hall, 1966; Friedman 1986) has been superseded by that on global cities (Sassen, 1991). In both accounts, the city has become the centre of global flows and transformations. The distinction between the former and the latter is that the former engaged in international transactions, while the latter consist of a set of command and control nodes for international business and commerce (Newman and Thornley, 2005). The world city/global city hypothesis, with its systems emphasis, attempts to fit and contain the ebb and flow of different cities with myriad characteristics and manifold differences into a functional straitjacket. Moreover, it ignores important historical trajectories, substituting the pencil and the map for a limited empirical template. It also accepts the contested concept of globalisation too readily. Benedict Anderson (1983) has famously termed nationalities 'imagined communities':

artificial nineteenth-century constructs. Similarly, global cities can be termed 'imagined places'. In London's case, it has been 'an imaginary addictive space' and 'an emporium for the whole Earth' for a very long time.

London's economy is very diversified and it has passed through various stages. In modern times one can distinguish between:

- *the Manufacturing City:* the geographical pattern of inter-war manufacturing development of the new craft-based and increasingly technological industries along centrifugal lines influenced the subsequent development of consumer-based and technologically dynamic manufacturing along radial lines (Scott and Walsh, 2004); and
- *the Service City:* the dominance of financial and business services in employment totals suggests that London is now a service city. The logic is that London has now moved from an industrialised economy to a tertiary one. Between 1984 and 1991 manufacturing's share of output declined from 17.9 to 13.7 per cent whilst financial and business services grew from 21.9 per cent to 29.3 per cent (Graham and Spence, 1995). However, this period covers the initial recovery from a very deep recession to the onset of another. Moreover, the deregulation of the City of London in 1986, known as the 'Big Bang', provided a significant boost for financial and business services. In looking at the relative performance of the two sectors and in comparison to the UK as a whole, we have been witnessing economic changes and *not* tertiarisation and deindustrialisation of the London economy *per se* (Graham and Spence, 1995). Once one conceives of the London economy as stretching significantly beyond the Greater London administrative boundaries, the relationship between the performance of manufacturing and services becomes more complex. Furthermore, in accounting for different sectoral growth contributions, the distinction between the two becomes increasingly irrelevant.

Manufacturing continues to play an important role in the London economy, as is evidenced by its contribution to gross value added per capita, as shown in Figure 14.3.

A similar pattern emerges when looking at the distribution of employment as shown in Table 14.2.

London's claims to global status rest on the comparative performance of its financial markets and associated services, like law, accountancy and management consultancy services, whose firms have established global brands. The key facts of the City of London for 2003 were:

- $504bn foreign exchange turnover each day in London
- 45 per cent of the global foreign equity market
- 70 per cent of eurobonds traded in London
- $2,000bn per annum traded on metals in London

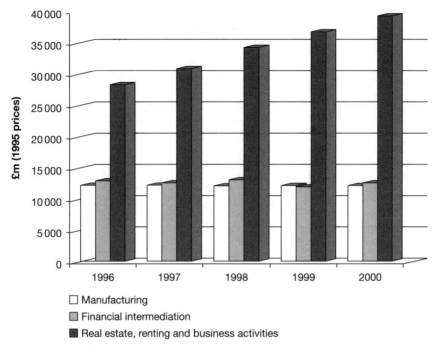

*Figure 14.3* GVA per capita by sector, 1996–2000 (£m: 1995 prices)

*Source:* Author's calculations from ONS (2004)

- world's leading market for international insurance: UK worldwide premium income reached £161bn in 2002
- $884bn a day traded on the London international futures exchange – Euronext.Liffe
- £2,619bn total assets under management in the UK in 2002
- £1,046bn in overseas earnings generated by the maritime industry in London
- 287 foreign banks in London
- 19 per cent of international bank lending arranged in the UK (largest single market)
- 381 foreign companies listed on the London Stock Exchange (LSE)
- Europe's leading financial centre: 23 per cent (76,000) of City-type jobs generated by continental EU business
- £1,200bn pension fund assets under management (third largest in the world)
- $275bn daily turnover in 'over-the-counter' derivatives (36 per cent of global share) (IFSL, 2004)

London's international provenance is rooted in its history as a port and financier of a growing empire that was based on international trade and commerce;

*Table 14.2* Number of employees by industry (SIC92), 2000

| Greater London | Number | Percentage |
|---|---|---|
| Manufacturing | 296,405 | 7 |
| Wholesale/retail trade, repairs, etc. | 639,114 | 16 |
| Financial services | 340,505 | 9 |
| Business services | 912,331 | 23 |

*Source:* Annual Business Inquiry, ONS (2003)

*Table 14.3* Comparative shares in international financial markets, 2003 (%)

| | UK | US | Japan | France | Germany | Others |
|---|---|---|---|---|---|---|
| Cross-border bank lending | 19 | 9 | 9 | 6 | 11 | 46 |
| Foreign equities turnover | 45 | 32 | – | – | 3 | 20 |
| Foreign exchange dealing | 31 | 16 | 9 | 3 | 5 | 36 |
| Derivatives turnover | | | | | | |
|     Exchange traded | 6 | 27 | 3 | 3 | 13 | 48 |
|     Over-the-counter | 36 | 18 | 3 | 9 | 13 | 21 |
| Insurance | | | | | | |
|     Marine | 19 | 13 | 14 | 5 | 12 | 37 |
|     Aviation | 39 | 23 | 4 | 13 | 3 | 18 |
| Fund management | 8 | 51 | 10 | 4 | 3 | 24 |
| Corporate finance | 11 | 60 | 10 | 2 | 3 | 15 |

*Source:* IFSL (2004)

for example, the establishment of the East India Trading Company in 1600. London's current financial prominence is demonstrated in Table 14.3. The international basis of London's financial comparative advantage is also shown in the distribution of financial services employment in Figure 14.4. It is the very internationalisation of London's financial market activities that is the basis of classifying London as a global city, but this has been the case throughout the long march of London's history. To classify London simply as a global city that dates from the late twentieth century ignores past and current complexity.

London has two global nodes: the City of London and its financial environs; and Heathrow Airport. The evidence base for the former is given above. The latter is the largest airport in the world for international traffic. The surrounding area is the location of the European headquarters of the ten leading companies in the world. It is the biggest port by value in the European Union (LDA, 2004). London's early dominance in international trade stemmed from connecting the Port of London, as the entry point for traded goods, with the developing commercial role of the City, financing the flows of internationally traded goods, Today, the City and Heathrow are connected by the flow of goods and services, both real and digital. However, the economic characteristics of Heathrow and

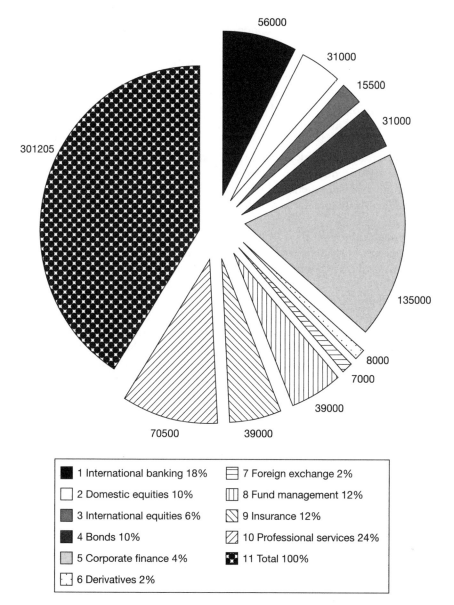

*Figure 14.4* City of London financial employment by market activity

its hinterland are different from those of the City to an almost significant degree. This subtle difference is not picked up by the promoters of the global city.

If the global city thesis of London is true, then one would expect an increasing degree of separation between the London economy and that of the UK. But Gordon (2004b) finds little evidence for this claim:

- The rest of the UK [outside the Greater South East] provides the core market for London's economic base [73 per cent of its employment in 2002/3];
- National cyclical influences have remained the key influence on London's unemployment rate (even in early 1980s) – both directly [at GSE scale] and then also indirectly [on London/GSE differential];
- London is very heavily integrated in both product & labour markets, possibly more than any other [sizeable region].

The relationship of London to the UK economy is also complex but over time does not significantly differ. However, given the relative size of the London economy, any small differential will be magnified over time. Evidence for this is contained in Figure 14.5, which shows real GVA per head in the UK and London.

Although the rest of the UK appears to be keeping track with London over time, once real prices are taken into account, this estimate of both income and productivity shows no sign of narrowing. For policy-makers, the Public Service Agreement (PSA) target of reducing the trend rate of growth of GVA per head by 2012 appears daunting.

The socio-economic characteristics of London compared to the other regions are set out in Table II.1 (p. 105). The interaction with the rest of the UK and London's neighbours also affects London's labour markets. London tends to correlate to UK trends, once short-run dynamics are taken into account. In other words, the London labour market tends to perform above national trends in upturns and underperform in downturns. Some evidence is advanced for this view in Figure 14.6.

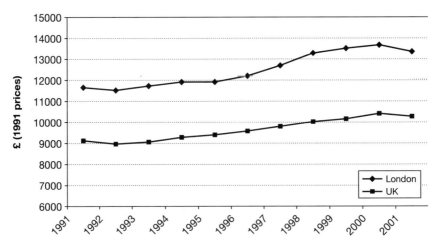

*Figure 14.5* London and UK GVA per capita, 1991–2002 (1991 prices)

*Source:* Author's calculations from ONS (2004)

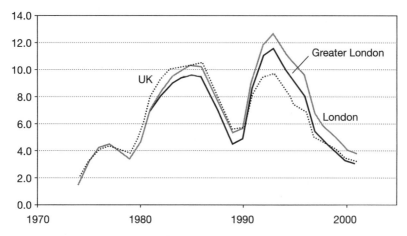

*Figure 14.6* Unemployment rates for Greater London, 1974–2001

*Source:* Gordon (2004b)

The importance of land markets and the interaction of financial institutions is often overlooked in discussions of the London economy and attempts to classify it functionally (Ball, 1996). The symbiosis of these interests could lead to London being termed 'Rentier City'. This would be a more appropriate term, given the way that land-use regulations and green-belt policy impact on real estate markets and their final use. The OECD (2004) recently pointed out that despite the good performance of the UK economy over the last few years, the housing market is contributing to downside risks. Land and real estate markets are major causes of economic congestion in London, but classifying London simply on the effect of these markets also restricts our understanding of this dominant city-region.

## Concluding remarks

The complexity of London and its patchwork quality defy definition by the pencil and the map. Similarly, attempting to lay a simple functional template on its topography prevents an understanding of the crucial role that London has played and continues to play. In this chapter, I have tried to examine London by means of the trajectory from city-state to city-region. The latter term is sufficiently general and descriptive to encompass the myriad and manifold interactions between London and its hinterland, as well as its different histories. The regional dimension to London is central to its current evolutionary position, as Mogridge and Parr (1997: 112) note: 'Indeed any attempt to trace the evolution of London from its earlier existence as a metropolis to its present discontinuous form as a complex metropolis-based urban system becomes virtually impossible without recourse to the notion of a region.'

In Michael Hebbert's (1998) paean to London, he concludes by referring to the Danish architect and urbanist Stein Eiler Ramussen. Ramussen's classic account of London, *London: The Unique City*, is based on his observations in the inter-war years, but they are still vibrant today: ready-made patterns do not fit London (Ramussen, 1948). Originally, this book sought to use London as a case study to express Ramussen's view on the twentieth-century city (Hebbert, 1998). London, however, has overwhelmed lesser mortals than Ramussen in defying typecasting. Even living with the seduction that a new century apparently engenders, through notions of rebirth, renewal, vitality and promise, London remains, as it ever was, a unique place. The basis of seduction has always been difference. In London's case, it was its very difference, from city-state to city-region, that James Boswell came to embrace:

> I have often amused myself with thinking how different a place London is to different people. They whose narrow minds are contracted to the consideration of some one particular pursuit view it only through that medium. A politician thinks of it as merely a seat of government in its different departments; a grazier as a vast market for cattle; a mercantile man, a place where a prodigious deal is done upon . . . But the intellectual man is struck within it, as comprehending the whole of human life in all its variety, the contemplation of which is inexhaustible.
>
> (Boswell, 1990: 79)

Samuel's Johnson's view of London as a tonic, expressed in his epigram that appeared at the start of this chapter, seems as appropriate today as it was in the eighteenth century. 'London: The Tonic City-Region' may be a productive starting point for classifying the dynamic complex that confronts us today.

## Notes

1   The Square Mile refers to the traditional boundaries of the City of London and became shorthand for the operations of its financial markets.
2   The original Greek meaning of 'megalopolis' is great city. It was first used in a modern sense to describe the densely populated urban area stretching from Boston to Washington, DC, that comprises the eastern seaboard of the United States by Jean Gottman (1957).
3   The United Nations coined the term 'mega-city' in the 1970s to designate all urban agglomerations with a population of eight million or more. In the 1990s, the United Nations raised the population threshold to ten million, following the practice of institutions such as the Asian Development Bank. From this definition, the United Nations (2002) estimates that there are currently nineteen mega-cities at the world.

## References

Allen, J., Cochrane, A. and Massey, D. (1998) *Rethinking the Region*. London: Routledge

Anderson, B. (1983) *Imagined Communities*. London: Verso

Association of London Government (1997) *The London Study: A Socio-economic Assessment of London*. London: Association of London Government

Bailey, N. and Turok, I. (2001) 'Central Scotland as a Polycentric Region: Useful Planning Concept or Chimera?', *Urban Studies*, 38: 697–715

Ball, M. (1996) 'London and Property Markets: A Long-term View', *Urban Studies*, 33(6): 859–77

Boswell, J. (1990) *The Journals of James Boswell*. London: Mandarin

Budd, L. (2000) 'Globalisation and the Crisis of Territorial Embeddedness in International Markets', in R. Martin (ed.), *Money and the Space Economy*. Chichester: John Wiley

Corporation of London (1995) *City Research Project: The Competitive Position of London's Financial Services*. London: Corporation of London

—— (2003) *London's Place in the UK Economy*. London. Corporation of London

—— (2004) *London's Place in the UK Economy*. London: Corporation of London

CURDS (1999) *Core Cities: Key Centres for Regeneration*. Final report, December, Centre for Urban and Regional Development Studies, University of Newcastle upon Tyne

Daunton, M. (ed.) (2000) *The Cambridge History of Britain*, III: *1840–1950*. Cambridge: Cambridge University Press

Friedman, J. (1986) 'The World City Hypothesis', *Development and Change*, 17(1): 69–83

Graham, D. and Spence, N. (1995) 'Contemporary Deindustrialisation and Tertiarisation in the London Economy', *Urban Studies*, 32(6): 885–911

Gordon, I.R. (2004a) 'A Disjointed Dynamo: The South East and Inter-regional Relationships', *New Economy*, 11(3): 40–4

—— (2004b) 'London's Place in the UK Economy'. DTI/Regional Studies Association Seminar, London and the Rest of the UK: The Economic Relationship, Department of Trade and Industry, 29 November

Gottdiener, M. and Budd, L. (2005) *Key Concepts in Urban Studies*. London: Sage

Gottman, J. (1957) *Megalopolis or the Urbanization of the Northeastern Seaboard*. Cambridge, MA: MIT Press

Hall, P. (1966) *World Cities*. London: Weidenfeld & Nicolson

—— (2004) 'Is the Greater South East a Mega-City Region?' Paper presented to a seminar held by the Institute for Public Policy Research, Institute of Community Studies, London, 10 December

Harvie, C. (1991) *No Gods and Precious Few Homes: Scotland 1914–1980*. London: Edward Arnold

Hebbert, M. (1998) *London*. Chichester: John Wiley

Hirmis, A. (2005) 'The London Region and Its Stakeholders Raising the Questions'. Paper presented to ESRC seminar, Business Cluster Urbanism and Regionalism, University of Westminster, 4 February

HMSO (1973) *Royal Commission on the Constitution (Kilbrandon Commission)*. Cmnd 5460–1, London: HMSO

IFSL (2004) *London's International Markets*. London: International Financial Services, London

Keene, D. (2004) 'Metropolitan Comparison: London as a City-State', *Journal of Historical Research*, 77(198), November: 459–80

Kloosterman, R.C. and Musterd, S. (2001) 'The Polycentric Urban Region: Towards a Research Agenda', *Urban Studies*, 38(4): 623–33

Llewelyn Davies, Bartlett School of Architecture and Comedia (1996) *Four World Cities: A Contemporary Study of London, Paris, New York and Tokyo*. London: Llewelyn Davies

London Development Agency (LDA) (2004) *Sustaining Success: Developing London's Economy*. London: London Development Agency

London School of Economics (2003) *London's Place in the UK Economy*. London: Corporation of London

Lovering, J. (2001) 'The Coming Regional Crisis (and How to Avoid It)', *Regional Studies*, 35(4), June: 349–54

Marquand, D. (1991) 'Nations, Regions and Europe', in B. Crick (ed.), *National Identities: The Constitution of the United Kingdom*. Oxford: Blackwell

Mayor of London (2004) *The London Plan: Mayor's Spatial Development Strategy*, London: Mayor's Office

Mogridge, M. and Parr, J.B. (1997) 'Metropolis or Region: On the Development and Structure of London', *Regional Studies*, 31(2), April: 97–116

Newman, P. and Thornley, A. (2005) *Planning World Cities*. Basingstoke: Palgrave

Organisation for Economic Co-operation and Development (OECD) (2004) *The UK Economy*. Paris: OECD

Office for National Statistics (ONS) (2003) *Annual Business Survey*. London: Office for National Statistics

—— (2004) *Regional Trends 38*. London: Office for National Statistics

Parr, J.B. (2004) 'The Polycentric Urban Region: A Closer Inspection', *Regional Studies*, 38(3), May: 231–41

Porter, R. (1994) *London: A Social History*. London: Hamish Hamilton

—— (2000) *Enlightenment: Britain and the Creation of the Modern World*. London: Allen Lane

Ramussen, S.E. (1948) *London: The Unique City*. London: Jonathan Cape

Sassen, S. (1991) *Global Cities: New York, London, Tokyo*. Princeton, NJ: Princeton University Press

Schwartz, L.D. (2000) 'London 1700–1840', in P. Clark (ed.), *The Cambridge History of Britain*, II: *1540–1840*. Cambridge: Cambridge University Press

Scott, A.J. (2001) 'Globalization and the Rise of the City-Region', *European Planning Studies*, 9(7): 813–26

Scott, P. and Walsh, P. (2004) 'Patterns and Determinants of Manufacturing Plant Location in Interwar London', *Economic History Review*, 57(1): 109–41

Syrett, S. and Baldock, R. (2004) 'Reshaping London's Economic Governance: The Role of the London Development Agency', *European Urban and Regional Studies*, 10(1): 69–86

Taylor, P.J (2000) 'World Cities and Territorial States under Conditions of Contemporary Globalization', *Political Geography*, 19: 5–32

United Nations (2002) *'An Urbanizing World': Population Reference Bureau Bulletin*, vol. 55, no. 3. Geneva: United Nations

Van Houtum, H. and Lagendijk, A. (2001) 'Contextualising Regional Identity and Imagination in the Construction of Polycentric Urban Regions: The Cases of the Ruhr Area and Basque Country', *Urban Studies*, 38(4): 747–67

# 15 Conclusions

*Paul Benneworth, Irene Hardill, Peter Roberts,
Mark Baker and Leslie Budd*

## Introduction

In this book we have striven to offer a more theoretically nuanced examination
of regional changes in England, thereby addressing a lacuna in recent publications on regions and devolution. In Part I of the book, situating our analysis
at both the national and regional scales, we went beyond description of current
modes of governance and institutional development, taking a more geographically informed and theoretically grounded critical analysis rooted in
concepts of uneven development, and drawing on the rich tradition of regional
geography. Regions were once the core of the discipline of geography, and
gave prominence to the connections between areas of land, on several scales:
it referred to *pays*, to regions and their combination with national borders,
and brought out their 'personality' (Claval, 1998: 18). Those who engaged in
regional geography emphasised the specific nature of areas and the lifestyles of
those who lived there, and, in Part II in a series of theoretically grounded
regional essays for all nine regions, we attempted to capture the unique atmosphere of the English regions. The contributors to this book have worked within
the constraints imposed by the English 'administrative region' map and used this
administrative structure to present a regional geography of England.

Regions were frequently defined in terms of their landscapes and their
distinctive social systems; such regions were regarded as the place-specific
outcomes of the interplay of physical and human systems. Beginning from a
particular place allowed the explorations and reflections to uncover truths and
relationships about that human–nature interplay, which in turn created better
understandings of those places. This is precisely what Tony Gore and Catherine
Jones do in their chapter about Yorkshire, showing how what appears to
outsiders as a homogeneous, 'straight-talking' region is in fact better regarded
as a mosaic of sub-regions, whose evolution bears a profound connection to
the landscapes (and seascapes) in which ancestor communities have evolved. The
Mersey axis, for example, around which the North West rotates, has emerged
precisely because of the Mersey's role as a natural communications route, with
Manchester's position on the Irwell, Medlock and Mersey a formative influence
on its domination of the regional industrial structure.

We have been inspired by the freedom of such an eclectic approach to circumvent the over-specification and taxonomies of political science and new institutionalism approaches to the English regions. Of course, the weakness of an eclectic approach is that the material hangs independently, unless drawn together, and that is what we seek to do in this final chapter. Our aim is to use the regional insights to develop a bigger and more problematic understanding of England, of an England at the crossroads, between very different versions of 'regions' with profound consequences for the kind of England that exists in the future.

To understand those choices that England faces, we first reflect upon the intellectual framework presented in the first half of this book in the light of the regional essays.

## The conceptual rise of the English regions

One of the problems with conceptualising the rise of the English regions which emerged in Part I of this book is that the concept of 'region' has emerged in so many different literatures. Moreover, there is a degree of interplay between the rationalisations and bases for regions, but quite frequently those interplays make assumptions about what makes the 'region' significant. Thus, what have been produced in totemic examples of the new economy are very complex stories of successful regions in which social, political, cultural, institutional and structural elements are tightly woven together, always against the bright background of past success. From such success stories, 'model' political or cultural concepts can be developed which purport to explain why particular regions are successful, and why regional political action or particular regional cultural formations produce economic benefits. The key challenge in this book in conceptualising regions is to avoid beginning from 'model' regions and concepts against which to evaluate a set of very different, real (English) regions. The opening chapters therefore offered a set of conceptual tools from which to understand the English regions. We considered the regularities and tensions that arise in conceptualising particular places as a means to provide a dynamic model of regional change – in its broadest sense – in contemporary England.

In Chapter 2, Peter Roberts and Mark Baker presented a conceptualisation of regions as a means of good economic management, and, of course, pointed out that good management would suggest a reshaping of the region in ways that embedded and institutionalised those management practices, thereby reshaping the region itself. This perspective of self-regions sits at odds with meso-nationalist perspectives, in which the region is regarded as a means of realising long-held cultural ambitions. The case of the West Midlands, highlighted by Anne Green and Nigel Berkeley, suggests that good management can drive a regional self-realisation process. Conversely, Allan Cochrane's analysis of the South East shows that several attempts to create an institutional structure for a South East, including SERPLAN, the Rest of the South East and the Government Office for the South East, failed to mobilise a corresponding culture which could informalise and embed regional institutions into something outliving government administrative reforms.

In Chapter 3, Paul Benneworth set out an array of different theorisations of how regions might be associated with economic success; and the regional chapters demonstrate that different places can be understood by reference to different versions of those theories. Perhaps the most interesting regional chapter in this light is Leslie Budd's portrait of London, whose success, as Gordon and McCann (2000) and Keeble and Nachum (2002) remind us, can be understood as the overlapping of many different success factors, such as the highly localised successes of Soho and the City along with a generally more buoyant regional economy offering urbanisation and agglomeration economies. Budd's chapter shows how the building up of success has been associated with a change in the very nature of London. Conversely, in Mia Gray *et al.*'s chapter on the East, two very different, and spatially separated, economies are visible: a Cambridge growth pole tightly linked into London nestles alongside an East Anglian rural economy whose poverty belies its proximity to one of the success stories of the twenty-first century.

An important part of the conceptualisation of English regions which emerged throughout the opening chapters was the idea of an 'internal colonisation' of England by London (after Peck). In Chapter 4, Andy Wood *et al.* noted that attempts to build regions through tripartite institutions failed because the business representatives which engaged with the new regional chambers lacked any kind of regional basis. This related to the centrality of London in the English political economy, and in particular the decline of regional industrial complexes, whose decline and associated territorial political demands were increasingly out of tune with the progressive nature of national neo-liberal economic policy. This theme recurred in many of the regional essays, but, again, manifested in many different ways.

Interestingly, Budd's chapter portrays London as a city itself long internally colonised by financial services and the City of London, with financial services squeezing out manufacturing beyond the limits of the green belt, and thereby increasing the dependency of the South East on the London core. Cochrane notes that the South East effectively exists as an economic hinterland, providing the raw materials, and particularly for the tertiary economy the skilled labour, to fuel London's market dominance. The language of internal colonisation provides an interesting heterodox perspective to consider some of the successful places beyond the Greater South East. Beyond the South East the rise of the English region seems much less impressive if pockets of success such as Leeds, Nottingham, Chester and Bristol are seen as enclaves of London's roaring economy rather than providing a regional counterweight to metropolitan success. Indeed, in Amer Hirmis's engaging portrait of the South West as a cleaved region, he presents compelling evidence that the region's eastern fringes are more part of the South East proper than a South Eastern enclave in the west.

In Chapter 5, Irene Hardill *et al.* add a gender perspective to explore how regionalisation is providing a means of mobilising diversity as a regional economic development asset. In the regional essays, a number of interesting issues arise concerning diversity. The first is the importance of particular forms of in-migration determining particular regions and their cultures, and leaving enduring economic legacies which shape regional cultural evolution. The North East and the North West were both recipients of huge nineteenth-century in-migration flows to feed their growth industries, but local specificities shaped the diasporic communities in very different ways, and the age profiles of regions such as the South West are being altered by retirement migration flows, which are creating new economic opportunities.

In the North West, Yorkshire and the Humber, and the East Midlands, migrants, including from Ireland, fed the textiles boom in the nineteenth century, going into industries with heavy reliance on female labour, resulting in high female economic activity rates. Conversely, in the North East, as Byrne and Benneworth show, the dominance of heavy engineering and extractive industries produced Irish diaspora communities with strongly gendered divisions of labour, which in turn created a greenfield labour situation for particular types of foreign investment from the 1960s onwards, which in turn increased the fragility of the labour market. In other regions, immigrant entrepreneurs have played a critical role in shaping regional cultures, such as in Leeds in the nineteenth century around finance for textiles, or in the twentieth century with ethnic entrepreneurship in Birmingham, Leicester and Brick Lane in London.

The theoretically informed empirical regional essays illustrate the way in which the conceptualisations have been played out in different ways in different regions, and it is possible to gain a greater insight into the nature of the various English regions. In some senses, the picture is a little stereotyped, akin to the view from the train window on a journey from London to the periphery. But what these various conceptualisations do allow is the creation of linkages between the regions, to understand with a greater degree of insight the 'English system' arising from both intra- and inter-regional relationships. To illustrate our approach, it is worth taking the wider story of one region that can be sketched using the four conceptual reference frames presented above. Because London is so dominant in all the regional essays, it is perhaps best to take a different region, and, for the sake of argument, we use the case of the West Midlands.

Green *et al.* conceptualise the West Midlands as a 'hinge region', and that conception is reinforced and supported by all four of the conceptual analyses outlined above. Central to a synthetic narrative about the West Midlands is that its position of the region at the 'heart' of England and English transport networks gave Birmingham an economic growth impulse. This then created a critical mass offering both economies and diseconomies of scale, associated pollution and congestion, and administrative interest in managing that growth. At first, in the nineteenth century, these demands led to the creation of effective local government to provide public services; and then, from 1945 onwards, to using Birmingham as the engine to reconstruct the wider West Midlands in the wake of the Second World War.

The West Midlands' central position and critical mass also allowed the emergence of a regional business complex, particularly in the post-war years, around clusters of automotives and aerospace engineering, which have in turn shaped national policies for the regional benefit. The region's position as a transport node has brought in significant numbers of immigrants in the post-war period, many of whom remain extremely well connected to offshore capital and enterprise activities, which has created 'borrowed assets' for the West Midlands. Birmingham as a 'hinge city' exists in the shadow of London, but nevertheless, unlike Leeds or Nottingham, it has some kind of claim beyond being a regional enclave of London. There are undoubted tensions in Birmingham's autonomous status, and Coventry and Warwickshire find themselves torn between Birmingham and London.

Similar synthetic stories can be told about each of the regions, and are embedded in each of the nine regional chapters in Part II of this book. However, what is interesting in the above narrative about the West Midlands is the wider picture, portraying the tension between Birmingham and London. In Germany or the Netherlands, Birmingham would be a leading national city in its own right, reinforced with political and administrative functions through a *Provincie* or *Land*. In England, Birmingham's success faces continual challenge from the dynamic London mega-urban region (MUR), which undermines and destabilises elements of the West Midlands economy, and re-embeds them firmly in an orbit around London. These pressures are also felt in other regions, and are creating a new set of tensions driving a new regional dynamic.

We now turn to look at how these regional and local dynamics are interplaying to change the regional geography of England at the national level.

## The changing regional geography of Britain

As we acknowledged in the introduction to this final chapter, our English regions are administrative regions, and it is perhaps worth reiterating that the significant regions of the early twenty-first century are not the same as the current Government Office regions. What is also clear from the regional chapters is that the regions themselves have continually been evolving, both in terms of the boundaries between them and in the nature of what is contained within them. As part of that, we have seen that the 1997 devolution process has had an impact on the nature of regions. Both the South East and East Midlands regions were created as something very different to the other regions, as a means of filling in the map, after all the 'strong' regions had been 'pencilled off'. However, what has emerged in these two regions is a very different form of institutional arrangement.

In the South East, there has been almost a defensive regionalism; on the one hand, SEEDA and GOSE have had to claim that there are pockets of deprivation on the South Coast and in the Kent coalfield, whilst SEERA has positioned itself as the guardian of the South East's rural character against the predations of London's growth. In the East Midlands, there has been a much more collaborative approach, in which several relatively new institutions have worked together to try to create a new managerial framework to shape regional growth in an economically, socially and environmentally sustainable manner. Common to both cases is that a set of institutions have emerged to fill the regional political space, although they have taken very different trajectories.

However, perhaps what is most striking about the current regional geography of England is the degree to which London has become central, and is more than ever before the axis around which regional fortunes turn. At the heart of this, as Budd indicated in his chapter, is the fact that London has become a centre of financial power and control, with an economy-in-an-economy, which in turn supports a highly competitive knowledge-based manufacturing and service complex in the Greater South East Region. Both Budd and Cochrane make a very compelling case that this economy is highly successful, and the competitive success of the UK is in turn highly dependent on the success of London. The second element of this is the fact that there is therefore a *de facto* South East and London macro-urban region (MUR) with significant influence on the rest of the country through its economic power, but also because of the eye-catching nature of its success for public policy-makers and private investors.

There are two additional dimensions to the London MUR that emerge in the course of the regional essays. The first is that the urban region is predominantly an economic space, rather than a lived, experiential or cultural space. As Cochrane points out, one of the key problematics of the South East (GO) region is the fact that people in Dover have little in common with those in Guildford, Portsmouth or Amersham. This problem is of course magnified if the London MUR includes the East of England and the South East as well as London. The second issue is that there are communities that have become disconnected from this urban space. Hastings, Thanet and Tower Hamlets are all in the 'pencil line on the map' for the London MUR, but their functional connections into the London knowledge economy are comparatively weak, so it is widely recognised that they do not play significant roles in the region.

The second dimension to this new London urban region is that it is not necessarily a contiguous region in a strictly cartographic sense. There are places across England whose economic success and strength are functions of their close connections to London. The Leeds financial services industry is a case in point; it is effectively an outpost of London's FIRE sector, with branches of London firms providing more cost-competitive services for businesses beyond London. Viewed of itself, Leeds seems to have a vibrant cluster, but that cluster is an inexpensive outshoot of London activities. Cheshire and parts of Devon and Cornwall are establishing themselves as places for 'downsizing', to where people tired of London's congestion relocate, whilst maybe continuing to do business in London. High-speed rail links continue to expand the extent of the London commuter belt, metro-dormitories serving London are springing up across provincial England. Whilst the walls around these communities might be as invisible, they can be as poorly connected to their local environment as are the poorest London communities.